£22.99

To our children. May they appreciate and seek to understand their heritage.

Themes in Tourism

Series Editor: Professor Stephen J. Page, *Scottish Enterprise Forth Valley Chair in Tourism, Department of Marketing, University of Stirling, Stirling, Scotland FK9 4LA.*

The Themes in Tourism Series is an upper level series of texts written by established academics in the field of tourism studies and provides a comprehensive introduction to each area of study. The series develops both theoretical and conceptual issues and a range of case studies to illustrate key principles and arguments related to the development, organisation and management of tourism in different contexts. All the authors introduce a range of global examples to develop an international dimension to their book and an extensive bibliography is complemented by further reading and questions for discussion at the end of each chapter.

Books published in the Themes in Tourism Series

S.J. Page *Transport and Tourism*
C.M. Hall *Tourism Planning*
S.J. Page and R.K. Dowling *Ecotourism*
R. Scheyvens *Tourism for Development*
S.J. Page and C.M. Hall *Managing Urban Tourism*

Forthcoming title

Williams, S. *Tourism and Recreation*

Heritage Tourism

Dallen J. Timothy and Stephen W. Boyd

An imprint of **Pearson Education**

Harlow, England · London · New York · Reading, Massachusetts · San Francisco · Toronto · Don Mills, Ontario · Sydney
Tokyo · Singapore · Hong Kong · Seoul · Taipei · Cape Town · Madrid · Mexico City · Amsterdam · Munich · Paris · Milan

Pearson Education Limited
Edinburgh Gate
Harlow
Essex
England
CM20 2JE

and Associated Companies throughout the world

Visit us on the World Wide Web at:
www.pearsoneduc.com

First edition 2003

© Pearson Education Limited 2003

ISBN 0582 369703

British Library Cataloguing-in-Publication Data
A catalogue record for this book is available from the British Library

Library of Congress Cataloging-in-Publication Data
Timothy, Dallen J.
  Heritage tourism / Dallen J. Timothy and Stephen Boyd. — 1st ed.
     p. cm. — (Themes in tourism)
  Includes bibliographical references (p.)
  ISBN 0-582-36970-3
     1. Heritage tourism. I. Boyd, Stephen W. II. Title. III. Series.
  G156.5H47 T56 2002
  338.4'791—dc21   2002074999

10 9 8 7 6 5 4 3 2 1
06 05 04 03 02

Typeset in 10/12pt Sabon by 35
Printed and bound in China
EPC/01

Contents

List of figures

List of tables

List of plates

Preface

The genesis of this book began long before it became part of Pearson's 'Themes in Tourism' series. Both of us have been interested in visiting heritage sites since childhood, but a serious academic interest in heritage tourism began during our years as graduate students together in Canada studying natural and cultural heritage landscapes within both the developed and developing world. This interest has continued since then, and a variety of issues have been explored and published individually and collaboratively on the contribution tourism has played in natural heritage settings, partnership development at world heritage sites, heritage interpretation, planning in built heritage landscapes, collaboration and co-operation, heritage marketing, principles of sustainable heritage tourism development, national examinations of cultural and heritage tourism, the examination of cultural and heritage tourism within specific geographic locales, to name a few.

The focus of much scholarly activity in tourism today has resulted in books that have a very specialised focus. Texts on tourism and heritage have followed this trend, examining specific themes like integrated heritage management (Hall and McArthur 1998), heritage as applied to particular geographical regions (Hall and McArthur 1993a, 1996), the context of the tourist-historic city (Ashworth and Tunbridge 2000), contemporary issues in heritage interpretation (Uzzell and Ballantyne 1998), and the nature of heritage attractions (Prentice 1993). Others have addressed heritage from the perspective of specific disciplines, such as geography for example (Graham *et al.* 2000), while still others have explored the social and political relationships between heritage and tourism (Herbert 1995b; Tunbridge and Ashworth 1996). These are all contributions to the furthering of our understanding of heritage and tourism, as is evident in the frequency to which they are referred to in this text.

Our purpose in writing this book was to provide a far-reaching overview of the primary issues and concerns facing students, teachers, researchers and managers of heritage tourism. The sources of this information are our own empirical research, personal experiences, secondary data sources and previously published documents and research works. It is our hope that this work will stimulate more scholarly debate regarding the nature of heritage tourism and its breadth of coverage and potential for growth.

Dallen J. Timothy   *Stephen W. Boyd*
Gilbert, Arizona   *Dunedin*
USA   *New Zealand*

January 2002

Acknowledgements

Many people have been instrumental in the development of ideas and concepts for this book. Dallen would like to extend a well-deserved thank you to Ross Dowling, Mike Hall, Dimitri Ioannides, Alan Lew, Bruce Prideaux, Geoff Wall and his colleagues at Arizona State University for their listening ears and genuine collegiality. A special debt of gratitude is due to his wife (Carol) and four children (Kendall, Olivia, Aaron and Spencer) for allowing him to be absent so much as the final draft of this book was being prepared.

The book started when Stephen was in the Geography Department at Staffordshire University, England, and the following colleagues were great sounding boards for ideas: Rick Ball, Stephen Williams and Louise Bonner. Others who were great colleagues and friends during a difficult time in my personal life are Janet Wright, Paula Addison, John Ambrose, Hamish Main, Derek Pratts, Liz Young and Gordon Walker and to them I say thank you. I am also indebted to Rosemary Duncan, the cartographer in the Geography Department who drafted many of the figures in this book. The later stages of writing were completed after I had joined the Department of Tourism at the University of Otago. Michael Hall, my colleague (and boss), has been a constant source of wisdom and advice, and also assisted in this work by freeing up time for me to complete my writing obligations in the book. Thanks also to my current colleagues David Duval, Brent Lovelock, Hazel Tucker, Anna Carr, James Higham, Frances Cadogan and Melinda Elliott for their support, suggestions and keeping me sane at times, as well as to my graduate students, Wai Loong, Shiva, Nick, Isabella, who slotted their agendas around mine towards the end of writing. I owe a great debt to my parents, sister and brother in Northern Ireland who had to endure a 2001 Christmas vacation with me, which I spent writing instead of visiting. I can only promise that it will not happen again in 2002. This book is dedicated to our children and in my case my three sons, Richard, David and Edward, who live with their mother but remain an important part of my life, and who are an ongoing inspiration to me.

We are both grateful for Stephen Page's enthusiasm for the series and our book in particular from the start. His patience is much appreciated. Our gratitude also goes out to an excellent colleague and editor, Matthew Smith, and to Morten Fuglevand of Pearson Education, and to both of you we thank you for your perseverance and patience.

Publisher's acknowledgements

We are grateful to the following for permission to reproduce copyright material:

Table 5.1 reprinted from Garrod, B. and Fyall, A. (2000) 'Managing heritage tourism' in *Annals of Tourism Research*, with permission from Elsevier Science, 691; Figure 5.5 reprinted from Moscardo, G. (1996) 'Mindful visitors: heritage and tourism' in *Annals of Tourism Research*, with permission of Elsevier Science, 383; Table 5.7 from Moscardo, G. (1999) *Making visitors mindful: principles for creating sustainable visitor experiences through effective communication*, Champaign, IL, Sagamore Publishing, Inc.; Figure 6.1 from Light, D. (1995) 'Heritage as informal education', in Herbert, D.T. (ed.), *Heritage, Tourism and Society*, Mansell, London, 117–45; Table 6.1 reprinted from Prentice, R.C., Guerin, S. and McGugan, S. (1998) 'Visitor learning at a heritage attraction: a case study of Discovery as a media product', in *Tourism Management*, with permission of Elsevier Science, 16; Table 6.2 from Light, D. (1995) 'Heritage as informal education', in Herbert, D.T. (ed.), *Heritage, Tourism and Society*, Mansell, London, 134; Table 6.8 reprinted from Stewart, E.J., Hayward, B.M. and Devlin, P.J. (1998) 'The place of interpretation: a new approach to the evaluation of interpretation' in *Tourism Management*, with permission from Elsevier Science, 261; Figure 7.1 reprinted from Cohen, E. (1979) 'Rethinking the sociology of tourism' in *Annals of Tourism Research*, with permission from Elsevier Science, 26.

In some instances we have been unable to trace the owners of copyright material, and we would appreciate any information that would enable us to do so.

CHAPTER 1

Introduction

Travel has come to play a very important role in the lives of people today. Numbers of global travellers have grown exponentially since 1945, and now tourism represents the largest form of temporary migration in the world, and it is expected that within the next decade almost a billion international trips will be taken. Tourism texts have stated from the mid-1980s that tourism is the world's largest industry. No further comment is warranted, other than to state that international travel, and domestic travel to a lesser extent, to view new spaces and places, meet new people, experience new challenges and soak up new experiences has, for many, become a lifestyle. The World Tourism Organization (WTO) has recognised that heritage and culture have become a component in almost 40 per cent of all international trips undertaken. The WTO defines heritage tourism as 'an immersion in the natural history, human heritage, arts, philosophy and institutions of another region or country'. While it was perhaps common in the past for people to take at best one international trip per year, today this number is rising as the nature and duration of trips become more varied. As a result, destinations must cater to a wider array of interests, constantly repackaging the tourist experience or product they offer, and many are starting to recognise the potential that exists in selling and retelling the past. While most tourists are not in the habit of branding themselves with labels – that is something the industry imposes on itself – the experiences within destinations often are branded and categorised. This book focuses on one of these categories, namely heritage tourism. It is not a book on heritage alone, nor how heritage ought to be managed, for these have been covered elsewhere, addressed in natural, cultural and urban contexts (Ashworth and Tunbridge 2000; Graham *et al.* 2000; Hall and McArthur 1993a, 1998). In addressing this topic, however, it examines key concepts, such as supply, demand, conservation, management, interpretation, authenticity and politics. However, any understanding of heritage tourism requires an understanding of heritage, and it is from this point the discussion begins.

The meaning of heritage and heritage tourism

There has been much debate within the tourism literature, suggesting that academics often get more caught up in the rhetoric behind concepts than researching the issues that matter (see Fyall and Garrod 1998). While this point might indeed be valid, it is still necessary to define terms if only to simplify what is meant by heritage and the issues surrounding it. The tourism industry has been quick to label different types of experiences, reflecting the fact that there are different types of tourists, and hence different types of tourism, perhaps because there is a marketing justification for doing so. Academics have been equally quick to assign labels to tourism experiences and to define and redefine what is included in different types of tourism. Often forgotten is the fact that tourists rarely, if ever, see themselves conforming to a particular type-set. Instead their ultimate goal is to take away from a trip enjoyable memories and good experiences.

Most researchers accept that heritage is linked to the past, that it represents some sort of inheritance to be passed down to current and future generations, both in terms of cultural traditions and physical artefacts (Hardy 1988). As many authors have pointed out, it is what elements of the past a society wishes to keep (Fladmark 1998; Graham *et al.* 2000; Hall and McArthur 1998; Tunbridge and Ashworth 1996). This infers that heritage is selective. The historical record is incomplete, and not all heritages are what society values; what is desirable to keep are selections from the past. This may be deliberate or intentional, but society filters heritage through a value system that undoubtedly changes over time and space, and across society. In this context, Fowler (1989: 60) expressed that 'the past per se, but perhaps not that part of its produce which we call heritage, is emotionally neutral. It is neither exciting nor dull, good or bad, worthwhile nor worthless without our intercession.' As heritage assumes some aspect of value, that which is of personal value is labelled as personal or family heritage, whereas those values dictated by nations or communities become 'our' heritage (Hall and McArthur 1998), the latter often shaping a collective identity by way of symbols, icons and even mythologies. Some observers focus on heritage within a regional context, arguing that the

> region product must be pervasive . . . heritage must be broadly defined to encompass not only major historic sites and institutions, but the entire landscape of the region with its geographic base: farms and field patterns, roads, harbours, industrial structures, villages and main streets, commercial establishments and of course, the people themselves and their traditions and economic activities (Bowes 1989: 36).

This was reiterated by Ashworth and Tunbridge (1999: 105) a decade later when they saw heritage as the contemporary uses of the past . . . The interpretation of the past in history, the surviving relict buildings and artefacts and collective and individual memories are all harnessed in response to current needs which include the identification of individuals with social, ethnic and territorial entities and the provision of economic resources for commodification within heritage industries.

The fact that different views exist about the meaning of heritage, is often because the term 'heritage' is being applied to two different sorts of phenomena. As Merriman (1991: 8) pointed out:

On the positive side the word is used to describe culture and landscape that are cared for by the community and passed on to the future to serve people's need for a sense of identity and belonging. In this context, the use of the term 'heritage centre' in for example natural parks, covers institutions, which aim to care for them. These positive values of care and identity are in sharp contrast to the more negative and pejorative views of the term heritage. In this sense, as used in the 'heritage industry', the word has become synonymous with the manipulation (or even invention) and exploitation of the past for commercial ends.

Heritage can be classified as tangible immovable resources (e.g. buildings, rivers, natural areas); tangible movable resources (e.g. objects in museums, documents in archives); or intangibles such as values, customs, ceremonies, lifestyles, and including experiences such as festivals, arts and cultural events. Heritage may be classified according to type of attraction (Prentice 1993). Some examples include natural heritage, which is usually associated with protected areas like national parks (Dearden and Rollins 1993; Boyd 1995; Butler and Boyd 2000), living cultural heritage (e.g. fashions, foods, customs) (Boniface 1995; Nuryanti 1996; Richards 1996; Butler and Hinch 1996), built heritage (e.g. historic cities, cathedrals, monuments, castles) (Ashworth and Tunbridge 2000), industrial heritage – elements of a region's past that were influential in its growth and development (e.g. coal, lumber activity, textiles) (Edwards and Llurdés 1996; Jansen-Verbeke 1999), personal heritage – aspects of regions that have value and significance to individuals or groups of people (e.g. like the Normandy beach landings, cemeteries, religious sites) and dark heritage (e.g. places of atrocity, symbols of death and pain, and elements of the past some would prefer to forget) (Lennon and Foley 1999). It is important that a holistic and inclusive understanding of heritage is present in thinking, as heritage has been too often abused for social, political and economic reasons (Graham et al. 2000).

The extent to which the term 'heritage' has been misused is well illustrated by Tunbridge and Ashworth (1996: 1–3), who commented on how the meaning of heritage has taken on different dimensions:

- a synonym for any relic of the past;
- the product of modern conditions that are attributed to, and influenced by, the past;

- all cultural and artistic productivity produced in the past or present;
- includes elements from the natural environment that are survivals from the past, seen as original, typical and appropriate to be passed on to future generations;
- a major commercial activity, loosely recognised as the heritage industry, that is based on selling goods and services with a heritage component;
- adopted by political extremism where heritage is used to disguise ethnic or racial exclusivism.

Such broad-based thinking about the meaning of heritage has meant that it has long since moved away from being associated with an inheritance or legacy, which some commentators view as myopic and rather restrictive, to claims that heritage is 'any sort of intergenerational exchange or relationship' (Graham *et al.* 2000: 1), where it is linked to broad concepts of identity, power and economy.

Associations are often made between history, heritage and culture. Many people erroneously equate heritage with history. History, however, is the recording of the past as accurately as possible in so far as it can be accurate given present-day limitations of knowledge. Heritage is part of our past too, but it includes a range of aspects such as language, culture, identity and locality, to name those that have assumed some degree of importance. Cassia (1999: 247) explained the differences well by stating that 'history as a scholarly activity is a means of producing knowledge about the past, and heritage is a means of consumption of that knowledge'. Thus, 'history is what a historian regards as worth recording and heritage is what contemporary society chooses to inherit and to pass on' (Tunbridge and Ashworth 1996: 6). In summary, this definition, those described above, and many others simply point to the fact that heritage is not simply the past, but the modern-day use of elements of the past. Whether tangible or intangible, cultural or natural, it is a part of heritage.

Associations are often made between culture and heritage, perhaps because there is an obvious link in that heritage is part of cultural landscapes of the past and present (Zeppel and Hall 1992). The association between culture and heritage is clearly evident in how Tahana and Oppermann (1998: 23) defined cultural attractions to 'range from historical monuments to handicrafts or artefacts, from festivals to music and dance presentations, and from the bustling street life of a different culture to the distinct lifestyle of indigenous people'. By linking history, culture and the land where people live, a range of heritage sites emerges that includes a mix of tangible and intangible elements:

- historic buildings and monuments;
- sites of important past events like battles;
- traditional landscape and indigenous wildlife;
- language, literature, music and art;
- traditional events and folklore practices;

- traditional lifestyles including food, drink and sport (Swarbrooke 1994: 222).

What has clearly emerged by escalating the intellectual and economic profile of heritage is an expansion of the term to apply not only to the historic environment, both natural and built, but also to every dimension of material culture, intellectual inheritances and cultural identities (Tunbridge 1998a). Richards (2001a) saw that the same trend of inflated meaning has been applied to the use of the term 'culture' in relation to tourism. The terms 'cultural tourism', 'heritage tourism', 'ethnic tourism' and 'arts tourism' are almost interchangeable in their usage, with limited consensus regarding whether or not people are talking about the same thing. Richards (2001a: 7) saw linkages between these types in the following way. He views culture as comprised of processes (e.g. the ideas and way of life of people) and the outcomes of those processes (e.g. buildings, art, artefacts, customs). Cultural tourism, therefore, goes beyond the visitation of sites and monuments, to include consuming the way of life of places visited. With cultural tourism involving cultural products, and contemporary culture, Richards argues that cultural tourism encompasses both heritage tourism (defined as being related to artefacts of the past) as well as arts tourism (that related to contemporary cultural production). This is very much in keeping with how Hall and Zeppel (1990a: 87) viewed the connections between cultural and heritage tourism, stating that

> cultural tourism is experiential tourism based on being involved in and stimulated by the performing arts, visual arts and festivals. Heritage tourism, whether in the form of visiting preferred landscapes, historic sites, buildings or monuments, is also experiential tourism in the sense of seeking an encounter with nature or feeling part of the history of a place.

In a later work Zeppel and Hall (1992), while maintaining the links between heritage and cultural tourism, placed heritage tourism within a broad field of special interest travel, as aspects of tourism ranged from the examination of physical remains of the past and natural landscapes to the experience of local cultural traditions. Molloy (1993) holds a similar view, stressing that natural heritage shares many of the same principles overall with cultural heritage. Other authors have made the distinction between heritage tourism and cultural tourism. For example, Moscardo (2000) views the former as focusing on the past, while the latter focuses on the present. Butler (1997) questioned the relevance of making a distinction, arguing that what is important to the tourists is not the label they are assigned, but whether or not they left satisfied and having enjoyed the experience. The link between the two is established when he echoed the view of Prentice (1994) that heritage tourism has been hailed as one of the fastest growing forms of cultural tourism, and that if one can assign meaning to the term 'heritage' it is generally related to culture in the form of buildings, art, well-known places, material artefacts, and modern-day people who practice ways of life that are thought to reveal their heritage (Butler 1997).

In sum, what exists is a wide heritage spectrum (Richards 1996), which embraces ancient monuments, the built urban environment, aspects of the natural environment and many aspects of living culture and the arts. While some claim heritage to be an industry, what often emerges is individual resources within this spectrum regarding themselves as unique players and 'making decisions about tourism markets with little or no reference to what others are doing, while hoping to attract the same audience' (Middleton 1997: 215). The idea of a spectrum of heritage is returned to later, but another important element in understanding heritage and heritage tourism is the context in which it exists.

An alternative approach to clarifying heritage tourism has been offered by Poria et al. (2001). They challenge the merits of heritage tourism as a subgroup of tourism based on the historic attributes of a site or attraction: a view common in the literature (Peleggi 1996; Seale 1996). Instead they suggest that heritage tourism is a phenomenon based on tourists' motivations and perceptions rather than on the specific site attributes. In making this distinction, Poria et al. (2001: 1048) identify three types of heritage tourists: (1) those visiting a site they deem to be part of their heritage; (2) those visiting what they consider as a heritage site though it is unconnected with their own; and (3) and those visiting a heritage site specifically classified as a heritage place although unaware of this designation. On this basis they offer the following definition of heritage tourism: 'a subgroup of tourism, in which the main motivation for visiting a site is based on the place's heritage characteristics according to the tourists' perception of their own heritage' (Poria et al. 2001: 1048). This was, however, strongly criticised by Garrod and Fyall (2001: 1049), claiming it was clearly a demand-side definition, failing to consider the perspective of those who actually supply the heritage tourism experiences. They also question its merit on tautological grounds, that it ignores the issue of dissonance in heritage, and places too much emphasis on relying on the perceptions of tourists. What this difference in opinion illustrates is that the debate over the meaning of heritage and heritage tourism is alive.

Another important point is that heritage cannot be divorced from the context of its setting. For instance, from a northern European perspective, heritage is not heritage unless it involves a visit to urban places, often the historical cores of old cities. In contrast, to North Americans, heritage is strongly linked to visiting natural places, particularly national parks, but also the cultures of first peoples, attractions such as museums and galleries in urban environments, festivals in both rural and urban settings, and those special celebrations that highlight national identity. While the natural component of places is important to the Australian and New Zealander, heritage is also linked to the uniqueness of the culture, people (Aborigine, Maori, European settlers) and their identity that coexist within natural places and the built environment. In sum, heritage and how it is understood are inextricably linked to the context in which it occurs.

Modelling heritage and heritage tourism

This discussion demonstrates that heritage and heritage tourism are complex. To simplify the myriad viewpoints and expressions described above, the following model is proposed as a general model of heritage and heritage tourism (Figure 1.1). The model is approached from a behavioural perspective and is based on ideas prominent within behavioural geography in the last century. It is suggested here that heritage exists within two types of environment, namely 'phenomenal' and 'behavioural'. The former is an expansion of the normal concept of environment that includes natural phenomena and cultural and built environments that have been either altered or created by human activity (Kirk 1963). Conversely, the behavioural environment is where the social and cultural facts existing within the phenomenal environment are passed through a filter of human values. According to Kirk (1963), these form the basis on which decisions are made which may, or may not, be acted upon to be translated into action within the phenomenal environment. A similar analogy can be taken from the study of resource management. Zimmermann (1951: 15) is famous for coining the phrase 'resources are not, they become', meaning that resources existed as part of a physical world as 'neutral stuff' and only became a resource when they were perceived as having some value to society. In the context of heritage then, what this infers is that 'heritage' exists as part of a world of physical and social facts, namely the 'phenomenal environment'. It only becomes part of the behavioural environment when it is perceived by society and cultures to have value and some utilitarian function. As noted earlier, Hall and McArthur (1998) illustrate this by saying heritage is therefore formed from those elements of our past that we want to keep. As such, not everything is selected and so heritage is a product that has passed through a number of filters. In the first case, it needs to be perceived or recognised as heritage in order to move from the phenomenal to the behavioural environment, and then secondly, it is only heritage that is valued as a commodity that forms the heritage that is marketed and 'sold' to visitors. As such the position shifts to where heritage that has passed through an economic filter takes on an economic function, and it is around this that a heritage industry has emerged (Tunbridge and Ashworth 1996).

At the centre of this lies the heritage tourism experience, the key outcome of tourism as people in the end want to take away good experiences from their trip. These are provided for within what is loosely termed the heritage industry. As the enlarged inner section of the model illustrates, the heritage tourism experience is formed within what is labelled here as the 'experiential heritage environment'. The heritage tourism experience is influenced and shaped by a mix of elements: supply and demand, the nature of the heritage landscape that has been conserved and protected, the impacts heritage creates and leaves within destination regions, how heritage attractions and resources are managed, how it is interpreted and presented, as well as the role politics plays in

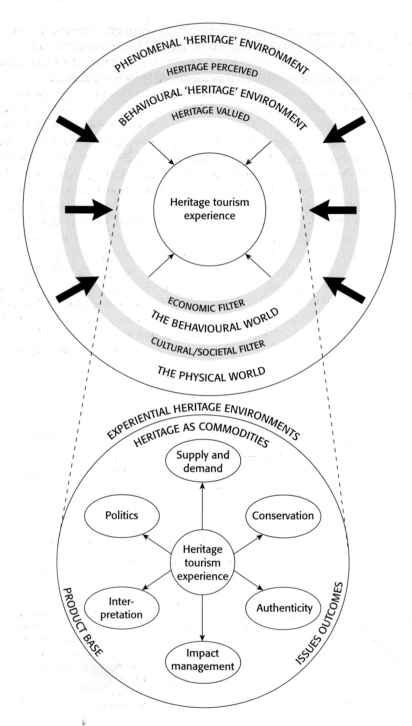

Figure 1.1   A model of heritage and heritage tourism

forming the heritage experience. Because the heritage tourism product is fashioned by tourism, the aspect of commoditisation features strongly within the experiences of tourists, experiences that are also influenced by the product base, issues and outcomes – all factors identified within the model.

It is important now to return to the question of a heritage spectrum as advocated earlier by Richards (1996). This concept is important as it helps to clarify the existence of many types of heritage experiences and heritage landscapes. Figure 1.2 suggests that the heritage landscapes traverse a multiplicity of settings ranging from the natural and pristine to the built-urban and artificial. As the figure also shows, this allows heritage tourism to have common characteristics with other types of tourism such as ecotourism (or nature-based tourism) within the left side of the spectrum, cultural tourism across the middle and urban tourism on the right. What this also demonstrates is that tourism types should not be viewed as mutually exclusive as overlaps most certainly exist. Because of this reality the model refers to heritage tourism as an overlapping concept. This overlapping of types also raises another important issue that ought to be addressed at the start of the book. This is not a book on ecotourism, yet much of natural heritage settings like national parks and protected areas are important venues for ecotourism. This book attempts to strike a balance by covering natural and cultural heritage, although many of the examples and issues lean more towards cultural, or built, heritage.

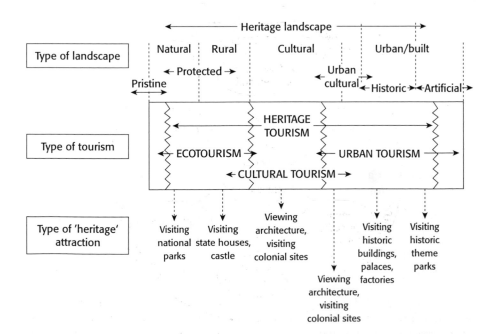

Figure 1.2 The heritage spectrum: an overlapping concept

Magnitude of heritage tourism

Heritage tourism has grown rapidly in recent years (Stebbins 1996) as a result of higher levels of education, more income, growing awareness of the world, globalisation processes that make the world a smaller place, technology, the effects of media and telecommunications (e.g. movies) and new types of heritage attractions. Even in times of recession, heritage tourism traditionally has continued to grow (Hanna 1993). What has emerged is that along with heritage, culture and arts have grown in importance at major destinations (Zeppel and Hall 1992). In fact, according to Richards (1996), change is taking place so rapidly that today's tourists are turning to periods as recent as the 1950s and 1960s for sources of heritage, an issue that Swarbrooke (1994) raised when asking how old something had to be to be considered heritage.

Research by Richards (1996: 261) revealed that heritage- and cultural-based tourism reflects a major shift in European tourism demand, although heritage and, more generally, cultural tourism is not an essential element in the tourism strategy advocated by the European Commission. In the USA 'cultural and historical attractions and destinations are the "in" thing, and . . . a new TIA marketing study [revealed] more than 65 million American adults made 86 million visits to arts/historic sites and events in [1996]' (*Travel and Tourism Executive Report* 1997: 1). Other examples that illustrate the magnitude of the market include the British Tourist Authority study of 1995 (cited in Hubbard and Lilley 2000), which stated that 20 per cent of all visits to tourist attractions in the UK were to historic properties, amounting to 67 million visits per year. A few years earlier Eastaugh and Weiss (1989: 58) were aware of the competitive advantages Britain had over other countries where heritage attractions were concerned, stating that '. . . our architectural and historic monuments are a major factor in making this country an attractive tourist destination for overseas visitors'. Light and Prentice (1994a) note that the heritage tourism industry has been one of Britain's growth industries of the past decade, important to both rural and urban tourism. In many parts of the world, heritage tourism is the primary form of tourism. For example, one study in Pennsylvania (USA) found that approximately 20 per cent of that state's tourism is heritage based. Heritage tourists, it was estimated, contributed nearly $5.5 billion to the state economy in 1997, including $1.34 billion in salaries, some 70,000 jobs and $617 million in tax revenue (*Travel Weekly* 1999). Pennsylvania has one of the richest reserves of national heritage sites in the United States, the Liberty Bell and Independence Hall being two of the most important.

A major factor in the growth of the industry has been the extent to which there has been a surge to preserve everything from the past and describe it as heritage. Carter (1994) argued that sentiment, nostalgia, local pride, tourism development, commercialisation and even desperation were at the forefront of converting past sites, particularly industrial-based ones, into attractions on the basis that there was no other suitable alternative left. This has created a situation where an oversupply of tourist attractions in general, and heritage sites in particular, has been reached (Middleton 1997). One cannot, however, challenge that heritage has been a key tool for bringing tourism into and regenerating declining urban and rural areas and bringing life to previously derelict industrial regions. The industry is not without its critics. Hewison (1987) and later Uzzell (1996) have condemned the heritage industry and tourism as evil forces that trivialise history and produce an inaccurate and shallow view of the past.

Recently, authors are trying to connect the interest of tourists in heritage and culture with the economics of the 1990s. Silberberg (1995) suggests that the economics of the 1990s triggered a change in peoples' perceptions from escapism to cultural enrichment. In one study he found that people in the 1990s valued cultural, historical and archaeological attractions as being more important than a good nightlife or fine food when planning a trip. Nuryanti (1997: 120–1) had this to say about the appeal of heritage for tourism:

> it is characterised by two seemingly contradictory phenomena: the unique and the universal. Each heritage site that is planned for tourism development has to maintain its unique attributes in order to be attractive and sustainable as a tourism destination. However, at the same time, although its meaning and significance may be contested, reinterpreted, recreated, and even reconstructed, the heritage site must have enough universal meaning to be shared by all the different visitors.

Development of heritage tourism

People have long used remnants of ancient and more modern pasts as recreational resources in urban and rural contexts (Newcomb 1979). Even in ancient days heritage tourism existed. It is the oldest form of tourism, and certainly not what some writers claim to be a new form of tourism (Prentice 1994). Within the context of modern tourism, there is justification to argue that heritage tourism has formed part of what is known as special interest travel (Zeppel and Hall 1992). Ancient records (to today's world inhabitants) tell of traders, sailors and adventurers travelling to see the Great Pyramids and the Nile. The ancient explorers were one early form of tourists. Even those who made the Grand Tour of Europe during the Middle Ages moved between ancient cities of culture to see grand buildings, cathedrals and artistic works (Marsh 1989). The Grand Tour, popular with the upper-class elite of Europe during the sixteenth and seventeenth centuries as an educational and culturally refining experience, included visits to such historic cities as Paris, Turin, Milan, Venice, Florence, Rome and Naples (Towner 1985, 1996). They followed a consistent route that took them from Paris through the lower Rhône valley into northern Italy, down to Rome and Naples to return to England via the German Rhineland and the Low Countries. The length of time spent on the Tour varied from as long as 40 months in the mid-sixteenth century to only four months in the mid-nineteenth century. The people who engaged in this travel phenomenon also varied over time. The early travellers were English, often of landlord aristocracy, but by the late eighteenth century the Tour was popular among lawyers, physicians, bankers and merchants. The aristocracy had long moved on to explore Portugal, Greece and the Near East (Towner 1996), suggesting that Plog's (1973) allocentric and psychocentric ideas were evident even in early forms of tourism. By the mid-nineteenth century, the Tour was popular among early American tourists. Today, many cities along the Grand Tour route remain popular sites of cultural and heritage tourism. Millar (1989: 14) noted that 'individual heritage sites such as Notre Dame Cathedral and the Eiffel Tower in Paris, or the Tower of London and Shakespeare's birthplace at Stratford-upon-Avon in England, provide the motivation for people to visit a country in the first place'. Butler (1996) denotes how travellers taking the Grand Tour in modern times are very different from the early travellers of the route (see Table 1.1).

While there exists some variation in the characteristics of modern-day Grand Tour consumers, tourists' fiscal and temporal constraints often mean they cannot retrace the travel patterns of the early tourists taking part in the Grand Tour. As will be commented on later in the book (see Chapter 3), it is possible to distinguish heritage tourists who conform both to the allocentric and psychocentric extremes of Plog's (1973) model. Heritage tourists travelling the slave routes of West Africa, the Silk Route across Asia, the routes between temples in South-East Asia and the routes throughout the regions of the former Aztec and Mayan civilisations of Latin America, are examples of allocentric heritage tourists; they are in a sense modern-day versions of the earliest travellers engaged on the Grand Tour. In contrast, modern-day tourists whose visit to Europe only takes in the major Western European cities (e.g. Rome, Paris, London) as part of a larger holiday where the focus is on pleasure over learning, qualify as heritage tourists towards the psychocentric end of the

Table 1.1 Comparisons between Grand Tour participants past and present

Characteristics	Early tourists	Modern tourists
Length of trip	Months to several years	Few days to a few weeks
Nature of experience	In-depth learning	Shallow experience
Places visited	Many and for long periods	Few and for short periods
Activities engaged in	In-depth learning	Shallow experiences
Purpose of the experience	Education (development)	Enjoyment (prestige)
Level of knowledge	High (informed on cultures)	Low (some preparation)
Market size	Limited to elite (small)	Large (open to masses)

Source: After Butler (1997).

spectrum. However one classifies the modern-day heritage tourist, new Grand Tours are being recreated and the original one still followed, so the idea of 'Grand Tours' will remain with heritage tourism for some considerable time.

Value and significance of heritage

Earlier in the chapter reference was made to values and value systems in determining what aspects of heritage have been conserved over time. The focus of value shifts to the significance people place on heritage. Hall and McArthur (1993a) identified four interrelated areas of significance in heritage: economic, social, political and scientific significance.

- *Economic significance*: heritage is preserved because of the value it offers in terms of expenditures of visitors to sites (Zeppel and Hall 1992). Tourism is big business, illustrated by private sector sponsorship as a means to generate income for sites, but sponsorship can also be used to target an audience that is socially responsible and has green tendencies. The economic significance of heritage may also be demonstrated in the development of the user-pays approach to entry of many heritage sites (see discussion in Chapter 5) as heritage is increasingly facing a situation of having to pay its own way.

- *Social significance*: this refers to the personal and collective identity that people and society have with 'their' heritage. A social conscience will often be the driving impetus to consider preservation in the first instance. Heritage can also help determine a sense of place; creating situations where people can use heritage to gain attachment to an area, and maintain a sense of place that remains virtually unchanged.

- *Political significance*: as will be illustrated in Chapter 8, the meaning and symbolism of heritage may serve political ends. As Hall and McArthur note, heritage by definition is political, in terms of reinforcing what is conserved, how heritage is told, and placing the wishes of private owners of heritage into conflict with government or public interests.

- *Scientific significance*: many national parks and protected areas may contain gene pools and ecosystems that will be useful to medicine. They also provide habitats for rare and endangered species. As benchmarks can be more easily established to measure change in protected areas, as opposed to settled environments, useful research can be undertaken on ecological processes often within a non-threatening context. There is also an educative component to heritage – providing visitors with information about the living history, culture, people of areas, lessons which are important in the relationship established between European settlers and the indigenous peoples of areas.

Scales of heritage

Heritage is not homogeneous; it exists at different levels or scales, namely world, national, local and personal (Graham *et al.* 2000; Swarbrooke 1994; Timothy 1997). Figure 1.3 illustrates these scales of heritage tourism experience, suggesting that they are all linked by the notion of 'shared heritage'.

World

Timothy (1997) noted that world-scale heritage attractions draw large masses of tourists from many countries. However, for most foreign tourists, these sites themselves are likely to be only a small part of a more extensive itinerary. Although these attractions may invoke feelings of awe, they probably do not invoke feelings of personal attachment. Visits to ancient monuments are largely motivated by the belief that such objects really are linked to the remote past. Indeed, for many tourists, visiting international heritage attractions is a way of appreciating universal civilisation and achieving some degree of human unity (Moulin 1991).

The early 1970s saw awareness for world sites turn into concern expressed at international conferences on national parks, and in the UN's Environment Programme and UNESCO's Man and Biosphere Programme. Each of the gatherings discussed and favoured the idea of a world convention. This resulted in the Convention for the Protection of the World's Cultural and Natural Heritage being adopted by UNESCO in 1972.

The World Heritage Committee (WHC) (an international non-governmental body) was formed under the terms of the Convention to carry out distinctive

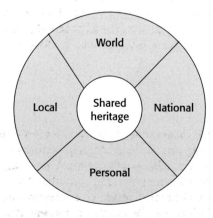

Figure 1.3 Scales of heritage tourism
Source: Timothy (1997).

functions (see Chapter 4). First, it was to produce a World Heritage List of cultural and natural properties 'of outstanding universal value' from nominations submitted by state parties, a term used by the WHC for a country that has ratified the 1972 Convention. The International Council of Monuments and Sites (ICOMOS) was charged with the assessment of cultural heritage, whereas natural sites were to be assessed by the International Union for Conservation of Nature and Natural Resources (IUCN). Second, from the accepted and inscribed properties, the WHC was to produce a List of World Heritage in Danger, for the purposes of emergency assistance. Third, the WHC was charged with administering a World Heritage Fund to assist needy state parties in protecting their World Heritage properties. A logical fourth function was added later – monitoring the state of conservation of all inscribed properties.

This multinational legislation has been considered one of humankind's most successful pieces of international co-operation, which has now been operational for over a quarter of a century, during which time 721 sites have been listed.

In light of the fact that heritage of global importance derives its status from the imprimatur of an international body, it is important to remember that only individual countries can nominate sites to be inscribed, meaning that world heritage is thus the sum of scrutinised national heritages, a situation which has the potential to create competition given that heritage becomes an expression of national self-esteem.

National

'Through time, certain heritage features come to symbolize a society's shared recollections' (Lowenthal 1975: 12). For example, to Americans, the Liberty Bell and Independence Hall in Philadelphia and Arlington National Cemetery in Virginia are representative of collective, national heritage attractions that may arouse strong feelings of patriotism. On this level, historical monuments often represent durable national ideals, and national pride can be an important stimulus of preserving the built environment in Western societies (Lowenthal 1975; Timothy 1997).

Local

Lowenthal (1979b: 554) noted that at the local level, communities need familiar landmarks so that they can remain in touch with their own collective pasts in a rapidly changing world. Many cities, towns and villages go to great lengths to conserve scenes and structures of the past that 'would never qualify for preservation grants as architectural gems or ancient monuments'.

Most of the world's historic sites are not internationally known, and only relatively few ever attract tourists from abroad, except perhaps in conjunction with other attractions. For every world-famous heritage attraction, there are

hundreds of other sites of more local fame (Wall 1989). These kinds of attractions stir emotions and contribute to a local heritage experience. 'Memorials
erected in memory of a community's earliest pioneer efforts, or a local historical
museum, can provide an important experience for locals to which outsiders
may not be able to relate' (Timothy 1997: 752). Throughout rural America,
small communities have recently been involved in a trend to establish and
support small historic sites of local concern (Ambler 1995). Many small
historic sites have common elements – churches, historic homes, schools,
businesses/shops and farmhouses (Ambler 1995). Richards (2001a: 11) has
pointed out that

> while [the] debate rages, however, the policy makers continue to invest in cultural
> attractions. This is often a matter of local pride and prestige. Every town and city
> feels that it is important enough to warrant its own theatre, concert hall, museum
> or heritage centre, regardless of the local demand for such facilities.

This has led to thousands of small villages and towns around the world
building community museums in an effort to demonstrate their heritage.

Personal

Lowenthal (1979b) asserted that modern-day destruction of historic relics
has deepened people's sense of nostalgia for the past. A search for roots and
historical identity and an increased appreciation for one's culture and family
legacy are evidence of this phenomenon. Of the four types of heritage presented
here, personal heritage has received the least attention in the literature and
hence is least understood (Timothy 1997). Personal heritage attractions draw
people who possess emotional connections to a particular place. These also
include heritage associated with specific interest groups to which a traveller
belongs, including religious societies, ethnic groups and career groups.

Family history research is an important aspect of personal heritage tourism.
In Salt Lake City, the Church of Jesus Christ of Latter-Day Saints operates the
world's largest genealogical library. Every year the library attracts thousands
of people of diverse backgrounds who travel from many parts of the world to
search for their roots and to support personal identities (Hudman and Jackson
1992). Family reunions are another important type of personal heritage experience that, for some people, can entail travelling great distances. Travel to
countries, regions and villages from which their ancestors migrated is common
among people trying to find their roots. For example, Franco-Americans are
becoming more aware of their ties to Quebec, and many are beginning to feel
a sense of belonging to the 'Mother Land'. In recent years, this has amounted
to increased numbers of French-speaking Americans travelling to Quebec to
discover their origins (Louder 1989). There are 60 million people worldwide
claiming to have Irish ancestry as a result of the Irish diaspora. In the United
States alone, the Irish community is estimated to be around 40 million. This

group is known for travel back to the homeland, and large-scale Irish kin reunions are held each year where people of Irish descent congregate by the thousand. Activities in personal destination areas commonly involve research in community archives, churches and cemeteries. Tracking down houses where grandparents grew up or churches where ancestors were married are also characteristic of this type of heritage experience.

Military reunions and travel to former battlegrounds by war veterans are one form of personal heritage tourism that is increasing in importance (Smith 1996). Timothy (1997: 753) notes that

> travel to historic places of religious, cultural, and vocational interest is another form of personal heritage tourism. Visiting a steam engine museum may stir up feelings of nostalgia for retired railway workers, and for Muslim pilgrims from Southeast Asia, a visit to historic Mecca can be a very personal, spiritual, and rewarding experience.

While the above discussion has highlighted different levels of heritage tourism experiences, significant boundaries between types of encounters remain blurred when a particular experience to one person may be different from what it is to another, even if it occurs at the same location. For example, an ancient Buddhist temple may be viewed as world heritage to one international visitor but personal heritage to another of the Buddhist faith. Similarly, for day visitors to Gettysburg National Military Park from nearby regions, the attraction and its related experience may be considered local heritage, but to millions of other Americans it is part of their collective national identity (Timothy 1997).

Structure of the book

This book is structured around the conceptual model illustrated in Figure 1.1. This is deliberate as the model shapes the authors' thinking of heritage tourism, and each chapter is an extension of it and the development of the argument around each of the key themes. As already stated, these key themes are supply, demand, reasons why the past has been conserved, the management of heritage tourism, interpretation, the authenticity debate within heritage and the association and role played by politics where heritage is concerned. Chapter 2, in addressing the supply side of tourism, examines different categories of attraction, the support services that operate at heritage locations, the contexts within which heritage exists and additional perspectives on scale from the perspective of supply. Chapter 3 examines heritage tourism demand, focusing on the nature of heritage demand, visitor characteristics, the motivations that drive people to visit heritage places and the obstacles that keep large portions of society from visiting heritage locations. Chapter 4 discusses the reasons why the past has been conserved, types of conservation, and the challenges that heritage operators face from the impacts this form of tourism creates. The longest discussion is given to the management of heritage tourism and is the focus of Chapter 5. A multifaceted array of issues are examined, such as ownership, economics, strategies for managing visitors and residents and how the marketing of heritage tourism can be approached with management in mind. Chapter 6 addresses heritage interpretation, involving an examination of first the origins of interpretation, followed by the various roles of interpretation, the interpretive planning process, the challenges managers face in delivering interpretive programmes, ending with useful tools to aid in heritage interpretation. Related to interpretation, Chapter 7 re-examines the debate on authenticity and asks some difficult and important questions regarding this matter. Chapter 8 offers a discourse on the politics of heritage, dealing with issues related to power, the use of heritage propaganda to create place image and nationalism, as well as the impacts of political conflict on the heritage infrastructure. Chapter 9 offers a brief summary and returns to key themes presented throughout the book, such as how conservation manifests itself, sustainability in heritage tourism, the challenges facing operators, interpretation and authenticity, and the role that politics plays in creating and shaping heritage. Within these chapters case studies of different lengths are provided to illustrate key points and smaller examples are alluded to frequently to illustrate examples from both the developed and developing worlds in the contexts of natural, cultural, rural and urban environments.

Questions

1. What factors account for the complexity that exists with the term 'heritage'?
2. What significance do you attach to heritage that is present in the region in which you currently live?
3. What is the evidence to support heritage tourism as one of the oldest forms of tourism?
4. How much support do you give to the idea that we are creating new 'Grand Tours' where heritage is concerned?

Further reading

Graham, B. Ashworth, G.J. and Tunbridge, J.E. (2000) A Geography of Heritage: Power, culture and economy. Arnold, London.

Herbert, D.T. (ed.) (1995) Heritage, Tourism and Society, Mansell, London.

Fowler, P. (1992) The Past in Contemporary Society: Then, now, Routlege, London.

Hewison, R. (1987) The Heritage Industry: Britain in a climate of decline, Methuen, London.

McKercher, B. and Du Cros, H. (2002) Cultural Tourism: The partnership between tourism and cultural heritage management, Haworth, New York.

CHAPTER 2

The heritage tourism supply

It is not uncommon to find a discussion on aspects of supply in most tourism texts today, and this book is no exception. Much research has focused on the supply side of tourism (e.g. Ashworth 1990a; Browne and Stevens 1996; Smith 1988; Wall *et al.* 1985; Wigle 1994), most general tourism texts devote an early chapter to supply issues, while most themed multi-authored texts cover the topic either within a dedicated chapter or through passing references to it within chapters addressing different issues, but where some discussion of supply has relevance. In general, supply means the tourism resources and services of a region. Where supply has been addressed within a specific context, such as urban places, it has been contextualised more precisely as consisting of primary, secondary and tertiary elements (Jansen-Verbeke and Lievois 1999). Attractions are usually viewed as the primary elements, comprising both activity places (e.g. cultural, sport and amusement facilities) and their leisure setting (physical characteristics and sociocultural features). Secondary elements focus on the service aspects offered within a region, namely accommodation, shopping and markets, whereas tertiary, or additional, elements are those relating to the infrastructure required to connect tourists to the attractions, such as transportation, information and parking facilities.

In this chapter, supply is taken to involve a mix of these features, as attention is paid not only to the types of heritage attractions offered to visitors, but also the setting and context in which the heritage exists, as well as the support services that have developed around heritage tourism. As already noted in the introductory chapter, greater attention is given over to cultural heritage than natural heritage in this book. Given this, heritage attractions described below include artefacts and places associated with wars and other armed conflicts, religious sites and events, living culture, industrial pasts and literary places. The chapter then describes the setting and context of heritage supply, addressing this for urban, rural and protected areas. It is within the protected areas section that natural heritage attractions, particularly parks, are discussed, in part because natural heritage is an important tourism resource for regions, but also because many parks are themselves popular tourist attractions. The support services necessary for heritage tourism are discussed in the following section. Those that may enhance or facilitate the continued existence and growth of heritage tourism are taken to be shops and catering services, transportation and accommodation. Aspects of scale and regional variation are addressed, and while both were addressed in Chapter 1, the focus here is to illustrate that similar heritage attractions exist at different scales, and that regional variation in the type of heritage supply is often a function of the context within which heritage exists. Heritage trails are used, by way of example, to demonstrate the presence of scale within heritage resources, and a case study is offered to readers of heritage trail development in Mombasa, Kenya, to illustrate the diversity of attraction that is needed to develop the supply side of heritage trails.

Heritage attractions

The foundation of heritage tourism is heritage attractions. Thousands of examples exist throughout the world of natural and cultural heritage sites that are of international acclaim and many more thousands of local notoriety. All of these play important roles in the supply of tourism, although they may draw different market segments (i.e. international tourists and local recreational users). In the United States nearly 350 cultural and natural heritage sites are owned and operated by the US National Park Service (Table 2.1). Likewise, almost 500 cultural attractions are operated by English Heritage (Table 2.2).

Table 2.1   US National Park properties, 2000

National battlefields	10	National parkways	4
National battlefield parks	3	National preserves	8
National historic sites	70	National recreation areas	17
National historical parks	37	National reserves	1
National lakeshores	4	National rivers	4
National memorials	28	National seashores	10
National military parks	9	National wild and scenic rivers	5
National monuments	68	Other parks	11
National parks	55	Total	344

Source: Compiled from US National Park Service (2001).

Table 2.2 Types of properties owned by English Heritage in 2002

Abbeys, churches and priories	83
Historic houses	49
Archaeological sites	83
Gardens/parks	22
Industrial monuments	10
Royal residences	7
Great antiquity	11
Romantic ruin	35
Castle/fort	110
Humps and bumps	1
Other (pot luck)	57
Total	479*

* Some attractions were counted in more than one category.
Source: Compiled from English Heritage (2002).

Many heritage attractions have been drawing visitors for centuries (e.g. the Pyramids of Egypt and Holy Land sites), while others are of more recent vintage (e.g. cathedrals and battlefields), and some are very ancient but only recently discovered by archaeologists (e.g. Native American ruins). Thus, throughout the world, there exists a wide array of heritage attractions of various age, size and historical significance.

The supply of heritage attractions can be changed in two basic ways. First, it can be widened. For example, new sites may be discovered, and sites that were not seen previously as significant attractions can be designated as such. Second, the supply can be deepened. This refers to the enhancement of existing attractions through actions like adding a visitor centre or bringing in additional relics and buildings to augment what already exists (Johnson and Thomas 1995).

Prentice (1994) offers a comprehensive, if overlapping, typology of heritage attractions based on the emerging heritage issues and themes that have developed in recent years and appeared in the literature (Table 2.3). Although many specific types of heritage attractions were identified by Prentice, space limitations do not allow a detailed examination of them all. Therefore, the following sections comprise a selection of some of the more common and timely heritage attractions today. These include museums, war sites, religious sites, living culture, industrial locations and relics, and literary heritage. It should also be noted that there may be some overlap between the types of attractions described here, and more than one of Prentice's (1994) types may be included within one type listed here.

Table 2.3   Types of heritage attractions

Natural history attractions – nature preserves, nature trails, aquatic displays, wildlife parks, zoos, caves, gorges, cliffs, waterfalls

Scientific attractions – science museums, technology centres, 'hands-on' science centres

Primary production attractions – farms, dairies, agricultural museums, vineyards, fishing, mining

Craft centres and workshops – water and windmills, sculptors, potters, woodcarvers, metal shops, glass makers, silk working, lace making, craft villages

Manufacturing centres – pottery and porcelain factories, breweries, cider factories, distilleries, industrial history museums

Transportation attractions – transport museums, railways, canals, shipping and docks, civil aviation, motor vehicles

Sociocultural attractions – prehistoric and historic sites and displays, domestic houses, history museums, costume museums, furniture museums, museums of childhood, toy museums, ancient ruins

Attractions associated with historic people – sites, areas, and buildings associated with famous writers, painters and politicians

Performing arts attractions – theatres, performing arts, circuses

Pleasure gardens – ornamental gardens, period gardens, arboreta, model villages

Theme parks – nostalgia parks, historic adventure parks, fairytale parks

Galleries – art and sculpture

Festivals and pageants – historic fairs, festivals, recreating past ages, countryside festivals

Stately and ancestral homes – palaces, castles, country houses, manor houses

Religious attractions – cathedrals, churches, abbeys, mosques, shrines, temples, springs, wells

Military attractions – battlefields, military airfields, naval dockyards, prisoner of war camps, military museums

Genocide monuments – sites associated with the extermination of other races or other mass killings of populations

Towns and townscapes – historic urban centres, groups of buildings, shops, urban settings

Villages and hamlets – rural settlements, architecture, pastures

Countryside and treasured landscapes – national parks, rural landscapes

Seaside resorts and seascapes – seaside towns, marine landscapes, coastal areas

Regions – counties and other historic regions identified as distinctive by residents and visitors

Source: Adapted from Prentice (1994).

Museums

Museums of one sort or another have existed for centuries. However, the original purpose of museums was somewhat different from what it is today. They were established to house relics for scholarship, curatorship and research, not necessarily for public viewing (Light 1995a; West 1988). However, in time, museums developed into places where artefacts and buildings were protected and shown to visitors. Formal museums as they are known today were established during the seventeenth century. England's first public museum, the Ashmolean, opened in 1683 and was the first modern museum designed specifically to display its collections to the public in addition to preserving artefacts for teaching and research purposes (Bennett 1995; Walsh 1992).

During the 1700s, museums began to open up in North America, one of the first being the Charleston Museum in South Carolina. The growth of museums in the United States was different from that in Europe. Public museums existed in the United States long before the private collections. In Europe, however, private museums preceded public ones. Early American museums, such as the Charleston Museum and Peale's Museum in Philadelphia, aimed to display their collections to the public, although their modes of presentation were lacking in sophistication and were more 'cabinets of curiosity' than organised interpretive displays (Walsh 1992: 21). Likewise, early museums were designed to be imposing places, frequently resembling cathedrals, in which the visitor felt awe and reverence (Light 1995a: 119).

According to Walsh (1992) the development of public museums is a result of the modern idea of progress (e.g. industrialisation and urbanisation) and the emerging historical disciplines, beliefs echoed by Lowenthal (1985). Likewise, Walsh (1992) argues that the development of local-level governance and social education programmes contributed significantly to this movement.

Many types of museums have developed during the past century. Almost every community in Europe and North America has some kind of museum, which it hopes will not only conserve some aspects of community heritage but also draw visitors to the town and provide leisure experiences for local residents. Some of the more prominent types of museums include the following:

- *Art museums* – commonly display paintings, sculptures, photography and handicrafts. The heritage value of most art forms is significant. Some of the most popular individual tourist attractions in the world are art museums (e.g. the Louvre in Paris and the Sistine Chapel in the Vatican City).

- *Sports museums* – celebrate local sport figures or those of more international acclaim (e.g. the Baseball Hall of Fame in Cooperstown, New York). Such museums commonly house relics such as uniforms, sporting equipment, certifications, photographs and other sport-related paraphernalia.

- *Music museums* – display photographs, musical instruments, clothing, awards, albums and other related equipment produced and used by famous musicians (e.g. the Rock and Roll Hall of Fame and Museum in Cleveland, Ohio).

- *War/armory museums* – celebrate war heroes and display remnants of armed conflicts. Weapons, ammunition, uniforms, letters, medallions, photographs, vehicles and evidence of atrocities are commonly found in war museums (e.g. Imperial War Museum in London).

- *Industrial museums* – can be based in functioning industrial centres and factories, in derelict buildings that have been renovated for use as a museum, or in purpose-built structures. These usually demonstrate manufacturing or extractive processes and exhibit goods extracted or produced in that type of establishment. Many of the mines and factories of the UK, Australia and the United States are good examples of industrial museums.

- *Stamp/coin/postcard museums* – are favoured attractions for many travellers. Collectors and non-collectors alike have a common interest in these types of museums, for they can reveal a great deal about the historical development of nations. Some small countries (e.g. Liechtenstein and San Marino) depend a great deal on stamps and coins in their tourism industries and have established impressive numismatic and philatelic museums.

- *Science museums* – reflect an interest in the heritage of technology and knowledge. These are popular for their innovative nature and often hands-on approach to interpretation and presentations. Transportation and other technological innovations, geology, climate and weather, animals, chemistry and vegetation are often the focus of these museums. The Canadian Science and Technology Museum in Ottawa is a good example of this type.

- *Local historical museums* – are popular throughout the developed world. They are commonly used to house artefacts of local importance ranging from maps and photographs to agricultural tools, clothing and building materials. The establishment of such museums is sometimes seen as a substantiation of a specific heritage or a statement of importance on the part of local communities.

Many museums are housed in older buildings that possess some degree of historical significance but which have been refurbished expressly for this purpose. Castles, churches, barns and farmhouses, schools, factories and stately homes are typical of this type of museum structure. Industrial and local historical museums frequently fall within this category. In many locations where such buildings do not exist, structures are built specifically for the purpose of housing museum collections. Science and sport museums generally fit this description.

One specific form of museum that has developed and gained popularity over the past century is the open-air folk life museum. These are known by several names including among others, living museums, historic theme parks and folk life museums. In response to the perceived threat of the Industrial Revolution and its impact on traditional lifestyles, traditional structures were rebuilt and preserved, and old ways of life began to be lived out (Gruffudd 1995; Richards 2001a). This notion first developed in Sweden in 1873 with the founding of the Museum of Scandinavian Folklore, which expanded and formally reopened

Plate 2.1   Open-air museum – Stockholm, Sweden

in 1891 (Walsh 1992) (Plate 2.1). Norway followed suit in 1894 and Denmark in 1909 with their versions of living folk life museums. As modernity began to replace many traditions and cultural practices in the late 1800s and early 1900s, many countries began to join the efforts to preserve rural lifestyles, cultural relics and folk traditions by establishing living heritage museums. This was particularly the case following the Second World War (Richards 2001a). Today, hundreds of these types of outdoor museums function in nearly all parts of the world, but they are particularly notable in Europe, North America and Asia. In most cases, volunteers and paid staff walk around in period costumes, some talking with visitors and others keeping to themselves, or demonstrating traditional ways of life and skills that might have been used in blacksmith shops, tanneries, bakeries, shipyards, cobbler shops and on farms.

Zeppel and Hall (1991) suggested that people like to visit historic theme parks because they are interested in history and have a desire to learn how people lived in bygone days. However, historic theme parks have received a great deal of criticism in recent years by observers who see them as presenting fake history and inaccurate lifestyles of the past (e.g. Barthel 1990; Gable and Handler 1996; Hewison 1991; Walsh 1992; Wells 1993). These criticisms will be discussed later in Chapter 7.

War/defence heritage

Another important type of heritage attraction is artefacts and places associated with wars and other armed conflicts. Several authors have examined war heritage in considerable detail (Ashworth 1991; Lloyd 1998; Smith 1996; Uzzell 1989c). Aside from regular museums, war heritage commonly takes the form of battlefields, cemeteries and memorials.

Smith (1996) discusses several forms of war attractions. 'Heroic' attractions, she notes, are designed to commemorate famous war heroes, such as George Washington, Alexander the Great and Napoleon – political figures who provoked war or heads of state and military chiefs. 'Remember the fallen' attractions are hallowed ground, where lives were lost in defence of national principles and personal freedoms. These often emanate an eerie sense of the supernatural and the mystery of the people who died there. Battlefields and war-related cemeteries are major attractions of this type, as are memorials to fallen soldiers (e.g. the Korean and Vietnam memorials in the United States). 'Lest we forget' war sites are those that remind visitors not to forget the freedoms and causes for which battles were fought. Anne Frank's house in Amsterdam and the Holocaust sites in Poland and Germany have this in common. Finally, 'reliving the past' attractions are overwhelmingly comprised of military re-enactments, usually held at historic forts and battlegrounds. This is a particularly popular activity in the United States and Canada in commemoration of the Civil War, Revolutionary War and the War of 1812.

Battlefields have become important conservation areas and major tourist attractions in eastern North America and Western Europe (Lloyd 1998). In the United States the growing importance placed upon war sites brought about legislation in 1990, namely The Civil War Sites Study Act, which aimed to establish a commission to study unpreserved Civil War sites, evaluate their short- and long-term threats and provide alternatives for their conservation and interpretation (Johnson and Sullivan 1993: 21). According to Smith (1996), visitors are attracted to battlefields for two reasons: because they are military history enthusiasts or they are intrigued by the sacred nature of the places that memorialise 'the fallen'.

War graves, memorials and cemeteries are another growing element of heritage tourism (Plate 2.2). The Pacific War Graves together with the *Arizona* memorial at Pearl Harbor are an important part of American military heritage that are visited by millions of tourists every year (Seaton 2002). Likewise, Arlington National Cemetery in Virginia is an evocative attraction where Americans can experience a deep sense of nationhood and increased levels of patriotism (Timothy 1997). There have long existed guidebooks to war graves and memorials for people making pilgrimage-like tours to battlefields and cemeteries such as those of the Somme and Flanders (Seaton 2000).

Governments and defence heritage managers approach conservation and interpretation from a variety of perspectives usually motivated by an underlying goal they wish to achieve, or an image they wish to create. Ashworth (1991: 179–83) identified six common approaches to the presentation of war heritage used by governments and heritage officers:

Plate 2.2 War graves at Arlington National Cemetery

1. A *nationalist approach* – refers to the ideological use of defence heritage to support a state's set of ideals. This can be called nationalism where it is used to legitimise the nation state. This aim is most commonly achieved through museum/historic site displays and interpretation, education pro- grammes and media images.

2. A *'romantic chivalry' approach* – is the most common approach to most medieval military architecture where attention is directed to knights and damsels. War is portrayed as a mixture of sport and the social responsibil- ity of a specific class. This view commonly involves re-enacting jousting tournaments and royal banquets.

3. A *cultural separatist or local patriotic approach* – is essentially a regional or local variation of the nationalist approach, but it uses defence heritage to defend a separatist identity. The emphasis is upon the role of military heritage and place associations in defence against the central authority. Basque and Scottish separatist efforts, while quite different from each other, are examples of this approach.

4. A *socialist approach* – From this perspective, the status of nobility is down- played and replaced with a stronger emphasis on the common person or peasantry, and how they suffered the effects of war or fought in national defence. This has a socialist slant as it tries to repress class distinctions and create a broader social equity in heritage representation.

5. A *technological/aesthetic approach* – is seen as a value-neutral approach, in so far as attention is directed to the form of the relict or reconstructed objects themselves and away from the actual purpose for which they were designed. Defence artefacts become part of industrial archaeology or architectural history.

6. A *peace and international understanding approach* – War heritage is sometimes used to support international understanding, rather than competition, and to advance peace instead of war. For supporters of this perspective, widespread interest in the sites and accessories of war represents an unhealthy trend that will likely contribute to a glorification of past conflicts and thereby make future conflicts more likely.

Most people's interest in war/defence heritage stems from a curiosity about the origins of the present world and the struggles endured to arrive at it (Ashworth 1990b), as well as a reinforcement of group identity, national pride and 'social, political and economic aspirations and their fulfillment' (Smith 1996: 263). Ashworth (1990b) agrees, as he suggests that organised physical conflict between people stirs up a distinctive, widespread and extremely powerful emotional appeal. War and its relics are of particular interest to historians, conservationists and public officials for its educational role. A common belief is that 'war will never be prevented by those who know nothing of it and thus it follows that defence heritage has an important educative task in ensuring that the past is not allowed to repeat itself' (Ashworth 1990b: 70).

While not necessarily a form of war or defence heritage, a related type of heritage exists that focuses on tragedies and atrocity. Tourism associated with death has recently received considerable attention from researchers and has been termed 'thanatourism', or dark tourism (Foley and Lennon 1996; Lennon and Foley 1999, 2000; Seaton 1996, 2002). Sites of mass murders, cemeteries, deadly accidents and deadly natural disasters are examples of attractions fitting this classification. The tunnel in Paris where Princess Diana was killed has become a virtual shrine for some people and a location of curiosity for many visitors to the city, just as the location where the World Trade Center towers used to stand in New York City is becoming a site of major tourist interest. Atrocities associated with war and other violent encounters also form part of the attraction base for dark tourism, such as the Holocaust museums in Europe, Israel and the United States. Concentration camps, too, play a significant role in atrocity heritage in Germany, Poland and other parts of Eastern Europe (Ashworth 1999, in press; Tunbridge and Ashworth 1996). Much of the tourism of war and death certainly fits well within the meanings and parameters of atrocity and dark heritage.

Religious heritage and pilgrimage

Travel to sacred places is commonly regarded as the oldest form of non-economic travel (Jackowski and Smith 1992). A great deal of travel within Europe and the eastern Mediterranean region was religiously motivated before and during the Roman Empire era. This trend has continued to the present day, and hundreds of sacred sites exist throughout the world that are important heritage attractions for adherents of all of the world's major religions (Ioannides and Ioannides 2002; Jutla 2002; Olsen and Timothy 1999; Shackley 2001; Vukonić 1992, 2002). Table 2.4 shows some of the primary pilgrimage/religious tourism destinations among five major religions of the world. Table 2.5

Table 2.4 A selection of major pilgrimage sites for five major religions

Religion	Major destinations
Buddhism	Shwe Dagon, Myanmar; O-Mei Shan, China; Bodh Gaya, India; Kamakura, Japan; Lumbini, Nepal; Temple of the Emerald Buddha, Thailand
Christianity	Međugorje, Bosnia and Herzegovina; St Anne de Beaupre, Canada; Mount Sinai, Egypt; Lourdes, France; Bethlehem, Israel/Palestine; Jerusalem, Israel/Palestine; Fatima, Portugal; Santiago de Compostela, Spain; St Peter's, Vatican City
Hinduism	Ayodhya, Badrinatha, Benaras, Davaraka, Haridwar, Kusi, Mathura, Puri, Ramaswaram, Ujjain, Varanasi, Ganges River – all in India
Islam	Meshad, Iran; Karabala, Iraq; Jerusalem, Palestine; Mecca and Medina, Saudi Arabia
Judaism	Jerusalem, Meron, Modi'in, Hebron, Mount Carmel, Safed, Tiberas – all in Israel/Palestine; Uman, Ukraine

Source: Adapted from Olsen (2000) and Russell (1999).

Table 2.5 Notable religious events and pilgrimages at Lourdes, 2000

Date	Event
31 December 1999–1 January 2000	Celebration of the Solemnity of Mary
9–20 February	Fast of Our Lady of Lourdes
17–24 April	Holy Week (Easter)
23 April–1 May	Pilgrimage for Handicapped Children
30 April–5 May	Monfortains Pilgrimage
19–21 May	Militaire International Pilgrimage
18–25 June	Eucharistic Week
17–22 July	Communauté des Béatitudes
11–16 August	French National Pilgrimage
13–14 August	Night for Peace
25–30 September	National Unitalsi (Italian National Pilgrimage)
20–24 September	Lourdes Cancer Pilgrimage
3–7 October	Rosaire Pilgrimage

Source: Adapted from Russell (1999).

demonstrates the variety of religious festivals that take place in Lourdes, France (one of Catholicism's most significant religious sites) each year.

Religiously motivated travel is usually called pilgrimage. Vukonić (1996) defines pilgrimage as a journey in search of the sacred. Similarly, Russell (1999: 46) defines it as 'a journey to one or more sacred places, undertaken for religious motives'. Some of these motives include visiting a site where a miracle took place or where one is expected to occur in the future; attending a family religious ceremony; fulfilling a commandment or religious requirement; obtaining forgiveness for sins; praying and seeking a cure for illness; attending a prayer meeting with a religious leader; witnessing a religious ceremony or performance; and participating in worship services.

Such activities usually take place in sacred space, or places that are designated as holy by religious associations. Shackley (2001: 6) identifies several types of sacred sites:

- places sanctified by events in the life of a prophet, saint or deity;
- sites of miracles and healing;
- places where apparitions or visions occur;
- locations dedicated to special religious rituals;
- tombs of saints/prophets/founders;
- shrines of a miraculous statue, icon or relic;
- the ancestral or mythical homes of the gods;
- locations that manifest the energy or mystical power of nature;
- places associated with great evil that have become a focus for remembrance.

To this list should be added specifically temples, churches, mosques, rivers, grottoes, forests, mountains, cemeteries, historic sites associated with the development of a religion, and various points along spiritual routes and pathways. Several of these types of holy places have gained such international prominence that they have been included on UNESCO's list of World Heritage Sites and are said to be of significant universal value.

Travel to sacred sites may be viewed on a motivation continuum where at one end it is required by formal religion as a means of gaining eternal salvation. On the other end of the spectrum is simple curiosity by secular tourists about places of interest (Cohen 1992; Morinis 1992; Turner 1973). Morinis (1992) wrote that sacred journeys are undertaken for a variety of reasons, ranging from pure religious obligation (pilgrimage is required to obtain eternal salvation) to a state of wandering where no ritualistic goals exist and where it is unnecessary to visit a specific shrine, more motivated by curiosity and a search for personal meaning and deeper levels of consciousness.

True pilgrims have traditionally been seen as travellers for whom a journey has truly been a difficult and rueful experience, where penance is gained through hardship. It is common for penitent pilgrims to walk the road or route, often long distances, to reach a holy location, which will lead to spiritual enlightenment. The Camino de Santiago route is a good example of this. For many travellers it is along the lengthy Camino de Santiago, a kind of rite of passage, where they 'become' true pilgrims on their quest for spiritual meaning (Graham and Murray 1997; Santos 2002). Thus, the search for spiritual cleansing and internal peace derives not only from visiting the Santiago shrine itself, but also from 'the hardships, joys and self-discovery of the nature of the journey to that place' (Graham and Murray 1997: 402). At Santiago de Compostela, 'motive meshes with mode' as walking or cycling visitors are regarded as true pilgrims, while those who arrive by car or bus are more secular.

Shackley (2001) sees visitors at religious sites as falling into one of two fundamental groups: those whose primary purpose is to gain a religious experience (pilgrim) and the potentially far larger group of those whose major motivation is visiting an element of the world's religious heritage (secular tourist). This suggests that variations exist in people's motivations for visiting religious heritage places. Many tourists desire to visit religious structures and sites not of their own faiths but out of interest in, or curiosity about, historic sites. Non-Buddhists visiting Borobudur, Indonesia or Buddhist temples in Thailand (Plate 2.3), would fit into Shackley's second group of religious site visitors and fit Smith's definition of secular tourists. While some scholars argue that differences exist between pilgrims and tourists or that they are two distinctively

Plate 2.3 Buddhist temples in Thailand

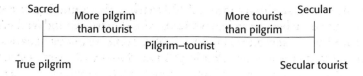

Figure 2.1 The pilgrim–tourist continuum
Source: After Smith (1992).

different groups (e.g. Graham and Murray 1997; Sizer 1999; Smith 1992), the distinction remains unclear, and researchers have been unsuccessful in drawing clear boundaries between them. In an effort to do this, however, Smith (1992) proposed a typology of the relationships and differences between pilgrims and tourists (Figure 2.1). She suggested that on one end of a spectrum are devout pilgrims, while at the other end are secular tourists, with some variations between the two located somewhere in the middle.

From the heritage tourism perspective, pilgrimage is a form of tourism under the broader heading of religious tourism. Simply stated, pilgrims can be seen as one type of tourist, and perhaps the distinction should be between leisure-based tourists and pilgrims rather than pilgrims and tourists. Owing to the negative stigma often associated with being a tourist and the negative impact that tourism can have in destination areas, religious organisations have been one of the primary groups attempting to promote the distinction between pilgrims and tourists (Vukonić 2002). In short, a pilgrim can be viewed as a type of tourist who is motivated by spiritual or religious needs (Timothy 2002a). In support of this argument, Gupta (1999: 91) argues:

> the fact that [pilgrimage] is often carried out on foot, is an older form and has many religious connotations, has made people overlook it as a form of tourism. Apart from the devotional aspect, looked at from the broader point of view, pilgrimage involves sightseeing, traveling, visiting different places and, in some cases, voyaging by air or sea etc., and buying the local memorabilia, almost everything a tourist does.

The pilgrim–tourist debate aside, it is clear that tourism to sacred sites, whether by adherents to one particular religion or another, is a major global phenomenon, and many destinations are beginning to broaden their attraction and service base to reflect this growth (Olsen and Timothy 1999). For example, Jordan is considering opening up a heritage park on the site of what appears to be the location of the baptism of Jesus in the Jordan River (Bredemeier 1999). This will no doubt influence tourism to the Jordanian side of the river and become a major stopping point on Christian tour routes.

With the beginning of the new millennium on New Year's Day 2000, religious heritage became even more of a drive for many people in 1999 and 2000. For optimistic secular tourists, the new millennium promised to bring in a better global society and offered a sense of fascination about the future. Among optimists with a spiritual motive, 2000 marked the beginning of a new age of faith – a period when many believe Jesus would reappear and lead his followers into paradise (Olsen and Timothy 1999). Some religious fanatics predicted catastrophic events and awaited impending doom and mass destruction. This belief led many thousands of apocalyptic fundamentalists to visit the Holy Land in 2000, where they anticipated witnessing the second coming of Jesus Christ and the destruction of the world (Brubacher *et al.* 2000; Olsen and Timothy 1999; *U.S. Catholic* 2000).

Living culture

Living culture forms the basis for tourism in many destinations. Included in this type of heritage are less tangible objects and activities, such as traditions, ways of life, ceremonies and rituals, dances, agricultural practices and culinary habits.

Many places are well known for their culinary heritage (e.g. China, France, Italy, Mexico, Thailand). Several countries and regions have focused significant promotional efforts on trying to attract tourists to try local gastronomical delights. In France, where food contributes a great deal to the country's tourist appeal, several forms of culinary heritage have been emphasised in recent years (Bessière 1998):

- farm fresh produce;
- farmstead inns that serve country-style food;
- food museums;
- traditional restaurants;
- regional culinary specialties.

Most tourists would hardly consider a trip to France complete without tasting a variety of regional wines, cheeses and pastries. It is not uncommon for tourists who are familiar with ethnic foods in their own countries to look forward to partaking of at least some local foods while on a foreign holiday.

Many other forms of intangible living heritage play an important role in the tourism attraction base, either as major attractions themselves or as ancillary attractions at larger, more visible tourist sites. For example, dances, shadow puppet shows, gamelan orchestras and cultural celebrations play a major role in the tourism supply in Indonesia, particularly on Bali and Java (Hughes-Freeland 1993; Picard 1990, 1995, 1997; Timothy and Wall 1995). These are particularly important in the local tourism environment as supporting attractions for cultural and heritage tourists in Yogyakarta and cultural and beach resort tourists in Bali. Similar cultural traditions and rituals have enhanced tourism to Native American reservations over the past century (Hollinshead 1992; Lew and Van Otten 1998) to the point where several tribes have had to limit tourist visits by closing their reservations to visitors for certain periods of time when some of the most sacred ceremonies take place (Lujan 1998) and limiting visitor access to certain parts of the reservation.

Plate 2.4   Amish/Mennonite lifestyle

Another clear example from North America is the Amish and Mennonite cultural communities in Pennsylvania, Ohio and Indiana (USA) and Ontario (Canada). What attracts visitors to these communities is their distinctive lifestyles, including their style of dress, modes of transportation (i.e. horses and buggies), foods, handicrafts, language, homes and farmsteads, and social and commercial institutions (e.g. blacksmith shops, markets, schools and churches) (Buck 1978; Fagence in press; Hovinen 1995, 1997; Luthy 1994) (Plate 2.4). These communities have become so popular to outsider gazers that tourism is beginning to affect their cultures and ways of life in what they perceive to be a negative way. So, there too, measures are under way to mitigate some of the effects of tourism (Fagence in press). Agricultural landscapes, such as rice terraces in parts of Indonesia and the Philippines, have become an integral part of the traditional ways of life type attractions that people travel to see.

Arts and crafts are another component of living culture that appeals to tourists, particularly in destinations where certain well-known crafts originate, such as batik cloth in South-East Asia and kente cloth in West Africa (Hitchcock and Nuryanti 2000). Purchasing souvenirs and handicrafts is a highlight of many tourists' trips, and watching crafters at work can heighten the experience and enhance the value of the items purchased in the eyes of the tourists.

Festivals and special events

Festivals and special events have become important cultural attractions (Getz 1991). As a form of attraction, they represent an element of supply that is highly diverse, covering many themes beyond that of heritage. Despite this, festivals make up another part of the heritage supply mix and deserve attention here. They range in scale from those that have international appeal (e.g. Mardi Gras, New Orleans, the Carnival held in Rio de Janeiro) to small seasonal community-based festivals that attract only local interest. This scale factor also becomes evident when festivals are examined at the level of individual countries. Boyd (2001), in his assessment of cultural and heritage tourism opportunities in Canada, noted that attendance at festivals was the second most important cultural and heritage activity after visits to national and provincial parks, and that opportunity existed to make greater use of this part of the country's heritage supply. The following example illustrates the diversity of Canada's festivals, where heritage themes are important.

CASE STUDY Festivals in Canada

As early as 1983, over 1,000 community-led festivals were estimated to be taking place across Canada (Getz and Frisby 1988). Based on a survey in 1986, Butler and Smale (1991) recorded that within the province of Ontario 363 festivals had taken place, 42 of which had a heritage theme. The majority were classed as seasonal (99), followed by food (66), arts (57) and ethnic (52), with the remainder classed as other (29), sports (11) and music (7). The study by Butler and Smale revealed that the majority of festivals were tied to communities, the number rising as community size increased. With respect to heritage festivals, they found these to occur in 'rural rather than urban areas, as many of the heritage events focus upon the traditional rural pattern of life in Ontario' (Butler and Smale 1991: 10). It is hard to distinguish tourists from local residents at these festivals, although given that the majority of festivals are community-based, the tendency to attract tourists, especially out of province and international, is relatively low. Clearly there are some exceptions though, such as the Oktoberfest, in the Waterloo–Kitchener–Cambridge area, with its emphasis on beer festivals and German culture, which attracts visitors from outside the region. Getz (1991) in his profile of eight festivals (Winterlude, Spring, Homelands, Italien, Franco, Dance, Jazz and the Arts) held within Canada's National Capital Region (Ottawa and Hull), demonstrated that while the majority are held within the peak tourist season, those taking place in the off season (Winterlude and the Festival of Spring) attracted the most visitors (605,000 and 350,000, respectively), as well as the most non-local visitors (28 and 21 per cent, respectively), revealing their tourism potential. The next most popular festival (the Franco-Ontarien) with 234,000 visitors attracts 15 per cent of its visitors from French-Canadian areas across Canada as well as performers from as far as Belgium and France (Dawson 1991). In 1996, attendance at festivals was less than 5 per cent of overall domestic travel activity, however, it should not be discounted as an important contribution to the make-up of heritage tourism in Canada.

Industrial heritage

Technological changes during the past century or so have contributed to a restructuring of older economies into more service-oriented systems. With this restructuring has come an abandonment of many traditional heavy industries and the resultant deterioration of many structures and landscapes associated with them. However, in recent years, post-industrial regions have begun to market themselves as heritage destinations. Outdated resources have been reinterpreted and industrial heritage marketed as a new resource, leading to efforts to conserve the industrial past (Alfrey and Putnam 1992; Fowler 1992; Hewison 1987; Ashworth and Voogt 1990; Robinson 1999b; Rudd and Davis 1998; Ward and Gold 1994; Urry 1995). Many urban and rural communities have had to make a conscious effort to reinvent their images from centres of industry to tourist destinations (Bramwell and Rawding 1996; Mansfeld 1992).

European efforts to conserve the industrial past began in earnest in the 1960s, and in North America in the 1970s. Although early attempts were made to conserve industrial relics in France, it has only been since the 1980s that they have been recognised as a significant part of the national heritage (Bazin 1995). This delayed recognition of the value of industrial heritage is not uncommon throughout the world.

Edwards and Llurdés (1996: 342) define industrial heritage as 'man-made sites, buildings and landscapes that originated with industrial processes from earlier periods'. They also included factory and extractive machinery later in their definition. However, they argue that such attractions will never achieve the level of interest among visitors that Romanesque churches or Gothic cathedrals have done since they do not hold the same romantic or aesthetic values. Nonetheless, more and more regions and countries are beginning to realise the potential for developing industry-based heritage tourism (Barke and Harrop 1994; Holcomb 1994; Brownill 1994; Harris 1989; Johnson and Sharpe 1994; Kerstetter et al. 1998; Kostyal 1996; Mansfeld 1992; Weiler 1984).

The primary resource base of industrial heritage includes mines, quarries, factories, harbours, ports, agricultural relics, railroads and railway museums (Balcar and Pearce 1996; Brown 1989; Harris 1989; Kerstetter et al. 1998) – items which Ward and Gold (1994) argue are transformed into sanitised, hyperreal artefacts of the modern world.

Based upon their work on mines and quarries, Edwards and Llurdés (1996: 349) suggest that most industrial heritage attractions can be divided into four categories, namely productive, processing, transport and sociocultural attractions (Figure 2.2). This can be expanded to include other types of industrial heritage in addition to mining. Productive attractions are those where natural resources are/were extracted, such as underground and open-pit mines and quarries. Processing attractions are places or structures where raw materials were previously or currently processed. Transport attractions are those that were used in moving raw materials, processed goods, and industry workers from place to place. Finally, sociocultural attractions make up the social side of

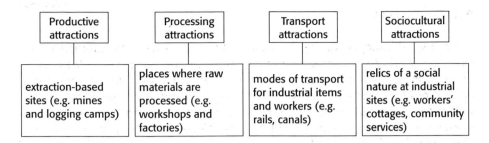

Figure 2.2   A typology of industrial heritage attractions
Source: Adapted from Edwards and Llurdés (1996).

Table 2.6   Mines and quarries as tourist attractions in Wales

Productive
Llechwedd Slate Caverns
Big Pit Museum
Rhondda Heritage Park

Processing
Welsh Slate Museum
Slate Workshop

Transport
Ffestiniog
Snowdon Mountain
Llanberis Lake

Sociocultural
Welsh Folk Museum
Welsh Miners' Museum

Source: After Edwards and Llurdés (1996).

industrial heritage, namely community spaces, retailing establishments, family sites and structures, and employee and employer lodgings. Table 2.6 lists some of these prominent types of attractions in Wales (Plate 2.5).

Natural resource industry attractions are particularly appealing because of their outdoor setting where the relationship between humans and nature is immediate and vital. There is also a growing trend internationally to recycle old factories and reactivate their machinery to offer visitors an up-close, and sometimes hands-on, experience of past manufacturing activities and processes (Weiler 1984).

Several countries are known for their wide range and large numbers of industrial heritage sites. The United States, Australia and the UK are three good examples. In the face of declining heavy industry towards a more service-oriented one, industry-based heritage tourism can allow places to take advantage of their 'forgotten past and its potential as a tourism attraction in

Plate 2.5   Slate mine in Wales

the face of widening cultural and recreational interests' (Edwards and Llurdés 1996: 358).

Related to mines and quarries are ghost towns. As natural resources like coal, gold and silver were exhausted, old mining towns were abandoned, and many still remain derelict reminders of wealth, wild lifestyles and cowboy mythologies. These rustic, if somewhat romantic, images of formerly bustling frontier towns have resulted in many of the ghost towns of the American (DeLyser 1999; Florin 1993) and Australian (Brown 1989) frontiers becoming important tourist destinations. Likewise, it is now common for formerly industrial villages that have not reached the stage of ghost town to reinvent themselves into tourist destinations. Mining and lumber towns, such as Leavenworth, Washington (USA) and Globe, Arizona (USA), and agricultural villages, such as St Jacobs, Ontario (Canada), are often transformed into tourist shopping villages (Getz 1993) where old buildings become new souvenir shops, restaurants and guest houses. Sometimes industrial cities are connected to form corridors/trails of industrial heritage (Llurdés 2001).

In addition to more elaborate industrial centres like Beamish, Ironbridge and Stoke-on-Trent, England, more mundane elements of the industrial urban and rural landscape have become significant attractions. Visits to whisky distilleries in Scotland and Ireland, for example, have become increasingly popular tourist activities over the past 25 years among various sectors of society (Boyd 1999; McBoyle 1996). By the mid-1990s, almost one-third of all malt distilleries in

Scotland had installed visitor facilities dedicated to catering to over 1 million visitors a year. A further 19 distilleries received visitors by prior arrangement (McBoyle 1996: 256).

Similar conditions exist in many wine-producing areas of Australia, New Zealand, North America and Europe, where many wineries offer tours and have opened visitor centres and gift shops (Dowling and Getz 2000; Hall and Macionis 1998; Telfer 2001).

Archaeological sites/ancient ruins

Another popular type of attraction, which overlaps with some of the others described here, are archaeological sites, ruins and ancient buildings. In many places these provide the essence of the heritage tourism base and much effort has been put into restoring or reconstructing sites that have fallen into disrepair over the centuries. Many of the ancient temple complexes in South-East Asia (e.g. Angkor Wat in Cambodia and Borobudur in Indonesia) are good examples (Plate 2.6). In North America, ruins of native homes and villages have become popular tourist attractions among domestic and international tourists, as these represent truly the only ancient civilisation on the continent. In Europe, Asia and the Middle East, large cities have developed around what were the original ancient centres of population and commerce.

Very often, museums and interpretive centres are established in close proximity to ancient monuments so that visitors can learn about the site before venturing on to experience it first-hand. In common with other types of heritage places, ancient sites vary in their degree of protection. Landscaping

Plate 2.6 Borobudur Temple in Indonesia

is usually an important part of site maintenance, but care must be taken not to allow this to detract from the attraction itself.

Literary heritage

There is a fascination about places associated with writers that has often prompted readers to become pilgrims: to visit a birthplace and contemplate the surroundings of an author's childhood, to see with a fresh eye places that inspired poems or books, to pay homage at a grave side or public memorial (Eagle and Carnell 1977: v, cited in Herbert 2001).

Herbert (2001: 314–15) outlines four main reasons why people visit literary places. First, they are drawn to places that are connected to the lives of writers. Former homes where writers lived and worked have a role to play in creating a sense of nostalgia, and they can inspire awe or reverence. Second, tourists may be drawn to literary places that form the settings for novels. Even in fiction novels, locations that writers were familiar with might have inspired their writing, and fictional characters located in fictional places can also create strong images in the minds of readers. Third, some tourists are attracted to literary places for some broader and deeper emotion than the specific writer or the story. Squire (1993, 1994), for example, discussed this in significant detail in the context of Hill Top Farm, a former home of Beatrix Potter, in Cumbria, England. Visits to this site are highly nostalgic, as among many tourists they evoke memories and emotions from childhood. Many people recall listening to these stories as children, which strengthens their bonds to home and family. The same is true of Montgomery's stories of the young Anne Shirley in the house of Green Gables on Prince Edward Island, where visitors can relive how the world was seen through the eyes of a child – a tranquil rural place with a blissful communion with nature (Fawcett and Cormack 2001). The fourth reason is generally less concerned with the literature than with some dramatic event in the writer's life, such as the location of his or her death, marriage, birth of a child, or some other major event. Figure 2.3 demonstrates these qualities of literary sites and suggests that other general qualities, such as attractive settings, facilities and services, and location relative to tourists' itineraries, may also contribute to the attractiveness of literary locations.

Figure 2.3 also sheds light on the fact that literary places are fusions between the real world in which the writers lived and the illusory worlds depicted in the stories (Herbert 1995a; Squire 1994). For tourists this distinction may be hard to make. 'Haworth, for example, is the landscape in which the Brontës lived, but is also that occupied by the characters in their novels. The writer infuses the novel with a sense of place but the novel in turn adds meaning to place' (Herbert 1995a: 33). Such a distinction between real and imagined places is not critical because most literary tourists, or 'literary pilgrims' as Pocock (1992) calls them, are less concerned with this distinction than with what stimulates their imaginations and nurtures their interest in literature (Herbert 2001: 318).

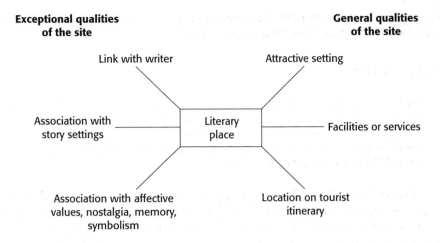

Figure 2.3 Qualities of literary places
Source: Adapted from Herbert (2001).

The fictional experiences and descriptions of places in literary works have influenced the ways in which most modern-day literary places are presented to tourists. Tourism founded on John Steinbeck's writings of Cannery Row in Monterey, California, has led to an otherwise ordinary urban industrial landscape becoming a major tourist attraction. Cannery Row holds an important social and economic place in Monterey's tourism industry, so city planners and interest groups have demarcated the area with heritage icons like signs and statues of Steinbeck to demonstrate the places he visited and imagined, and the images he created in his writings. Thus,

> on Cannery Row . . . markers will be placed on actual sites as well as on the places that existed only in Steinbeck's imagination. The reproduction comes to transcend the real so that the Row is legitimated in so far as it offers participation in the fictionalized landscape created by Steinbeck. Steinbeck's fiction, in turn, only becomes acceptable to the tourist landscape when it has been redigested, caricatured (Norkunas 1993: 95).

This is also the case at Hill Top Farm, where visitors can see Peter Rabbit's garden, and at Dorothy's farm of *Wizard of Oz* fame in Liberal, Kansas, tourists can visit the famous farmhouse and skip along the yellow brick road. Similarly, the setting and interpretation of Green Gables House on Prince Edward Island are heavily influenced by Montgomery's fictional descriptions of Anne's experiences. Parks Canada allows this form of less than realistic representation because of its nationalist mandate to celebrate Canada as a natural and cultural landscape that nurtured Montgomery's creativity (Fawcett and Cormack 2001).

As these examples demonstrate, places associated with famous literary figures become significant tourist attractions. In 1999, Key West, Florida, and

Plate 2.7 Café frequented by Hemingway in Havana, Cuba

Havana, Cuba, were heavily promoted and visited on the 100th anniversary of Ernest Hemingway's birthday. Places associated with his writings are now major tourist destinations in both locations (Plate 2.7). The gentleman who is said to have inspired the story of the *Old Man of the Sea* was still living in 1999, and even he and his village in Cuba had become tourist attractions (Landy 1999; Stoddard 1999).

In addition to literary places themselves, literary festivals have become the focus of significant tourist attention. Sometimes these events are located at places directly tied to authors, but more often they are held in places with few or no connections to the stories or authors themselves. Stratford, Ontario (Canada) and Cedar City, Utah (USA) celebrate annual Shakespearean festivals that attract thousands of visitors from around the world – not because of any real association with Shakespeare, but simply because they initiated the festivals and have been successful in maintaining them. In an incongruous way, these communities are now associated with Shakespeare, and fortuitously he and his plays have become part of these two North American communities' own adopted heritage.

Clearly the issues and concepts in this section are not limited only to authors and playwrights. Places associated with other famous people, such as film stars, artists, politicians and musicians, have also become a heritage of notoriety, a mixture of fact and fiction. Elvis Presley's Graceland, considered by some to be the second most famous house in America after the White House, is a prominent example of this. Nearly a million people visit each year to pay their respects and to experience Elvis's beloved home, which influenced his life and his music (Alderman 2002).

Settings/contexts of heritage supply

Urban areas

Heritage attractions, primarily in the form of museums, monuments, houses, historic buildings, theatres, factories, businesses, parks, cemeteries and markets form a large part of the urban milieu. Indeed in many of the oldest cities of Europe, for example, the city centres are almost entirely comprised of historic structures, squares, fountains and archaeological ruins (Plate 2.8). Many of the oldest cities have developed into major tourist destinations with their primary point of attraction being their historic centres (Jansen-Verbeke and van Rekom 1996; Stabler 1998). Many cities have purposefully targeted tourism as an economic growth mechanism, particularly those places that

Plate 2.8   Rome, Italy, a tourist-historic city

have a rich array of historically significant buildings, museums and monuments. Cities more so than rural areas have been the focus of intentional tourism development owing to a fairly rapid decline of age-old manufacturing activities in recent decades, the need to stimulate the local economy and boost employment levels, the common perception that tourism is a growth industry, and the perception that tourism development will result in the regeneration and revitalisation of urban cores (Cameron 1989; Chang *et al.* 1996; Law 1993; Page 1995a).

The 'tourist-historic city' has been defined as a particular area within the city where architectural forms and morphological patterns together with their artefacts and edifices have been consciously used to mould a place-bound heritage product (Ashworth 1990a, c; Ashworth and Tunbridge 1990). In other words, certain districts in urban areas, usually apart from the modern sections of the city, function as a historic area for several groups of users, including residents, city planners and tourists.

Research has shown that urban areas have fairly distinct spatial patterns of tourism supply, namely hotels, restaurants and souvenir shops (e.g. Ashworth and Tunbridge 1990; Law 1993; Page 1995a; Pearce 1987, 1998; Wall *et al.* 1985). As tourism develops in urban areas, support services are built to satisfy the needs of tourists, although local people use many of the same services as well. The development of tourism can bring about changes in the form and function of cities, and cities' images are often influenced by the types and extent of hotels and other services they offer (Wall *et al.* 1985). The location of tourist services relative to other urban functions reveals some interesting patterns about tourist cities. Smith (1985) concluded that proximity to busy highways and main streets, shopping malls, residential neighbourhoods, and central business districts (CBDs) contributes to the success or failure of various eating establishments. Similarly, many of the hotels in Christchurch, New Zealand, are clustered near the city centre, although several newer ones have been constructed in a linear fashion along main highway axes, and these patterns are allowing the accommodation sector in that city to flourish (Pearce 1987). Such findings can be useful for urban planning and for assessing what types of locations different services are likely to experience their greatest success.

In most historic cities, food services and souvenir shops are located in close proximity to attractions and along historic waterfronts and primary pedestrian routes (Prentice 1993). Lodging has similar tendencies. Ashworth and Tunbridge (1990) propose a model of hotel locations specifically within tourist-historic cities, which are defined, as alluded to previously, by their touristic importance based on historic buildings, centres and various other artefacts. They suggest that hotels of similar types have a tendency to cluster within the historic city itself, near railway stations, along major access roads, and in the zone of overlap between the CBD and the historic city. This model demonstrates the importance of location in relation to historic urban regions and the role that these regions play in the heritage tourism production process. Other studies have confirmed this pattern described by Ashworth and Tunbridge in various parts of the world (cf. Timothy and Wall 1995).

Heritage tourism in cities normally does not extend throughout the whole community. Instead, it is usually located in a compact centre, which was most likely the original urban core, and from there the city developed into more modern regions and suburban areas. In Prague, for example, tourism has not developed extensively throughout the entire urban area, but rather it has remained focused in the city's small and densely built historic core (Simpson 1999). This is much the same in most historic cities. Nonetheless, in some cases, the historic city extends beyond the tourist-historic city, as many heritage elements are located in nodal fashion or are spread throughout even residential areas (Ashworth 1988). This is certainly the case in Rome.

Rural areas

Rural areas provide the setting for some of the most spectacular heritage attractions. In particular, many of Europe's most beautiful castles are located outside of major cities because of their historical aristocratic context and the need for large spaces. Other important rural attractions include small villages, rural lifestyles, farms and farmhouses, covered bridges, mines and quarries, archaeological sites of indigenous peoples, and national parks. Until quite recently, cities and natural landscapes were the main focus of conservation efforts throughout the world. However, during the past few decades, the value of conserving the rural cultural environment has received considerably more attention as rural areas and small towns/villages have become more urbanised and have threatened to lose their traditional form (Grenville 1999; Holdsworth 1985).

Much of the rural landscape has recently begun taking on a new form as it has itself become not only the attraction but also part of the service function. Farm-based tourism, for example, has become a very popular way of increasing rural incomes and providing rural tourists with places to eat, sleep and recreate. This is particularly so in Europe, New Zealand, Australia and North America. For a long time farmers have let out rooms, converted farm buildings into holiday accommodation, created caravan and camping sites, and developed trails and farm walks for visitors. As many as a third of farms in the Austrian Tyrol offer accommodation to visitors and approximately one-sixth of the farms in some counties of Scotland (Clout 1998). The tradition of tourism being centred primarily in and around cities is now changing as rural and peripheral areas become increasingly more important venues of heritage attractions and tourism support services (Page and Getz 1997; Prideaux in press; Prideaux and Kininmont 1999; Timothy 2001a).

Castles and large estates have become important tourism services too as they have been transformed into hotels, and small cottages, barns and covered bridges become guesthouses, restaurants and gift shops.

Protected areas

Protected areas and/or relatively untouched regions are important places to observe natural heritage. While the concept of parks has a long, if indistinct, history dating back several thousand years, it has only been in the past two centuries that national parks have been formally established (Boyd and Butler 2000). From the outset of their establishment, tourists have been drawn to such places because of the natural heritage they offer. With their spouting geysers, towering plinths of granite, volcanic peaks, mountain ranges, valleys and lakes, wetlands, tundra deserts and isolated outback regions, the national parks in many countries rank as internationally renowned visitor attractions and often the most visited heritage attractions. For instance, Banff National Park in Canada receives over 5 million visitors per year on average, the Grand Canyon over 3.5 million and Uluru (Ayers Rock) in Australia over 400,000 (Butler and Boyd 2000). Furthermore, in many countries the imagery of many national parks is used in the promotion of international tourism. For instance, Uluru (Ayers Rock) is often featured in how tourism is sold to the international market by Australia, just as Yellowstone, Yosemite and the Grand Canyon are featured in American tourism promotional literature.

National parks and other protected spaces can often represent the heritage landscape of certain regions. This is particularly the case for countries like Canada and New Zealand, where their relatively short history (depending on how history is read) means that most heritage features are from the natural environment. The Canadian National Parks system is now widespread with properties throughout the country and is a valued part of the national landscape (Figure 2.4) (Plate 2.9). While tourist attractions are more diverse than this form of heritage in such countries, it would still be valid to say that the grandeur of the naturalness of regions is an essential element in the heritage supply they offer. As such, this type of supply is attractive to other types of tourism (e.g. ecotourism) as parks offer opportunities to observe, admire and learn about existing flora, fauna and natural processes.

While national parks usually contain natural heritage features, some also contain cultural heritage sites related to ethnic groups and indigenous peoples. A good example of this is the Anangu in Uluru, Australia, where the rock and the Aboriginal villages are both key features of any visit. In the past, it was not uncommon for traditional peoples to be removed from their land with the formation of large wildlife parks and reserves (Lilieholm and Romney 2000; Boyd 2001), and only recently have local peoples been encouraged to visit these areas – once the preserve of elite members of society and an international clientele. Only in the past two decades have there been sufficient developments in legislation to bring local people and indigenous groups into the realm of park management. Traditional activities and practices are now accepted as part of park functions, and representatives from native groups work alongside park managers. In Uluru National Park, Australia, the local Anangu have a voice in how the park is managed and run for tourism. They want to control tourist

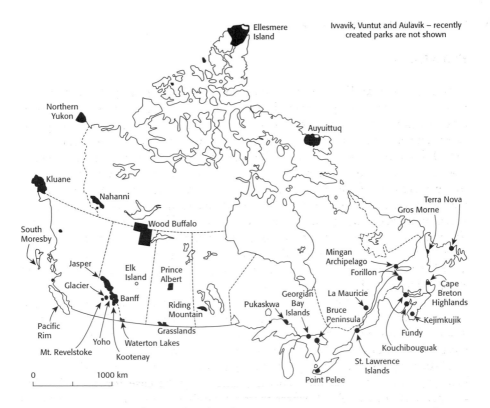

Ellesmere Island

Ivvavik, Vuntut and Aulavik – recently created parks are not shown

Northern Yukon

Auyuittuq

Kluane

Nahanni

Terra Nova

Gros Morne

South Moresby

Wood Buffalo

Jasper

Elk Island

Prince Albert

Mingan Archipelago

Forillon

Glacier

Banff

Georgian Bay Islands

La Mauricie

Cape Breton Highlands

Pacific Rim

Riding Mountain

Pukaskwa

Bruce Peninsula

Kejimkujik

Yoho

Grasslands

Fundy

Mt. Revelstoke

Waterton Lakes

Kouchibouguak

Kootenay

St. Lawrence Islands

Point Pelee

0   1000 km

Figure 2.4   The Canadian National Parks system

Plate 2.9   Waterton Lakes National Park, Canada

numbers and product development, and encourage tourists to learn about their culture (Hall 2000a; Boyd 2002). They also want to promote the cultural resources of the area, dissuade visitors from climbing the rock, widen the interpretative services, and educate visitors about Aboriginal culture, history and traditions.

National parks and protected areas are important places to present natural and cultural heritage. They should not be discounted as part of the heritage landscape and heritage supply. Provided they can be maintained and the culture they contain be presented in a positive manner, they will most likely remain key heritage tourism features for both domestic and international visitors in much of the world.

Support services for heritage tourism

In addition to the attractions themselves, the heritage tourism supply includes various other services that enhance or facilitate the continued existence and growth of heritage tourism. Shopping facilities, catering services, accommodation and transportation can be successfully developed at or near heritage sites to provide for the needs of visitors and to earn additional revenues (Plate 2.10). The use of these facilities as sources of income will be discussed in greater depth in Chapter 5.

Plate 2.10 Tourism service village at the Great Wall of China

Shops and catering services

Shopping is one of the most important activities that tourists undertake while travelling. Aside from accommodation, tourists generally spend more money on shopping than for any other purpose while in the destination area, usually in the range of 20–50 per cent of total on-site expenditures. Prentice (1993: 141) found that meals, snacks and gift purchases totalled approximately one-fifth of tourist expenditures on the Isle of Man, and this included activities of visitors to heritage attractions as well as other locations. Thus it is hard to overestimate the value of providing eating and shopping opportunities for heritage visitors, and heritage managers are beginning to realise this. In one study, Marsh (1991) found that nearly 80 per cent of responding museums had some kind of retail sales opportunities.

Catering services allow visitors to take a break and enjoy a meal, a drink or a snack. Barthel (1990: 89) puts it this way: 'when they tire of visual and cognitive pleasures, tourists can indulge in oral pleasures'. Referring to open-air museums, she goes on to suggest that 'it is no accident that inns, restaurants, candy stores and snack bars figure prominently in village layouts, and, in terms of traffic, prove some of their most popular attractions' (Barthel 1990: 89).

When managers decide to go into retailing, they must determine why they are doing it. Usually the motive is threefold: to provide services to visitors; to draw visitors to the museum/site; and, more often, to generate funds (Marsh 1991). As discussed earlier, the goals of most museums are not to make money. Instead their aim is to collect, conserve and present artefacts for visitors and researchers. In general, they should not have to rely on sales of food and souvenirs to survive; however, with volatile economies throughout the world during the late 1990s and early 2000s, public support for museums and other historic sites has been cut significantly, which has led many heritage managers to seek alternative sources of funding from commercial activities (Marsh 1991).

When snack bars, restaurants and souvenir shops are located in historic buildings an additional motivation is created for people to spend. Souvenir stores in restored grain silos and restaurants in basement prisons can indeed become part of the attraction. While it is important to earn money from eating and shopping facilities and provide these services to visitors, it is critical that these facilities, as well as the types of souvenirs and food on sale, do not detract from the visitor experience, for there is potential for these to overpower the special qualities of a site (Millar 1989). According to Orbaşli (2000: 171), 'the importance of heritage value over commercial and economic gain must be recognized and commercial activity remain appropriate and sensitive to the qualities of an historic area'. Although offering souvenirs that have little connection to the site might make economic sense, it might leave some negative impressions among visitors as they reflect back on the 'tacky' souvenirs they saw.

Transportation and accommodation

Just as shopping and eating facilities can be an important part of the heritage supply, so can transportation and accommodation. Without a doubt transportation and proximity to gateways and transportation routes are necessary for good access and for the successful development of tourism. Nonetheless, when transportation forms become part of the heritage experience, the value of the experience can be enhanced. The best examples of this include journeys on historic trains and railway lines, stagecoach rides, travel by canal and barge, and lift rides down deep mine shafts. In common with shopping, these services can create additional funding while at the same time providing entertainment and memorable experiences for visitors.

Some outdoor heritage theme parks have developed inns and other forms of accommodation. In some historic villages, bed and breakfast establishments have been created as a way of getting people to stay longer and enjoy more of what the community has to offer. Clearly, if historic communities or large heritage attractions have little to offer in the way of accommodation, they will have a difficult time retaining people on more than a very short-term basis. This, like the examples before, can add a sense of romance and historical ambience that becomes part of the attraction base. In some instances large hotels, which have significant heritage attributes on their own accord are utilised in certain destinations, perhaps one of the best examples being the Raffles Hotel in Singapore.

Scale and spatial variation

A discussion of scale was offered in the introductory chapter to show that heritage is found at different levels, ranging from those attractions that receive international status to those that exist for a small and local market. However, scale can also be used to distinguish differences within similar types of attraction. Heritage trails are used below to demonstrate this point. With regard to spatial variation, similar heritage features can mean different things for different groups of people over space and time, and that heritage can take on greater importance in some geographical regions than others.

Heritage trails

For the most part, linear tourist attractions have received considerably less attention than those that are characterised as points or areas (Wall 1997). This lacuna is particularly noticeable when heritage tourist attractions are considered. While attention has been paid to attendance at heritage institutions within the built landscape (e.g. museums), or to natural heritage areas such as national

Plate 2.11   The 'point of no return' on the Slave Route in Benin

parks, the use of heritage trails as linear tourist attractions has been some-
what understated. In short, heritage trails provide another context within
which heritage-based tourism takes place. They can be found at different scales
such as mega (international), large (national and regional) and small (local).
Examples of mega heritage trails would be the Silk Road throughout Central
Asia and the Middle East (Airey and Shackley 1998), or La Ruta Maya in
Central America, or the Slave Route in West Africa (Bruner 1996) (Plate 2.11).
Familiar large-scale or intermediate-sized heritage trails might include the
Mormon and Oregon trails in the USA, the Los Caminos Del Rio, along the
Rio Grande border between the USA and Mexico (Timothy 2001c), several
Black History and Civil War trails in the south-eastern United States (*Ebony*
1990; Mahoney 1999), long-distance national trails in England and Wales
(Boyd and Timothy 1999) and winery routes within the Niagara region of
Canada (Telfer 2001). Well-known small-scale heritage trails include the
Boston trail in the USA, Gamla Stan (Stockholm) in Sweden, and the walking
trails of Toronto or industrial heritage trails around Stoke-on-Trent, England.

Heritage trails are unique in context in that they can encompass both urban
and rural areas, and sometimes a combination of the two. Broadly speaking,
it is possible to argue that the setting in which mega and large-scale trails are
found is predominantly rural with a certain urban component, whereas small-
scale trails are almost exclusively found within urban areas. In terms of their
subject matter, while each trail offers a specific heritage theme and tells a different story, in general terms it is possible that most mega and large-scale trails

focus on pilgrimage and/or religious history, migration and trade routes, connected urban centres, or observation of the natural heritage of the region. In contrast, small-scale trails are specifically theme driven, including industrial, cultural and literary heritage, to name a few.

In all cases, the primary physical characteristic of heritage trails is their linear and nodal properties. In most cases, they are a composition of specific individual attractions connected by a walking, cycling and/or driving route. Of course the scale of the trail will determine the mode of transportation. For instance, the Boston Freedom trail can be travelled entirely by foot in only a couple of hours, or by car and foot in an hour or so. Along this route are located American heritage sites of national importance, such as the cemetery where Paul Revere is buried, Benjamin Franklin's bookstore and the site of the Boston Tea Party. It is a popular tourist attraction in Boston, and is marked on the ground by a red footpath that passes throughout the city's historic centre.

Where intermediate or long-distance scales are concerned, and where these involve rural and some urban areas, transportation requirements can range from a car to a bicycle or horse to complete. For those that exist within the urban–rural interface, they commonly include sites in cities, such as historic houses and factories, as well as countryside features like farmsteads and rural monuments. The predominantly rural routes often have egress points to connect to nearby cultural and historical features such as monuments, cemeteries, churches, castles and museums. This is a common feature, for example, of Hadrian's Wall national trail in England (Cole 1994). Again, generalisations may be made, but at this scale features more often than not are to be found as nodes, but within certain sections of the complete line.

Large and mega-type trails connect cities, smaller communities and rural areas, and while they cover varying distances they are normally linked by some common features in the form of nodes *along* lines. This is illustrated in the following example. Murray and Graham (1997: 515) describe the Camino de Santiago, a long-distance religious pilgrimage route, as being comprised of a complex attraction of four separate but similar elements. First, the route itself, its traditions and historicity function as the primary attraction, giving route-based tourism its *raison d'être*. Second are the tourist-historic cities along the route, with the most famous being Burgos, Léon and Santiago de Compostela itself. These function as the principal nodes of tourism attraction along the route. Third, surviving remnants of medieval infrastructure create a succession of intermediate nodes for tourists along the modern route. These too include a number of important towns, such as Pamplona, Logrono and Lugo, and several smaller market towns, villages, churches, shrines and other monuments along the way. Finally, the route acts as a spine from which travellers deviate to visit other places, including the monastery of Santo Domingo de Silos.

When considered as a whole, all scales and types of heritage trails are becoming more commonplace throughout the world as individual sites, cities and other communities are beginning to realise the significant benefits in being linked to other heritage places through routes and trails (Cheung 1999; Koščak

1999; Muinzer 1993; Patullo 1997). The following case study illustrates the attractions required to develop a heritage trail as part of a region's appeal.

CASE STUDY Heritage trail development in Mombasa, Kenya

Introduction

The Kenyan tourist product focuses on four S's: sand, sun, sea (coastal tourism) and safari (wildlife/nature-based tourism). The opportunity that old city centres offer as heritage places is often undervalued. This example, which is based on an ongoing study (Boyd 2002a) looks at the old city section of Mombasa and assesses its heritage tourism potential. Three broad research questions are asked. First, what currently exists in terms of heritage tourism in the Old Town? Second, what are the opinions of tourists regarding visiting the Old Town? Third, is there potential within the Old Town to develop a heritage trail to raise tourist awareness? There are many features within the Old Town that could easily be classed as having heritage appeal. Fort Jesus is the key attraction, but throughout sections of the Old Town a diversity of architectural styles 'paints' the picture of myriad cultures and historical periods that could be put on display to tourists. Sadly, however, much of the built fabric is in need of repair. A recent conservation scheme may go some way to making improvements and boosting tourism in the Old Town. In terms of how tourists regard visiting the Old Town, a pilot survey in 1999 revealed that visits were based on tours designed by local operators and that further improvements to the Old Town, and better marketing in the tourist hotels, were needed to encourage tourists to visit. Tour operators accept that at present the Old Town does not have the necessary appeal to be a full-day excursion destination, but that half-day trips are favoured. The development of a heritage tourist trail throughout the Old Town was favoured by tourists surveyed, and this case study puts forward a possible route that takes into account the safety of tourists while respecting the culture and daily activities of residents.

Coastal tourism along a short strip north and south of Mombasa on the east coast and safari experiences within the country's system of national parks and nature preserves dominate tourism in Kenya. Gateway surveys have revealed that over 70 per cent of visitors listed safaris and beaches as their first and second reason for taking a trip to Kenya. Despite the cultural resource base that exists throughout the country, very limited development of cultural and heritage tourism has taken place. One opportunity to develop a heritage/cultural dimension to the existing and dominant four S experience (sand, sun, sea, safari) is the promotion of old town quarters within major cities. Mombasa, Kenya's second largest city and principal port, offers that opportunity.

Attraction base

Mombasa has a long history. First mentioned in the writings of Roger II of Sicily in 1154, there are references as early as the second century AD to trading towns on Africa's east coast. While only architectural remains of a medieval period exist, Mombasa today is a composite of its development within certain periods of history: Portuguese (1498–1697), Arab (1697–1888), British (1888–1963), post-colonial (1963–present day). Given such a diverse history with many different cultures and empires influencing its development, a wealth of attractions has survived. While these empires left their distinctive mark on the built fabric of Mombasa, the majority of these features have survived intact within the Old Town section of modern Mombasa. These include the old town streets, houses, architecture, carved doors, and the ethnic diversity of Mombasa's population. Two heritage trails have been created: one that focuses on the old port, the other taking in a walk of the town wall around the old quarter. The following list describes the range of heritage features available within a combined heritage trail.

Architecture

Two key features dominate here:

- Swahili, Arabic, Indian and European carvings on 100 plus doors throughout the Old Town – Mombasa was renowned for being a cosmopolitan trading town, and this fact is reflected in the designs of doors throughout the Old Town. New residents of importance were known to have brought their doors with them, or had them carved according to their status and allegiance.
- Narrow side streets and balconies – the size of the streets adds to their appeal for visitors. Never designed to accommodate motor vehicles, they are often referred to as *Kitoto* (the place of small children). Many of the balconies reflect either functional usage or cultural requirements. In the case of the former, they form part of the basic design of the house, many being beautified through carvings (floral designs and birds), decorative wooden brackets and supported by wood or cast-iron pillars.

Principal tourist feature

Fort Jesus was built by the Portuguese at the end of the sixteenth century to secure their position on the coast of East Africa. The fort was built in 1593 as a military base on the edge of Mombasa's natural harbour. Its name reflects the flag of the Order of Jesus, which the Portuguese sailed under. Built according to the rules of military defence by the Italian architect Joao Batista Cairato, the fort's angular shape consists of a central court with bastions at the four corners and a rectangular projection that faces the sea, covering an area of approximately two acres. Tours of the fort describe its rather turbulent history: under siege by the Arabs in 1696, starvation and plague in 1697, Arab possession in 1698, mutiny and the Portuguese takeover in 1728, retaking of the fort by Arabs in 1729, Arab rule until the British bombardment in 1875, use as a government prison between 1895 and 1958, and restoration of the fort as a historical monument and opened to the public in 1960.

Harbour

The old port is a dhow harbour where traditional techniques are still in use and where ships from India, Somalia and Pakistan are often berthed. The area known as the Leven Steps contains a tunnel, wharf and jetty that were built by the British Lieutenant James Emery in 1824 as a base for the British Royal Navy. The steps down to the wharf were recently renovated to allow for ease of access to the wharf. The harbour itself is not open to visitors unless accompanied by a guide.

Religious icons

Within the Old Town there are no churches despite the European influence over much of the history of Mombasa. The community is predominantly Muslim, which is reflected in the high number of mosques located within the Old Town. The Mandry Mosque is the oldest, built in 1570. Others are the Bohra Mosque and the Memon Mosque with its carved pillars, staircases and balconies of interest to visitors. The only Indian presence is reflected in the Jain Temple that was built in 1937 and which is often visited by tourists on tours of the Old Town.

Cultural and people features

The culture and activities of people within the Old Town are displayed at markets and workshops. Vendors selling items ranging from spices to fresh produce and traditional clothing crowd many of the main streets. Streets known for their markets are Biashara Street, which is business-oriented with its cloth and food stalls, and Langoni Street where local residents purchase their meat, fish, fruits and vegetables for daily consumption. Two furniture workshops are open where demonstrations of local wood-carving skills are given.

Tourist appeal

The following results were derived from a pilot survey of 50 visitors staying in hotels on the coastal strip north of Mombasa undertaken in December 1999. The majority (84 per cent) of visitors were European with only a token North American (3 per cent) and African presence (13 per cent), where the length of stay was predominantly one to two weeks (87 per cent). This is somewhat influenced by the schedule of flights in and out of Mombasa International Airport. Asked what attracted them initially to Kenya, responses ranged from weather (27 per cent), safari and price (17 per cent), good beaches (10 per cent), with culture only being mentioned by 3 per cent. Regarding what attractions they had visited or were intending to visit, going on safari and staying by the beach were very popular, with 63 and 23 per cent, respectively. Somewhat surprising was that a third of respondents mentioned Mombasa as an attraction they had visited. Directing questions specifically to visits to the Old Town section of Mombasa, over 70 per cent had visited some section of the Old Town, 43 per cent doing so with a tour operator. The majority (62 per cent) spent half a day, mostly in the morning viewing the Old Town, with Fort Jesus being the most popular attraction (76 per cent) followed by the streets and their shops (57 per cent), the port and harbour (43 per cent), with the markets and the mosques being of less interest, 38 and 14 per cent, respectively. Asked what they most liked about their visit to the Old Town, the top responses were present culture (33 per cent), history (24 per cent) and architectural features (19 per cent). In contrast, what tourists most disliked about their visit, which has implications for further developing old quarters as tourist features, were the presence of rubbish (38 per cent), general deterioration of the built fabric (33 per cent), and the pestering they suffered from some vendors and residents (29 per cent). When introduced to a designed heritage trail that takes in the majority of features within the Old Town, the majority of visitors were not aware that these existed and that signs and information boards were needed before a clean-up of some sections of the Old Town was undertaken. Despite not knowing about the trails, over 70 per cent of respondents would recommend others to visit if a heritage trail were formally created, and over 86 per cent of those who had visited believed this would increase visitation levels. While the pilot survey only surveyed a small sample of the tourist population, the results would suggest that a heritage trail around the Old Town is a viable attraction where the infrastructure needs to be further developed.

Improving the existing supply/infrastructure

Since an Old Town Conservation Plan was initiated in 1990 it was not until funding was received from UNESCO and the European Union that improvements have been made. Actual schemes for improvements were not started until 1999. The first scheme involved building and renovating along Bachawry Road, but with local involvement as well as students working on the project this work will not be completed until 2002. The overall plan is to preserve the Old Town structure to boost tourism while at the same time conserving the historical architecture and preserving local values. A number of schemes have been identified that will add to the quality of experience tourists will get from a visit. These include:

- renovation of buildings and façade frontages along main streets;
- land by the harbour to be landscaped and converted into a public park to be attractive to both residents and tourists;
- improvements to be made to the wider infrastructure within the Old Town: roads, paving, sewage and drainage system and streetlights;
- improving the Leven Steps that lead down to the wharf as they have somewhat deteriorated;
- erecting new kiosk stalls outside of Fort Jesus in the traditional wooden style and creating an official place for local vendors and hawkers to sell their crafts to tourists.

Conclusion

While this case study has described a heritage trail in the stages of development, improvement of this existing element of Mombasa's tourism supply will improve its use and enjoyment by tourists. While the infrastructure exists to develop a heritage trail, it should nevertheless focus on the themes of culture, architecture and other heritage. It should incorporate key tourist attractions, so that a visit to the old section of town does not just take in a visit to the fort. There is the need also to ensure the safety of visitors, particularly in those sections of the trail that go through residential quarters and market regions. At the same time, the privacy of local residents needs to be respected. Apart from the long-term initiatives to revive the heritage base, there is the immediate need to have some information boards and directional arrows to assist people who visit the Old Town on their own.

Spatial variations

Heritage tourism and heritage attractions demonstrate a number of interesting spatial patterns. Properties viewed as old in one place may not necessarily be considered old in all places. Age, or antiquity, is thus relative to location. Events throughout history occurred at different times, so places associated with certain events vary in the degree of antiquity. For example, a historic building in Oregon or Washington in the western United States would hardly be considered old in relation to the age of many sites in Virginia or Maryland, or even more so in Europe and Asia. Events had occurred, communities were established, and buildings were constructed on the US east coast long before the first Europeans even began settling the American west. This consideration is primarily in Eurocentric terms, for the ruins of homes and communities of indigenous Americans in the west are generally more pervasive and impressive than those in the east.

Although tourist agencies in most countries attempt to market historic sites to some degree, heritage tourism has been most successful in Europe and North America. Many countries in the developing world possess extraordinary historic attractions like ancient temples, ancient cities and virgin rainforest. However, their financial resources are much more limited, and their infrastructure often remains underdeveloped, both of which frustrate the successful development of tourist destinations. Similarly, there exists an uneven distribution of heritage sites in North America as a result of the earlier history associated with the eastern part of the continent. For example, according to Seale (1989), 72 per cent of Canada's national historic sites are located in Ontario and further east, and in the United States, a disproportionate number of sites are located near the Atlantic coast. While California hosted the largest number of heritage and cultural tourists in 1997, New York was next, followed by Pennsylvania, Texas, Virginia, Florida, North Carolina, Tennessee, Illinois, with a tie for number 10 by Georgia and Ohio (*Travel and Tourism Executive Report* 1997: 4).

Likewise, the character of historic properties often differs from one place to another. Much of what is viewed as heritage in the eastern United States is directly related to the Civil War and the Revolutionary War (Winks 1976), while western American built and cultural heritage focuses on Spanish missions, Native Americans, cattle ranching and mining (Timothy and Wall 1997). Examples of spatial differences also exist within the UK between England and Wales. In England, according to Edwards and Llurdés (1996: 348), heritage sites are comprised primarily of properties associated with the lives of aristocracy, whereas in Wales, the legacies of wealth were largely absent. As a result, the presence of industrial and folk-life attractions is more prominent in Wales.

Although many prosperous international tourist attractions are specific sites, many are also areas or collections of individual buildings and monuments (Wall 1989). Ashworth (1988) suggests that an ensemble of historical relics and buildings offers a level of attractiveness that an individual site is rarely able to offer, which contributes to the appeal of cities. Of this, Tunbridge (1981: 272) contends: 'area conservation provides a framework of compatible scale and functional sympathy within which individual conserved buildings have meaning; it creates a geographical feature of which urban models must take account, in a way that piecemeal conservation does not'. In places like New Orleans (USA), Old Quebec (Canada) and Paris (France), buildings that may seem rather ordinary by themselves become part of an overall attractive setting if they are located in groups with other buildings:

> The aesthetic appeal of an historic place may result from the combination or juxtaposition of many buildings rather than the individual merits of any particular building. Most cities are made up of buildings from a range of periods in a variety of styles and idioms. Thus, the past may be valued because of its juxtaposition with the present. In particular, older buildings provide a potent contrast to the interminable sterility and monotony of much modernist architecture. Such diversity is usually viewed positively . . . even relatively mundane historic buildings will have value through their contribution to the aesthetic diversity of the urban scene (Tiesdell et al. 1996: 13).

The ongoing trend in many small North American communities to revive their historic downtown areas attests to the importance of grouping common structures together to achieve an overall appealing display (Holdsworth 1985).

Another spatial concern relates to scale of appeal. Places such as Stonehenge, the Pyramids of Egypt, the Great Wall of China and St Peter's Square, are major tourist attractions that draw large numbers of people from long distances. However, the majority of the world's historic sites do not draw great numbers of international tourists. Instead, they contribute to the overall attractiveness of an area for people already visiting a place for other reasons, and they are usually geared towards a more local or regional market. To illustrate this point, Wall (1989) suggested that, for every world-famous attraction, there are 100 other sites of more local renown. 'This does not mean that the latter are unimportant, rather it suggests that historic sites of international fame, such as the pyramids, are the exception rather than the rule' (Wall 1989: 13). Furthermore, the tendency of tourists is to associate places with a select number of internationally recognised landmarks such as the Leaning Tower of Pisa in Italy, or the Eiffel Tower in France, which have been the foundations for the international tourist images of many places. Tourists often confine their visits to such landmarks, largely ignoring the lesser-known attractions (Ashworth 1988).

Summary and conclusions

This chapter has presented the supply side of heritage. As can be seen, a multitude of heritage attractions exists for the visitor: museums, war sites and atrocities, religious sites, living culture, industrial places and literary locations. For each one a typology emerges: museums (art, sports, music, industrial, science, philatelic, local history), war sites and atrocities (battlefields, war graves, cemeteries, memorials), religious sites (pilgrimages, sacred sites), living culture of distinct groups (traditions, ways of life, ceremonies, dances, agricultural practices, culinary habits, arts and crafts), festivals (heritage being one of many), industrial places (mines, quarries, factories, harbours, ports, agricultural relics, railroads and railway museums), literary sites (fictional and real-life places of authors and playwrights). As Figure 1.2 illustrated, the heritage landscape traverses urban, rural and protected/natural areas.

The discussion presented in this chapter would clearly suggest that the majority of heritage supply is urban in location, partly because of what is viewed as heritage and the emphasis within supply given over to the built environment. Caution needs to be exercised here, as natural environments can take on a greater importance for some cultures and regions where heritage is concerned. Much of Canada and New Zealand's heritage, for example, is connected to nature and the systems of protected spaces that have been established. While the point about culture influencing heritage is made in the introductory chapter, it is important that in any discussion of supply, it is reiterated as it influences the type of supply created.

Any heritage attraction base requires a good support service infrastructure. This point has been stressed in this chapter within a section devoted to this topic as the two, to a certain extent, depend on each other. Heritage attractions cannot exist by themselves; they require an infrastructure around them to bring tourists to them and cater to their needs while there. Likewise, the presence of heritage attractions necessitates that accommodation, food, shopping facilities and transportation are developed. While these can exist in the absence of attractions, the extent to which they play a role in the economic development and well-being of regions, and the scale at which they exist, is clearly tied to there being attractions near by. As such, the support infrastructure becomes an equally important element of any supply, and must be seen to be on a par with the attractions themselves.

The question of scale and spatial variation has been raised in this chapter. It was done so to demonstrate that within a similar type of supply feature, in this case heritage trails, these can be found at varying scales and as a result can have implications as to the type of supporting infrastructure required and the importance accorded to the attraction itself. As for spatial variation, the importance of context and cultural thinking needs to be kept in mind in explaining why similar features are viewed differently from one place to another, and why certain types of heritage take on greater importance than others.

Opportunities exist to create new supply. This can be accomplished in two ways: by adding extra dimensions to existing supply and by generating a new type of heritage supply from the heritage setting itself. The development of gold heritage and gold trails in central Otago, New Zealand, from the broader base of the industrial past of the area, the creation of the Titanic quarter in Belfast, Northern Ireland, building on the industrial heritage of the harbour region, or the development of literary festivals as part of the heritage of literary places, are all examples of the former. There is less scope to create new heritage landscapes. Some exceptions to this can be found within rural and coastal environments such as the development of heritage coasts in England and Wales and the development of a heritage rivers system in Canada, where stretches of river are set aside for their historical, recreational and cultural values and are seen as part of the natural heritage of regions (Boyd 2001).

Is there too much heritage supply? Writing about cultural heritage, Berry and Shephard (2001: 159) comment that in many regions 'heritage sites now have to fight for survival, not only against other categories of attraction but also against each other. This is principally because the supply of cultural heritage sites has outgrown demand.' The heritage tourism industry relies on a varied supply base. Without good attractions and related support infrastructure, there would be no heritage tourism. But equally, this form of tourism requires visitors to make use of the supply. In today's society, where tourists are seeking more meaningful visitor experiences, does there exist sufficient demand to meet the supply that has been created? This is one question addressed in Chapter 3, which examines the demand side of heritage.

Questions

1. Describe the type of heritage attractions that can be found in the area in which you currently live. To what extent do you see scale playing a role here?
2. Why are components of heritage supply often connected with mainly urban places?
3. Do you think that heritage attractions can exist in the absence of support services and facilities?
4. Is there a danger of over segmenting the heritage tourism supply?

Further reading

Herbert, D.T., Prentice, R.C. and C.J. Thomas (eds) (1989) *Heritage Sites: Strategies for marketing and development*, Avebury, Aldershot.
Prentice, R.C. (1993) *Tourism and Heritage Attractions*, Routledge, London.
Richards, G. (ed.) (2001) *Cultural Attractions and European Tourism*, CAB International, Wallingford.
Shackley, M. (2001) *Managing Sacred Sites: Service provision and visitor experience*, Continuum, London.
Walsh, K. (1992) *The Representation of the Past: Museums and heritage in the post modern world*, Routledge, London.

CHAPTER 3

Heritage tourism demand

The previous chapter examined the supply of heritage tourism. Attention in this chapter shifts to demand and the opportunity that is or is not taken to make use of the facilities, attractions and infrastructure that exist for tourists. Prior to discussing demand as it relates to heritage tourism, a useful starting point is to explain what is meant by the concept of demand in general. In traditional economic terms, demand refers to the quantities of products and services that are consumed at various prices. Generally it is assumed that when prices are high, consumption will be low, and by the same token, when prices are low, consumption will be higher. In the realm of tourism, in common with other service industries, it is usual to talk of other types of demand as well. Current demand means the portion of the population that actually participates in tourism, or those who travel. Latent, or unmet, demand refers to the difference between the potential participation in tourism within the population and the current level of participation. Option demand is the value people place on being able to travel in the distant future, as they appreciate the option of being able to travel at some other time. When attention focuses on heritage tourism alone, the same types of demand (current, latent, option) exist. The key difference is that participation or the decision not to visit is directed at people who are attracted to places because of the heritage products they offer.

This chapter starts by looking at heritage demand, noting the growth of this sector of tourism and the various perspectives by which heritage tourism can be viewed. On the basis that one can segment tourists into specific types depending on the experiences they seek, broad generalisations are then made about the characteristics of heritage visitors, grouping them under the headings of demographics, geographic origins, psychographic and other. The chapter also discusses motivations, the heritage tourist's pursuit of knowledge and personal benefits, and the role that is played by nostalgia. In contrast, a final section looks at the non-use of heritage and the latent demand market and why people choose not to visit.

Heritage demand

As discussed in Chapter 1, the demand for tourism has grown notably during the past two decades, and few places exist in the world today that have not been affected by it in one way or another. Just as demand for tourism has grown, so has demand specifically for heritage-related experiences. In common with ecotourism and other types of special interest travel, heritage tourism is one of the fastest growing segments within the global phenomenon of tourism (Chen 1998). In the United States, visiting heritage sites has become one of the most popular tourist activities, and visitor attendance at historic sites had a 25–30 per cent annual growth rate during the 1980s (Hall and Zeppel 1990a, b) and still continues to grow. Table 3.1 demonstrates that, despite some fluctuations in visitations from year to year, overall visitation to US National Parks natural and cultural heritage sites has increased dramatically during the past 20 years,

Table 3.1   Total visitation to US National Park properties by property type

Property type	1980	1990	2000
National battlefield	2,563,644	2,647,631	2,428,383
National battlefield park	7,795,027	3,599,427	12,413,897
National historic site	7,545,290	12,745,422	10,470,921
National historical park	21,666,675	33,778,243	41,890,838
National lakeshore	2,726,470	4,191,104	3,727,563
National memorial	11,648,225	14,945,372	27,755,746
National military park	19,718,364	16,576,322	19,476,141
National monument	13,943,457	22,911,027	26,722,727
National park	62,665,290	80,891,271	90,035,043
National parkway	40,173,267	37,872,512	70,434,124
National preserve	n/a	221,341	1,695,366
National recreation area	47,488,900	50,564,202	53,368,479
National reserve	n/a	n/a	66,252
National river	2,371,192	3,834,019	4,299,672
National seashore	14,983,966	19,940,362	19,431,476
National wild and scenic river	457,284	812,367	951,685
Park (other)	30,598,733	29,364,115	44,687,810
Total	286,345,784	334,894,737	429,856,123

Source: Compiled from US National Park Service (2001).

totalling some 430 million visits in 2000. Similarly, the American Association of Museums estimated that around half a billion visits were made to museums in the United States in 1990 (Falk and Dierking 1992). Such high numbers of demand place visiting heritage sites among the most important tourist activities in the United States (Makens 1987). Zeppel and Hall (1992: 50) attribute the growing strength of heritage tourism to increasing awareness of heritage and arts, more leisure time, greater affluence, greater mobility and higher levels of education.

According to Johnson and Thomas (1995: 178), within the specific realm of heritage tourism, demand can be viewed from four perspectives. First is current or use demand, meaning the number of people who visit historic sites. It may also include the demand for using a historic building for facilities like offices or other services. The second type is option demand, which is where potential visitors wish to retain the option of visiting a site in the future. They may receive some kind of benefit from knowing that the opportunity exists for them to visit a heritage attraction, but they do not actually do so. Existence demand is the third type of demand. This suggests that value is placed on heritage that is unrelated to any actual or potential use; it is based on the notion that there is some intrinsic value placed on heritage that is not directly related to any actual or potential use. It is simply a demand value of knowing something exists. Finally is bequest demand – a desire to be able to pass on to future generations the heritage acquired from preceding generations. Another type of demand that Johnson and Thomas did not explicitly consider is latent, or non-use, demand, which refers to the number of people who could visit heritage attractions but do not.

Demand can also be viewed from the perspective of demand source. The most significant source, perhaps, in the realm of tourism, is individual people and groups that promote visits to heritage attractions. They are the tourist consumers to whom managers direct their marketing efforts and interpretation programmes. A second source is various levels of government, which is commonly equated with 'society' or 'the public' at large. It is assumed that because governments are in theory set up to represent the wishes of society they do so. The third and final group is heritage guardians, such as national trusts, civic groups, preservation societies and the workers who assist in protecting the resource (Johnson and Thomas 1995: 178).

The term 'demand' is also commonly used to mean the market (the tourists/visitors) for heritage sites and attractions. Heritage visitors can be seen as either passive or serious. Passive tourists and visitors are those for whom a visit is simply something they do to pass time or who view a historic property as a secondary or ancillary attraction. American tour participants in Europe, for example, whose travels take them to many locations, including mountain ranges, Rhine River cruises, Mediterranean beaches, and a mix of chateaux and churches, might be considered passive heritage tourists. They are in fact visiting many heritage sites, such as churches, chateaux and castles, but this is not necessarily the primary motive of the trip. Serious heritage seekers are those whose purpose is to undertake a specific heritage experience of one kind or another. These are more inclined to have educational experiences or a sense of personal nostalgia as their primary motivations, while more passive visitors are simply there to see the world-famous sites they have heard about since childhood (e.g. the Eiffel Tower, the Colosseum, the Great Wall of China and the Tower of London). In common with the recent trend in tourism towards niche travel, Confer and Kerstetter (2000) conclude that heritage tourists will also become more specialised in their pursuits of heritage experiences.

Much of the argument within ecotourism suggests that not every tourist activity that takes place in a natural setting can be described as ecotourism. The same should be true of heritage tourism. Serious heritage tourists tend towards what is known as special interest travel. Generally, the passive visitors demonstrate characteristics of mass tourists, and therefore are not motivated by the same kinds of issues that motivate serious heritage tourists, and their impact may be different as well.

Another way of looking at heritage visitors is by the specific type of attraction they visit (Kerstetter *et al.* 1998). Thus, there may be industrial, religious, political, natural, ethnic/cultural and literary heritage tourists, and indeed such classifications might be useful in understanding various specific market segments whose interests lay in specific elements of heritage. An awareness of groups, and an attitude that heritage visitors are not an undifferentiated group of people who all like to visit all types of heritage sites, is an important management tool that must be considered in development, interpretation and marketing policies for historic sites (Thomas 1989).

Heritage visitor characteristics

Three of the most common ways that managers and marketers divide the market for their products and services are based on their demographic, geographic and psychographic characteristics. Demographic characteristics are important to know for understanding the types of people who participate in heritage tourism. Level of education, gender, age, income level and employment types are among the most important visitor attributes for heritage managers to understand. It is commonly accepted that this knowledge will help managers and marketers determine people's desires and needs based on generalised patterns. Geographic segmentation has traditionally been dominated by a classification based on where the tourists live, although some observers argue that this can be misleading, as many people do not travel directly from their home environments to heritage properties. Instead, they might be travelling from other places they are visiting on holiday or from the homes of friends and relatives. Thus, marketers 'may have to target these people not where they live, but in the place where they are staying' (Swarbrooke 1995: 65). Another aspect of geographic segmentation is where tourists visit. It would be helpful for managers to understand the spatial/geographical patterns of behaviour, travel and visitation once tourists are in a destination or a specific heritage region. Finally, psychographic characteristics are based on the notion that people's attitudes influence their behaviour, and these attitudes come from aspects of their individual lives such as lifestyle, social class and personality (Middleton 1994). Active outdoors-oriented people, middle and upper classes, and workaholics are ways of segmenting the market according to psychographic characteristics. Swarbrooke (1995) identified several other ways of segmenting the tourism market, which would also be useful in looking at heritage tourism. These include, but are not limited to, mode of travel (e.g. by coach, private car, train), behaviour (e.g. awareness of the place, enthusiasm, loyalty, regularity of use), visit party composition (e.g. family groups, individuals, couples) and visit type (e.g. parties, educational). According to Hall and McArthur (1998), this three-part segmentation can be refined even further (Figure 3.1). They suggest that the demographic, socio-economic and geographic (including visitors' previous travel patterns) are objective measures, for these are more readily visible and measurable. Psychographic and behavioural characteristics are referred to as inferred measures and are not as easy to measure.

Scholars and site managers have conducted a great deal of research on the market characteristics of heritage tourists over the past 20 years, and

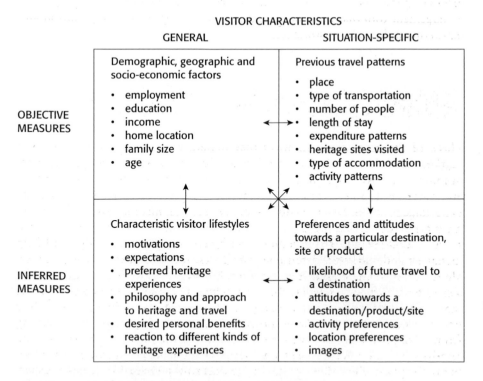

Figure 3.1   Characteristics of visitor market segments
Source: Hall and McArthur (1998).

their findings are consistent and interesting. Studies like that of the European Association for Tourism and Leisure Education (ATLAS) in 1997, reported by Richards (2001b), are important milestones in this regard, where 8,000 surveys were completed at 50 heritage/cultural sites in 9 European countries.

Demographic characteristics

High levels of education appear to be one of the most important characteristics possessed by heritage visitors. On average, heritage tourists are more educated than the general public. In fact, according to a study involving 6,400 respondents (Richards 1996), more than 80 per cent of heritage/cultural tourists in Europe had some form of tertiary (university/college/trade school) education, and nearly a quarter had postgraduate education – a finding similar to that reported by Hall and Zeppel (1990a). In addition to being well educated in a formal sense, literary tourists in particular tend to be well versed in the classical literary works and in possession of 'the cultural capital to appreciate and understand this form of heritage' (Herbert 2001: 313). Thus, education is seen as a mechanism for broadening people's interests in, and knowledge about, times, places, people and events, which draw them to heritage places.

Closely related to education is socio-economic status and employment. Since the heritage public is better educated, it is also reasonable that they are better off financially than the average citizen and have better-paying jobs. Research in North America and Western Europe during the 1980s and 1990s confirmed this theory, leading several observers to conclude that the majority of museum visitors overall belong to a higher economic class than non-visitors (Balcar and Pearce 1996; Hooper-Greenhill 1988; Light and Prentice 1994b; Merriman 1989; Prentice 1989b; Richards 2001b). Even compared to the travelling public, heritage tourists have considerably higher levels of income and education (Travel Industry Association 1997), in some places as much as 30 per cent higher (Richards 2001b).

In terms of gender, there is some evidence that more women than men visit historic sites, although the opposite is true with science museums (Hooper-Greenhill 1988: 218). A US National Trust for Historic Preservation study reported by Hall and Zeppel (1990) showed that nearly 70 per cent of the visitors to Trust properties were female. Likewise, the ATLAS research found that 52 per cent of the European respondents were female, which might reflect the general tendency of cultural activities to attract more women than men (Richards 2001b: 40).

The heritage market is usually younger than that of other tourism types. Over 35 per cent of the ATLAS respondents were younger than 30 years, while only 26 per cent were over age 50. This partially indicates the age composition of the destination country's own population, as many respondents were domestic consumers (Richards 2001b: 40). Age variations have also been reported between different types of attractions. For example, castles have a substantially greater appeal for family groups compared to churches and many museums. This is in part a result of the interests of the children in the stories, lore and memorabilia associated with castles. For teenagers, however, there seems to be less interest in the historical aspects of sites. Instead, they appear to want the more 'entertaining' dimensions to enhance their visit (Thomas 1989: 91).

Geographic characteristics

The geographic origins of heritage tourists, whether international or domestic, are closely related to the scale of an individual heritage attraction. Places of international fame will bring in large numbers of visitors on their own merit, while smaller regional sites will draw more domestic tourists and local recreationists, although some international tourists may visit in conjunction with larger package tours and because they are already near the site for other reasons.

Heritage visitors can be broken down into several types based on their places of origin and residence (Robinson *et al.* 1994; Uzzell 1985). The first group is local residents. These are people who live in the immediate vicinity and who generally make same-day visits to historic properties. These people are very important in supporting all scales of historic sites – local, regional, national and international. The second group is domestic tourists who visit sites but stay overnight in some form of accommodation, including with friends and relatives. Third is international tourists. They generally either stop by a historic property on their way to somewhere else, or desire to spend enough time at a heritage location that it merits their spending a night in local commercial accommodation or with acquaintances.

Richards's (1996) earlier survey results indicate that over half of the heritage consumers in Europe (57 per cent) were international tourists, travelling from outside the country in which the survey was being conducted. An additional 28 per cent were domestic tourists. In a later study, Richards (2001b) reported that 60 per cent of visitors interviewed were out-of-town tourists, and 40 per cent were local residents. Similar results were found between international and domestic tourists. In the ATLAS survey of European sites, 40 per cent of the foreign tourists were from the UK, Germany, France and Italy, although Americans, Australians and New Zealanders were also well represented (Richards 2001b).

Psychographic characteristics

Plog (1973, 1991) proposed that tourism places develop differently as a result of the types of visitors they attract. He argued that tourists could fall between two extreme poles on a psychographic spectrum, where psychocentrics display tendencies towards nearness, comforts of home, and familiarity in their surroundings. At the other end of the spectrum, allocentrics seek out the distant, unusual and challenging experiences. In a similar way, psychographic thinking can be applied to heritage tourism. By visiting some of the cities on the original Grand Tour circuit and other typical tourist locations, modern-day tourists to Europe are displaying psychographic tendencies to visit well-established urban tourism places. In contrast, those visitors keen to tour the temples of Asia, the rainforests of Africa and South America, the ruins of the Mayan and Aztec civilisations, and experience the culture of first peoples in the Arctic, the outback regions of Australia, and the Amazon basin are in essence creating a new Grand Tour (Hall and Zeppel 1990a) and are displaying more allocentric tendencies. Culture and heritage are becoming important motives for people's travel, and there exists demand to satisfy all populations along the psychographic spectrum.

Other visitor patterns

Several other visitor patterns and trends are present but do not fit clearly within the categories outlined above. As most people attend heritage sites in groups, it is worth noting the types of groups that travel together. Families comprise the largest group of heritage visitors (Prentice 1989b). Falk and Dierking (1992: 20) concluded that most people (60 per cent) who visit museums in groups are in family groups. This usually entails parents travelling with children, although extended family members (e.g. grandparents and cousins) frequently travel together as well, forming another subtype of family group. School groups are perhaps the second most important type of crowd at the majority of heritage sites. Field trips by primary and secondary classes are an integral part of the formal education system in most of the developed world and comprise a considerable portion of visitor numbers to most sites. University sessions also often require visitation at sites, particularly those associated with disciplines like history, anthropology, geography, archaeology and cultural studies. Other groups, such as church youth, senior centre groupings, boy and girl scout troops and hobby associations, are more likely to visit specialised attractions that are more pertinent to their individual interests. Church groups, for example, are inclined to visit churches and sites of historical importance to their denomination; senior groupings to war memorials; boy and girl scout groups to science centres, ruins of indigenous peoples and forts and castles; and hobby associations to places related to their pastimes, such as railroad or aircraft museums, stamp and coin exhibits and industrial locations.

In common with other special interest groups, such as ecotourists (Fennell 1999; Newsome et al. 2001; Page and Dowling 2001), heritage tourists tend to have greater empathy with local customs and environments than traditional mass tourists or those who travel in search of sun, sea and sand experiences (Fletcher 1997). Other profiles suggest that heritage tourists have a tendency to spend more time on holiday, resulting in higher levels of spending. They are more inclined to stay in hotels than in other forms of accommodation or with friends and relatives, and they have a greater propensity to shop (Fletcher 1997; Silberberg 1995), with a preference for local artefacts and food, as opposed to mass tourists who commonly purchase imported goods and consume food and beverage of a familiar (imported) variety (Fletcher 1997: 144).

In Richards's (1996) study, cultural/heritage tourists were found to be not only more frequent visitors at heritage attractions than other groups, but they generally travelled more than the average population, especially on short holiday trips. Krakover and Cohen (2001) support this finding in their suggestion that non-visitors to heritage sites, on average, are less attracted to all other types of tourist attractions as well. Similarly, heritage visitors are more likely to be regulars at other heritage locations (Jansen-Verbeke and van Rekom 1996), although according to Prentice (1989b: 48), repeat visitation at the same site is fairly unusual, as some 1980s studies found that over 80 per cent of visitors were on their first or second outing to specific sites. In the same way, evidence implies that across Europe, high levels of cultural consumption at home translates into high levels of heritage and cultural consumption on vacations away from home (Richards 1996).

Demand for heritage is less elastic than that for general tourism. For example, while heritage tourists would no doubt be affected by acts of war and terrorism in their choices to travel or which destinations to visit, they appear to be less affected than general tourists. General tourists have the opportunity to change their destinations of choice, for resources like sunshine, clear waters and white sandy beaches can be found in many different locations around the world. However, there is only one Taj Mahal, one Grand Canyon and one Great Zimbabwe. As Fletcher (1997: 144) points out, the 'sun, sand and sea vacation is very price competitive. A price differential of as little as $5 can determine the destination choice', but in the realm of heritage, people are more willing to pay for the 'once in a lifetime' experience of visiting places of global fame.

Heritage tourists demonstrate less seasonal variation than many other tourism niche markets. Fletcher (1997) argues that this might be because a large portion of heritage tourists travel without children and are therefore not as constrained by school holidays. It probably also has something to do with the fact that they are more education and knowledge oriented, a motivation that can be manifest regardless of weather and time of year. The activities of other types of tourists (e.g. beachgoers and outdoor enthusiasts), however, are constrained more by phenomena such as weather and time of year.

Motivations

In his study of motivations, Chen (1998) found that heritage visitors are driven by two broad motives: pursuit of knowledge and other more personal benefits. According to some observers (Boyd in press; Prentice 1995; Light 1995a), the learning dimension and the perception of a greater willingness to learn on the part of the tourist are one of the most critical defining distinctions between heritage tourists and other types. In their pursuit of knowledge, Chen's respondents claimed that learning about culture and nature, as well as generally enriching personal knowledge, were their primary motivations. In a recent study by Confer and Kerstetter (2000), approximately one-quarter of the heritage tourists they surveyed indicated an interest in culture, heritage or ethnicity as one of their primary motives for visiting heritage sites in southern Pennsylvania (USA). While there was not a huge difference in motivation between local visitors and tourists in Richards's (2001b: 45) study, tourists were somewhat more likely to be searching for new experiences and learning new things than local visitors. Learning new things and satisfying curiosity about unique and interesting places are definitely among the most important reasons why people visit heritage properties.

Chen's (1998) second motive, personal benefits, includes a wide range of intentions. He found that people desire to visit heritage sites because of perceived health benefits, relaxation, gaining some kind of spiritual reward, recreation activities and enjoying sightseeing. Richards (2001b) found many similar motives in his study and also that people commonly visit sites not out of their own interest, but also because they might want to accompany visiting friends and relatives who want to learn more, relax or simply sightsee. Some people's visits are also motivated by business, as a significant number of local people in the Richards study also said that their attendance at heritage sites was connected to their work.

Different types of people demand different heritage experiences, although there are some commonalities between them of course. With reference to the United States, Makens (1987) pointed out that as the population ages, there appears to be an increased interest in understanding one's roots, leading to increased interest in historic sites as visitor attractions. Trends show that older people are more inclined to travel for personal heritage reasons. The growth of genealogy, or family history research, as a form of serious leisure and the travel that it provokes to ancestral lands, genealogical centres, churches and cemeteries, attest to this fact (Timothy 1997). Deeply religious people often travel to sacred sites as a way of affirming their faith and seeking divine blessings. Outdoor enthusiasts and people interested in natural landscapes comprise a huge segment of the total visitors who visit national parks, while history buffs and education-oriented tourists might appreciate experiences at ancient ruins and museums. Tourists at thana (death) attractions might be motivated by a morbid curiosity about death or simply a fascination with famous people. To visit a literary location or a site associated with one's personal heritage could be about a great sense of nostalgia or discovering one's roots.

There is a recent line of research that shows when people are exposed to museums and other heritage sites as children, with school groups or families, they have a tendency to visit them more as adults compared to people who did not visit regularly as children (Krakover and Cohen 2001). According to Falk and Dierking (1992: 21),

People learn that different activities reinforce their lifestyles and desires at different times of their lives. For example, many people associate museum visits with
their childhoods because their parents took them to museums when they were
children. As they became adolescents and young adults, they focused more on
athletic or club events. But when they became parents, they returned to museums
for the benefit of their children . . . parents resume about half of the activities they
themselves participated in when they were young.

This reflects positive experiences from childhood that manifest themselves
later in a desire to see the places they visited as children, to begin traditions
and memory building with their children the way they remember, and their
own sense of nostalgia for their childhood days.

This brings up another critical underlying motive behind many of the
reasons why people desire to visit heritage sites – nostalgia. Many scholars and
observers have recently directed a great deal of attention to understanding
heritage visitation from the perspective of nostalgia. Thus, it is discussed
here for its timeliness and applicability in understanding underlying drives for
heritage site visits.

Baker and Kennedy (1994: 169) defined nostalgia as 'a sentimental or
bittersweet yearning for an experience, product, or service from the past'.
Belk (1990: 670) called it a 'wistful mood' sometimes triggered by an object, a
variety of music, a familiar scene or a recognisable smell. Thus,

it is not surprising that family and friends are important elements in the nostalgic
experience . . . the smell of freshly baking cinnamon rolls at a nearby bakery may
evoke nostalgic feelings of a grandmother. The playing of a song from the past
may bring back memories of an earlier time of laughter and friendship with childhood companions (Baker and Kennedy 1994: 169).

There is in this sense a bittersweet longing associated with a memory or image
of the past and a combination of happiness, excitement and sadness (Baker and
Kennedy 1994). The notion of nostalgia – from Greek terms meaning a yearning to return home – was a seventeenth-century medical term used to describe
the melancholia experienced by Swiss soldiers fighting far from their homes
and families. The symptoms of those with the 'disease' included depression,
sadness, weeping, anorexia and frequent attempts at suicide (Davis 1979;
Schofield 1996). In modern terms, nostalgia is commonly used to describe the
feeling people experience, which motivates them to visit heritage places of a
strong personal connection (e.g. homelands, cemeteries, old homes), national
landmarks that evoke strong feelings of patriotism and pride (e.g. national
cemeteries, war memorials, battlefields), and perhaps even sites of global
importance that induce emotions of awe, reverence and respect for people and
events of the past (e.g. Holocaust sites, ancient temples, castles, mines).

Lowenthal (1979b: 549) has argued that rapid modernisation and 'accelerated destruction [of the past] has deepened nostalgia for the supposedly
simpler, safer, more livable world of the past, a search for roots and historical

identity'. People are proud of and intrigued by their pasts and the pasts of others. Such pride and fascination lead travellers to places that represent values and lifestyles that are rapidly being lost in the modern world. A new industrialised society has been created with no precedent and no roots in the past (Merriman 1991: 11). For these reasons, people constantly attempt to discover the past and return to it. Hewison (1991) contended that the world's travelling population has turned to the past not only as an economic resource but also as a psychological one, and in the words of Dann (1998: 29), 'today a great deal of time and energy is devoted to looking backwards. Our quest is the capture of a past which, in every conceivable manner, is portrayed by the media as far superior to the chaotic present and dreaded future.'

According to one study (Merriman 1991), people generally think that people were happier in the past, because life was simpler and less complex. In the study cited by Merriman, people were asked their perceptions of what the best things about life in the past were. A selection of the primary answers is found in Table 3.2. For these and other reasons people honour their ancestors (Lowenthal 1992), as portrayed in the following example:

> This rekindled her adult interest in weaving as a hobby. She longed to purchase one of the now-marketed reproductions of these older looms, but even the least expensive was priced far too high for her. She recalled with irony the fate of her grandmother's loom, which, although in good condition and still operative, was discarded as junk by her mother shortly after the grandmother's death. In this intergenerational cycle of a silk-weaving tradition, a craft process that the grand-mother learned, probably due to necessity, was rejected and easily abandoned by a daughter-in-law grateful for the ease and convenience of buying ready-made clothes, and nostalgically returned to as a hobby by the granddaughter. In such

Table 3.2 What people consider to be the best things about life in the past

Families were a lot closer

There was very little pollution

There were few or no cars

Life was at a slower pace

There was a common bond of neighbourliness

Less emphasis was placed on money earned

The rate of change, both technically and socially, was slower and meant a greater degree of stability

There were no nuclear weapons

Life was simple with no economic worries

Values were higher

Source: After Merriman (1991: 28).

cases, what was a creative but predominantly essential work for former generations has become a leisure pursuit for modern, relatively affluent Japanese (Creighton 1997: 247).

In this way, people ascribe meanings to their environments. The same is true of tourists when they visit historic sites in an effort to understand themselves as they relate their experiences to their personal lives. Bruner (1994: 410) provides two good examples of this:

> One farmer from Illinois entered a log house where one of the interpreters was spinning wool. The farmer stated that when he was a child there was a spinning wheel in his home very similar to the one at New Salem, and he recalled images of his farm in the prairies.

Likewise,

> A judge told me how he loved to come to New Salem very early on snowy winter mornings so that he could walk, in solitude, on the same hallowed ground that Abraham Lincoln had walked. The judge had practiced law in the same district as had Lincoln. He had a bronze bust of Lincoln in his office, he had played the part of Lincoln in local theatrical productions, he was tall and thin, he physically resembled Lincoln, and clearly he had made a personally meaningful identification (Bruner 1994: 410).

Both the education and other personal reasons for visiting heritage sites come together to create various levels of demand for various heritage products. Based upon a study reported by Merriman (1991) wherein 301 interviews were conducted with residents of Cambridge, Southampton, York and Lancaster, UK, Table 3.3 shows the primary reasons why people think they should know about heritage. Their answers fit into three categories: to orient people in the present, sheer interest and curiosity, and to help direct the future.

Latent demand/non-use of heritage

As mentioned earlier in this chapter, one of the most important types of demand is unmet, or latent, demand, which means the difference between the potential number of people who could utilise a heritage resource and the number who presently do. Latent demand can be viewed as people who have never visited and never think about visiting, people who used to visit but no longer do, and people who infrequently visit (Davies and Prentice 1995; Swarbrooke 1995). Although non-visitors are more difficult to enumerate and research, it is important for managers to understand them in order to figure out how to attract new visitors and bring back those who seldom or no longer visit.

Table 3.3 People's perceptions of why people should understand the past

To orient people in the present
'The past is the key to the present'
'Comparison with present day'
'To discover what made the world the place it is now'
'To establish origins and the development of humanness'
'So we know where we came from'
'One must know of the past to appreciate the present'
'Without a knowledge of the past you are living in a vacuum'
'Increased understanding'
'As background for today and interesting in its own right'

Innate interest and sheer curiosity
'Curiosity'
'It is interesting for us to know what happened in the past'
'To find out about places and people who lived years ago'
'Interest'
'Because man's curiosity will never be satisfied'
'It is worth learning how people in the past did things'
'To know more about history and what happened years before our time'
'It is nice to know how people lived, and to know what they lived in and the things they
   used'
'Curiosity about the past'
'See how people lived'

To help direct the future
'To help the future'
'To learn for the future'
'Because lessons can be learned'
'To enable us to make a better future'
'To see where we went wrong'
'To gain knowledge to help in the future'
'We need to know our past history in order to rearrange the course of our future'
'To learn from our mistakes'
'With knowing the past helps the future'
'Ideally that we should learn from the struggles of the past . . .'

Source: After Merriman (1991: 24–5).

A fairly wide range of constraints can be identified why people do not
participate in leisure activities and tourism. Crawford and Godbey (1987)
classified such constraints into structural, intrapersonal and interpersonal
categories. Structural barriers are factors that block people's intentions from
becoming actions. Intrapersonal constraints exist when people fail to develop
leisure preferences because of problems or misconceptions associated with
personality needs, prior socialisation, personal abilities and perceptions of
reference group attitudes (Jackson and Scott 1999: 307). Finally, interpersonal
barriers result from social interactions with other people. The following
sections examine some of these constraints.

Inaccessibility

Two types of accessibility exist in the realm of tourism – physical and market. Physical access means physically being able to get to a place. Physical inaccessibility might be caused by harsh weather, topographic barriers, lack of infrastructure and transportation, and a lack of handicap access. Market accessibility is more of a perceived notion, where no literal physical barriers exist, but where other less tangible obstacles keep people away from heritage places. In terms of market access, two of the most popular and obvious reasons people give for not visiting heritage sites and museums are lack of time and money (Hood 1983), due largely to work and domestic responsibilities and low amounts of disposable income (Davies and Prentice 1995). Even if they desire to visit, many people do not because admission fees and transportation may cost too much and take time from other important responsibilities.

Lack of educational preparation

While generally an intrapersonal constraint on the part of the latent visitor, a perceived lack of educational preparation keeps many people from visiting (Davies and Prentice 1995). To some people, the world represented by museums is not their world. Instead, it is a world structured by scientific laws, nomenclature and segmentation into periods that are not at all common ground for the layperson. Museum professionals have a tendency to forget that what is obvious to them is not clear to everyone else (Schouten 1995b: 259). Schouten (1995b) also asserts that communications in museums are rather conventional, and everyone is presumed to start from the same point and undergo the same types of knowledge-enhancing experiences at the same pace.

Related to this is a lack of visitation during childhood, which may be viewed as informal education. Research shows that people who visited heritage sites during childhood are more inclined to do so during adulthood as well (Krakover and Cohen 2001). Thus, not having a history of attendance could be seen as a constraint.

Disabilities

One critical constraint common among large segments of society who choose not to visit heritage sites is physical disabilities. Somewhat paralleling Crawford and Godbey's (1987) categories of leisure constraints, Knudsen et al. (1995: 111–12) outline three types of barriers that exist for people with disabilities who do not participate in leisure activities, including visits to heritage attractions. Intrinsic barriers are those that result from an individual's personal limitations involving physical, psychological or cognitive disabilities, including several situations that may inhibit desires to go to heritage destinations and attractions:

- skill gap, where a person's skills may seem inadequate to allow enjoyment of a place;
- physical dependence on another person or machine;
- health problems;
- social ineffectiveness;
- lack of knowledge of places and facilities to make informed choices.

Environmental barriers are the second constraint for this group of latent visitors. This involves external forces that create constraints on individuals with disabilities. These limitations include but are not limited to:

- negative behaviours of other visitors towards people who are different;
- architectural structures that do not allow easy access;
- natural and topographic obstacles such as hills, rocks, snow and trees;
- lack of adequate and user-friendly transportation;
- economic barriers, such as low income and high expenses.

Communications barriers, the third form of barrier suggested by Knudson *et al.* (1995), result from the failure of message senders and/or receivers to interconnect adequately. The clearest cases are people with sight and/or hearing impairments. For example, even though a heritage interpreter is speaking in a way that most people can hear and showing slides that most can see, some individuals will have difficulty and may become frustrated with their visits.

In some parts of the world, legislation has been enacted as a means of assuring rights of access for people with physical disabilities. The 1992 Americans with Disabilities Act (ADA), for example, is far-reaching in its treatment of people with disabilities. It deals with issues of employment, insurance and communications, but perhaps more importantly for the purposes of this discussion are its requirements that 'no individual with a disability shall be excluded from participation in or be denied the benefits of services, programs or activities of a public entity or subjected to discrimination of any such entity' (West 1991: 37) and 'no individual shall be discriminated against on the basis of disability in the full and equal enjoyment of the goods, services, facilities, privileges, advantages, and accommodations of any place of public accommodation by any person who owns, leases or operates a place of public accommodation' (West 1991: 38). Public in this sense means public use, not government ownership, which means that in the United States, all businesses, including most heritage sites, transportation and accommodation services must provide access to people with disabilities and assure that they have opportunities for high-quality experiences on a par with people without disabilities. This often means that historic city centres and individual heritage sites have to undergo some physical transformations, such as building ramps and elevators, or adding interpretive media for blind or hearing-impaired visitors. The exception to this is where it is unfeasible to provide physical access in a way that does not threaten or destroy the historic significance of the building or structure. However, alternative methods of access should still be provided.

While most places in the developed world have begun to adopt similar guidelines, in the developing world relatively few places of historical interest offer access to people confined to wheelchairs and walkers and information to those who are visually and hearing impaired, although this is beginning to change. This issue will be addressed in more detail in Chapter 6, but it is important to note here that lack of access is one of the most significant roadblocks to participation in heritage tourism for a significant segment of the world's population.

Psychological constraints

There is also a common belief that historic sites are boring ruins, 'always the same' and 'only for tourists' (Davies and Prentice 1995: 492). For many people it is the nature of the site itself and its subject that is unappealing, not necessarily the presentation. 'In other words, history – no matter how it is presented – may not be of interest to those people who currently choose not to visit heritage sites' (Light 1996: 188). In light of this finding, Light (1996) points out the implication that presentation might not be the best tool for widening the heritage market. Instead it appears to be more useful in consolidating and reinforcing the existing core audience. To the non-specialist, most museum objects tend to look alike, especially if they are in large quantities (Schouten 1995b). Heritage managers and curators often consider words and letters the best or only medium for transferring ideas. For members of the younger generations, who have been raised on television and video games, reading is merely a secondary means of processing and collecting information. Their learning focuses more on visual and electronic images. For many of these individuals, museum set-ups are poor, incomprehensible and boring (Schouten 1995b: 260).

Perhaps the most common psychological reason people give for not visiting heritage attractions is a lack of interest or desire. In this case it is usually a matter of taste. Some people simply have no desire at all to visit historic sites and museums. Some people have little interest in undertaking recreational activities outside the home, and more still have no desire to travel away from their home environments. Often these people will make excuses relying on simple problems that could be overcome if there were real interest. Such an attitude prevents many people from even thinking about visiting (Davies and Prentice 1995).

One of the most important reasons people give for visiting museums is the social interaction. Thus, some people are reluctant to go to museums and historic sites if they have nobody to go with (Schouten 1995b).

Other constraints

Because a large percentage of museums and other properties are owned by the public and volunteer sectors, and therefore not as profit-oriented as private-sector establishments, they have developed a reputation of not being concerned about high-quality customer service. Schouten (1995b) provides an example of museum shops closing precisely at closing time and people taking their items for purchase to the cashiers only to find that the registers have been closed for the evening.

'Museum fatigue' is another reason why some people do not visit historic sites. This is when people begin to feel exhausted, have sore feet and their head begins to swim. As a result, the longer they are in a museum the faster they move towards the exit, and the longer they spend in the galleries the less attention they pay to the exhibits (Schouten 1995b: 260).

The following case study tells of heritage tourism demand in Northern Ireland, as well as some of the political constraints moulding the face of demand.

CASE STUDY   Heritage tourism demand in Northern Ireland

Background

In most cases, travellers search for safe and interesting places to visit. The absence of safety within a destination region often overrides the quality of experiences and attractions on offer and so an alternative destination is sought. Terrorism represents a form of violence that has a dramatic and immediate effect on tourism within destinations, whether the terrorist threat is targeted at the tourists or the tourism infrastructure in place (Sönmez and Graefe 1998; Aziz 1995). This form of conflict between 1969 and 1994 in Northern Ireland was a key factor in why the region did not develop its full tourism potential (Boyd 2000b; Wall 1996; Buckley and Klemm 1993). Others argue that the Northern Ireland Tourist Board (NITB) failed to promote the region and encourage tourist development despite the ongoing threat of terrorism (Leslie 1999). It is hard to be critical of the tourist board given that an image of violence is not easily overcome when this fact alone shaped many people's perceptions of Northern Ireland.

Image is important for any tourism destination. It is often the image an area conveys which attracts visitors or which causes them to select an alternative destination. It is not surprising to see then how images of the Irish Republican Army (IRA) and Protestant parliamentary activity and the devastation that sustained bombing campaigns inflicted on the region's infrastructure, masked the wealth and diversity of tourism attractions the region could offer (NITB 1993; Browne 1994). As a consequence, the period 1969–93 has been described as 'lost years' in terms of tourism growth and development, when compared to the growth that the rest of northern Europe enjoyed during the same period (Baum 1995).

Importance of culture and heritage

Northern Ireland as a holiday destination not only has had to address a negative image, but it also has had to accept that its geographic position on the periphery of Europe and its cold-water resorts do not set it out as an obvious holiday destination. Visitors come to Northern Ireland because they have reason to visit as opposed to adding a stay as part of a larger trip itinerary. On saying this, the majority of attractions within Northern Ireland are designed to provide visitors with a cultural and heritage experience, with heritage fundamentally tied to the product base of people, landscape, culture and activities (Northern Ireland Tourist Board 2000).

Heritage attractions in Northern Ireland can be subdivided into several distinct categories:

- historical (elements within the built landscape, e.g. houses, castles, monuments, cathedrals);
- industrial (links to products indicative of the region's past, e.g. linen, pottery, whiskey, crystal, shipbuilding);
- cultural (links to past societies, lifestyles, customs, e.g. early Irish settlement, settlement from early British presence in Ireland);
- natural (elements of the natural landscape, e.g. causeway, country and forest parks, caves);
- educational (links to attractions where the ultimate purpose is the dissemination of information for the purposes of learning, e.g. museums, visitor centres, libraries, planetariums).

A review of the top tourist attractions listed in Table 3.4 shows that heritage is key to the visitor experience offered in Northern Ireland. While there is some fluctuation in the position individual attractions held from year to year, the overall picture from Table 3.4 is that heritage attractions have strong and consistent attendance, and that Northern Ireland has a reliable brand related to heritage, which it should continue to promote.

In a study by Boyd (2000b) heritage tourism emerged as a dominant theme in Northern Ireland's tourism product between the first IRA ceasefire in 1994 and the signing of the Good Friday Agreement in 1998. Table 3.5 records visitor numbers to different categories of heritage attractions, and this table reveals that in the event of the ceasefire, Northern Ireland enjoyed its best visitor numbers since the time records were kept by the Northern Ireland Tourist Board. What the table also reveals is the volatility of the market due to unrest, as the breaking of the ceasefire in early 1996 witnessed a considerable drop in visitor numbers for that year across all categories.

Key markets

Having to contend with being a peripheral location, a cold-water destination and a negative image abroad, may explain why visiting friends and relatives (VFR) has remained the principal reason people choose to visit Northern Ireland. Table 3.6 records the main purposes of visits, and apart from 1995 when less than 40 per cent declared their main reason for visiting, it has remained relatively constant between 41 and 44 per cent for the years thereafter. Pure holiday visits as a percentage of all visits were placed third behind those visiting for business reasons. The only year this pattern changed was 1995, when more holiday visits were recorded. What this table reveals is that since the Good Friday Agreement was signed and a ceasefire maintained, Northern Ireland has remained unable to capitalise on this event to draw in more holidaymakers. However, one needs to exercise caution, as both VFR and business travel are important niche markets, and just because people do not declare pleasure holidays as their reason for visiting, does not mean that tourism has not been growing since 1997. An examination of the total trip numbers in Table 3.6 reveals that this has been the

Table 3.4 The top 20 tourist attractions visited between 1994 and 2000 in Northern Ireland

Attraction	1994	Rank	1996	Rank	1998	Rank	2000	Rank
Giant's Causeway Visitor Centre	330,000	1	395,000	1	407,806	1	395,247	1
Ulster Museum	256,020	2	240,859	2	235,594	3	217,811	3
Pickie Family Fun Park*	230,000	3	100,000	12	300,000	2	350,000	2
Exploris*	211,129	4	137,023	8	127,000	9	124,500	9
Belfast Zoo	188,946	5	177,984	4	183,273	4	204,458	4
Ulster Folk Park	186,656	6	198,211	3	168,623	6	155,847	7
Belleek Pottery	148,386	7	161,000	5	171,757	5	193,672	5
Murlough Nature Reserve	128,000	8	160,000	6	129,000	8	–	–
Dunluce Centre	118,116	9	80,088	14	78,000	14	78,000	15
Ulster American Folk Park	117,081	10	134,650	9	111,250	10	120,464	11
Fantasy Island*	100,000	11	103,453	11	103,000	11	–	–
Portstewart Strand	95,433	12	127,749	10	100,620	12	140,000	8
Waterworld*	95,139	13	68,385	17	–	–	57,236	19
Linen Hall Library	94,755	14	–	–	–	–	80,000	14
Oxford Island Nature Reserve	88,526	15	149,200	7	158,000	7	190,951	6
Tannaghmore Farm and Gardens	75,000	16	74,000	16	77,000	15	78,000	15
Carrick-a-Rede Rope Bridge	65,952	17	61,704	20	71,952	17	120,579	10
Old Bushmills Distillery	63,691	18	99,847	13	97,454	13	104,608	12
Newry Arts Centre	61,000	19	–	–	75,500	16	90,000	13
Navan Centre	60,000	20	–	–	–	–	–	–
Tyrone Crystal	–	–	75,000	15	68,755	18	68,936	17
Streamvale Open Farm	–	–	63,000	18	–	–	–	–
Malone House	–	–	62,000	19	62,500	20	62,500	18
Carrickfergus Castle	–	–	–	–	63,215	19	56,356	20

* Denotes those attractions that have no association with heritage.
Source: Boyd (2000b) and Northern Ireland Tourist Board (1999a, 2001a).

Table 3.5 Visits to heritage attractions by type, which received over 5,000 visitors between 1994 and 1997

Types	No.	1994	1995	%	1996	%	1997	%
Historical	14	276,896	326,820	+15	304,744	−7	293,578	−4
Cultural	8	549,586	599,325	+8	506,861	−18	525,595	+4
Industrial	4	236,979	384,879	+38	351,353	−9	383,564	+8
Educational	6	210,651	273,747	+23	215,047	−27	219,000	+2
Natural	21	1,598,047	1,984,564	+19	1,854,678	−7	1,853,017	0
Total	53	2,872,159	3,569,335	+20	3,232,683	−10	3,274,754	+1

Source: Boyd (2000b).

Table 3.6 Purpose of visit to Northern Ireland, 1995–2000

	1995		1996		1997		1998		1999		2000	
	Trips*	%	Trips	%	Trips	%	Trips	%	Trips	%	Trips	%
VFR	564	36	590	41	577	41	617	42	684	41	743	44
Holiday	461	30	297	21	263	19	277	19	305	18	306	18
Business	402	26	409	28	419	29	434	29	501	30	464	28
Other	130	8	140	10	156	11	149	10	165	10	159	10
Total	1,557		1,436		1,415		1,477		1,655		1,672	

* Trips are numbered in thousands.
Source: Northern Ireland Tourist Board (2001b).

situation, where the declines in 1996–98 have been turned around from 1999 to the present day.

The opportunity of culture, heritage and the arts is seen as a niche market that has potential to capitalise on a market trend where interest in the culture of destinations is growing. The World Tourism Organization recently stated that around 37 per cent of all tourism trips have a cultural and heritage component to them. This is in part because today's traveller is seeking more than what the Sunkist destinations can offer (sun, sand, sea, sunburn and skin cancer), as well as the reality that an ageing population within the key tourism source regions are interested in visiting places to learn about different cultures, as well as being willing to be educated while on holiday. Tourism is essentially about an intangible product, namely an experience. Culture and heritage lie at the heart of the Northern Ireland experience.

Since the cessation of violence in Northern Ireland, there has been growth in the European, North American and the overseas markets, with minimal growth and sometimes loss in the market regions of Great Britain and the Republic of

Ireland. However, when market regions are considered in terms of total numbers of trips taken, the two key markets remain Great Britain and the Republic of Ireland. Following the terrorist attacks in the United States on 11 September 2001, it is even more essential that Northern Ireland is sold as a holiday destination in its principal market regions, including continental Europe, as the likelihood of growth from the North American market and from other regions cannot be assured. While Australians, New Zealanders and Canadians may travel as part of the VFR market, there can be no certainties of this in the foreseeable future. Hence, if culture and heritage are to remain key attractions they must be found outside of the USA. This is important, for the current (draft) corporate plan for 2001–4 has projected an increase in discretionary visitors from 50.6 per cent (1999) to 57.3 per cent by the end of 2003. This translates into an increase from 837,000 to 1,150,000 visitors (Northern Ireland Tourist Board 2000). Heritage and cultural tourists are recognised as a key element of the discretionary visitor market. In terms of the average spending per trip, this is projected to rise over the same period from £137 to £200. Boyd (2000b) noted the contribution heritage tourists and business tourists played in the rise in average spending prior to this period, and it is expected that yet another rise in spending will rely on maintaining a strong demand for heritage tourism across the province. One particular subset of heritage tourism, where out-of-state demand exists, is that of industrial heritage.

Demand for industrial heritage attractions and products

With the emergence of a new political climate within Northern Ireland and the cessation of terrorist activity, the opportunity exists to promote the province as a holiday destination, but one that focuses on specific products. In the past, there has been a lack of emphasis on developing the domestic market. This, along with key themes such as roots tourism and an interest in local studies, education and languages, as well as the many facets of what constitutes heritage, are all areas where tourism can grow in Northern Ireland. One particular niche market where demand exists is industrial heritage. While the industrial heritage category shown in Table 3.5 constitutes the smallest number of attractions, visitor surveys in 1997 and 2000 (NITB 2001b) revealed that industrial heritage remains the most favoured category of heritage attraction by out-of-state visitors, particularly those from North America. The industrial heritage product in Northern Ireland is mixed and includes:

- linen;
- shipbuilding;
- distilling;
- steam and waterways;
- pottery and glassmaking/crystal;
- brewing;
- other industrial heritage (gas production, spade-making and printing).

A SWOT analysis undertaken by the NITB (1999b) for this sector (see Table 3.7) revealed that while a market and demand exist for this type of heritage tourism attraction, weaknesses were greater than strengths as were the threats over the opportunities existing for this sector.

Table 3.7   SWOT analysis results for the industrial heritage tourism sector within Northern Ireland

Strengths
 1. An attractive industrial heritage product already in place and easily accessible to the visitor
 2. Authenticity
 3. Unique products such as spade mill (last in UK) and *Titanic*
 4. World-renowned industrial products
 5. Quality product particularly in linen, brewing, distilling and glassmaking
 6. International reputation of Irish linen
 7. Superb collection of archive and historical materials in museums across NI
 8. Excellent collections, resources and local knowledge

Weaknesses
 1. Low marketing profile
 2. Limited human resources
 3. Product is not given proper recognition
 4. Tourism is not perceived as important to the industry
 5. Poor promotional and marketing campaigns
 6. Not enough advertising and exposure
 7. Lack of co-ordinated development initiatives
 8. Poor communication within the sector
 9. Visitor inertia

Opportunities
 1. More exciting interpretation at sites
 2. Co-ordination of development and marketing activity
 3. Marketing collaboration within and between sectoral interests
 4. Millennium opportunity – contrast between past and present technology
 5. Potential to increase visitor numbers to Republic of Ireland levels
 6. Matching the needs of the discerning visitor
 7. Provide excitement and entertainment at sites
 8. Coherent planning
 9. Identification of clear objectives
10. Reclaim the *Titanic*
11. Special events and themed festivals

Threats
 1. Doubts about the peace process and political stability
 2. Narrow agendas and competition between industrial heritage organisations
 3. Poor planning and co-ordination
 4. Low profile leading to insufficient interest
 5. The dark, satanic, dirty, unattractive image in the public imagination
 6. Poor networks
 7. Property developers and delisting
 8. International competition
 9. Expectations of sophisticated overseas visitors
10. Internal competition between attractions
11. Authenticity sacrificed to commercial gain
12. Lack of support from the Northern Ireland Assembly

Source: Northern Ireland Tourist Board (1999b).

What the SWOT analysis revealed is that problems exist within the make-up of the industrial heritage product group within Northern Ireland, and that these internal factors need to be overcome if they are to capitalise on the demand for such types of tourist attraction. There is a need for effective communication structures, building of external networks, as well as development of strategic and marketing plans. In spite of these huge challenges facing sectors such as industrial heritage, places like Northern Ireland which must deal with violence and the reality of a peripheral location should capitalise on the uniqueness of this aspect of heritage.

Summary and conclusions

Upon completion of this chapter the reader should be familiar with the following facts regarding heritage tourism demand. First, as a form of special interest travel, heritage tourism has witnessed phenomenal growth as of late, whether visitation is to natural heritage attractions like national parks or to cultural and educational attractions like museums. Second, heritage tourism demand can be viewed from different perspectives: current or use demand, option demand (visiting in the future), existence demand (intrinsic value placed on heritage that is not actually consumed), bequest demand (heritage passed down to future generations) and latent demand. Third, demand can be viewed according to source, including those that promote visits to heritage attractions, various levels of government, and heritage guardians who protect the resource, or according to the market and type of heritage visitor, be they passive, serious or focused on a specific subset of tourist attraction (e.g. industrial, natural, literary).

While it is difficult to equate different types of tourists with similar characteristics, the argument put forth in this chapter is that heritage tourists can be distinguished by certain demographics (i.e. they are highly educated, often hold well-paid jobs within professional and managerial positions, gender slant towards women, with varying ages attracted to different types of heritage attraction), geographic origins (closely related to the scale of the attractions visited), psychographics (tendency to be more allocentric in type), and other characteristics (e.g. travelling as part of a group as opposed to on their own, have greater empathy with local customs, respect environment, spend more, stay longer, display less seasonality and not be as influenced by external factors that could prevent travel).

Motivational aspects are important in understanding the pattern of demand for heritage tourism. First, there is greater emphasis placed on learning about the places and culture visited, as well as a mix of personal benefits. Second, motivation is often tied up with a person's connection with place. With a larger grey market within generating regions, roots tourism has become a significant part of heritage tourism. For example, in the United States alone it is claimed that there are over 40 million people who can trace their roots back to Ireland. This has led to many Irish-Americans travelling back to the 'motherland' to investigate their roots, which the Irish Tourist Board has capitalised on by offering personal heritage, or genealogy, tours and massive family reunions (Timothy 2001b). Third, and linked to the roots identity, is the factor of nostalgia, the allure of the simpler lifestyles from the past, and the educational and personal reasons that attract people to heritage places.

While making the best use of the heritage supply is important, of equal importance is the reality that many choose not to avail themselves of the heritage experience. In discussing this, key constraints were identified as those classed as structural (lack of physical and market accessibility), intrapersonal (lack of educational preparation, desire and interest) and interpersonal (disability as a result of intrinsic, environmental or communication barriers, as well as psychological constraints of visiting attractions on their own). Within demand research in heritage there is a need to focus more attention on non-use. In the context of heritage, managers must not discount this potential market and attempt to address many of the factors that explain their non-attendance. At the same time, caution needs to be exercised in assigning labels to visitors. While there is a case to be made sometimes that certain visitors are interested solely in things of heritage, understanding the demand that exists for heritage tourism is to understand that above all tourists are interested in gaining an overall experience of the places they visit. In this instance, the experience is centred on things heritage. Having discussed supply and demand, the next chapter shifts to examine why people desire to conserve the past.

Questions

1. What factors, as of late, explain the growth in interest in heritage tourism?
2. Do heritage visitors have certain key characteristics that make them distinctive?
3. To what extent is latent demand the most important type of demand where heritage tourism is concerned?
4. Using heritage places in your locality, what factors best explain their non-use in terms of visitation?

Further reading

Drummond, S. and Yeoman, I. (eds) (2001) *Quality Issues in Heritage Visitor Attractions*, Butterworth Heinemann, Oxford.

Herbert, D.T. (1995) *Heritage, Tourism and Society*, Mansell, London.

Herbert, D.T., Prentice, R.C. and C.J. Thomas (eds) (1989) *Heritage Sites: Strategies for marketing and development*. Avebury, Aldershot.

Hewison, R. (1987) *The Heritage Industry: Britain in a climate of decline*, Methuen, London.

Richards, G. (ed.) (2001) *Cultural Attractions and European Tourism*, CAB International, Wallingford.

CHAPTER 4

Conserving the past

Heritage is not about the past. Rather, it is a reflection of what exists at present. Graham *et al.* (2000: 2) in their book, *A Geography of Heritage*, support this notion, stating that 'people in the present are the creators of heritage, and not merely passive receivers or transmitters of it [as] the present creates the heritage it requires and manages it for a range of contemporary purposes'. As noted in Chapter 1, the 'industry' around which heritage tourism operates is a relatively recent phenomenon, but one that is reliant on the past as a resource, shaped by contemporary structures of society. It is therefore fitting that this discussion shifts from the supply and demand side of heritage tourism to address why society over time has felt it necessary to conserve elements of its past as a resource to be presented to visitors.

The term 'conservation' has been used in a wide variety of contexts and at different times. It is often used to mean the same as preservation, although most conservation specialists agree that there are differences between them. About these differences, Pearce (1997: 89) asserts that conservation is widely accepted to mean the wise use of resources, while preservation means no use at all. Pearce (1997) defines conservation as preserving purposefully. According to the New Zealand Conservation Act of 1987, conservation is 'the preservation and protection of natural and historical resources for the purposes of maintaining their intrinsic values, providing for their appreciation and recreational enjoyment by the public and safeguarding the options of future generations' (Pearce 1997: 89). Thus, there are various interpretations of conservation, but their primary premise is the protection of cultural and natural resources.

Among all other areas of land use management, conservation seems to have succeeded the best and most often. Duerksen (1992: 110), writing from a North American perspective, offered several pieces of evidence for this assertion. First are the numerous local conservation ordinances that have been enacted in recent years and the hundreds of extant ones that have been given more power to protect historic resources. Second, state conservation laws have improved and broadened including many that give states real authority, which has resulted in more states including historic conservation elements in their land use plans. Third is the growth in financial incentives for heritage properties, including tax reductions for conservation and tax breaks for historic properties. Finally, moves to protect archaeological sites at the federal and state levels have become so pervasive that archaeology has become a growth industry, especially in the western United States.

This chapter commences by looking at why Western societies have lately acquired an obsession with the past. Reasons for this include the drive for industrialisation/modernisation, nationalism and collective nostalgia, science and education, economic benefits to be gained by society from showing its heritage, its artistic value, environmental diversity and/or simply because heritage is deemed to have some functional value. Types and perspectives of conservation are also presented, including approaches such as preservation, restoration, renovation, urban renewal (regeneration), with specific discussion given to waterfront developments in heritage places. The conservation process is also examined, and brief commentary on conservation legislation and bodies is provided before addressing the challenges managers face to conserve heritage and the impacts that heritage tourism brings about.

Why conserve the past?

Heritage planning has emerged from broader concerns of preservation and conservation (Ashworth and Tunbridge 2000). Concerns for preservation within Western societies have been around since the early eighteenth century and are reflected in the writings of authors in the Romantic period (e.g. Byron and Rousseau), where the values of simple living and preserving of wilderness were the antecedents to establishing natural heritage landscapes such as national parks (Butler and Boyd 2000). This was followed by conservation and Gifford Pinchot's guiding philosophy of 'the greatest good for the greatest number', better known as the wise use of resources. He advocated that the principal objective of conservation was the control over, and usage of, natural resources for the benefit of all, but in doing so alienated those who viewed conservation from a strongly preservationist stance, such as John Muir (Boyd 1995). As for heritage and its conservation, this has become a paramount concern in Western societies during the past 50 years, and several reasons have been identified in the literature why this 'Western obsession with the past' (Merriman 1991: 3) has emerged. These reasons are set out below.

Industrialisation/modernisation

Rapid industrialisation and high-tech development have characterised the consumer societies of the 1980s and 1990s, which, according to Barthel (1996), has resulted in historic preservation as a display of dissatisfaction with it. Through the process of modernisation, people and societies become nervous about the present and the future, for it is only the past that is known and understood. 'The preoccupation with the past is created out of the experience of continual change . . . Far from being a symptom of a supposed "post-modernity", the preoccupation with the past, and the typical means for evoking it, lie in the very foundations of modernity' (Brett 1996: 15). Thus, a hold onto the past, particularly in terms of preserving tangible objects, provides comfort, familiarity and a grounded sense of identity (Lowenthal 1979a, b) in a world, which, compared to the past, is considered more bleak, grim, wretched, ugly, unfulfilling and frightening (Davis 1979). As an outcome of this, rapidly changing Western societies have 'sought to retain buildings, townscapes and objects which help to maintain a link with the past and therefore build a sense of continuity in their lives' (Hall and McArthur 1993a: 1) – hence the roots of the expansive movement during the past 30 years to preserve the small town environments in North America (Holdsworth 1985; Ziegler and Kidney 1980).

Part of the prescription for modernisation appears to be the loss of tradition, as the populations of most modernised nations have become consumed with conserving rural lifestyles and landscapes out of a fear of losing them. In Japan, which is densely urbanised and highly westernised, there are many fears of a vanishing countryside and loss of Japanese identity, which is commonly equated with rural life by city dwellers. This has resulted in traditional pasts and rural landscapes being promoted persistently by the tourism industry, especially for domestic tourists, as a way of replacing 'temporal distance . . . by a geographical one' (Creighton 1997: 252). In the United States and the UK, modern society longs for the simpler and safer landscapes of rural life, instead of the harried life of the city. In Lowenthal's (1977) view, what people like most about the countryside is the belief that it is more natural and therefore more virtuous.

Heritage critic, Hewison (1991: 25), argued that such mass conservation efforts are an illusion marketed by a profitable industry as a way of offering the public some kind of phoney reassurance in the present. As such, the search for safety even leads societies to develop contrived places that never existed. 'Indeed, it is even possible to gaze upon the burial site of Alice in Wonderland, the House that Jack Built, the birthplace of Dick Whittington, and the precise spot where George slew the dragon' (Dann 1998: 29–30).

Nationalism and collective nostalgia

Closely related to, and often stemming from, modernisation-induced preservation is collective nostalgia. Just as nostalgia can be a motivator for individuals to travel to heritage sites, as discussed in the previous chapter, it can also be seen in a broader context as a reason heritage is valued and conserved by collective groups and societies. Collective nostalgia, just as it does on an individual level, can evoke bittersweet yearnings within entire societies – emotions shared by people of a similar background (Baker and Kennedy 1994), such as generations, cultures and nations (Belk 1990). The difference between individual and collective nostalgia is that the latter involves symbolic objects of a highly public, widely shared and socially familiar character. Such symbolisms from the past under proper conditions can generate nostalgic feelings en masse among millions of people at the same time and can range from awesome events to something as seemingly insignificant as cartoon characters and other media creations (Davis 1979: 122).

Heritage helps establish individual, community and national identities, which enable people to define who they are (Hall and McArthur 1993a: 1). In national terms heritage sites and historic relics are a product and evidence of different traditions and achievements of the past, and are thus an essential element in the personality of patriotic citizens. They are also an indivisible part of the cultural landscape that provides emotional and physical linkages and continuities with national pasts (Pearson and Sullivan 1995: 15). However,

> it is not merely an aesthetic or visual continuity, but also a continuity of cultural memory that seems important. Since the mid 1960s this justification for preservation has been of increasing significance, broadening the original elitist concern and preoccupation with the aesthetic properties of historic artifacts. Visible evidence of the past can contribute pedagogically and educationally to the cultural identity and memory of a particular people or place, locating a contemporary society in relation to a previous tradition and giving meaning to the present by interpreting the past (Hewison 1987: 85).

The value of heritage to ethnic minority groups is an important consideration when considering nationhood. For indigenous peoples, for example, the significance of heritage sites may be traditional, historic or contemporary. Traditional places may be sacred, having an important religious worth where ceremonies are/were held or a place associated with a cultural hero. Places with historic meaning may have their origins before or after European colonisation and relate to locations where major events occurred or places that were used for other essential purposes (e.g. cemeteries). Contemporary sites may have no traditional associations but do in modern times. An example might be an archaeological site previously unknown to present aboriginal peoples, but when discovered may acquire cultural importance because of what it symbolises (Pearson and Sullivan 1995: 19).

Scientific and educative importance

Many properties are seen to have scientific and conservation significance because they are representative of certain natural and cultural environments (Hall and McArthur 1993a: 1). As such, they have potential to provide information of great value in many areas of research (Pearson and Sullivan 1995), particularly if sites of recent discovery are considered 'one-of-a-kind' attractions. This is commonly the case at many archaeological sites.

Akin to scientific value is educative importance. Clearly, the teaching role of heritage attractions and museums is irrefutable. Educating the public about important people, places and events from history is one of the premier responsibilities and goals of most heritage managers, which requires careful and intentional conservation endeavours.

One key aim of conservation at sites associated with death and atrocity is to educate the public about how malevolent some aspects of history were so that history will not repeat itself. In the words of Lennon and Foley (1999: 48–9) in reference to the Holocaust Memorial Museum in Washington, DC, 'the primary purpose of the museum [is] to make visitors understand how attempts to annihilate an entire people came to be and how this was executed'.

Heritage is good economics

In places where tourism is dominated by heritage attractions, the economic impact can be very profound. As heritage tourism has grown, destinations have begun to realise the potential value it has for local and national economies in terms of job creation, increased tax bases, more regional income and stimulating local entrepreneurial activity. Very often, therefore, economics forms the basis for conserving heritage. Several historic cities in Central and Eastern Europe have recently begun to realise the potential of developing urban-based heritage tourism as a means of economic development.

> If cities such as Edinburgh or Florence can be seen to successfully base their development upon cultural resources, and even cities with few previous cultural pretensions such as Frankfurt am Main, Lille or Glasgow are investing in aspects of culture for its perceived economic benefits, then the temptation for the Central European cities to follow such examples is almost irresistible. One of the few comparative advantages that they possess are relatively heritage-rich cities and high quality cultural industries, often cosseted by the previous regime and now in search of new financial support (Ashworth and Tunbridge 1999: 111).

Tiesdell *et al.* (1996) argue that in the private sector, unless there is a clear economic rationale for a particular policy or practice, it is unlikely to occur. This goes for heritage conservation as well, and in a worldwide situation where public funding is scarce, the economic justification of tourism often wins over the arguments of activists who fight against the tourist use of heritage.

Artistic and aesthetic value

It is common for historic towns and old buildings to be valued simply for their aesthetic value, or because they are old and therefore have a 'scarcity value' (Lynch 1972). Many conserved sites throughout the world are marvellous examples of high artistic and creative achievements. Much of the reason for the general appreciation of historic buildings is the insipidness of modern and postmodern styles of architecture, which lack the types of appeal and artistic value that so much of society longs for today. 'Historic buildings and areas have picturesque qualities; they are redolent of a period of genuine craftsmanship and individuality that has been lost in a period of modern industrialized building products and systems of construction' (Tiesdell *et al.* 1996: 12).

Environmental diversity

In its broadest sense, environment refers to both human and natural elements. Environmental diversity and sustainability are a critical consideration in heritage conservation, particularly since heritage is a non-renewable resource. Once sites of historic value are gone, they cannot be reintroduced or regenerated, and even if lifelike replicas are created, they cannot replace the original in scientific, aesthetic or educational terms (Pearson and Sullivan 1995). Owing to their irreplaceable environmental value many cultural heritage sites have been included in recent years in the World Monuments Fund's (WMF) list of threatened sites – places under threat of destruction by human-induced and natural processes. This list is compiled by the New York-based non-profit WMF, which aims to highlight the plight of certain places that are considered most in need of rescue and conservation funding, and their goal is to aid countries in protecting important heritage sites through international financial donations. Table 4.1 records some of these threatened sites in Eastern Europe and Asia, although dozens more from around the world are listed with the WMF.

Heritage as functional resource

In addition to the heritage values described above, there is also a use, or functional, value. It is common for historic properties to be renovated and used for purposes other than their original objectives. Old factories transformed into office buildings, prisons into restaurants and railway stations into souvenir shops, are good examples.

In evaluating the utility of old buildings and historic urban areas, planners need to examine the relative value of such places in relation to current needs. Thus, the diminished utility, or level of obsolescence, should be weighed against the costs of constructing new buildings taking into account the heritage conservation value as well. In many cases buildings are better used as modern resources than replaced with new structures that have little historic attachment to place (Setiawan and Timothy 2000; Tiesdell *et al.* 1996).

Table 4.1   A selection of the World Monuments Fund threatened sites

Country	Name of site	Location
Albania	Butrint Archaeological Site	Sarande
Bosnia-Hercegovina	Mostar Historic Centre	Mostar
Bulgaria	Ivanovo Rock Chapels	Rousse region
Cambodia	Banteay Chlmar Temple	Thmar, Puok
China	Palpung Monastery	Bagang village, Sichuan
China	Xuanjian Tower	Yuci City, Shanxi
Czech Republic	Kuks Forest Sculptures	Kuks
Georgia	Tbilisi Historic District	Tbilisi
India	Basgo Gompa Temples	Ladakh, Leh
India	Jaisalmer Fort	Rajasthan
Indonesia	Tanah Lot Temple	Tabanan, Bali
Malaysia	Kampung Cina River Frontage	Kuala Terengganu
Mongolia	Bogd Khaan Palace Museum	Ulaanbaatar
Nepal	Itum Monastery	Kathmandu
Romania	Banffy Castle	Bontida
Russia	Irkutsk Historic Centre	Irkutsk
Russia	Viipuri Library	Vyborg
Slovakia	Basil the Great Church	Krajne Cierno
Turkmenistan	Merv Archaeological Site	Bairam Ali
Ukraine	Zhovkva Synagogue	Zhovkva
Uzbekistan	Abdulazizkhan Complex	Bukhara
Vietnam	My Son Temple Complex	Quang Nam
Yugoslavia	Subotica Synagogue	Subotica

Source: *Travel Weekly* (2000a, b).

Conservation types and perspectives

Time has shaped the heritage resources that exist today. Sadly, many have been lost, ruined or substantially changed from their original condition as the interests of preservation, conservation and, more recently, heritage planning have fought against the interests of modernisation, economic development and growth, and an absence of interest in some quarters about the past. With the decay of heritage resources over time, there are two courses of action that can be taken in response to this, acceptance or prevention. Ashworth and Tunbridge (2000) refer to the former as euthanasia, where it can be passive with no action taken, or active where heritage resources are demolished. The focus here is with the second response to preventing the decay of heritage resources, where a range of perspectives on conserving heritage, and the location it is situated within, can be taken. Invariably, the goals for each site generally shape the strategies embraced by management that are in turn heavily influenced by visitor expectations. Depending on these goals, heritage managers must decide which of several approaches to conservation they will adopt: preservation, restoration, renovation (repair) and regeneration, where much of the latter is often centred on developments around heritage in waterfront locations.

Preservation

Preservation refers to a situation wherein the choice is made to maintain the site in its existing state. A great deal of effort and expenditure are involved in this work to maintain the property and impede deterioration (Timothy and Wall 1997). Obviously this is not a hands-off policy, for much work is needed to retain the present situation (Wall 1989).

Two of the best examples of this from North America are ghost towns and ruins of ancient Native American communities. Most ghost towns are left in a deliberate state of dereliction, for this is the notion of their being ghost towns. Thus, the attractiveness of ghost towns is their run-down and abandoned atmosphere. Any efforts to restore them to their earlier glory would in fact reduce their heritage and touristic value (DeLyser 1999). Leaving a site in its present situation is appropriate 'where the cultural significance would be diminished by a higher degree of intervention, where the present state of the site is itself significant, where there is insufficient information or resources to restore or reconstruct the place, or where sufficient well-restored examples already exist' (Pearson and Sullivan 1995: 233). This is much of the reason that nearly all Indian ruins in the American West have been left in the condition they were found by Europeans and frontier settlers. Consequently, 'there is an excitement about seeing the original, even if it is faded or eroded, which restoration or reconstruction would spoil' (Pearson and Sullivan 1995: 233).

Restoration

Restoration, sometimes known as reconstruction (although there are subtle differences), refers to the act of returning a property to some previous condition. Restoration refers to two activities: putting displaced pieces of a building or site back together and removing pieces and amendments that have been added through time (Pearson and Sullivan 1995) (Plate 4.1). In purely theoretical

Plate 4.1   Restoration works at Prambanan temples in Indonesia

terms restoration means that not even new materials can be used in the process (e.g. nails and staples). When new materials are used to restore a structure, the process becomes one of reconstruction rather than pure restoration (Pearson and Sullivan 1995). Thus, from this purist perspective,

> it is impossible, for nothing can be restored to be exactly what it was. The act of restoration itself marks a change: a shattered Greek urn meticulously restored is not the same urn as made in 300 BC. Indeed, the very skill of its contemporary restoration may well shift the emphasis of our admiration from then to now. Restoration can induce change and may indeed be carried out for that purpose, the achievement of which may itself produce further, perhaps unintended results (Fowler 1992: 11).

According to Pearson and Sullivan (1995: 235), 'restoration is appropriate only if there is sufficient evidence of an earlier state'. As a result, a great deal of research may be required to determine exactly what the property was like in the past. In cases where the site has had a long history, a decision will have to be made regarding which of a number of previous states is to be restored (Wall 1989). Such efforts are arduous, time consuming and expensive, which led Fowler (1992: 12) to comment in a joking, if mordant way, 'if only people in the past had kept it simple, our task would be so much simpler; but of course they changed and adapted their buildings through time just as we continue to do'.

Renovation

Renovation, also known as adaptation, entails making changes to a site while still maintaining a portion of its historical character. Attaching an additional wing to a historic building for administrative purposes or for living space for interpreters, while maintaining the historic nature of the rest of the building, would be a case of renovation. Perhaps one of the most common practices of renovation is to keep a building's original façade while modifying the interior. This is common where there is a desire to give an illusion of historic integrity (Timothy and Wall 1997; Wall 1989). The guideline offered by Pearson and Sullivan (1995: 238) for this managerial practice is that 'adaptation must be limited to that which is essential to establishing a compatible use for the place'.

Urban renewal/regeneration

When decisions are made not to demolish obsolete buildings (depending on what conservation controls are in place), it is not at all uncommon for all three of these approaches to conservation, as discussed previously, to be utilised in urban renewal and regeneration projects. With the rapid growth of technological change and the resultant diminishing role of heavy industry in urban areas in the developed world, cities have recently become centres of service industries and consumption rather than centres of heavy production. This has resulted in cities throughout the world changing to accommodate post-industrial, information-based economies. Part of this movement attempts to deal with obsolescence in an effort to extend the useful lives of buildings and historic urban centres. Such endeavours are known as urban renewal (Larkham 1992; Page 1995a; Tiesdell *et al.* 1996).

As a means of revitalising historic urban quarters, many cities have attempted to attract new activities. Among the most common are tourism and cultural activities. Such strategies have encouraged the exploitation of the area's historic legacy for tourist development and combated obsolescence by bringing in new uses and enhancing the urban environment. This according to Tiesdell *et al.* (1996: 68–70) leads to increased local confidence and the likelihood of various forms of investment. Often, as part of tourism-based strategies, historic buildings are used for tourist functions. This has the potential to benefit historic quarters positively in the following ways:

- Historic buildings are restored.
- It provides a living function for a historic building that might otherwise sit empty.
- It decreases the number of empty properties, providing a more desirable urban environment, which may reduce crime and violence associated with empty city centres and create safer and more desirable places to live.

- It might avoid the environmental impacts of the same function being located in a newly constructed building.
- It has the potential to create environments that will help historic towns retain the qualities that make them attractive (Orbaşli 2000: 161).

Despite these benefits, urban renewal is not necessarily an easy or problem-free process. Orbaşli (2000: 161) identified four difficulties in initiating urban regeneration projects (see Table 4.2). First, there is often a clash of policies regarding new development and conservation. This usually results from conflicting interests and a lack of co-ordinated efforts between government agencies that are charged with different responsibilities. Second, in the developing world context, there are higher aspirations for modernisation than for maintaining traditional urban forms and architectural designs (Mohit and Kammeier 1996). In the Western world the opposite is generally true. Third, it is difficult to balance the needs of a tourist culture and those of the local culture in a way that does not offend or alienate residents but which caters to the needs of the tourists. Finally there is the problem of maintaining a sustainable and high-quality urban environment as tourist arrivals increase. Van der Borg *et al.* (1996) noted a similar concern with urban congestion and crowded conditions, which can detract from the experience but also erode the area's environmental integrity.

Table 4.2 lists other challenges that also exist in urban centre renewal. It is difficult to measure success in urban revitalisation. As Tiesdell *et al.* (1996: 207) argue, 'there are no magic thresholds above which it can be claimed empirically that revitalization has occurred. Revitalizing – bringing areas back into active use – is a dynamic process.' Another challenge is the place of historic quarters in the overall function of the city. It is critical for planners to understand that historic areas are not separate cities, but instead function as only one part of urban agglomerations. Thus, while it is still uncommon in many places, the tourist-historic city must be considered as a part of the city as a whole, for there is usually a symbiotic relationship between historic

Table 4.2 Challenges to urban historic quarter regeneration

Clash of policies on new developments and conservation
Modernisation versus maintaining traditional forms
Balancing the needs of tourists and needs of local residents
Maintaining high-quality environments as tourist arrivals increase
Difficulty in measuring the success of renewal
In planning, historic centres are often viewed in isolation from the rest of the city
Tourism is often left out or ignored in urban planning strategies

Source: After Orbaşli (2000), Tiesdell *et al.* (1996) and van der Borg *et al.* (1996).

cores and other urban areas (Tiesdell *et al.* 1996: 22). Finally, it is very common for tourism to be left out entirely from urban planning strategies, which is an unfortunate oversight on the part of city planners, for very few cities in the world today exist without some form of tourism. According to van der Borg *et al.* (1996), in fact it is still quite rare to find municipalities involved in making political actions that pertain to tourism. In most cases, tourism is simply considered in terms of traffic and parking, although in Europe exceptions to this include Bruges, Oxford, Salzburg and Venice, where tourism and its pressures on the built environment hold a prominent place in urban planning.

Tiesdell *et al.* (1996) have written extensively on historic urban quarter revitalisation. While much of what has been written in the general literature deals almost entirely with physical regeneration, they have suggested that urban renewal must include other forms of revitalisation as well: physical, economic and social. Physical revitalisation indicates the traditional view of urban renewal, which involves keeping buildings in good condition, the streets clean and rehabilitating areas to create an environment of cleanliness and comfort. Economic revitalisation implies that property development is insufficient in creating a livable urban environment. Instead, the economic infrastructure must be considered, and economic growth must be stimulated by bringing in additional services, diversifying the existing economic base and utilising existing buildings.

> In the short term, physical revitalization can result in an attractive, well-maintained public realm that projects a positive image and encourages confidence in the location. In the longer term economic revitalization is required, as ultimately it is the productive utilization of the private realm that pays for the maintenance of the public realm (Tiesdell *et al.* 1996: 209).

Social revitalisation entails creating a usable location where residents and tourists alike can enjoy walking, sightseeing, shopping and spending time with others. Historic quarters should be lively places that exude a comfortable ambience and are attractive to visit. It also means that crime rates will be low and the revitalised structural elements are usable as space for living and working.

In the United States, movements have been under way for many years to improve the lot of declining centres in large cities and smaller towns. The Main Street Program and the Business Improvement Districts are two programmes that have been key in these efforts. The Main Street Program includes economic development aims within the broader context of historic preservation, meeting local needs in terms of promotion, design, economic restructuring and organization (Balsas 2000).

The following case study of Stoke-on-Trent, England, provides an example of how one community/region is taking strides to recreate its image and enhance its local economy through industrial heritage tourism.

CASE STUDY   Stoke-on-Trent: rejuvenation as a result of industrial heritage tourism

Stoke-on-Trent is not a typical city; it consists of a conurbation of six towns: Tunstall, Burslem, Hanley (city centre of Stoke-on-Trent), Stoke, Fenton and Longton. As a region it has a long history of industry; it was at the heart of the Industrial Revolution recognised for its steelworks, coalmines and pottery industry. Stoke-on-Trent became dubbed the 'Ceramics capital of the world', home to, and the birthplace of, ceramic entrepreneurs such as Doulton, Wedg-wood and Spode. The plight of Stoke-on-Trent during the twentieth century has been characterised by the closure of pits, steelworks and a downsizing of the ceramics industry. Tourism, particularly industrial heritage tourism, has been viewed as one means to assist in regional regeneration.

This case study examines several programmes of regeneration that have taken place within the six towns. As an area that has suffered decline, it has qualified under European Union structural funds as having Area 2 status: regeneration of regions or parts of regions seriously affected by industrial decline. In addition, most of the areas within the six towns are part of a larger programme of renewal by the British government called Single Regeneration Budgets (SRBs). Twenty separate regeneration programmes, run by five different government depart-ments, were amalgamated into the SRB that came into operation in 1994 with an initial total of £1.4 billion (Ward 1997). Opportunity existed within what was titled the Challenge Fund to bid for up to seven years. Caffyn (1998: 112) notes that the Department of the Environment (DoE) identified that the strategic objectives for the SRB Challenge Fund were to:

- enhance the employment prospects, education and skills of local people and promote equality of opportunity;
- encourage sustainable economic growth and wealth creation by improving the competitiveness of the local economy;
- promote and improve the environment and infrastructure and promote good design and landscaping;
- improve housing conditions for local people through physical improvement, better maintenance and improved management;
- promote initiatives of benefit to ethnic minority communities;
- tackle crime and improve community safety;
- enhance the quality of life and capacity to contribute to regeneration of local people, including their health, cultural and sports opportunities.

There is a lack of vision within the Stoke-on-Trent region as tourism has often been limited to visits to a few household named pottery attractions (e.g. Royal Doulton in Burslem, Spode works in Stoke and Wedgewood in Barlaston) (Plate 4.2). There is a need to broaden the appeal of the area to tourists. Part of the problem in achieving this has been that much industrial heritage has been based on tour packages that can only accommodate a one-day visit to the region and therefore they take in the big three attractions named above. The challenge has been to market the region to the day-trip and domestic market, as well as the international market not restricted by a packaged itinerary.

Plate 4.2   Spode Works: industrial heritage in Stoke-on-Trent, UK

According to the Stoke-on-Trent visitor survey of 1997, the majority of visitors are domestic day trippers (47 per cent) compared to international tourists (20 per cent) where only 4 per cent of these actually stay overnight. The majority of domestic visitors are resident in the adjacent counties as well as from across the north-west region of England. The majority of international visitors are from North America (47 per cent), Japan (7 per cent), the Netherlands (6 per cent) and New Zealand (5 per cent). The majority of visitors (both domestic and international) cited 'pleasure' and 'pottery/shopping' as the main purpose of their visit, supported by the fact that 51 per cent of all activities undertaken in the region were connected to factory shopping. Asked what they liked most about Stoke-on-Trent, the main response was again 'shops' and 'shopping related to pottery' (22 per cent), as opposed to 'industrial heritage' which only received 7 per cent, suggesting that many fail to make the connection between pottery attractions and industrial heritage. Nevertheless, tourism is important to the city. According to the visitor survey (Stoke-on-Trent 1997) it is responsible for 3,839 direct jobs and 1,346 indirect jobs, where the majority of these are within the retail sector.

A number of programmes have been initiated in recent years where tourism is assisting with regeneration schemes. For instance, the town of Burslem has initiated a townscape heritage initiative since 1998 and launched a Millennium project entitled Ceramica in 2001. Hanley has developed the Festival Park area into a tourism and leisure space, and launched the scheme to develop the Cultural Quarter in 1999. Stoke since 1998 has been engaged in a seven-year regeneration programme entitled 'The Stoke Approach' and there are future plans to redevelop the canal system that passes through the region, and develop a leisure, tourism and residential district called 'Festival Waters' in the near future. Two of the above are examined in detail below.

Burslem

The town has the appeal of a unique architectural and historical character. It is largely a nineteenth-century town that has received very minor post-war redevelopment. In fact it is one of the oldest centres for industrial pottery manufacturing in the UK. It is the setting for many of Arnold Bennett's novels in which he wrote of the realities of life in a growing nineteenth-century industrial town. Recent years have seen the town suffer from economic decline where there has been a lack of investment in the built fabric. The response by the town has been twofold. First, the city council has adopted a long-term regeneration strategy to turn the town's fortunes around, with particular focus on what they declared as the Conservation Area Boundary. Second, the Burslem Community Development Trust (BCDT) was set up as part of an informal partnership with Stoke-on-Trent City Council and English Partnerships. The objectives of the BCDT were as follows:

1. to encourage the participation of local people in broad regeneration schemes;
2. to encourage and participate in practical schemes of development, environmental enhancement and building repair;
3. to encourage pride and awareness of the heritage qualities of Burslem.

The focus to date has been in securing funding to assist with regeneration. Under the Burslem Conservation Area Partnership Scheme Action Plan an analysis of special architectural and historical interest, problems and opportunities, regeneration, design and development strategy and an audit of the built fabric of the conservation area have been completed. Heritage regeneration and tourism have been undertaken within the Burslem 1998–2000 SRB by improving street lighting, paving and street furniture. Furthermore, under European Regional Development Funding (ERDF) objective 2 status, monies have been secured to enhance the Royal Doulton visitor facilities, heritage regeneration and tourism have taken centre stage, and the School of Art has undergone a feasibility study to cater to tourists' interests in the arts. Other feasibility studies have been carried out on the Wedgwood Institute building both to refurbish it and provide for a range of arts-related uses for visitors and residents.

Another project that superseded the above initiatives has been the development of the Bursley trail within the centre of the town. Tracing places within Arnold Bennett's novel, individual buildings have a small plaque on the wall that signifies their presence within one of his novels. The brochure that is provided for tourists gives some history of each landmark, but the plaques are extremely small, and no directions are given on the ground to assist tourists walking the trail, unlike the red line that demarcates the Boston trail.

The flagship project within Burslem has been the rather controversial Ceramica project that received over £3 million of Millennium funding. The intent was to reuse the Old Town Hall in the centre of the town as an exhibition and interactive visitor centre linking the area's industrial past with a vision of how the manufacture of ceramic products may develop in the future. It has been controversial as it failed to open during 2000, the millennium year, and it had to apply for additional funds (an additional million to complete the project), as well as there being criticism over the modern building that was built and attached to the existing Old Town Hall. The purpose of the new addition was to provide visitors with a linked pavilion that contained a café, shop and public amenities. The project was due to open in late 2001.

Stoke

Stoke is engaging in a seven-year programme, costing £56 million to 'put heart back into the forgotten town'. Some projects that have been completed are a more pleasing environment after exiting the Victorian train station. The area surrounding the Wedgwood monument, immediately across from the entrance to the train station, has been relandscaped with new cobblestones and areas for seating. An industrial heritage walk is being created around Stoke, starting and ending at the station, that takes in more than just the Spode visitor centre, but includes the clock tower, canal, Stoke market and the St Peter's churchyard. The signs are in place, but much landscaping is needed to make sections of the walk appealing to visitors. It is being planned as one of the regeneration walks within the SRB that takes in the region of Stoke, and neighbouring areas of Eturia, Hanley and Shelton. While the walk is designed as a tourist trail, it is also part of an initiative by North Staffordshire Health Authority to get local residents to use the walks as part of a health campaign for healthier living.

Much of these regeneration programmes are linked to tourism and sharing the heritage of the region's industrial past with visitors. A key part in enabling schemes like these to advance has been the regeneration budgets and European programmes encouraging such development. Stoke-on-Trent has to date been relatively successful in securing funds to create the necessary infrastructure against which more tourism can result. Hewison (1987) was critical of places turning to their past as a means of economic growth, but places like Stoke-on-Trent should be proud of their industrial heritage and the legacy it leaves for future generations and visitors to enjoy.

Waterfront development

Another specific form of revitalisation that is usually found in the urban context and is a major player in heritage tourism is waterfront redevelopment. Many of the world's largest and most interesting tourist cities are located on waterfronts because this is where water-based transportation hubs were developed throughout the centuries and industrial complexes assembled. As part of the broader movement to revitalise urban areas and to utilise former (and current) industrial resources for tourism, many cities throughout the world have turned to developing their waterfronts into attractive tourism and recreation resources. Some of the most prominent examples include the London Docklands (Brownill 1994; Page 1995b), Toronto's Waterfront (Kieron 1992), Baltimore's Inner Harbour, Sydney Harbour, Liverpool (Craig-Smith 1995; Waitt and McGuirk 1997), Wellington (Page 1993) and the Cape Town Waterfront (Worden 1996, 1997). Even smaller cities (e.g. Toledo, Ohio, USA and Windsor, Ontario, Canada) have begun to join this trend in an effort to make their industrial waterfronts into more attractive recreation resources.

Waterfront development almost always focuses on heritage and its interpretation as part of its development efforts (Page 1993). This ranges from the industrial heritage upon which harbours and docklands were based to shipbuilding traditions and immigrant processing. The most common features of waterfronts that are developed for tourism include parklands and walkways, gardens and fountains, museums, shopping facilities, restaurants and snack bars, historic buildings, and elements of the industrial past, such as machinery used for loading and constructing ships.

Craig-Smith (1995: 34) outlined eight lessons that can be learned for waterfront developers from his examination of Liverpool, Sydney and Baltimore. They are:

- Large-scale redevelopment is sometimes the only solution to some serious local problems. In the cases he examined, the areas had become so run-down that only large-scale development would have had any chance of success.

- To achieve revitalisation on the scale necessary to succeed, governments must become involved either as financiers and/or development agents.

- Large projects, such as those mentioned here, should not be expected to occur quickly and show instant results. In most cases, success will only be achieved after many years of development.

- Site location is a crucial issue. Locations adjacent to city centres are more likely to succeed than sites in more peripheral places.

- It is important to involve local residents in decision-making about water-front development. There is generally very little local criticism of these types of development efforts, which in the case of Liverpool, Sydney and Baltimore, may have reflected the fact that there were relatively few people living and working in the area under consideration.

- Whenever possible, historical buildings and structures should be kept rather than torn down and new ones built. People can and want to relate to history and historical buildings.

- Tourism and recreational use of renewed waterfronts is very important and can be a legitimate economic reuse of dilapidated and redundant buildings. Visitation to these linear attractions is significant, running into the millions each year.

- The wider the variety of uses for the development, the better. Tourism, while very important, should not be considered the only legitimate use. A greater mix of uses will help withstand lower visitation levels when economics takes a downturn.

The following case study provides a glimpse of some of these waterfront development issues in the context of Belfast, Northern Ireland.

CASE STUDY   Laganside, waterfront redevelopment and heritage

As most European cities go, Belfast does not have a long history associated with it. Planned at the start of the reign of James I (1603) as a model plantation town and granted a charter of incorporation in 1613, Belfast has had a varied and interesting history marked by discernible eras of development and change. Beckett (1988) listed these up to 1914 as:

- settlers' town (*c*.1603–1750);
- radical town (*c*.1750–1801);
- cotton town (*c*.1801–40);
- linen town (*c*.1840–70);
- shipbuilding and engineering city (*c*.1870–1900);
- years of uncertainty (*c*.1900–20).

The remaining years of history have seen a city that faced depression (*c*.1920–39), war (1939–45), hope (1945–68), violence and decline (1969–*c*.1986), only at last to enter an era of new thinking, growth and rejuvenation (*c*.1987–present day). Belfast grew up around its waterfront, river mouth and harbour, which allowed it to flourish as a place of commerce, export and industry. However, when decline set in, Belfast abandoned its waterfront and river. With rejuvenation occurring over the past decade, as with many other industrial cities (e.g. Birmingham and Glasgow), Belfast has once again rediscovered its waterfront.

The river Lagan and the area surrounding it have re-emerged as an important part of Belfast – a place of culture, heritage and general appeal to tourists. This revival began with the Laganside Concept Plan of 1987, where a vision for the waterfront area was set out. The British government created the Laganside Corporation in 1988, giving it a remit to 'tackle the social and economic regeneration of an identified 140-hectare area of inner-city land straddling both banks of the river Lagan' where public investment was used as a catalyst to secure private development capital. The area encompasses around a 5 km stretch of the river Lagan. An additional 60 ha was added in 1997 with the inclusion of a region known as the 'Cathedral Quarter', one of the oldest areas of the city and in the past (c. eighteenth century) an important merchant and finance region. It is within the Cathedral Quarter that opportunity exists to develop cultural and heritage tourism. Rejuvenation of Belfast's waterfront region has included projects like:

- A new weir over the Lagan in 1994 at the cost of £14 million, which has controlled the water level, obscuring the mudflats and bringing life back to the river.

- Completion of riverside pathways between 1992 and 1994, which have become part of the Sustrans Millenium National Cycle Route.

- Development of 'Lagan Lookout' Visitor Centre in 1994, which offers visitors displays about the weir, the waterfront region, and Laganside Corporation.

- Development of Lanyon Place in 1997 with the building of the Waterfront Hall with a seating capacity of 2,235 adjoined by a 500-seat studio. This venue has hosted cultural conferences, competitions, and has been the venue for AGMs for companies like Ford, British Telecom, Price Waterhouse and will be the venue in 2006 for the British Medical Association. Other developments in Lanyon Place include the five-star Hilton Hotel, and the BT Riverside Tower. In 1999 a Thanksgiving Square was completed in Lanyon Place with the purpose of creating a space to 'bring people together to reflect and share their diversity'.

- Executive apartment development has also occurred alongside the Lagan, for example, the apartment complex at Gregg's Quay in 1999.

- The Odyssey entertainment complex (Northern Ireland's millennium project), which opened in 2001 at a cost of £91 million. Built on the Abercorn Basin (formerly created from dredging the main channel in the 1840s to form a people's pleasure park, only to be taken over by shipbuilding in 1870) on the east side of the Lagan it comprises an Imax theatre, Time Warner multiplex cinema, a science museum (W5: what, where, why, when, who), retail outlets (e.g. Hard Rock Café) and a 10,000-seat indoor hockey arena.

The Laganside Corporation has been successful in transforming Belfast's waterfront (Plate 4.3). It is expected that by 2002 over 10,000 people will have jobs in its designated area. One project that is still in its early stage of development

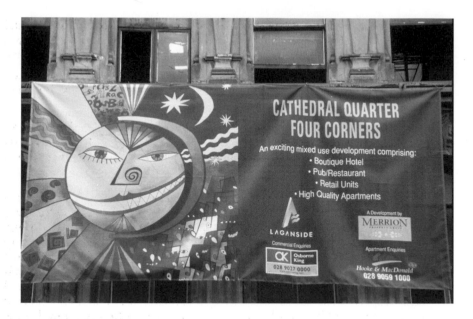

Plate 4.3   Sign for Laganside Waterfront Development

is completing the Cathedral Quarter. The idea to revive this area of Belfast adjacent to the waterfront had its genesis in 1997. The following year, a strategy was launched where the area was given the following vision:

- a cultural and entrepreneurial quarter;
- Belfast's specialist retail area;
- a tourism and visitor destination;
- a growing residential community;
- a unique example of urban conservation and regeneration.

At present, key strategic programmes within the Cathedral Quarter include:

- Diversification of uses and key opportunities to create a mixed use urban quarter.

- Conservation and urban design, ensuring preservation of the intricate streetscape pattern of the region, ground floor refurbishment and support for conservation.

- Business development that promotes new economic activity to the area, with a focus on professional and business services, software and IT, advertising, multimedia and cultural industries.

- An access to opportunity programmes that includes training and employment opportunities for communities in north and west Belfast, and social and community projects aimed at the youth.

- A cultural development programme that acts as a catalyst for physical and environmental renewal. Projects include developing a range of cultural venues, space for artistic production, a café culture and a place for public art.

- Public realm and movement, with integrative activity nodes, urban spaces, pedestrian, cycle and vehicle circulation, pedestrian-based corridors, and transformation in how the area is used and perceived.

- Promotion and marketing campaign to include the Cathedral Quarter as an essential element to how the city promotes its heritage to tourists, festival attendees and the business and conference segment (Laganside Corporation 1999).

At the time of writing, Belfast is currently preparing a bid to become European Capital of Culture for 2008. The completion of the Cathedral Quarter is an essential element in this process. Glasgow was awarded this title in 1990, and subsequently has developed into one of the most important tourist venues in Scotland. Belfast hopes to follow in its footsteps. Currently, the British Tourist Authority website (www.visitbritain.com) has identified Belfast as a 'city of culture worth seeing'. The revival of the waterfront region, along with the planned rejuvenation of the whole sector of the city, is hoped to create in the minds of tourists an image of Belfast with culture and heritage worth seeing and that the experiences and memories they take away from a visit will be positive, unlike most of the images people have of the city and its surrounding environs at present (see the case study in Chapter 3).

The conservation process

In common with other processes, such as regional tourism planning, the conservation process is not the same in every situation. While there is a rational set of steps that should be taken, adaptations must be made to fit local conditions, needs, goals and objectives. These steps, or phases, are not mutually exclusive, for there is likely to be some degree of overlap. This is especially so throughout the longer phases of the process (e.g. restoration and development, and management and interpretation) (Pearce 1997: 92). The exact nature of these phases cannot be generalised, because they experience different degrees of variation in different circumstances and in specific contexts. Figure 4.1 illustrates an overview of the general conservation process, which can be taken as a template to be adapted to suit individual circumstances. The sequencing of the stages is as follows:

- *Identification of the heritage place or object* involves locating, identifying and documenting the feature(s) being considered (Pearson and Sullivan 1995).

- *Research and inventory* entails identifying and classifying the various features of a heritage site or area to be conserved. This generally involves

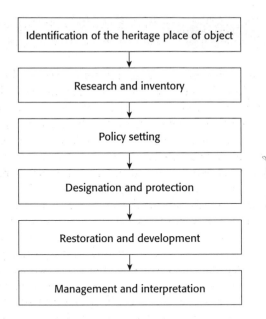

Figure 4.1 The heritage conservation process
Source: Based on Pearce (1997) and Pearson and Sullivan (1995).

significant historical, ecological and archaeological research to discover the cultural value and extent of the site. Potential management constraints and opportunities are also identified (Pearce 1997; Pearson and Sullivan 1995).

- *Policy setting* is where the goals for conservation and its institutional frameworks are established, largely based on cultural significance and management constraints (Pearce 1997; Pearson and Sullivan 1995).

- *Designation and protection* occur as a site is deemed worthy of conservation with some degree of legal protection. This might entail listing the property with a heritage sponsoring body, which may assist eventually in providing protection and securing funding. If the site is owned by some person or organisation different from the one attempting to protect it, there might be a need to purchase the site (Pearce 1997).

- *Restoration and development* emphasises the more physical tasks, such as restoration, renovation, developing the infrastructure and building visitor facilities (Pearce 1997). In many cases, the most immediate task will be to stabilise any structures that are in danger of collapse and taking actions to prevent additional deterioration (George 1976).

- *Management and interpretation* is the final phase, which requires a long-term commitment to continuous monitoring and evaluation. This is the operational phase that must consider visitation rates and the need for, and goals of, interpretation (Pearce 1997; Pearson and Sullivan 1995).

Conservation legislation

Very often nations enact legislation that aims to protect historic places and historically and culturally significant artefacts of material culture. Legislation also sometimes restricts the amounts, types and ages of cultural artefacts that can be exported. Heritage-oriented protective legislation began to be enacted in various parts of the world as early as the 1800s as people began to be more environmentally conscious as a result of the stewardship concept, which was prominent in the second half of the nineteenth century and which generated the first legislation on preservation in many countries (Aldridge 1989: 77). The early national parks in the New World countries owed much of their existence to the passing of Acts and then benefiting from an era when conservation and preservation of natural elements were of importance to society. Protective bodies and organisations began to be formed whose primary purpose was to push for protective legislation and uphold the laws and ordinances already in place. The systems of natural heritage places in most countries that tourists enjoy today would not have been possible if legislation had not been enacted to ensure that more areas were protected from development. This section of the chapter describes the development of heritage conservation legislation where some of the key organisations/agencies in several countries that have responsibility for the protection and maintenance of heritage sites and attractions are examined.

Legislative action

Among the first countries to enact legislation for the protection of built heritage was the UK. In 1882, the Ancient Monuments Protection Act was passed, paving the way for significant efforts to protect archaeological and historic sites throughout Great Britain. This Act led to the 'listing' process and scheduled 29 monuments in England and Wales, 21 in Scotland, and 18 in Ireland for state protection (Delafons 1997: 136). The listing of historic buildings began in earnest later in the twentieth century as a reaction to wartime bomb damage, and the system was formalised in the 1944 and 1947 Town and Country Planning Acts (Larkham 1995: 95). Following the Second World War, many legislation actions were taken throughout the British Isles in an effort to conserve the built environment. Several of the primary legislative Acts for the protection of built heritage in the UK are listed in Table 4.3. These laws and regulations have set a trend in heritage conservation. As of the mid-1990s, there were approximately half a million buildings listed in England alone and more than 9,000 conservation areas that included some unlisted objects of historical interest. These listings include more than just buildings. Objects such as fences, gravestones, historic telephone booths, gardens and battlegrounds are also included (Delafons 1997: 137).

Table 4.3   A selection of heritage legislation in the United Kingdom

Legislation	Year
Ancient Monuments Protection Act	1882
Housing, Town Planning Act	1909
Housing Act	1923
Town and Country Planning Act	1932
Town and Country Planning Act	1944
Town and Country Planning Act	1947
Historic Buildings and Ancient Monuments Act	1953
Local Authorities (Historic Buildings) Act	1962
Town and Country Planning Act	1962
Civic Amenities Act	1967
Town and Country Planning Act	1968
Town and Country Planning Act	1971
Town and Country Planning Act	1972
Ancient Monuments and Archaeological Areas Act	1979
National Heritage Act	1980
National Heritage Act	1983
Town and Country Planning Act	1990
Planning (Listed Buildings and Conservation Areas) Act	1990

Source: Compiled from Delafons (1997) and Stansfield (1983).

In the United States, early legislation focused on preserving elements of the nation's natural heritage. In 1872 Yellowstone was created as the world's first national park, and the Yellowstone Act of the same year provided the precedent of setting public land aside for pleasure purposes and established that private exploitation of natural resources was not necessarily the best public policy (Boyd and Butler 2000: 17). Following on from the Yellowstone Act, the Antiquities Act of 1906 (8 June) gave presidential blanket authority to proclaim and reserve historic landmarks, historic and prehistoric structures, and other objects of historic interest. The powers under the Act were responsible for the establishment of almost a quarter of the national park system that exists today and which enjoys over 250 million visitors each year (Boyd and Butler 2000: 20). Another piece of American legislation, the National Park Service Act of 1916, set in place that the mandate of national parks was to conserve the natural heritage (objects, flora, fauna) contained within and to allow the enjoyment of this heritage by current and future generations. In so doing, this legislation put in place the means to safeguard natural and cultural heritage features and established many previously 'worthless' regions of the USA as tourist places.

In spite of these developments with respect to natural heritage, conservation and listings of important places are not as well developed and centrally co-ordinated in the USA as they are in the UK. Instead, with the exception of a few organisations like the National Trust, most efforts are undertaken by individual communities (Howell 1994). Nonetheless, the National Historic Preservation Act, which was passed in 1966, has facilitated the listing of thousands of rural buildings, sites and structures in the National Register of Historic Places (Stokes 1992), and bills passed as recently as 2000 are allowing the designation and protection of several additional national monuments in the American west.

Canada quickly followed the USA in taking steps to safeguard its natural heritage, and which led to the development of its early national parks. The Dominion Lands Act of 1883 placed the management of public lands under the auspices of the Minister of the Interior and allowed government to reserve forestlands and forest parks in a state of preservation. Banff was established as Canada's first national park in 1885, to be quickly followed by five parks all in western Canada (Glacier 1886; Yoho 1886; Waterton Lakes 1895; Elk Island 1906; Jasper 1907). Other parks were added through the passing of the Dominion Forest Reserve and Parks Act of 1911. With its strong preservationist tones, the Act provided the necessary legislation to protect large areas from mining and timbering activities (Boyd and Butler 2000: 21). The passing of the National Parks Act in 1930 took the system of national parks in Canada in the same direction the USA had followed, namely to conserve for the pleasure of all peoples. It is because of such early legislative developments that Canada is today renowned for its natural heritage tourism attractions, with the majority of tourists visiting the western parks as part of their overall trip experience (Boyd in press).

Heritage conservation Acts in New Zealand over the years have been a unique blend of edicts that mixed concerns both for indigenous Maori culture as well as that of the country's European heritage. The concern for maintaining artefacts and places of significance to the Maori people was evident relatively early (1901) compared to the concern for indigenous heritage in many other multicultural societies (e.g. Australia and the United States). As a result, many of the conservation Acts passed in recent years in New Zealand have focused on Maori heritage (Barnett 1997; Cloher and Johnston 1999; Hall 1996; Hall *et al.* 1992; Ryan 1999; Ryan and Crotts 1997; Tahana and Oppermann 1998; Zeppel 1997). One of the earliest was the Maori Antiquities Act of 1901, which was intended to avert the export of Maori cultural property of historic or scientific value from New Zealand. Other Acts throughout the twentieth century amended the original Act, and the 1975 Antiquities Act was more specific and restricted the export of any Maori artefact made before 1920. It also restricted relics of European (*pakeha*) importance that were over 60 years old (Butts 1993: 173). The Historic Places Act 1980 established the New Zealand Historic Places Board of Trustees to clarify and protect historic buildings, historic areas, archaeological sites and traditional sites. The Act allows buildings to be classified into four different categories based on their historical significance and/or architectural quality by degree of urgency rather than by type of structure:

- buildings whose permanent preservation is essential;
- buildings that merit permanent preservation;
- buildings that warrant preservation;
- buildings that merit recording (Butts 1993: 177–8).

Several other bills have been passed in New Zealand in the 1980s and 1990s that work to conserve the cultural and natural heritage environments. The Historic Places Bill of 1992 again concerns the heritages of the two primary ethnic groups in the country. Its objectives include:

1. increasing Maori representation on the Trust Board;
2. providing more appropriate means for protecting Maori cultural heritage;
3. integrating the Historic Places Act with the Resource Management Act of 1992;
4. integrating the registration and protection of all historic and archaeological sites;
5. increasing penalties for convictions under the Act (Butts 1993: 81).

Conservation bodies

Most countries of the world have established bodies that are responsible for the listing and protection of heritage properties. These range from being full government agencies to quasi-governmental agencies that resemble non-profit organisations and associations (see Table 4.4). In the developing world, heritage is usually listed and protected at the national level by government agencies (e.g. ministries of culture, environment and tourism). In the developed world the tendency is towards more quasi-public forms of guardianship through various associations and conservation groups. Conservation may also be done on a subnational level where states, provinces, counties or departments are charged with these tasks. Several examples exist where protection is carried out at several levels. In the United States, for example, heritage conservation areas are found under the control of various levels of government, including national, state, county and municipality.

The United States

The historic protection movement in the United States has seen significant success since the enactment of the 1966 National Historic Preservation Act. At the national level, the number of properties listed in the National Register

Table 4.4   Organisations in charge of heritage protection, UK, USA and Canada

United Kingdom
Ancient Monuments Society
Association of Independent Museums
Association of Industrial Archaeology
CADW: Welsh Historic Monuments
Civic Trust
Civic Trust for Wales
Conservation Bureau (Scotland)
Countryside Commission
Department of the Environment
English Heritage
Historic Buildings and Monuments Branch (N. Ireland)
Historic Scotland
ICOM UK
Museums and Galleries Commission
National Museums of Scotland
National Trust
National Trust for Scotland
Northern Ireland Museums Advisory Committee
Royal Commission on the Ancient and Historical Monuments of Scotland
Royal Commission on the Ancient and Historical Monuments in Wales
Scottish Civic Trust
Society for the Protection of Ancient Buildings
United Kingdom Institute for Conservation

United States and Canada
Advisory Council on Historic Preservation
American Association of Museums
American Association for State and Local History
American Institute for Conservation of Historic and Artistic Works
Association for Preservation Technology (Canada)
Canadian Museums Association
Conservation Foundation
Getty Conservation Institute
Heritage Canada
Heritage Conservation and Recreation Service
National Park Service
National Trust for Historic Preservation
Parks Canada

Source: Compiled from Stratton (1994).

of Historic Places grew from an initial 900 to more than 58,000 by the early 1990s (Boasberg 1992). The National Trust for Historic Preservation in the United States is more involved in urban conservation than its British equivalents, which are more involved in protecting rural landscapes and artefacts (Tunbridge 1981). Since its foundation in 1948, its emphasis has been 'to increase public awareness and promote public involvement in the preservation of buildings and districts. It coordinates preservation efforts and provides advice, as well as maintaining a variety of properties' (Stratton 1994: 227). Of high significance are the conservation bodies grouped in the US Department of the Interior. The National Park Service administers the nation's national historic sites and national parks, and the Interagency Resources Division maintains the National Register of Historic Places, which reviews nominations based on recommendations from each state's historic preservation offices (Stratton 1994: 227).

In addition to national-level agencies, each state in the USA has its own state parks system, which has stewardship over both natural and cultural resources that are of statewide significance. Likewise, county parks systems throughout most of the USA have charge over places of more local importance, and the same is true of municipalities. Most towns and cities have established their own museums in an effort to preserve icons of local pasts, and several major cities, such as Chicago and New York, have Landmarks Commissions that act as protectors of designated buildings and areas (Stratton 1994).

The United Kingdom

England's primary public sector agency in charge of recording historic sites is the Royal Commission on the Historical Monuments (Bold 1994). The Historic Buildings and Monuments Commission for England, more commonly known as English Heritage, is one of the primary agencies involved in protecting and conserving the built heritage. English Heritage was created under the National Heritage Act of 1983 and formalised in 1984. Although funded by the government and under the sponsorship of the Department of the Environment, English Heritage is an independent agency responsible for maintaining England's historic monuments and buildings, most of which were formerly in the care of the Department of the Environment. The objectives of English Heritage aims include increasing public understanding and enjoyment of the past through site presentation and educational facilities (Prentice and Prentice 1989: 155). The counterparts to English Heritage in Scotland and Wales are Historic Scotland and CADW: Welsh Historic Monuments (Stratton 1994).

The National Trusts and Countryside Commissions (now known as the Countryside Agency) for England, Wales and Scotland, are the main governing bodies for historic places and attractions located specifically in the countryside throughout the UK. While the Commissions (Agencies) themselves do not own land or facilities, they work with other organisations to achieve conservation goals. Much of their efforts focus on tourist and recreational use and interpretation of rural landscapes and sites (Prentice and Prentice 1989). The National Trust for Places of Historic Interest or Natural Beauty leads the private sector in supporting heritage. Its interest encompasses not only historic properties, but also gardens and other lands, including coastlines (Eckstein 1993). In 1992, the Department of National Heritage was created as a public agency, which shared its responsibilities with the Department of the Environment (Delafons 1997).

UNESCO

The United States and the United Kingdom provide good examples of organisations and agencies charged with heritage listing and conservation at the national level. Beyond the national realm, though, several international agencies have been formed that have as one of their primary responsibilities the care of the world's heritage. Perhaps the most widely recognised of these is the United Nations Educational, Scientific and Cultural Organization (UNESCO), whose mandate is far-reaching in all aspects of culture, science and education, but whose World Heritage List aims to protect and provide global status to properties of high cultural and natural value. To have heritage properties on the World Heritage List adds prestige to states, particularly smaller and less affluent nations. In some cases, having a few World Heritage Sites reinforces nationhood and can be a legitimating influence for new governments. Countries also seek UNESCO recognition for the potential financial assistance involved as well, and according to research by Hall and Piggin (2001), over two-thirds of the World Heritage Sites they surveyed reported an increase in visitor arrivals since gaining World Heritage status. This was impressive enough to most site managers that nearly two-thirds of the sites began using their World Heritage status as a marketing tool.

Through a series of conventions, UNESCO has been able to incite widespread interest and commitment from world governments to work towards protecting the world's heritage, places that are considered of 'outstanding universal value'. The first UNESCO convention related to cultural heritage took place in 1954 and was titled the Convention for the Protection of Cultural Property in the Event of Armed Conflict. This is more commonly known simply as the Hague Convention. This agreement was followed in 1970 by the Convention on the Means of Prohibiting and Preventing the Illicit Import and Transfer of Ownership of Cultural Property, but the most influential meeting occurred in 1972, the Convention Concerning the Protection of the World Cultural and Natural Heritage. This accord, more commonly known as the World Heritage Convention, has been the primary drive and directing influence in the conservation of the most significant cultural sites (Leask and Fyall 2001; Shackley 1998b). The World Heritage Convention established the World Heritage Committee, whose primary responsibility is to establish and keep a World Heritage List of cultural and natural properties submitted by countries and considered to be of outstanding universal value. One of the Committee's most important responsibilities is the provision of technical co-operation under the World Heritage Fund in states whose resources are insufficient. As of December 2001, 167 nations had ratified (joined) the Convention (UNESCO 2001).

As of 16 December 2001, there were 721 properties in 124 nations inscribed on the World Heritage List – 554 cultural sites, 144 natural sites and 23 mixed properties. Between 1980 and 1989, 266 properties were added to the List. From 1990 to 2000, 372 sites were inscribed, and 31 were inscribed in 2001 (UNESCO 2001). Based upon research by, and recommendations from, three bodies that are charged with emergency rescue and information exchange – the International Council on Monuments and Sites (ICOMOS) and the International Centre for the Study of Preservation and the Restoration of Cultural Property (ICCROM) for cultural sites and the International Union for the Conservation of Nature and Natural Resources (IUCN) for natural sites – the World Heritage Committee selects sites to be added to the World Heritage List on an annual basis (Ashworth 1995; Boniface 2001; Drost 1996; Leask and Fyall 2001; Peleggi 1996). Essentially the World Heritage Committee has three basic functions (Shackley 1998b: 2–3):

- to identify properties, based on states' recommendations, which are to be protected under the Convention and to inscribe them on the World Heritage List;
- to decide which sites on the World Heritage List should be inscribed on the List of World Heritage in Danger;
- to establish how and under what conditions the resources in the World Heritage Fund should be used to aid governments in protecting their Heritage Sites.

According to the Heritage Convention, only member states that have adhered to the Convention can make nominations to the World Heritage List. These nominations must demonstrate that the site is truly of exceptional universal value, that it meets specific criteria imposed by the Convention, and that it is assured of adequate protection (UNESCO 1999). The main problem here for developing countries wishing to propose sites for UNESCO designation is the need to demonstrate their financial, technical and political capacity to manage, conserve and open access to their prospective sites (Evans 2001: 82). This lack of finance and expertise, together with political reasons, has kept many countries from applying for World Heritage status for their significant cultural and natural sites (Shackley 1998b). Nevertheless, States Parties can request international assistance under the Heritage Fund for the preparation of tentative lists and nomination forms, expert missions, work necessary for preserving sites, training of specialised staff, and supply of equipment when appropriate. They can also apply for long-term loans and, in some special cases, non-repayable grants. Limited emergency assistance is also available under the Fund for those properties placed on the List of World Heritage in Danger. In December 2001, 31 sites were listed, some of which correspond to those on the World Monument Fund's list in Table 4.1. This includes cases of properties severely damaged by specific natural or human disasters or threatened with imminent destruction of some other kind (UNESCO 2001). Unfortunately, the Fund's meagre budget ($3.4 million in 1996), which is derived from member state dues and voluntary contributions, does not go far when so many countries are seeking technical help, emergency aid and training to protect their listed sites (Shackley 1998b: 6).

When a nation joins the Convention, it has the responsibility to nominate sites it deems appropriate for inclusion on the List and to pledge to protect these sites for future generations (Leask and Fyall 2001). The operational guidelines provide all the relevant criteria for nominating sites to the List, which include both cultural and natural features. While the process of nomination is rather involved and takes a great deal of preparation and research, simply stated, the process involves the submission of a dossier for a site by the national government, which must be accompanied by archival information. This is then considered by the Committee to decide whether or not the site merits inclusion in the List (Shackley 1998b).

UNESCO's cultural heritage sites are divided into four different categories: monuments, groups of buildings, sites and cultural landscapes. By this definition, monuments include architectural works, works of monumental sculpture and painting, elements or structures of an archaeological nature, inscriptions, cave dwellings and combinations of features that are of outstanding universal value from the point of view of history, art or science. Groups of buildings are assemblages of separate or connected buildings which, because of their architecture, their homogeneity or their place in the landscape, are of outstanding universal value from the point of view of history, art or science. Third, sites comprise works of human beings or the combined works of nature and humans, and areas including archaeological sites that are of outstanding universal value from the historical, aesthetic, ethnological or anthropological points of view. Finally, cultural landscapes represent the interactions between humankind and nature. They represent the evolution of societies and settlements over time, under the influence of the natural environment and social, economic and cultural forces (UNESCO 2001).

According to the operational guidelines (UNESCO 2001), from which this information is derived, if groups of buildings are found in urban areas, special considerations must be given. Groups of urban buildings eligible for inclusion in the World Heritage List fall into three main categories:

- towns that are no longer inhabited but which provide unchanged archaeological evidence of the past;
- historic towns that are still inhabited and which may continue to develop under the influence of socio-economic and cultural change;
- new towns of the twentieth century that paradoxically have something in common with the prior two categories.

The consideration of uninhabited towns does not raise any special difficulties other than those related to archaeological sites in general. Unique architectural style and exemplary character, concentrations of monuments, and important historical associations are critical components of the evaluation, just as they are for other clusters of buildings. In the case of inhabited historic towns and cities, they should not be considered solely on the role they might have played in the past, but also on their current roles. However, the spatial organisation, structures, materials, forms and, where possible, functions of a group of buildings should essentially reflect the civilisation or succession of civilisations that have prompted the nomination of the property. Four categories can be distinguished:

- Towns that are typical of a specific time period or culture and which have been almost entirely preserved and avoided major effects of subsequent developments. In this case, the entire town is listed together with its surroundings.

- Towns that have been preserved containing major elements of typical successive stages of history in the midst of other development. In these cases, the historic portion of the city is taken separately from the modern environment.

- Historic quarters that are located in the same place as ancient towns but are enclosed within modern cities. The precise limits of the historic sectors need to be delimited and protected.

- Areas of cities that even if surviving in residual condition, provide consistent evidence of the composition of a historic town that has disappeared. In these cases, surviving buildings should be representative of what the entire town would have been like previously.

The criteria for inclusion in the list of cultural and natural sites are described in Table 4.5. While these do not need to be described in detail in the text, it is important to note that the primary consistencies between them are their superlative characteristics, their high level of representation of distinct cultures and places worthy of protecting, and their irreplaceable value to humankind.

Management plans exist for each World Heritage Site, which typically specify policies towards visitors, addressing issues such as entry charges and local tourism business development, the impacts of various visitor types (e.g. large tour groups, visiting scholars, schoolchildren), and potential injury to resources from overcrowding and natural processes. Management plans also consider issues related to information and interpretation, ancillary services (e.g. shops, guides, catering) and accessibility (Shackley 1998b: 7). Despite the existence of good management plans and support from UNESCO, critics of the World Heritage Site programme argue that UNESCO does little for the world's heritage in actual practice. In the words of Sakya (1996: 205), the Commission is 'unable to finance but always there to complicate projects'. These criticisms notwithstanding, according to Shackley (1998b), several problems or issues exist at UNESCO properties that offer challenges to their management, including issues of jurisdiction and management responsibility, strict management controls, change brought on by the World Heritage Site designation (e.g. increased visitor numbers and overly ambitious restoration), and in common with all other heritage attractions, litter, vandalism and pollution.

Table 4.5   Criteria for inclusion in UNESCO's list of World Heritage Sites

Cultural sites must fulfil one or more of the following criteria:

- represent a masterpiece of human creative genius
- demonstrate human values over a span of time or within a cultural area of the world in terms of architecture, monumental art, landscape design or town planning
- be representative of a cultural tradition or civilisation that is living or has disappeared
- exemplify outstanding buildings, technological or architectural ensembles or landscape that illustrates important stages of human history
- be an exceptional example of traditional human settlement or land use that is representative of a culture, particularly when it has become susceptible to impacts of irreversible change
- associate tangibly or directly with events, ideas, living traditions, beliefs, artistic and literary works of outstanding universal importance

Natural sites must fulfil one or more of the following criteria:

- be exceptional examples of major stages of the earth's natural history, including ongoing geological processes, record of life, and geomorphic features
- exemplify significant ongoing ecological and biological processes, such as those related to marine ecosystems and communities of animals and plants
- contain outstanding natural phenomena or areas of superlative beauty and aesthetic importance
- contain the most important and significant natural habitats for conservation of biological diversity

Source: Based upon UNESCO (1999, 2001) and Shackley (1998b).

Challenges to heritage conservation

Heritage conservation faces many challenges from economic, political, environmental and sociocultural perspectives. While these challenges exist universally, they tend to be much more pronounced in the less developed countries of the world – an observation made for many years by scholars who have recognised differences in the dynamics of tourism in developing and developed countries (Britton 1982; Mathieson and Wall 1982). While contextual factors create challenges that are specific and different by region, the following subsections present broad challenges to heritage conservation.

Lack of funds

Maintaining historic sites in whatever form is an expensive task, and a lack of adequate financial resources for heritage conservation is one of the most profound difficulties facing heritage managers in most of the world (Henson 1989; Isar 1986), forcing them to search continuously for new sources of revenue. In much of the developing world, this situation results in inadequate restoration materials and equipment, insufficient numbers of skilled staff, and an inability to monitor, manage and mend historic properties (Myles 1989; Rasamuel 1989).

As a result of inadequate funding and lack of effective training, much of the maintenance work done to heritage properties in many parts of the world is purely cosmetic, and heritage resources commonly fall into various states of disrepair or are repaired poorly by inexperienced and untrained personnel (Chance 1994; Jones and Bromley 1996). According to Hills (1997: 29), in Eastern Europe, 'old-fashioned excavation techniques have been ruinous' and in other places 'well-meaning but faulty restoration, such as stone injections with epoxy resins and metal intrusions . . . inevitably fractured the very monuments they were meant to protect' (Sadek 1994: 41).

Another problem is that scarce public funding is often utilised for other purposes that have short-term benefits, such as mass tourism promotion, rather than for conservation, which might better ensure the long-term viability of tourism. Additionally, in most developing countries, the money earned from donations and gate receipts is seldom put back into maintaining the site (Timothy 1999a). Olinda (1991), writing about tourism in Kenya, noted that less than 7 per cent of the receipts from tourism were reinvested in the country's protected areas system of national parks and reserves, despite the fact that the safari experience was the principal reason for visiting.

Modernisation

Economic disparities and the challenges of basic survival in many developing countries lead to situations where, according to the founder of the Bandung Heritage Society in Indonesia, 'Development pressure is so great that we are in danger of losing buildings before the economic rationale for saving them has a chance to work' (quoted in Burton 1993: 37). For example, although protective legislation now exists in Yogyakarta, Indonesia, it was common practice in the 1970s and 1980s to demolish many of the traditional houses to create space for developing small hotels, guesthouses, restaurants, souvenir shops and tour agencies (Timothy and Wall 1995). However, this was not uncommon in the developed world in the past either. For example, in the early 1800s, the state of Pennsylvania (USA) attempted to demolish Independence Hall and sell the land to commercial developers (Wallace 1996), and in Great Britain, '1,000 Georgian buildings were demolished in Bath between 1950 and 1973, of which 350 were listed; over 1,000 churches have been declared redundant; and between 1945 and 1975 over 700 major country houses were destroyed' (Eckstein 1993: 32). Similarly, over the years, in an effort to modernise for tourism, many small business owners in Nepal have changed the original architecture of their homes and businesses, including features inharmonious with traditional designs (Shackley 1996).

Sometimes the cost of maintaining historic sites is so high that governments see heritage buildings as an unaffordable luxury, so buildings are torn down in favour of new construction that will generate more economic benefits (Wahyono 1995). Very often, community members, developers and government leaders view the protection of ancient monuments and historic buildings as an obstruction to modern development, and opinions are usually divided regarding the priority of each (Rghei and Nelson 1994; Sadek 1990).

While recent history shows that people and societies in the Western, developed world have an increasing desire to conserve the past, residents of developing countries commonly associate preservation with backwardness (Timothy 1999a), which often results in a lack of desire to conserve. According to Shackley (1996), this is of great concern when traditional architectures, decorations and styles are abandoned or replaced with large concrete buildings, all in the name of modernisation. Trotzig (1989) and Norton (1989) both argue that from an anthropological perspective, the destruction of heritage in developing regions is more serious than in developed areas because in the former, archaeological remains constitute the only real, objective and material sources of data pertaining to precolonial history. In places where traditional societies wandered through mountains, forests or deserts, little material culture is left, particularly dwellings and other community structures, to inform modern-day science about their lifestyles.

Environmental pressures

Aside from modernisation and inadequate funding and training, five primary pressures exist within the realm of physical environment. The first is flow of visitors. Some locations are visited so intensely during high seasons that heritage managers have had to resort to ways of limiting access as a means of preventing wear and tear. Large numbers of visitors crowded into relatively small spaces can have significant implications for the conservation of both built and natural heritage. This will be discussed in greater detail later in this chapter.

The second environmental pressure is that of resident use of heritage features. Examples abound where residents of developing countries have established their homes and villages inside historic sites/ancient ruins or immediately adjacent to them (Dove 1993; Timothy 1994; Nuryanti 1996; Evans 1998). This situation creates obvious issues that conservationists must address. Deterioration of the physical fabric of ancient sites becomes problematic, and this is further accentuated when artefacts are removed and utilised in other ways (e.g. cut stones or statue pieces being used for building materials or as souvenirs for tourists). One example of this is in Indonesia, where Ratu Boko, the ruins of an ancient palace complex near Yogyakarta, became home to an entire village for many years. During the 1990s, the Indonesian government began to develop the site as a tourist attraction, and difficulties were encountered in trying to locate all of the missing pieces of the temples that were scattered throughout the village (Timothy 1994; Nuryanti 1996).

A similar situation exists in Egypt, where Nazlet al-Simman, a squatter settlement at the foot of the Sphinx and Pyramids of Giza, has raised legitimate concerns about its effects on the ancient sites (Dove 1993; Gauch 1991; Evans 1998). Villagers do not want to leave their homes, and the Egyptian government has offered few economic incentives for moving. In this case the tension between villagers and the national government is intense. The government claims that the people are thieves who steal and forge antiquities and sell them to tourists. From the villagers' perspective, the government wants to relocate them and keep the money earned from tourism entirely for itself (Gauch 1991).

Mother nature is the third environmental pressure. Angkor Wat, Cambodia, one of the world's most impressive ancient temple complexes, has been ignored and neglected for many years by conservation groups, the Cambodian government and tourists as a result of the bloody civil war that engulfed the country during the 1970s, 1980s and early 1990s. As a result, nature has wreaked havoc on the temple structures resulting in broken stones and crumbling walls, much of the complex having been overgrown by forest (Wager 1995). If the trees are left in place, parts of the half-ruined structures will possibly collapse. If the trees are removed, however, the structures also might collapse. This situation has created a serious dilemma for conservationists in Cambodia in recent years. According to some observers, it is necessary to save the trees because some of them are saving the structure (*New York Times* 2001: A22). A similar situation existed at Indonesia's Borobudur Temple, which was almost entirely overgrown with forest and soil sediments when a farmer discovered it early in the twentieth century. In this case the decision was made to remove the soil and vegetation so that restoration could be done (Surgohudujo 1971; Morton 1986; Shoji 1991).

Fourth is pollution, which in most cases is not directly caused by tourism, but rather by heavy industry, high volumes of traffic, and inadequate waste disposal systems. At the Taj Mahal, for example, factories and other elements of heavy industry have for many years created conditions wherein chemicals and other pollutants released into the air have begun to deteriorate the monument.

> Up close the picture begins to crumble. Acid rain and condensation from the former Mughal capital's coke-fueled factories and, environmentalists say, a nearby oil refinery are eating away the marble and turning what remains the color of unloved teeth . . . plastic bottles litter the lawns; the canals are dirty; guides offering tours for an inflated price are maddeningly insistent. The colored engravings are chipped and in places have fallen off. In the basement, the graves of the Emperor and his beloved are off limits, the entrance blocked with untidy wire mesh. The inner sanctum smells of bats and pigeon droppings. Enormous beehives hang from the arches; black smoke stains mark where other hives have been burned off. The river behind the tomb is sluggish with sewage (Ganguly 2001: 6).

Similar conditions are creating problems at the Pyramids of Giza (Gauch 1991; Dove 1993) and other world-famous heritage sites.

Finally, looting, or theft, is a major problem at many archaeological sites, largely a result of international demand for authentic antiquities. Much of what is stolen from historic locations is sold illegally on the international collectors' market, and the perpetrators are usually local people attempting to earn money. At the Angkor Wat temples in Cambodia in recent years, statues have been chopped to pieces and the carved base relief chiselled off and stolen. Looting at this site began in the 1960s, but during the 1990s, following the civil war, looting damage has increased dramatically. Weak security, the impoverished state of the nation, and corrupt governments have created conditions where such illicit activity has flourished. The market for these items abroad is so large that, according to Dauge (1997: 170), 'videos and catalogues circulate in buying countries for prospective clients to preview'. Similar problems have plagued places like China, New Zealand and the United States for many years (Min 1989; Simons 2000). This problem is very difficult to address because simply enacting laws cannot stop it, and taking steps within the heritage source country alone is not sufficient as action must also be taken within the buying countries (Dauge 1997).

Public perceptions

In many Third World countries, the idea of heritage conservation is relatively new, and comparatively few people appreciate the need for it (Cohen 1978; Henson 1989; Myles 1989). It is often the case that appreciation for conservation increases only with the promise of economic benefits (Cohen 1978; Soemarwoto 1992). According to Norton (1989), this is because people's primary concern is survival. It is difficult to rouse enthusiasm for heritage conservation in societies where the poorest segment of the population is hungry, inadequately clothed and sheltered, and health care and education are largely inaccessible to the masses.

In most of the developed world, people have a tendency to grow more interested in their personal heritage as they age (Lowenthal 1996). In developing regions, however, the elderly have little interest in preserving the past. Instead, it is the younger generations who are interested in conserving their heritage. In South-East Asia, 'preservation is essentially the passion of the affluent young; their elders have little sentimental attachment to buildings that remind them of their humble beginnings' (Burton 1993: 37). Preservation in this context is often viewed as stagnation or worse, the opposite of progress (Rodgers 1982; Myles 1989), and with modernisation comes the attitude that traditional equals unfashionable (Shackley 1996). As a result, villagers pride themselves on progress, not preservation, because progress is nearly always measured in economic terms (James 1995). This results in significant differences in the meaning of heritage, the values ascribed to conservation, and techniques associated with heritage tourism management between the developing and developed worlds (Crookston 1998; Timothy 1994, 1999a). Residents of less developed countries, who have lived for generations in a single place, would, in Dann's (1998: 39) words, 'be baffled by nostalgia. It is the dislocated Western traveller of today who experiences nostalgia to its fullest, and who incidentally, travels precisely on account of such disorientation.' Thus, for most people of the world, conservation and its motivations are alien to indigenous practices and unreasonable in circumstances where even basic survival is sometimes in question.

Nonetheless, there is a real need to educate local people about the value of conserving historic structures and environments. Proponents of conserving the ancient Yemeni city of Sana'a, for example, suggest 'apart from raising money for conservationists, the campaign must also raise the consciousness of Sana'a residents, impressing upon them the significance of Sana'a's cultural heritage and the need to create a fine balance between modernization and conservation' (Kia and Williams 1989: 33).

Colonial legacy

Some metropolitan powers were slow to enact laws and practices related to protecting the built and natural environments in their colonies. In fact, until quite recently, heritage conservation, including national parks and historic sites, was basically non-existent in the developing world (Sutton 1982). Most conservation legislation in the Third World followed independence, sometimes as late as the 1970s and 1980s. Ghana's ordinance for preservation was instated in 1957, the same year the country achieved independence. Heritage laws in Ecuador were not established until 1945 and 1979, and in 1989 Togo had still not initiated antiquities legislation (Jones and Bromley 1996; Myles 1989; Norton 1989). Henson (1989) and Trotzig (1989) argued that this delayed response to heritage conservation is the reason why so much archaeology was destroyed during and after the colonial era.

Substandard maintenance by ruling authorities also contributed to the weak condition of colonial antiquities, and as James (1995: 56) submits, nineteenth-century world powers were notorious for dispatching untrained public works officers into the field to reconstruct, restore and preserve buildings and artefacts of which they had no practical or aesthetic understanding.

The colonial legacy might also have contributed to an underappreciation of heritage among residents and administrators of developing countries (Timothy 1999a). Very often, the rule of foreign powers delayed, and sometimes prohibited, the rise of indigenous historical consciousness and feeling of national identity. It was not uncommon for colonial powers to use extreme measures to control independent thinking and to muffle emotions of national pride on the part of native residents (Ansprenger 1989; Trotzig 1989). This has had long-term implications, as countries like Indonesia, India and Rwanda are today facing great difficulties in trying to create a spirit of nationalism and common heritage.

Impacts of heritage tourism

As tourism develops in destination communities, it brings with it recognisable ecological, social and economic impacts. Likewise, individual types of special interest travel also bring with them the same types of impacts in a variety of settings. This section discusses the physical and social impacts that can be attributed specifically to the development of heritage tourism, for they are located most significantly in heritage locations. The economics of heritage tourism will be addressed in Chapter 5.

Physical impacts

Serious damage can occur to historic site environments as a result of excessive visitor pressures, particularly at peak times, and several authors have devoted considerable attention to examining this phenomenon in recent years (Edwards 1989; Gilbert and Clark 1997; Page 1992; Strange 1997). Sadly, the behaviour of heritage visitors and their sheer numbers are slowly destroying the very things that attracted them in the first place, although it is actually unclear to what degree damage is caused by tourists and how much is caused by local residents. This is particularly so in historic cities (Page 1992). The most important aspects of physical damage at historic properties are wear and tear, litter/pollution and vandalism (Plate 4.4). The wear and tear experienced by a site can range from very minor to very significant. Clambering tourists at ancient monuments, such as the Egyptian Pyramids, Hadrian's Wall and Stonehenge, have played a major role in the deterioration of the sites themselves. A number of English cathedrals have reported deterioration of stairs, paving stones and memorials as a result of thousands of tourist feet, while other site managers are concerned with the slow disappearance of decorative motifs and carvings due to thousands of hands touching the delicate artwork (English Tourist Board 1979). Many visitors may have waited all of their lives to visit some of these places and are eager not only to see for themselves but also to touch and photograph (*Culture Plus* 1992: 16).

A similar concern is the moisture and condensation created by breathing, sweating and touching, which can affect delicate surfaces and paintings. In museums and other places where delicate objects are preserved, inside environments are planned and controlled. The light, heat, air and humidity are closely monitored and set at levels suitable for the objects on display to prevent death, decay and fading. This is where visitors become part of the problem as they 'bring with them dirt and damp from an uncontrolled, polluted atmosphere into the purified space of the museum. The heat generated by their bodies and the breath that visitors expel add to the traces of impurity which will have to be eradicated after they have left the building' (Hooper-Greenhill 1988: 227). At Thebes, where capacity levels tend to be ignored by guardians,

Plate 4.4   Vandals' names carved in an ancient temple, Indonesia

one calculation suggests that at the Tomb of Nefertiti, 125 people in one hour produce the equivalent of 12 litres of water poured on to the walls (Shackley 1998a: 203).

Perhaps one of the best-known examples of wear and tear and subsequent management response is Stonehenge. After experiencing years of clambering tourists, often numbering more than 2,000 an hour during the summer, Stonehenge began suffering visible degradation. Many of the stones were being worn smooth by thousands of hands, and the earthworks around them were being heavily trampled. This was beginning to result in irreversible changes to the site such as leaning formations and stone deterioration. In response to these negative impacts, the British Department of the Environment (DoE) erected a perimeter fence in the spring of 1978 to protect the site. Though not allowed inside the fence, visitors to Stonehenge are permitted to wander freely outside the barrier for a fairly close-up view of the stones (Plate 4.5). Furthermore, as a result of an increase in unnecessary erosion caused by layers of gravel on the ground around the stones, the DoE replaced the gravel with turf (Bainbridge 1979). Bender and Edmonds (1992) argue against the extreme measures of preservation taken at the Stonehenge site and recommend that the rock formations should be more accessible, though on a limited basis, to both tourists and

Plate 4.5   Stonehenge and efforts to restrict tourist access

non-tourists (e.g. academics and Druids) alike for purposes of enjoyment, research and religious worship.

Litter is another negative effect of tourism at heritage sites. Fast-food containers, cigarette butts, broken bottles and soda pop cans can not only ruin the ambience of an attraction, but also are expensive to clean up. In the late 1970s at Canterbury Cathedral in England, rubbish left on the grounds filled at least three waste bins every week during the summer (English Tourist Board 1979). In the interiors of certain buildings, ice cream, sweets and chewing gum often cause a sticky mess which, if not cleaned up immediately, can leave permanent stains on some delicate surfaces. Such remnants damage delicate surfaces and show disrespect on the part of visitors towards historic sites, and they are often difficult and expensive to clean up. Litter has become a major concern for natural heritage environments. Trekking trails in the foothills of the Himalayan mountain range have been dubbed the 'Andrex' trails as a reflection of the amount of rubbish that tourists leave behind at designated camps as well as along the route of the trail itself.

The third major impact of heritage tourism, vandalism, is another problem at most locations. Graffiti can become a permanent part of a heritage property as a result of careless fun-seekers, as in the case of Stonehenge, the Temple of Poseidon in Greece and various sites in China (Leung 2001). Timothy (1994) noted the tragic impacts of spray-painting by vandals on several sixteenth- and seventeenth-century tombstones within the ruins of St Paul's Church in the historic district of Melaka, Malaysia. Environmental damage of this nature is often irreversible; however, even if a clean-up is possible, historic relics are difficult to clean since the process may cause additional damage to the delicately carved stone surfaces.

A similar problem faced by many site managers is souvenir hunting. Gathering artefacts from historic properties, either loose ones or by means of breaking and chipping, may cause irreversible damage, and can make the process of restoration much more difficult and costly. At Westminster Abbey, for example, small shields are regularly stolen from the monument to the Marquess of Winton and require continual replacement (English Tourist Board 1979; Timothy 1994). Furthermore, visitors periodically break off pieces of mosaic at the same site, while hands and other movable objects are frequently stolen from the figurines. Similar problems were noted by Shackley (1998a: 203) in Bukhara, Uzbekistan, where domestic visitors and Muslim pilgrims commonly remove tiles or pieces of plaster as souvenirs from holy places.

Though fewer in number than negative effects, a few positive impacts of heritage tourism can be noted. The need to offer historic attractions to visitors has led to the maintenance and protection of monuments, buildings and other artefacts. For instance, Niagara National Historic Sites (comprised of a number of properties operated by the Parks Canada along the Niagara River) have recently undergone environmental changes to become more 'green', to meet the needs and concerns of visitors, and to present a more accurate nineteenth-century setting which will add to the tourist experience. If the experience of tourists is a positive one, they will probably be more amenable to preserve the site rather than contribute to its degradation. Landscaping the grounds around historic structures can add enjoyment to tourist visits as long as it is done in an appropriate manner. The purpose of landscaping is to enhance the main attractions at a heritage property. Hence, every effort should be made to prevent the landscaping and additional structures (e.g. museums, offices, restaurants, gift shops and ticket booths) from distracting the attention of visitors away from and obstructing the view of the main attraction (Soemarwoto 1992). It is suggested here that the manicured grounds (Taman Wisata) around the Prambanan Temple complex in Central Java represent quality landscaping, which does not take away from the tourist experience, but rather adds to the ambience of the entire complex.

Tension often exists between conservation and the use of heritage sites by tourists. Many people favour direct experiences with the past by engaging in activities which provide opportunities to see, touch, utilise and even climb on historic artefacts. Some people, however, consider this hands-on tendency by tourists to be potentially disastrous to the preservation of antiquity (Konrad 1982). On the other hand, several writers have argued that, through education, entertainment and the proper use of heritage attractions, it is possible to instil a spirit of conservation awareness in visitors (Ashworth 1997; Butler 1991; Carter and Grimwade 1997; Cossons 1989; Herbert 1989b; Millar 1989). If the use of heritage sites is to build awareness and a spirit of conservation, then education based largely upon interpretation is probably the most credited method for accomplishing this (see Chapter 6).

Sociocultural impacts

Turning attention now to social and cultural impacts, one social effect of tourism that prevails in the less developed world is the conflict that so often ensues between government agencies and local communities pertaining to the development of historic sites into objects of tourism. These actions on the part of development agencies often disturb the lives of local residents who have established their homes and sometimes their entire communities within the historic site itself or immediately adjacent to it. Conflicts often occur between residents and government bodies involved in the restoration and conservation of such sites (Nuryanti 1996; Thorsell and Sigaty 2001). Timothy (1994) observed examples of this at several properties in Indonesia in the provinces of Central Java and Yogyakarta, including Ratu Boko Palace complex near the Prambanan Temple complex and at Taman Sari water palace near the city of Yogyakarta. These two sites have great potential for tourism, and the government has taken steps to develop them further. However, conflicts have arisen between the modern-day inhabitants of the ruins and the development agencies. Questions of community relocation and adequate compensation have been raised, but they have not yet been resolved. Confrontations of this type often take years to resolve and a great deal of negotiation.

Similarly, the development of a tourism industry that utilises religious relics of the past may cause further friction between locals and/or out of town pilgrims who still use the site for religious purposes, and tourism at heritage sites can have the effect of not allowing local people access to their own sacred sites and to places associated with their own heritage (Crain 1996). Many of the most historic temples in South-East Asia are still used for worship by adherents to Buddhist and Hindu beliefs. Some of the most impressive Buddhist temples in Thailand, for example, serve not only the needs of believers, but also attract large masses of tourists. Boisterous tourists and flashing cameras may be considered a major disturbance to many temple worshippers (Timothy 1994).

A major negative social consequence of tourism has been the removal of traditional peoples and original owners from their own land. This type of action was all too common in the creation of natural heritage landscapes, particularly in the establishment of national parks in Africa where this draconian action was taken to shape pleasuring grounds for elite societies of the past as well as the modern safari tourist (Adams and McShane 1992; Butler and Boyd 2000). It has only been through the use of partnership agreements that local peoples have started to reclaim and share in the benefits of presenting their natural heritage to visitors (Goodwin 2000; Boyd and Spawforth 2001).

Masses of tourists in historic communities and at heritage places create anxiety and discord among local residents that can lead to blatant animosity in some cases. In the case of Stratford-upon-Avon, England, a heritage town of only 23,000 residents, which attracts some 2.5 million tourists a year, there is a 'love–hate' relationship with tourism. As mentioned earlier, the industry provides over 8,000 jobs, yet a recent survey showed that 40 per cent of the local population felt there were too many tourists, and 28 per cent claimed that from their perspectives, the disadvantages of tourism outweighed the advantages (Drohan 1995: 2). According to one local resident, 'the locals just keep their heads down when the tourists come . . . I have to come [to work] early in the morning to avoid the tourists' (quoted by Drohan 1995: 2). Such sentiments are unfortunate, but it is common for tourism to develop 'despite' the locals. In fact, in the words of Boniface and Fowler (1993: 34), there is no

> hint of a reference to the fact that other people actually live in such places. The whole is couched in terms of an assumed right of foreigners to be invited by third parties to enjoy, and possibly improve, themselves in someone else's country, and to arrive uninvited by the citizens and not notice nor speak to them.

This 'inevitably generates . . . tensions between those who work and live in (and around) heritage sites and those visitors who view heritage through the "tourist gaze"' (Hubbard and Lilley 2000: 222–3).

Tourists feel other effects of the sheer pressure of numbers at peak times as well. Crowded conditions create safety hazards, which may be a real concern for some visitors, reducing the pleasure of the visit by ruining the local ambience and blocking good views of attractions (Shackley 1998a).

Again, on a positive note, with respect to built heritage, as people in the developing world realise the monetary value of ancient monuments and historic areas as attractions for affluent tourists, they have become more enthusiastic about preserving them. There is often limited appreciation among a developing country's native population for its natural beauty and historic features until tourism rouses such an appreciation (Cohen 1978). Soemarwoto (1992) claims that if the local people could benefit economically from these kinds of restoration projects, they would feel that it would be in their best interest to support it. He also suggests that such local involvement may create a sense of co-ownership of the sites within the community, and residents would become its stewards and guardians.

Summary and conclusions

The premise of this chapter is based on the argument that the heritage on display for tourists today is mainly a result of elements of the past being conserved. Although not specifically addressed in the form of questions, each section of the chapter provided answers to key questions regarding conservation in its broadest sense.

First, why have societies, mostly Western societies, decided to safeguard elements of their past? A myriad of reasons have emerged in the literature, but those that have greater explanatory power include the desire to offset feelings engendered by change and modernism with its loss of connection to the past;

nationalism and collective nostalgia where heritage becomes valued as a means of maintaining identity; scientific and educative importance because of what heritage resources can tell us about our past and what lessons we can learn; because they hold aesthetic value and represent such diversity that we cannot afford to lose them for ever; and finally because heritage resources can be reused and it makes good economic sense to conserve heritage that can be marketed and sold to tourists.

Second, what perspectives can one take regarding heritage conservation? A spectrum ranging from passive to active measures has emerged in this chapter regarding the approaches to conservation adopted. Preservation and restoration are passive measures where change in the heritage resource and/or feature is minimal. In contrast, active measures of conservation involve renovation of existing heritage buildings, the renewal of heritage places such as historic quarters of cities, and the role heritage tourism is often found to take in waterfront development, where heritage and its interpretation are often key developments in changes to waterfront regions.

A third question to emerge from the chapter is what form should the conservation process take? One needs to be careful here and not suggest that the process presented in this chapter has universal acceptance and is appropriate for all situations and heritage contexts. However, the authors argue that a general conservation process includes identification of the heritage place and/or object, research and inventory, setting goals that are in line with the policy context in which the heritage is present, designation and protection of features, restoration of structures and development of a visitor infrastructure, and long-term management and interpretation of the heritage being conserved and presented.

Fourth, what role have legislation and conservation bodies played in conserving the past? Discussion on this topic exclusively focused on how specific developed world nations took steps to conserve elements of their past as well as establish specific conservation-related organisations, as the impetus and desire to achieve this were clearly present in the thinking of Western societies. While there is a lack of interest in conserving heritage in developing world nations in some circles, international organisations, such as UNESCO, provide the means to ensure that their heritage is cared for, provided it is considered to have world appeal. Although much discussion was provided on the World Heritage List, the most important fact to remember is that UNESCO does not provide financial resources to sites that are nominated to the List, and as such the actual conservation falls to its managers. For sites in the less developed world, monies are too often diverted to other priority projects that are less relevant.

The reality of lack of funds led the discussion on to a final question, namely what challenges do heritage managers face? Apart from a lack of funds, other challenges include modernisation, environmental pressures, low public perception particularly in Third World countries where heritage conservation is relatively new and not considered important or even necessary by many, and dealing with a colonial legacy often in developing countries where conservation has been delayed, resulting in the loss of some heritage. Like other forms of tourism, heritage tourism is not impact free, and the reality is that managers need to address the physical and sociocultural impacts that this form of tourism creates. Within the section on impacts, a number of examples of well-known heritage attractions were used to illustrate the pressures they face from the natural elements as well as from society and local peoples that live around and in some places within them. The next chapter follows on from this discussion by looking at how heritage tourism can be managed.

Questions

1. Why have we conserved our past(s)?
2. How useful is it to classify perspectives of conservation as passive and active?
3. Why are conservation bodies and legislation predominantly found in developed world nations? Are there any exceptions?
4. What are the major challenges facing heritage conservation in your locality?
5. With reference to heritage in your own locality, what are the major physical and socio-cultural impacts that heritage managers have to face?

Further reading

Butler, R.W. and Boyd, S.W. (2000) *Tourism and National Parks: Issues and implications*, Wiley, Chichester.

Holdsworth, D. (1985) *Revising Main Street*, University of Toronto Press, Toronto.

Norton, P. (1989) *Archaeological Heritage Management in the Modern World*, Unwin Hyman, London.

Orbaşli, A. (2000) *Tourists in Historic Towns: Urban conservation and heritage management*, E & FN Spon, London.

Pearson M. and Sullivan, S. (1995) *Looking after Heritage Places: The basics of heritage planning for managers, landowners and administrators*, Melbourne University Press, Carlton.

Tiesdell, S., Oc, T. and Heath, T. (1996) *Revitalizing Historic Urban Quarters*, Architectural Press, Oxford.

CHAPTER 5

Managing heritage tourism

Heritage resources are irreplaceable; they are non-renewable resources that require conservation and good management. Heritage sites provide a tangible link between the past, the present and the future, and are often subject to the conflicting aspirations of conservation and tourism. It is therefore essential that heritage sites are well managed. Millar (1989: 14) used the analogy of juggling eggs when talking about the management of heritage tourism, claiming that 'done well, it is the key to conservation and commercial success, done badly, it may mean a significant part of our heritage is lost forever'. More recently, Garrod and Fyall (2000: 684) see management as the critical aspect of any heritage mission by managers, claiming that mission to be 'primarily one of caring for the property and maintaining it in as pristine a state as possible, with issues such as financial solvency and public access entering into the decision making process only as secondary considerations'. These authors go on to state that many heritage managers do not even consider themselves to be in the tourism business, instead preferring to view their role more as guardians of the national heritage than providers of public access to it (Garrod and Fyall 2000).

Linked to management is the theme of sustainability. While this topic will be addressed in more detail later, it is important at the outset of this chapter to establish the connection between good heritage management and sustainability. Sustainability principles are evident in the elements of the mission of heritage attractions as shown in Table 5.1, supporting the notion of sustainable heritage tourism development.

However, these ideas are not new, as Millar (1989: 13) writing at the end of the 1980s noted that 'long-term planning for heritage tourism with an integral, continuing conservation policy, is essential in ensuring a quality experience for the visitor at each heritage site, village, town, seaside resort or area of countryside'. Keeping to the sustainability theme, Hall and McArthur (1998) note that in the past heritage has often been treated as a static commodity, where managers are often not aware that this resource and its associated values are

Table 5.1   Elements in the mission of heritage attractions

Conservation
The role of the heritage manager is to safeguard the heritage for posterity; to ensure that the use of heritage by the present generation does not compromise the ability of future generations to use and benefit from those assets; and to ensure that the present generation properly manages the heritage assets it holds in trust for the nation as a whole

Accessibility
Heritage only has significance in so far as it benefits people. If people are prevented from experiencing heritage objects, it can no longer be considered part of their heritage. However, high levels of accessibility can lead to heritage assets being damaged. At the same time, conservation requirements can prevent the present generation from enjoying heritage to the fullest extent

Education
Education plays a crucial role in achieving accessibility. To appreciate heritage, visitors must be able to understand its nature and importance, including why it needs to be conserved. This requires the use of various interpretive techniques, ranging from the very formal to the very informal. Education is most effective if it is also entertaining

Relevance
Heritage sites must be relevant to as broad an audience as possible. They should not simply be the domain of a small minority of 'heritage enthusiasts'. Ideally, all visitors should leave with a better appreciation of why the heritage asset is relevant to them, the local area, and to the nation as a whole. Heritage attractions should also seek to be something with which the local community can identify, giving them a greater sense of place and pride

Recreation
Part of the mission of heritage attractions must be to entertain visitors and provide recreational opportunities. If they do not enjoy themselves, visitors will be less likely to make return visits or to recommend the attraction to others. Nonetheless, conservation requirements may by necessity limit the recreational potential of a heritage place

Financial
Heritage attractions need to be financially sound if they are to achieve their aims. Finances need not, however, be generated entirely by charging for admission, and some external funding, particularly for expensive conservation work, will most certainly be required

Local community
The heritage site should seek to work in harmony with the host community. Visitors should not be permitted to use the heritage attraction at the expense of residents. Heritage places can also have important economic multiplier effects throughout the community

Quality
Heritage sites must provide high-quality service to their customers if they expect to compete in an ever more crowded tourism marketplace. This includes providing a range of facilities, flexibility, a high standard of cleanliness, well-trained staff and adequate car parking. If a charge is made for admission then the attraction should aim to exceed visitors' expectations

Source: Adapted from Garrod and Fyall (2000: 691).

constantly changing, and any serious attention to achieving sustainability requires the development of management strategies that can accommodate change. While visitor management frameworks form a latter part of this chapter, a few comments on planning principles for heritage tourism are offered here to emphasise the association between heritage tourism management and sustainability. First, for visitation to be sustainable it must be at a scale appropriate for the specific location and should produce no permanent degradation of the values associated with the heritage site. Second, visitation must be placed within a strategic planning framework that identifies values, goals, objectives and appropriate actions for heritage management and site visitation. Third, and most critically, it is important for local communities to be involved in the heritage management process (Hall and McArthur 1993c: 276).

This chapter commences by looking at the ownership of heritage sites and how management issues vary between sites that are under public, private and voluntary ownership, and how issues are conditioned by the different goals set by each sector. An important part of the ownership debate is the role that partnership plays in co-operation across and within sectors. Attention then shifts to heritage economics and how managers fund attractions. While a range of options is offered, particular focus is directed to the merits and disadvantages of imposing fees on the users of heritage sites. The next sections of the chapter examine how staff and visitors are managed, visitor management involves discussion on three levels. First, the importance of sustainable heritage management is returned to; second, different visitor management models are presented that are considered to be relevant to heritage managers; third, specific tools and conventional methods used by managers are presented. Next, a discussion is presented about managing local residents, where the focus is placed on ensuring their participation both in decision-making and in the benefits of tourism. The penultimate section looks at management from the perspective of how heritage tourism is marketed.

Ownership

The ownership of heritage sites is important to understand, for each type of ownership has unique management issues, economic implications and human resource repercussions. The three sectors that tend to own different types of heritage attractions are the public, private and voluntary. Based to some extent on the work of Swarbrooke (1994, 1995), Table 5.2 demonstrates these three types of ownership, provides examples of historic buildings that each type of ownership might include, and describes the primary and secondary motivations for each sector. For the most part, the goals of public and non-profit ownership are conservation and education, while for private ownership, profit and recreation are usually the primary motivations.

Table 5.2 Ownership of heritage attractions

Sector	Examples of attractions owned	Primary and secondary motivations for ownership
Public	Archaeological ruins Ancient monuments Historic homes/buildings Parks Forests Museums	Primary – conservation Secondary – public access, education, revenue, catalyst for tourism development
Private	Historic theme parks Museums Wineries and distilleries Culture centres Art galleries Industrial plants and mines	Primary – profit Secondary – boost visitation, entertainment, public image enhancement
Voluntary	Historic buildings Museums Heritage centres Trails	Primary – conservation by self-sufficiency Secondary – entertainment, education

Source: Adapted from Swarbrooke (1995).

Public

Public ownership means that a site is owned and possibly operated by a government agency, such as a national parks service, department of environment or a ministry of culture and education. Perhaps the best example from the UK is English Heritage, which is a government agency that operates a large number of the most visited heritage attractions in England (Swarbrooke 1995: 9). As discussed in Chapter 4, public ownership can exist on national and subnational levels, as well as in the domain of special administrations, such as Native American reserves. Monument Valley, Arizona/Utah, is a good example of natural heritage and the Four Corners Monument where the states of Colorado, New Mexico, Arizona and Utah meet, is a good example of a political/cultural attraction that is owned and operated by the Navajo nation and its tribal council.

The public sector in most countries has assumed a major role in heritage conservation. Pearce (1997: 89–91) identified several interrelated reasons for this:

- *Market failure* – This occurs when market forces are unable to support heritage places because of inadequate financial resources/earnings. Government budgets usually provide a means for overcoming this shortfall to some degree. Likewise, the market is inclined to be more short-term-oriented despite the fact that environmental effects of tourism are long-term issues.

Finally, environmental values need to be preserved notwithstanding their potential tourist attraction.

- *Public interest* – Historic features might be of such high universal value that their rescue is reasoned to be in the 'public interest' rather than in the control of any particular group.

- *Historical public ownership* – State-owned buildings that have been state-owned throughout much of history usually continue to be once they have achieved some degree of heritage status.

- *Political considerations* – Many monuments commemorate state achievements (e.g. winning wars, political independence) and constitute an important part of nation building.

- *Economic considerations* – Public agencies almost always have an interest in creating jobs, earning regional income and establishing a strong tax base. Therefore, they realise that conservation may be encouraged through economic motives, such as tourism development. Because of the administrative complexities of such programmes and the need to provide infrastructure, public sector agencies are usually involved in this process.

There tends to be a degree of uniformity among national-level publicly owned sites in terms of facilities, presentation and interpretation. The emphasis is on preservation, and little, if any, marketing is undertaken. According to Balcar and Pearce (1996: 208), however, the community-managed sites have less uniformity and few explicit management plans and strategies.

Private

Several types of heritage attraction, namely mines, industrial heritage sites, wineries, distilleries, farmsteads, plantations, stately homes and some museums (e.g. the Corning Museum of Glass), are commonly found under private ownership. Less common are natural heritage areas, although a nice example of a privately owned piece of nature is Meteor Crater in Arizona, USA – one of the world's best specimens of meteor craters. Although the primary goal under private ownership is profit, heritage managers at these places must also consider the conservation and education domains. A long-term perspective is necessary in terms of managing sustainable resources if their business will continue into the future.

Privately owned sites are acquired most commonly in one of two ways. First are historic properties that were purchased by an individual or company prior to the enactment of regulations and legislation that would prevent it from being purchased privately today. This can also be buildings and places that when purchased had a utilitarian value, and the heritage value accrued later on by being associated with famous people or events. Second (which can also be in the first category) are properties that have been passed down from one generation to another and whose owners have had little interest in selling or donating to public or non-profit organisations.

The Tussauds Group is one of the largest private sector attractions operations in Great Britain and the Netherlands. The company operates many tourist sites that can be classified as heritage attractions, the most prominent being Warwick Castle, Madame Tussaud's Museum in London and Alton Towers. Some of these sites were purchased by the group early on, while others have been developed from the beginning (Swarbrooke 1995). The wineries of California, USA, and the Niagara Peninsula of Canada, which have become an integral part of each region's agricultural heritage, are another example of privately owned attractions that have probably been passed down from one generation to the next and are becoming increasingly popular tourist destinations.

Volunteer/non-profit

Among the most common types of heritage attractions owned and operated by non-profit organisations are museums, cemeteries, heritage trails and historic buildings. As their primary goal is to earn enough revenue to continue to exist, they usually charge entrance fees, a large portion of which should be expended directly back into site maintenance.

Perhaps the best known and most widespread non-profit heritage body in Britain is the National Trust. Its properties include agricultural lands, historic houses and other structures and landscapes, primarily in rural areas. Its purpose is to raise enough money every year to continue to maintain its conservation activities (Swarbrooke 1995). Many comparable volunteer and non-governmental organisations (NGOs) can be found in most countries of the world.

Intersectoral co-operation

Co-operation, collaboration and partnership (e.g. between private, public and volunteer ownership and between places) have become more prominent in recent tourism literature, as researchers have begun to realise that partnerships have the potential to promote the principles and practices of sustainable development (e.g. Bramwell and Lane 2000). Co-operation is increasingly being viewed as an important practice in addressing management concerns and problems that arise when heritage resources overlap jurisdictional boundaries and ownership sectors (Boyd and Timothy 2001). Writing from the context of the management of World Heritage Sites (WHS), Boyd and Timothy (2001) recognised that co-operation was an essential element of successful management, others being the type of partnership best suited for the situation (formalised or informal) and the best approach to forming partnerships (grassroots or agency led) (Figure 5.1).

CONTEXT

	Protected landscapes	Mixed-use landscapes
Local/ regional	**Type A** • Mostly formalised type of partnership, with an equal relationship • Emphasis on grassroots approach • High degree of co-operation expected, involving both the private and public sector Example: Banff National Park (Canada)	**Type B** • Formal or informal partnerships, where relationships are unequal • Emphasis on an agency-driven approach • Limited degree of co-operation, greater between government agencies as opposed to private versus the public sector Example: Hadrian's Wall (UK)
Binational/ international	**Type C** • Mostly informal type of partnership, with an unequal relationship • Local-level agency-driven and grassroots approach • Limited degree of co-operation, mostly between national governments and their respective agencies responsible for protected lands Example: Waterton–Glacier IPP (USA–Canada)	**Type D** • Informal partnership at best, with likelihood of none existing • Local-level agency-driven approach • At best, limited degree of co-operation where issues of mutual benefit warrant it or where similar range of mandates are involved Example: None at present

SCALE is indicated along the left vertical axis.

Figure 5.1   Scale of co-operation in heritage places
Source: After Boyd and Timothy (2001).

⊕ Co-operation is needed where heritage sites, particularly WHS, exist within mixed-use settings, as 'managers have a dual challenge of not only safeguarding and promoting the site itself, but also ensuring that a balance is kept with the needs of the working landscape around it' (Boyd and Timothy 2001: 50). The example of Hadrian's Wall in northern England (inscribed as a WHS in 1987) is a prime example where ownership of land around a heritage feature changes across its entire 118 km length. While the wall is recognised as the best relict frontier of the entire Roman Empire and an important heritage attraction, it runs through a varied array of land uses, including heavily popu-lated areas, rural working landscapes and conservation areas. Co-operation was needed in the development of a management plan for the wall and the corridor it passes through. In 1996, English Heritage took the lead in produc-ing a plan that would ensure a satisfactory balance between conservation of the site and its setting, as well as attending to the interests of the host farming communities, accessibility requirements, tourism and economic benefits. With the wall being a popular tourist attraction, receiving on average 1.25 million visitors a year, of which approximately half a million confine their visitation to forts and museums open to the public, a strategy for tourism was developed that takes into account the views of the local community, ensures a sustainable level of visitors, strives to improve the visitor experience and co-ordinates access, transportation and facilities. In fact, a tourism partnership was formed as early as 1994, prior to the completion of the management plan for the wall in 1996, involving a diverse range of private and public partners which co-operates with English Heritage and operates within the bounds of the WHS management plan (Hadrian's Wall Tourism Partnership 1999).

Other examples where mixed ownership necessitates that intersectoral co-operation is in place include world heritage features such as Stonehenge in England and the Giant's Causeway in Northern Ireland. Writing about Stonehenge, Fowler (1992: 99) had this to say:

> One of the practical curiosities about Stonehenge is that, while the monument itself and its little triangle of land between the main roads is managed by English Heritage, all the other land around about is owned by the National Trust. The Trust is imbued with the ethos of management, notably in the sense of estate management. As it has taken aboard an awareness of its archaeology, most of which was acquired unknowingly, the thousands of sites and landscapes involved have therefore been absorbed into a well-founded and increasingly sophisticated system of land management within the concept of the 'estate' as a whole.

A similar type of situation exists for the Giant's Causeway, inscribed as the UK's first WHS in 1986. As Boyd and Timothy (2001: 50) note:

> Management occurs in the form of an informal partnership between the National Trust, the Moyle District Council, and the Department of the Environment for Northern Ireland (responsible for the provision of scientific advice and liaison) where a high level of co-operation exists.

Co-operation is also needed where heritage attractions are located in border regions, either across or adjacent to international boundaries. Timothy (1999b) noted that levels of cross-border partnership range from alienation to integration where co-operation is seen as the halfway point. In his book, *Tourism and Political Boundaries*, Timothy (2001c: 153) suggests, 'cooperative networks are characterized by initial efforts between adjacent administrations to solve mutual problems'. In the case of WHS that straddle international borders, 'co-operation is needed to assist with management concerns like conservation, marketing, and the development of tourism infrastructure' (Boyd and Timothy 2001: 51). The lack of cross-frontier co-operation can result in the overuse of resources on one side, creating severe ecological problems as well as having an impact on the quality of built attractions within the neighbouring region (Timothy 1999b). A good example of binational co-operation is the case of the

International Peace Park (IPP) WHS formed by Waterton Lakes National Park (Canada) and Glacier National Park (USA), inscribed as a WHS in 1995, although symbolically connected by Canadian and US government legislation as early as 1932. While two different management systems work alongside each other for the management of essentially one ecosystem, co-operation exists in the marketing and promotion of the IPP, and in how community groups on each side of the border work co-operatively to produce newsletters to inform residents and tourists and organise special events (Timothy 1999b). The case study below shows the role of cooperation across borders in difficult political situations.

CASE STUDY   Nicosia, Cyprus: cross-border co-operation

After the fall of the Berlin Wall, Nicosia was the only internationally divided city left in the world (Rossides 1995). The Attila/Green Line divided the city in 1974, when Cyprus became a divided island, Greek in the south and Turkish in the north. The years following (1976–89) were difficult, with the city experiencing considerable economic problems. Rossides (1995) states that although the inner city's employment base remained constant in absolute terms, its share fell considerably, while in the ensuing decade the decline was accelerated in both absolute and relative terms. To tackle the problems arising from the division of the city and the city's outward, unplanned expansion, a master plan was prepared under the auspices of the United Nations Development Programme (UNDP). It was conceived by the Greek city's progressive mayor, who along with his Turkish Cypriot counterpart, undertook the difficult task of creating a joint vision for the city's development and ensuring that programmes would be formulated to meet that vision (Rossides 1995). With the absence of a central planning authority, a bi-communal team acted as a de facto planning commission and sought to chart a development course for the city that would preserve its cultural heritage while luring back residents and businesses to the decaying core area. This demonstrated that co-operation between the two communities across a political divide was possible, where co-operation was viewed not as an objective for some indefinite period in the future, but for the present. While this action is small scale, it demonstrates that co-operation can work even in places of conflict.

It may also be argued that co-operation can create situations where a wider range of tourism attractions are made available to visitors, as well as ensuring higher rates of success for specific types of attractions. In their examination of industrial heritage tourism, Edwards and Llurdés (1996: 360) commented that:

> mines and quarries as industrial heritage attractions would seem to have the greatest chance of success if they are part of a wider range of tourism attractions in the locality. In this respect, Wales is quite fortunate. The Dolaucothi gold

mines in Dyfed are linked with the nearby Llyn Brianne Dam reservoir complex, the breeding area of the rare red kite bird and the folklore associated with Twm Shon Catti, the Welsh equivalent of Robin Hood.

Co-operation is not a new idea. Fowler (1992) was quick to point out that over the past 25 years environmental, agriculture and historic preservation organisations have increasingly recognised the interrelationships among natural areas, farmland and historic resources, given that many rural scenes incorporate both cultural and natural elements important to both historic preservationists and environmentalists.

> The preservationist views farmland and wooded hillsides as providing the setting for agricultural buildings, representing the historic source of the farm owners' livelihood: the fields allowed them to raise crops and pasture livestock, the forest provided lumber for construction, wood for the stove, habitat for game, and sap for maple sugar. For the lover of the natural environment, the farm is a welcome transition – and buffer – between the city and the forest (Fowler 1992: 82).

Co-operation also exists between organisations, in terms of co-ordinating the management and marketing of heritage. Characteristically, the organisational structure dealing with the past is complex. It exists on global, international, continental, national, regional, district and local scales. One of its major preoccupations is therefore not so much managing the past as attempting to co-ordinate the management of the past. Many of the plenitude of organisations, especially the large ones, are also inevitably concerned with running themselves. For instance, the staff costs of English Heritage, for example, take up some 75 per cent of its budget. Management of the UK's heritage is inevitably bound up with supranational organisations. For example, one of the great world bureaucracies, UNESCO, is the parent of the World Heritage Committee, which receives nominations of sites from its state party members. At the level of individual attractions, heritage managers cannot solve every problem unaided; they must network with organisations that can advise them on specific issues and concerning possible sources of financial support (Stratton 1994). For example, the National Trust for Scotland, which is a voluntary charitable organisation, relying on a membership of 250,000 (5 per cent of the population), seeks support not only from its members and commercial enterprises, but produces income from many sources and relies on government support for only 10 per cent of its budget. Because the National Trust for Scotland owns 125 properties of historic importance in the human and natural environments 'on behalf of the nation', it has always worked harmoniously with government and non-government enterprises in partnerships that recognise the overall need of meeting the requirements of the marketplace. While there is clearly competition for available resources, there is little unwillingness to collaborate in joint promotion (Borley 1996: 185).

Heritage economics

Heritage is not cheap! Although the value of learning experiences provided by interpretive services is vast and contributes to the enjoyment, education and appreciation of an attraction by visitors, the cost of telling the story is enormous, as is site conservation in light of increasing visitor and other environmental pressures. By way of example, Fowler (1992) tells that the cost of obtaining most historic houses can cost upwards of £5 million. Restoring a property, maintaining it, installing necessary facilities (i.e. toilets) and establishing and running an interpretive programme can easily cost twice as much. In the past, heritage property managers have depended on government financial support for operating and preserving historic places. In 1995, for instance, English Heritage earned £17 million but spent £61 million for conservation, reflecting that agency's dependence on public funds (Powe and Willis 1996). However, public funds have become increasingly scarce during the past 20 years as administrators have become more budget conscious and as other social programmes and national priorities have been established. Government cutbacks for heritage programmes throughout the world have become the norm (Broadhurst 1989; Garrod and Fyall 2000; Smith 1989), and managers have come to expect budget reductions. Such a prospect has led some 30 per cent of museum managers in the UK to describe the situation as 'bleak' and some 65 per cent to express it as 'challenging' (Davies 1993), reflecting an economically induced lack of confidence in the future of heritage.

Given that it can cost millions of dollars or pounds to 'save' heritage, site managers have had to become more fiscally responsible on their own in attempting to devise ways of increasing revenue. Such a turnaround is not new to privately owned attractions, but for the public and non-profit sectors, this prospect is an uncomfortable one.

The source of money for maintaining historic areas has sparked a great deal of debate in both private and public circles. Cossons (1989) argues that, in addition to government spending and corporate sponsorships, heritage users should pay for their experiences by way of more widespread entrance fees. According to a British study, this pricing change would not likely deter many potential visitors since heritage demand has been found to be generally inelastic to price (Prentice 1989a). Prentice found that visitors generally expect to pay for admission to the major attractions, despite the large number of sites under public ownership. This is probably due in large part to the fact that most visitors are well off economically, and are willing to pay for the upkeep of the sources of their recreational learning experiences.

Sources of revenue

Difficult financial times have required heritage facilities to take fiscal matters into their own hands by increasing revenues and controlling operating

Table 5.3   Common sources of revenue at heritage sites

Direct funding	*Events*
Government funding	Festivals
Local authority funding	Craft fairs
Grants	Historical re-enactments
Donations	Plays/concerts
Legacies	Horse/dog/car shows
Membership	Battle games
Endowments	Exhibitions
Sponsorship/joint promotions	Sporting activities
Affinity cards	
	Interpretation
Retail	Guidebooks
Merchandising	Other publications
Mail order	Audio tours
Farm shops	Audiovisuals
Garden centres	Guided tours
Franchise reproduction	Machines/simulators
Off-site shops	
Currency exchanges	*Catering*
Plants	Restaurants/cafés/snack bars
Specialty shops	Banquets
	Corporate entertainment
Accommodation	Conferences
Bed and breakfasts	
Training courses	*Admissions*
Residential conferences	Site/entrance fees
Holiday cottages	Car parking fees
	Activity participation fees
Private hire	
Film sets	*Leasing property*
Photography	Land cultivation
Product launches	Caravan parks
Renting artefacts	Golf courses

Source: After Stevens (1995).

expenditures (Broadhurst 1989; Fowler 1992; Marris 1985; Silberberg 1995; Smith 1989). As a result, heritage managers have begun offering a variety of services to visitors in an attempt to keep them longer and get them to spend more (Table 5.3). The rest of this section focuses on some of the various income sources available to heritage site management.

User fees

Aside from direct government funding, the most widespread and most traditional means of earning money has been user fees, the most common being entrance and admission fees. The primary difference between entrance and admission fees, according to Edginton *et al.* (2001), is scale and spatial concentration. Entrance fees are monies paid to enter large open areas like parks, zoos and gardens. Admission fees, however, are more related to entrance into buildings and other structures like museums, galleries, castles and houses. Entrance/admission fees usually provide the largest majority of revenue at historic properties. During the 1980s, approximately 90 per cent of the Ironbridge Museum's (UK) income was from visitor admission charges. While this is an impressive figure, Smith (1989) brings up a valid point. This is obviously an enormous achievement, but is dangerous as it places far too high a reliance on the vagaries of the English weather and other external factors which can affect visitor numbers.

Rental costs may also be considered a user fee where visitors purchase the right to utilise some part of a historic site or artefact. Letting out rooms for wedding receptions, professional meetings and family reunions are common examples of this. Some heritage attractions, such as museums and parks, have begun offering memberships, which might be seen as a form of sponsorship, but more likely is a user fee, since individual members and families by being members often have almost unlimited admission to the attraction. Car parking and participation costs for special events and additional activities are also becoming more common fee-based sources of revenue.

In many less developed countries, managers have a desire to bring in revenue while at the same time provide opportunities for less affluent local populations to enjoy their own heritage. One way of doing both is to put in place a dual pricing system, which means that local people pay a significantly lower admission/entrance fee than foreign tourists. This is very common in Asia and parts of Africa and Latin America. At the Taj Mahal in India, for example, entrance tickets for Indians cost approximately US$0.40, but foreigners must pay 48 times more (US$20), which comes as a significant shock to many international visitors (Duff-Brown 2001; Ganguly 2001).

Management decisions concerning entry/user fees must consider a range of variables. One issue of critical concern is where to charge (i.e. at the entrance, at the exit or in the car park). Another question is whether or not charges should be high enough to be inclusive of interpretive media, guides, etc., or should each item be charged separately. A third concern is when to charge. Should the full fee be imposed during low season, or should a discount or complimentary entrance be offered? Perhaps seasonal rates should apply. Fourth is the matter of whom to charge. Should children be admitted at no cost, should family specials be offered, and will we honour student discount cards? These are all important questions that need to be answered in pricing policy formulation (Prentice 1989a: 233).

Special events

Supporting special events and extracurricular activities, particularly during the off season, can also offset operation costs. In addition to the participation fees just described, event organisers (if the event is organised from outside the heritage location) can be charged rental, utility and other service fees, or they might be required to pay a percentage of their proceeds to the hosting attraction. Theatrical performances, concerts and sporting events are particularly suitable activities for properties that have significant seating and action room. Art displays and craft shows may be fitting events for large spaces, but also for smaller areas. Although these sorts of events have the potential to bring in significant quantities of revenue, it is important to remember not to allow these occasions to detract from the primary aims and objectives of the site.

Retailing

It is obvious that people have an unusually high propensity to spend money while on vacation. This inclination is illustrated by the development of shopping districts in many communities (both large and small) and other tourist areas. This spending tendency can have major economic impacts upon tourist destinations, especially in small communities (Timothy and Wall 1997). It is also known among managers that heritage tourists are more likely to have more disposable incomes and have a tendency to spend more while on vacation (Silberberg 1995). With this realisation, and based on visitors' expressed interests in having more spending opportunities, many heritage managers during the past 20 years have begun to expand their services into the retailing sector (Butcher-Younghans 1993; Prentice 1993; Smith 1989; Thomas 1989). With careful planning, the development of tourism in areas of historic significance can play an important role in providing not only money for conservation and day-to-day operations, but jobs and increased community income as well.

Edwards (1989) discovered that heritage tourists in Wales who were on vacation away from home were more likely to purchase items than either home-based recreationists or other people not on vacation. He suggested that these findings reflect the greater tendency of holidaymakers to buy souvenirs to document their travels than home-based visitors. Several different retail items at heritage attractions are very popular, including: miniature replicas, guidebooks, photo albums, camera film and batteries, postcards, posters, sweets, T-shirts, calendars, salt and pepper shakers, coffee mugs, wood carvings, pens and pencils, and especially handicrafts or skill works that are unique and representative of the place (e.g. model ships at a dockyard, copper pots at a coppersmith's shop and souvenir bricks at a brickyard). Some locations have become very creative in their retailing endeavours. For example, in 1988, Ironbridge Museum in the UK introduced its own token coinage, which represented the older system of coinage that was used in Great Britain before 1900. The exchange rate was 40 modern pennies for one old penny, and shop prices were set accordingly – they appeared to be at 1800s price levels. The money had the look and feel of the old currency and thus was an interesting education tool, but perhaps most important of all for this discussion, the management found that over 45 per cent of the coinage went home with visitors as souvenirs, which was pure profit (Smith 1989: 26).

There are a few spatial patterns that can be useful management tools when it comes to retailing. First is controlling the flow of visitors. This can be a useful tool for making money from souvenirs if visitor flows are directed so that they pass through or near the souvenir selling areas, so that visitors will be tempted to buy (Prentice 1993). Second is the concentration of tourist commercial areas. It is sometimes useful to cluster gift shops together and to place these near other important services such as cafés, restaurants and restrooms. Third, the location of gift shops can affect people's purchasing behaviour. It might be that people are more inclined to purchase larger items if the shop is located adjacent to the exit gate rather than the entrance, as many people will be reluctant to buy something they have to carry around all day. This will also offer visitors a last-chance opportunity to pick something up on their way back to the car. Finally, shop location can also be useful for interpretive purposes. According to Smith (1989), placing retail locations inside museums can be a useful form of interpretation that provides information for visitors and allows them to make contact with interpretation staff.

As in the case of hosting special events, gift shop managers must be careful not to allow the range and types of souvenirs to detract from the heritage experience or lessen the aesthetic value of the place. Good quality and locally made handicrafts and souvenirs will probably be better received among visitors than cheaper souvenirs manufactured in faraway lands that have little to do with the attraction itself. Likewise, the design and scale of retail structures should be balanced against local need and appropriateness to place. Such features, if uncontrolled, can create tourist ghettos at the expense of a community's historic character (Orbaşli 2000: 171).

Lodging and catering

Lodging and catering are other sources of income that might be considered at historic sites (Smith 1989). Since accommodation buildings are generally quite large, it is especially important to ensure that any new structures do not divert from the goals of conservation or trivialise the heritage value of the main attraction. In historic villages, it is common for old homes to be converted into guesthouses. Hotels in urban historic quarters can be established quite effectively in existing historical buildings. The extent to which this can be done, however, will depend on extant land use plans and zoning regulations. In rural areas some of the most successful and aesthetically amicable lodging establishments are bed and breakfasts, cabins, farmhouses, campsites and cottages.

Accommodation facilities have the potential to lengthen visits and increase additional spending. Thus, attracting higher-spending tourists, rather than large masses of tourists, can be an important way of approaching environmentally sustainable heritage tourism. In the words of Smith (1989: 28), 'for too long heritage attractions have gone for maximum numbers, when they should have been looking for optimum numbers'.

Food services provide for the dining needs of visitors, sometimes more than once if they are there for an extended period. At locations where visitors could spend many hours, a range of catering options should be provided, such as sit-down cafés, fast-food restaurants, snack bars and catering carts. Short visits can be enhanced by opportunities to be refreshed with snacks and treats like ice cream, chips, pastries and soft drinks. One concept that appears to have caught on in recent years is themed food. For example, at historic re-enactments (e.g. jousting tournaments and battles) visitors sometimes have the option of eating food and using utensils that might have been typical during the period in question. Eating from pewter plates without knives and forks and drinking from pewter goblets at a jousting tournament or in a medieval prison can add to the entertainment factor and help educate visitors in a small way.

Interpretation

To a limited extent interpretation can be used to increase visitor expenditures. The most common way is through audiotape rentals, selling maps and guide-books, and offering inexpensive group tours. In most cases, brochures are offered free of charge or are included in user fees, although special leaflets and postcards can be sold separately. In conjunction with interpretive tours, baby carriages, wagons and bicycles can also be rented to visitors who feel the use of such items would enhance their experience.

Grants

Where there is no direct line to government coffers, organisations can submit grant proposals to various public agencies. Often, public agencies that have an interest in conservation and education may have a limited budget for providing one-time gifts to private and non-profit sector places. This is normally done on a highly competitive basis, and justification has to be made why the individual site is deserving of the money. Most national governments in the developed world have programmes of this nature, and the European Union, at the supra-national level, has funds (e.g. Leader and Interreg) that can be tapped for community-based heritage and tourism projects. In like manner, grants can be obtained from philanthropic organisations such as the Ford Foundation, the Kellogg Foundation and the Rockefeller Foundation in the United States. Most of these large-scale, non-profit foundations have programmes for both domestic and international work and have a tendency to focus on development-oriented projects. Generous organisations like these usually offer a one-time gift, which is attached to a reporting-based process of accountability.

Sponsorship

Sponsorship has become one of the most important generators of direct and indirect income. This entails a form of 'in-kind' exchange, whereby some sort of service is provided in exchange for another service or money. One example would be an airline offering monetary gifts or plane tickets to a trust property in exchange for using its name and logo on trust brochures and signage. Wigle

(1994) gives the example of a regional newspaper offering advertising space to a historic fort in exchange for admission passes, which it uses as prize give-aways. It is also common for organisations to sponsor special events, which allows a great deal of visibility for their products.

Goodey (1994: 307) clarifies a few points related to sponsor relationships. First, sponsors expect a positive association with the heritage product. This has implications for content, values expressed and promotional opportunities in design and retailing. Second, sponsors need to understand the specific details of a project or management plan and know the projected image. Third, the sponsor will nearly always desire to be involved in determining the market segments to be targeted and the approaches to be used in attracting them. Finally, sponsors, as sources of direct or indirect funding should be consulted about changes and future plans, and regular contact should be maintained.

Donations

Unlike sponsorship, donations generally do not have in-kind intentions attached to them. To elicit small-scale and personal donations, managers at public, private and non-profit attractions place donation boxes near entrances and exits as a way of motivating people to put spare change or more into the site's conservation fund. This is commonplace even at attractions where entrance fees are required, and a donation may be considered an adequate admission fee at sites where official user fees are not levied. Perhaps the most sought-after form of donation, however, is done primarily by the non-profit sector and entails larger gifts from estates, corporations and philanthropic individuals. The advantage of non-profit heritage sites is that they are usually considered to be trusts or foundations – in essence charities – that can offer tax benefits to contributors. This funding is usually limited to places where individuals, families or organisations have a personal stake in site preservation. For example, the Wall of Honor located at Ellis Island, New York/New Jersey, where thousands of immigrants entered the United States in the early twentieth century, is funded by donations from individuals and families whose ancestors migrated to North America via this notorious immigration post. For a sub-stantial donation individuals and families can have their ancestors' names engraved on the wall. Donations by American ethnic associations and cor-porations also contributed to the $161 million Ellis Island restoration project (Kirshenblatt-Gimblett 1998; Wallace 1996).

The charitable foundation status of many heritage places has several benefits over other forms of ownership and management (Edginton *et al.* 2001: 311; Mallam 1989: 44–5). These benefits are as follows:

- Foundations generally have a good public reputation. Their motives, usually, are altruistic, which makes promotion for self-interest difficult.
- Trusts and charities have the ability to raise free investment capital without the need to provide financial returns to investors.

- They are independent, free from bureaucratic control and government impediments.
- They can offer tax benefits to contributors.
- Sometimes they can acquire private sector products and services at discount prices.
- Foundations are in a good position to leverage donations.

The user pays debate

Considerable debate has ensued in recent years over whether or not the public should have to pay for the experience of visiting its own heritage. The pro-payment activists argue that in such difficult times there is no other way to finance conservation and interpretation except with the help of user fees and other sources of earnings (Smith 1989). Anti-payment observers suggest that the fundamental concept of heritage is that conservation and interpretation exist for the good of the people whose past it is. The question, 'whose heritage is it?' is a large part of this debate, and the conclusion is often drawn that heritage belongs to the people, therefore they should not be required to pay for something that is already theirs. Fyall and Garrod (1998: 222–3; Garrod and Fyall 2000: 685) highlight several reasons why some heritage managers are opposed to the user pays philosophy in the context of heritage:

- Managers tend to associate the pricing of access with commercialisation or commodification of the past, which focuses more on a site's commercial value than its personal and conservation value.

- Many managers find the notion of price contradictory to their ideological views of the wider mission of heritage operations. If potential visitors are unable to experience heritage because of cost, then whose heritage does the property represent and for whom is it being protected? Thus, an elitist demand is created for something that everyone should have the right to enjoy. This, Fyall and Garrod suggest, disenfranchises much of the public from their own heritage.

- Similar to the second point, having to pay admission fees probably decreases impulse attendance. A large portion of the heritage market is comprised of spontaneous visits by casual visitors, who may be put off and decide not to visit if the price is high or if a charge is levied at all.

- User fees are also considered wrong by some observers because they tend to preoccupy managers with commercial management matters at the expense of the more important cultural, ecological and educational goals of most heritage attractions.

- Finally, there is a concern that secondary spending, such as food, lodging and souvenirs, will decrease if entrance fees are imposed because people will have less money to spend and will have to economise by refraining from buying commercial items. While important, this point is less of a concern than the previous ones because entrance fees are generally pure profit, while retail and other service fees involve overhead and upfront expenses.

On the opposite side of the debate, Fyall and Garrod (1998: 220–1) argue that there are positive outcomes of charging admission fees at heritage attractions that can contribute to the sustainable management of heritage properties:

- Entrance earnings can be used effectively to protect and conserve. In this sense, since visitors are the ones who damage heritage through their use of it, then it is sensible that they should pay for its prevention or repair.
- While there is some danger in this as described above, fees can help reduce visitor traffic flows through sensitive areas and at critical periods of time.
- Fees can assist in educating the public and public officials about the value of specific sites and conservation generally. Site profiles can be enhanced, which might be rewarded later in competition for scarce public resources.
- Earnings help the attraction improve site quality in terms of landscaping, facilities and interpretive programmes, which can act to improve visitor satisfaction and increase repeat visitation.
- Accountability on the part of managers might be improved. Fyall and Garrod argue that free heritage attractions tend to be more responsive to the whims and wishes of visitors than those that charge admission fees.
- When visitors are required to pay a fee, they tend to be less destructive and more respectful.

Managing staff

Paid workers

From the general human resource management body of knowledge, many authors have drawn out staffing issues specifically in the context of tourism and recreation (e.g. Edginton *et al.* 2001; Middleton 1994; Newman and Hodgetts 1998). Many of the issues associated with human resource management in the service industries in general and tourism in particular are the same or similar to those in heritage tourism (e.g. hiring, training, salary issues, dismissal), perhaps with the exception of volunteers (addressed in the following section). Thus, published resources for dealing with staffing issues in tourism are plentiful and will not be addressed in much detail here. This section, however, does examine some of the problems and issues that are particularly relevant to heritage site staff.
Swarbrooke (1995: 227–8) identified several problems that attraction managers face in human resource management in the private and public sectors.

Private

- Seasonality of demand, which is less significant in the heritage context than other areas of tourism, means that much labour is temporary and casual. This can result in lower levels of commitment on the part of members of staff and leaves little time for training.

- High turnover rates are generally a result of relatively low pay, long hours and the monotonous nature of some jobs. While other types of tourist attractions (e.g. amusement parks) might experience this more noticeably, it is still the case to some degree at heritage sites.

- In most of the developed world, tourism-related jobs have a relatively poor status. This can make it difficult to hire and retain good staff.

- Lack of career structures can result in a lack of opportunities for diligent and highly motivated staff.

- Heritage tourism jobs are time and effort intensive. They are unusually demanding and staff members are expected to be service oriented and cheerful at all times. Finding people who can perform well in this stressful environment is not easy.

- A lack of management expertise is another problem facing heritage managers. Very often, as a result of budget limitations, museum curators or site conservationists are expected to fill managerial shoes that are beyond their areas of expertise. Relatively few curators or interpretation specialists also have extensive training in areas like staff recruitment, marketing, budgeting and general operations management. Likewise, managers specialising in common managerial trends may have little understanding of conservation, interpretation and impact management.

- In tourism there is a lack of widely recognised qualifications, training certifications and standardised competencies in tourism in general, although this is changing in the realm of heritage as some universities and technical schools are beginning to offer certifications in museology, curatorship, heritage resource conservation and cultural heritage studies.

Public

- Low turnover rates are common in the public sector. This means that with tight budgets and fewer opportunities for creating new positions, fewer people with new experiences and creativity can be brought in.
- Public sector working practices are usually quite inflexible. This is not always compatible with operating in the tourism industry, such as not being open on Sundays.
- Public sector wages are often fixed in clearly defined levels based on time served rather than by performance.

- Recruitment procedures and disciplinary actions are standardised and not developed with heritage attractions in mind, which may result in their being inappropriate to the specific situation.

Retaining high-quality paid staff is an important management task. This can be done by ensuring that new employees are well established in the organisation and that they understand clearly the nature of their positions. Providing good motivations or incentives, such as financial rewards, public recognition or additional training, will also go a long way in making the heritage attraction a better place to work. Periodical staff evaluations are important, for this will allow managers to gauge individual work performance and make disciplinary corrections if necessary or offer rewards when they are deserved. Staff members may have to be trained in specific and multiple tasks, such as crowd control, repairs to artefacts, interpretation and conservation measures if this is not a part of their backgrounds.

Volunteers

Volunteers play a critical role in the tourism industry, especially at visitor information centres and tourist attractions. Likewise, in the context of heritage, volunteers are fundamentally crucial to the viable operation of historic sites, as they usually work at two levels: on the board of directors and at the operational level (Jago and Deery 2001). Without volunteers, non-profit sector attractions would hardly exist, and many public sector sites also benefit a great deal from volunteer workers. This section is less applicable to the private sector, although some cases might exist where services are offered free of charge by volunteer workers.

Recruiting volunteers is an important task, for there are certain characteristics, behaviours and attributes that will contribute to the success or failure of a heritage project, place or programme. There is a widespread and erroneous view among heritage managers that nobody should be passed up because they cannot afford to be too choosy. In the words of Jago and Deery (2001: 205), this attitude

> greatly increases the likelihood of taking on volunteers who are totally unsuitable for the organization and the tasks at hand. This approach also adds to the view of many that voluntary programmes do not work. It is critical to the success of voluntary programmes that the recruitment function of volunteers is conducted in the same rigorous manner as occurs in many organizations for the recruitment of candidates for paid positions.

Different sources of volunteer workers can have different effects as well. Some people's volunteer activities simply reflect an extension of their employment activities or hobbies, which will allow them to bring in existing knowledge and skills for the good of the heritage attraction. Other volunteers, while highly valuable, may have to be trained in several areas in order to function effectively.

Government agencies are an important source of volunteers. There are public agencies in North America and Europe whose singular purpose is to recruit and refer volunteers to programmes they have an interest in. Such public bureaux are valuable resources for they serve the non-profit sector and the volunteers themselves through lobbying, research, communication, training, developing skills and information sharing. The Voluntary Action Centers (VAC), also known as Volunteer Bureau in the United States, operates hundreds of volunteer distribution centres throughout the country. VAC offers its volunteer recruitment services to museums and other similar heritage locations. In addition many state governments have offices dealing specifically with volunteerism (Butcher-Younghans 1993: 228). Other examples of these organisations include the Association for Volunteer Administration, American Association of Museum Volunteers, National Volunteer Center, Nonprofit Management Association and Retired Senior Volunteers.

Corporate programmes for retired employees are another useful source of volunteer labour. Many companies offer volunteer services through their corporate programme for the retired, matching former employees with appropriate volunteer positions in the community. Butcher-Younghans (1993: 228) offers an example of Honeywell, Inc., a large corporation based in Minnesota, which offers such a programme. The service is staffed by former Honeywell employees and is able to tap into a wide range of expertise. They have long provided museums, historic houses and other such sites with retired people skilled in areas like photography, lighting, office work and management consulting. In this company, requests for volunteers are recorded on a computer database that matches qualified retired people to volunteer needs.

Universities and colleges are also important sources of volunteers. Internships in museums and park properties are quite common. These provide students with a challenging environment that gives them opportunities to earn academic credits while gaining practical experience. Interns are generally involved in activities like researching collections or assisting in registering, storing, inventorying and categorising relics and records. Since they are usually attempting to obtain a well-rounded and comprehensive experience, interns can also help to plan and prepare exhibits by researching and writing labels and assisting in brochure and website design. Curators have the right to restrict applicants to students with a background in history, ethnic/cultural studies, environmental studies, resource management, museology and other related fields. For students to receive university credit for their experience, internships should include a written agreement between site management, the student and the academic institution (Butcher-Younghans 1993: 229).

Other community groups can also become valuable sources of volunteers. Church groups, youth organisations (e.g. boy and girl scouts), and school-based associations can provide valuable assistance on a short-term basis. Somewhat still unusual, but ever more commonplace, is putting tourists themselves to work as volunteers. One recent growth area in tourism is volunteer vacations or volunteer tourism, where people travel in search of meaningful experiences that can assist in making the world a better place to live (Singh and Singh 2001; Wearing 2001). Physicians and dentists travelling to less developed parts of the world on a short-term basis to provide free medical and dental assistance to people who could not otherwise afford it is a good example. In the context of heritage, tourists sometimes assist in archaeological digs and restoration projects. Such experiences give travellers an opportunity to get away from home, to change their routines and to contribute altruistically to a good cause.

The careful selection of volunteer workers is vital for successful operations. Although it is unlikely that the selection of a volunteer will be as formal as that for a paid member of staff, there should still be a structured process with interviews and an evaluation of selective criteria. Bad volunteers can ruin a place, an interpretive programme or a visitor's experience (Jago and Deery 2001). Good personality, cheerful disposition, creativity, an understanding of events and peoples related to the site, good communications skills and diligent work habits are characteristics that make good-quality volunteers.

Researchers have identified several motives that drive people's willingness to volunteer (Table 5.4). These range from somewhat selfish reasons at one end

Table 5.4 Motives for volunteers at heritage attractions

Altruism – People volunteering because they feel they want to do something to improve the world around them

Self-fulfilment – People get some kind of personal fulfilment, happiness, or self-development out of giving of themselves in this manner to a cause they believe in

Social interaction – This is led by a desire to meet and interact with people and make new friends. It is also seen as a useful way of integrating into a new community and getting to know other people with similar interests

Skill development – Many people see volunteering as an opportunity to polish their skills and improve their level of marketability. Skills such as computer programming, writing, researching and building are usable beyond the scope of the historic site

Academic credit – Student interns may be motivated in part by the need to fulfil a certain number of academic credits before a degree can be awarded

Social status – To work in certain attractions or with certain well-known scholars and curators might improve one's visibility and social status within a particular circle of people

Interest in history/nature – Some people desire to work in a setting that they find intellectually stimulating because of their interests in history and nature

Spare time filler – It is not uncommon for retired persons and people on disability pensions who might have significant amounts of free time to fill their time and add diversity to everyday life by working as volunteers

Self-esteem – For some people, volunteering may provide a sense of authority or allow them to be recognised for doing something good

To get in – It might be important to get one's foot in the door in case a paid position becomes available later on

Source: After Butcher-Younghans (1993), Jago and Deery (2001) and Pearce (1993).

of the spectrum to completely selfless, altruistic reasons at the other (Pearce 1993). Regardless, it is important for managers to understand volunteers' motives, as this will assist them in recruiting, selecting, maintaining and rewarding volunteer staff and can help them understand different performance levels and willingness to perform certain tasks.

Regardless of the reasons people choose to volunteer at heritage places, it is important to remember never to view them as sources of cheap labour. Their roles should be clearly defined and their responsibilities clearly outlined. This will create an environment of order and give volunteers a sense of purpose and direction with the organisation (Butcher-Younghans 1993). This can be helped by assigning one individual responsibility over volunteer staff. This enables quality control and helps identify volunteers that are more committed to the cause and who might benefit most from additional training (Jago and Deery 2001).

It is important to reward all employees (including volunteers) for hard work and high-quality service. Rewards, recognition and positive feedback create high levels of morale and maintain a work environment that is conducive to continued hard work and successful co-operation. While volunteers do not seek financial rewards, they usually appreciate some kind of recognition. Surprisingly, relatively few heritage visitor attractions have any type of volunteer recognition system in place (Jago and Deery 2001).

Butcher-Younghans (1993: 232) suggests several ways of rewarding volunteer staff that have found considerable success at heritage visitor attractions. These include annual banquets/celebrations, profiles in museum newsletters, discounts at the museum store, plaques and certificates of award, free parking, desk space, daily refreshments, complimentary tickets to exhibitions and special events, free museum membership and letters of recommendation. More subtle recognitions can also be offered, such as counting their opinions in management decisions, using their skills, recognising their work in media releases, keeping them informed about developments, providing social functions on their behalf, giving them discounts and free entry for families (Jago and Deery 2001: 214). Such recognitions and awards strengthen volunteer camaraderie, and even the most subtle forms of recognition can be most satisfying for volunteers. These simple and quite inexpensive measures will allow managers to demonstrate their appreciation for the time and efforts donated by their unpaid assistants.

Managing visitors

Most traditional views of heritage management have focused on the supply, or the resource itself. Perhaps this is because traditionally heritage managers have not wanted to recognise or deal with tourists, and indeed many adopted (consciously or not) a 'leave us alone' view that only considered tourists in their role as a necessary evil (Hooper-Greenhill 1988; Pearson and Sullivan 1995). The situation has changed somewhat, however, during the past three decades as it has become clear that visitors (i.e. the public) in some way own the heritage; therefore, they have a right to see and experience it, and the existence of natural and cultural conservation is dependent on how they feel about them (Knudson *et al*. 1995: 104). As a consequence, as tourism, and heritage tourism in particular, is booming, heritage managers can no longer ignore the quandaries of tourists and their impacts. Indeed, observers have begun arguing for the need for heritage management to consider seriously both the resource and the visitor experience (Hall and McArthur 1993a; McArthur and Hall 1993c; Middleton 1994) and have even gone so far as to argue that tourists should be valued guests. 'The idea that museums might value, or even cherish, their visitors and their user groups is a new one, although increasingly curators will be adopting this point of view' (Hooper-Greenhill 1988: 215).

The goals of sustainable heritage management, therefore, should be twofold: to maximise visitors' appreciation and enjoyment of heritage places and to minimise the negative effects described in Chapter 4 (Glasson *et al*. 1995; McArthur and Hall 1993c; Pearson and Sullivan 1995). Implicit in this argument is the concept of carrying capacity, which emerged from research in the field of wildlife management where it was discussed in terms of the maximum number of grazing animals that could be maintained on a site without causing damage to their food supply or the soil. The concept was borrowed and adapted by outdoor recreation specialists in the early 1960s to determine the maximum number of people who could use a recreation area without 'destroying its essential qualities' (Glasson *et al*. 1995: 44). Since then it has been extended into the realm of tourism not to mean how many tourists will fit into a given area, but instead a threshold or limit (number of people) that when crossed will begin to result in negative effects in terms of both the physical environment (ecological capacity) and visitor experiences (social capacity) (Lindberg *et al*. 1997; McIntyre 1993). In tourist-historic cities, the main consideration is concentration of visitors in specific areas at certain times.

> While a narrow medieval street may have the physical capacity to accommodate a given number of persons, the valued image and context of a medieval quarter are lost once it is overcrowded. Acceptance of capacity, however, is all too often left to 'saturation', at which point there is overcrowding and a place starts losing its attractiveness, its deterioration in value leading to a subsequent decline (Orbaşli 2000: 164).

Good examples of this can be found throughout Rome, Italy. For instance, the Spanish Steps, one of the city's most popular tourist attractions, are a beautiful part of the city's historic urban milieu; however, during busy times of the year and week, the steps and surrounding areas are so crowded with people that they cannot be climbed or even seen from the base. This certainly affects some people's experiences, as the authors have observed, for they commonly 'give up' and move on to the next location without ever having experienced the Spanish Steps. The Trevi Fountain and other important sites in Rome face similar problems. These conditions cause wear and tear and graffiti to become major pressures at these sites during periods of dense traffic.

Carrying capacity goes beyond mere visitor crowds, for the number of shops, hotels and other services can also become excessive. 'A balance must be retained with the size and character of the place and oversupply avoided, both of which will lead to the cheapening of the place and the quality of the environment being compromised' (Orbaşli 2000: 164).

In the past heritage managers have attempted to define and set carrying capacities with varying degrees of success. Universal success is difficult because there is no defined formula for calculating carrying capacity in a living environment, and maintaining set targets is very difficult (Page 1995a). This is especially so owing to the fact that carrying capacity is not simply a number, but also involves the variables of season, space, culture and nature (Orbaşli 2000). Thus, capacities are not absolute, and there is no universal formula for measuring them. Rather, each location is unique and has a different threshold, or level of tolerance for use, from that of other places, depending on many variables, not least of which is physical or cultural resilience. These complications have led some scholars to conclude that the notion of carrying capacity is erroneous and flawed (Lindberg et al. 1997; Wall 1982). Wall (1982) argued that any established criteria for measuring carrying capacity will be purely subjective because every location on the earth is different, and even at one specific site, what might be unsatisfactory conditions to one visitor might be satisfactory to someone else (Lindberg et al. 1997). Thus, there are critical questions about the measurement of carrying capacity or setting acceptable limits that have yet to be resolved. Despite the doubts about the utility of carrying capacity, what is clear is that there is a need to manage the risks of tourism by managing the tourists themselves well. As the next section demonstrates, there has been considerable work in developing management frameworks and procedures that have addressed the issue of carrying capacity and imposing limits, but which have also capitalised on maximising opportunities within regions.

Visitor management procedures and frameworks

Over the last three decades a number of management procedures have been developed with particular reference to natural heritage environments, but recently have been applied to cultural and urban contexts. In general, these frameworks have placed a focus on visitor opportunities rather than identifying specific capacity limitations, although the issues of numbers of users, quality of experience and quality of environment underlie all of them. The first, and most widely adopted, framework was the recreation opportunity spectrum (ROS) by Clark and Stankey (1979), which has received much attention by academics since (see Payne and Graham 1993; Boyd and Butler 1996; Hall and McArthur 1998). The ROS incorporated relationships between setting, activities, user expectations and the role of management. The framework took a behavioural approach, defining the recreational setting as the combination of physical, biological, social and managerial attributes. It established a spectrum of recreational settings that varied from pristine wilderness to high-density urban areas. It utilised six specific attributes to define the nature of opportunities for recreation which are deemed possible within each setting: access, management, social interaction with other users, non-recreational resource uses, acceptability of impacts from visitor use and acceptable levels of control. The ROS has proved attractive to managers of natural heritage resources because it has a high degree of flexibility where opportunities are supplied by integrating the setting with visitor priorities and preferences. By incorporating the spectrum concept into management plans, specific sensitive areas can be identified and protected, and other settings more capable of withstanding heavier levels of use can be earmarked for more intensive forms of visitor use.

Since its development, ROS has been adapted to suit tourism, and then subsequently modified for specific types of tourism. Butler and Waldbrook (1991) developed the tourism opportunity spectrum (TOS) and applied it to the Canadian Arctic, using the framework to provide a background and setting against which tourism development and change could occur. The purpose of TOS was to provide a context and framework within which information and data can be examined prior to decision-making as regards the activities that should be allowed or prohibited, and the kind of facilities that should be developed. Boyd and Butler (1996) modified TOS to apply specifically to ecotourism (ECOS). Using eight factors viewed as important to ecotourism: (1) accessibility, (2) relationship between ecotourism and other resource uses, (3) attractions in a region, (4) presence of existing tourism infrastructure, (5) level of user skill and knowledge required, (6) level of social interaction, (7) degree of acceptance of impacts and control over level of use and (8) type of management needed to ensure the viability of areas on a long-term basis, managers of natural heritage regions can determine the nature of that opportunity as it applies to visitors across the spectrum from specialist and dedicated to generalist and casual ecotourists (see Figure 5.2). Other adaptations of the opportunity spectrum approach include IPCOST (indigenous peoples' cultural opportunity spectrum for tourism) developed by Sofield and Birtles (1996) and more recently UTOS (urban tourism opportunity spectrum) by Jansen-Verbeke and Lievois (1999).

Where cultural heritage tourism is concerned, the IPCOST model has relevance for managers. The framework consists of three phases. Phase 1 identifies characteristics of indigenous communities around the themes of community (structure, cohesion, decision-making and conflict resolution, self-reliance, interaction and attitudes to change), resources (land and sea, relationship with the land, retention of culture, and people), and business (skills, communications, tourism industry experience and capital). Community characteristics

| | Ecotourism spectrum |
| | ....Eco-specialist........Intermediate........Eco-generalist |

ACCESS

(i) Difficulty

arduous and hard..................
.....difficult and vigorous......
moderate and easy...

(ii) Access system

Transportation

waterways, trails........................
......aircraft (float planes)......................
...............roads (loose surface)...............
...............roads (logging)...........................
.......roads (paved)...........................

Marketplace

personal experience............................
friends
local tourism.................................
operators (camps and outposts)
travel companies...........

Information channels

word of mouth.........................
advertisements (local tourism brochures)
.............travel company tours.......

(iii) Means of conveyance

Transportation

foot, canoes, horses......................
motorised vehicles.............................

OTHER RESOURCE-RELATED ACTIVITIES

(i) Relationship

incompatible..........
......depends on nature and extent......
...........compatible on a larger scale

ATTRACTIONS OFFERED

more oriented to natural environment..........
focus on cultural and urban aspects.........

EXISTING INFRASTRUCTURE

(i) Extent

no development
development only in.......
isolated areas
moderate development........

(ii) Visibility

none...........
......primarily natural......................
........obvious changes..........

(iii) Complexity

not complex.................
level of complexity increasing.........................

(iv) Facilities

none..........
search and rescue........
rustic accommodation
(camps and outposts)
some comforts..........
(lodges)
.......many comforts
(hotels and cottages)

Figure 5.2 Ecotourism opportunity spectrum (ECOS)　　　　　　　(cont'd)
Source: Boyd and Butler (1996).

SOCIAL INTERACTION

(i)	Other ecotourists	avoid or little contact..........
		some contact.........
		(travel in small groups)
		frequent contact..........
		(travel in large groups)
(ii)	Hosts (local population)	little contact....................
		some interpretation.............
		and use of basic services
		frequent contact............
		services and source for
		handicrafts

LEVEL OF SKILL AND
KNOWLEDGE

professional..........
and extensive
        extensive to limited.........
               minimal to..........
               no knowledge

ACCEPTANCE OF VISITOR
IMPACTS

(i)	Degree of impact	none.............
		...........low to moderate...........
		............high degree..........
(ii)	Prevalence of impact	minimal or uncommon.........
		prevalent in small areas........
		prevalent.............
(iii)	Level of control	no control............
		minimum control..........
		moderate to strict control

Figure 5.2   *(cont'd)*

are set around a development wheel, where each characteristic can be scored between 0 and 10 (see Table 5.5).

Phase 2 of IPCOST assesses cultural opportunities within communities on the basis of how much contact with tourists and degree of access by visitors to cultural elements is permitted. This exists along a spectrum from no contact and a close environment to direct and open interaction for mass tourists. The specific grades along the spectrum are as follows:

- no contact;
- controlled access;
- indirect participation;
- passive contact;
- embryonic direct contact;
- occasional, organised activities;
- seasonally determined activities;
- more active involvement;

Table 5.5 Range of options regarding characteristics of indigenous communities

Characteristic	Continuum score	
	Nil	**10**
Community		
Structure	Closed	Open
Cohesion	Fragmented/individualistic	Solidarity/unity
Decision-making	Autocratic	Democratic
Self-reliance	Dependency	Autonomy
Interaction	Indirect	Direct
Attitudes to change	Conservative	Innovative
Resources		
Land and sea	No territory	Ownership
Relationship with the land	Lost	Alive
Retention of cultural resources	De-acculturation	Dynamic culture
People resources	Inadequate	Strong
Business		
Business skills	Lack of skills	Possess skills
Communications	Poor ability	Good ability
Tourism industry experience	No experience	Experience
Capital	No capital	Capital

Source: Adapted from Sofield and Birtles (1996).

- interactive opportunities (day trip only);
- interactive opportunities (longer term);
- total cultural immersion experiences (Sofield and Birtles 1996: 426–7).

Building on the previous phases, the third and final phase uses a range of existing tourism models and variables to allow managers to assess the sustainability of cultural opportunities for tourism development. These include Butler's (1980) tourism area life cycle and principles such as authenticity, carrying capacity, accessibility and employment variables.

As a framework IPCOST has utility for both managers and community members as it can:

- provide tools for a community to carry out its own assessment of its capacity to undertake development generally;
- help to catalogue culture in terms of potential opportunities for tourism ventures;
- help in reaching decisions on whether appropriate resources for cultural tourism are present in a region;
- help in deciding whether a community should venture into cultural tourism;
- enable decisions on which options represent the best opportunities, given cultural and social values and economic considerations (Sofield and Birtles 1996: 419).

With respect to the urban tourism opportunity spectrum (UTOS), Jansen-Verbeke and Lievois (1999) see the potential of developing opportunity sets to integrate tourism better, both spatially and functionally, into the urban system. Opportunity is defined in a more restricted way of having accessibility to core elements of the cultural tourism product (e.g. heritage buildings, museums, events, festivals) as well as secondary elements that add value to the tourist experience (e.g. restaurants, shops, street markets). Six specific factors play a role in the development of the UTOS. These are:

- accessibility to and within the destination area;
- the possibility of choosing from a wide range of activities and meeting a diversity of preferences;
- the combination of activities within a specific time–space budget;
- the spatial arrangement of interesting places (e.g. networks, trails);
- the functional synergy between urban facilities;
- the interaction between activities (Jansen-Verbeke and Lievois 1999: 99).

Within a pilot study of the historic city of Leuven, Belgium, development models of UTOS brought out the importance of clustering of complementary tourist products, synergy and the multifunctionality of tourism combined with other urban functions, as well as the potential of themed trails and capitalising on intervening opportunities. What lies behind these development models is assessing 'the role of heritage clusters in the development of an attractive spectrum for different types of tourists' (Jansen-Verbeke and Lievois 1999: 99).

In the above spectra, the emphasis is on opportunities. However, it is also important to balance this with the effects of visitor use on the resource base, and approaches to managing both the resources and the visitor. While managers may want to provide the greatest opportunity to visitors, at times they will have to set maximum limits of use (Butler 1996). One attempt to solve some of the problems of identifying maximum use levels was the limits of acceptable change (LAC) approach, proposed by Stankey et al. (1985). This concept accepted that, as the solutions to the issues of carrying capacity were likely to be found and instituted by resource managers, a process to assist them in identifying acceptable use levels was required. The LAC concept places an emphasis on positive planning and management pre-empting inappropriate or overuse, thus avoiding the need for remedial or after-the-fact management actions. However, it places a considerable responsibility on managers, with no guarantees that managerial values and decisions will be in line with use preferences, particularly as both of these elements are dynamic (Payne and Graham 1993).

Several other management concepts that have relevance to management of natural heritage places include the visitor activity management process (VAMP) (Graham et al. 1988), the visitor impact management process (VIMP) (Graefe 1990) and visitor experience and resource protection (VERP) (Vaske et al. 2000). VAMP was developed by the Canadian Parks Service (CPS) for use in national parks, and is incorporated into the CPS natural resources

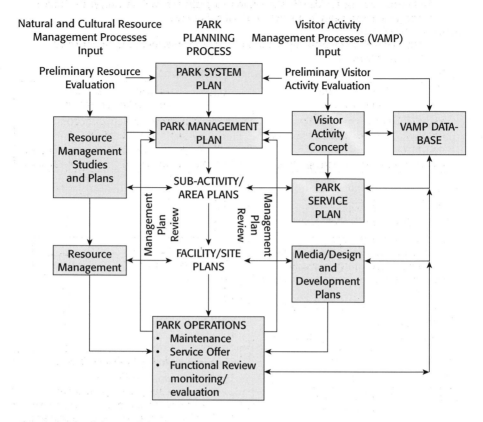

Figure 5.3   Visitor activity management process (VAMP)
Source: Payne and Graham (1993).

management planning process (Figure 5.3). It is aimed at producing management decisions that are based on both ecological data and social information, and is, in reality, a generic planning model, incorporating objectives, terms of reference, analysis of data, options, recommendations and implementation. Its counterpart, VIMP, was developed for use within the US national parks, with the aim of reducing or controlling negative effects of use (see Figure 5.4). It focuses on identifying problems and unsuitable conditions, on identifying likely causal factors resulting in undesired impacts, and on identification of management strategies for mitigating or preventing unacceptable impacts. It has proved reasonably effective as a management strategy where a system of control, data collection and analysis and management is in place. VERP has several basic elements. First, it stresses managerial responsibility not to create experiences, but create opportunities for experiences. Second, like VIMP and LAC, it provides managers with indicator variables and standards to match appropriate conditions for particular types of experience. Third, actions are linked with standards, either by managers employing strategies like technical fix, education, regulation or imposing use limits. Finally, the VERP process

BASIC APPROACH:
  Systematic process for identification of impact problems, their causes, and effective management strategies for reduction of visitor impacts.
CONDITIONS FOR USE:
  Integrated with other planning frameworks or as management tool for localised impact problems.

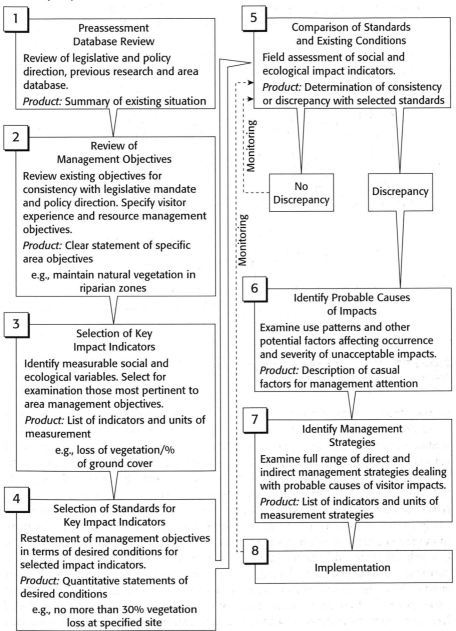

1 Preassessment Database Review

Review of legislative and policy direction, previous research and area database.

Product: Summary of existing situation

2 Review of Management Objectives

Review existing objectives for consistency with legislative mandate and policy direction. Specify visitor experience and resource management objectives.

Product: Clear statement of specific area objectives

  e.g., maintain natural vegetation in riparian zones

3 Selection of Key Impact Indicators

Identify measurable social and ecological variables. Select for examination those most pertinent to area management objectives.

Product: List of indicators and units of measurement

  e.g., loss of vegetation/% of ground cover

4 Selection of Standards for Key Impact Indicators

Restatement of management objectives in terms of desired conditions for selected impact indicators.

Product: Quantitative statements of desired conditions

  e.g., no more than 30% vegetation loss at specified site

Monitoring

5 Comparison of Standards and Existing Conditions

Field assessment of social and ecological impact indicators.

Product: Determination of consistency or discrepancy with selected standards

No Discrepancy

Discrepancy

6 Identify Probable Causes of Impacts

Examine use patterns and other potential factors affecting occurrence and severity of unacceptable impacts.

Product: Description of casual factors for management attention

7 Identify Management Strategies

Examine full range of direct and indirect management strategies dealing with probable causes of visitor impacts.

Product: List of indicators and units of measurement strategies

8 Implementation

Figure 5.4 Visitor impact management process (VIMP)
Source: Graefe (1990).

involves the public and stakeholders in decision-making through adopting a collaborative approach to natural resource area management. In summary, VERP, as do LAC and VIMP, outlines the following sequential process of assessing and managing visitor impacts:

- defining appropriate experience opportunities for specific management objectives;
- identifying key impact indicators;
- setting quantitative standards for the selected impact indicators;
- inventorying and monitoring existing conditions against the standards;
- linking management actions to standards when impacts exceed standards (Vaske *et al*. 2000: 218).

Specific management tools and techniques

In contrast to visitor management frameworks, a range of specific techniques and tools are at the disposal of managers. For the most part, these deal with regulating access directly or indirectly, although visitor management must also include imaginative efforts to enhance visitor experiences, maintain a favourable reputation, and secure a high-quality environment that both residents and tourists can enjoy (Orbaşli 2000: 163). The tools and methods most commonly used to manage heritage visitors are the focus of the following subsections.

Controlling traffic, visitor flows and congestion

Some of the most notable negative impacts of tourism are directly related to the flow of traffic and crowded conditions. Crowdedness can not only ruin the resource being conserved, but it can also spoil the visitor experience. Seasonal closures can be a useful tool on an annual basis to allow the local environment to recuperate from the onslaught of visitors during the high season and let local residents recover from intense host–guest interactions (McArthur and Hall 1993c). One of the best ways to control site-specific tourist traffic is to restrict the sizes of certain groups at certain times of the day or week. Similarly, it is useful to limit large groups, say bus tours and school classes, to certain days of the week and specified periods of time. Tuesday afternoons, for example, at most locations would probably be a less harried time that could accommodate large groups better. Drawbacks to these measures include lost revenue as some groups cannot always adhere to selective schedules such as these, and the level of dissatisfaction might be high among people who could not gain entry at convenient times. Allowing groups to visit by appointment only is also catching on as a management tool in some locations (Drohan 1995).

Similarly, quota systems have been implemented at times or discussed at considerable length in various heritage cities, although physical restriction should be a last-resort approach to overcrowding (Orbaşli 2000). One quota system proposed in Venice would have charged a fee to enter the historic districts, which would close once the permitted number of visitors was met (Fyson 1991). Efforts along these lines have been implemented on occasion with some degree of success in cities such as Venice and Prague. Orbaşli (2000: 164) argues that in the long term, restricting access can pay off as destinations become and remain comparatively unspoiled and are viewed as 'exclusive'. On a national level perhaps the best-known example of this is Bhutan, the small kingdom in the Himalayan mountains. As a means of controlling tourist traffic into the country, strict quotas are in place to allow only limited numbers of tourists to enter each year, and visitors are required to pay a significant sum of money for each day they are in the country.

Zoning and good land use planning can assist in this as well in reducing crowded conditions and negative interactions between pedestrians and motor vehicles. Pedestrianisation of historic areas has since the 1970s become a more common visitor and traffic management tool in European historic cities. This entails zoning changes to prohibit vehicular traffic in specified areas of the city and land use planning to provide pedestrian malls (Plate 5.1). The primary aims of this are to reduce the impacts of vehicular traffic on significant

Plate 5.1 Pedestrian mall, Stockholm

buildings and historic areas (Slater 1984) and to provide enjoyable and safer environments for tourists. Some pedestrian zone regulations are a compromise where vehicular access is permitted in the early morning and late evening hours. Despite some problems related to access and parking, in most cases shopkeepers and heritage managers view pedestrian-only zones as being good for 'business' (Orbaşli 2000). According to Orbaşli (2000), urban pedestrian zones need to be well designed to provide optimum enjoyment among historic quarter visitors. Building fronts, shops, variety, signage, street furniture, parks, the types of surface material to be used (e.g. cobblestones) and information booths can all contribute to the visitors' enjoyment of the pedestrian area.

Heritage managers can also limit masses of tourism by directing tourists' attention away from critical locations. The principle of dispersion is useful in this regard (Page 1992). For example, in France, managers at Chartres Cathedral have long encouraged tourists to recognise the cultural and historic value of the entire city and region, not just the cathedral itself. Their hope is that the cathedral will be viewed as part of a whole historic community rather than a wonder in itself and that people will decide to spend less time at the cathedral itself and more time exploring other parts of town. Similarly, Versailles introduced a project in the early 1990s, which aims to integrate the chateau into the broader context of the historic community. According to site managers, this should help to alleviate some of the physical pressures on the properties by dispersing the concentration of tourists at one specific site (*Culture Plus* 1992).

Similarly, community-wide, traffic congestion in central urban areas can be reduced by routeing vehicles in a pattern that will avoid the town centre. Enacting and enforcing lower speed limits can calm the traffic situation, as can establishing park-and-ride programmes and facilities at the edges of historic cities, and creating efficient and user-friendly urban transport systems (e.g. light rails and shuttle buses) (Page 1992).

Limiting contact between visitors and artefacts

There are several ways managers can limit physical contact between historic artefacts and tourists. Perhaps one of the most widespread measures is roping off sensitive areas. In historic houses and museums, ropes and chains are widely used to keep people from wandering into places that might be harmed by large numbers of visits (Plate 5.2). An antique rocking chair, for example, can be made off limits by placing a rope across the seat or setting it behind the rope line. Covering artefacts with plastic or glass also prevents people from touching fragile relics. Such coverings require regular maintenance throughout the day to keep the surfaces free of fingerprints. Video cameras can also be effective tools for deterring people from touching or vandalising artefacts. Not only is evidence provided in case it does happen, but people will be less inclined to do it if they feel they are being watched. Itinerant or stationary staff members can have the same effect. It is common for European museums and historic sites to require the use of overshoes on visitors to minimise the effects of shoes

Plate 5.2   Ancient cauldrons protected from tourists in Beijing's Forbidden City

on floorboards and other walking surfaces. Thousands of shoes can do serious damage to original wood, marble and carpet floors, with their accompanying small particles of stones, sand and dust. Overshoes provide protection and reduce cleaning costs. In the past, these kinds of visitor controls have found various degrees of success in many of England's historic buildings (English Tourist Board 1979).

Fees and pricing

Many observers have commented that initiating entrance fees can be effective in reducing visitor numbers. While this has some negative implications, as described earlier (e.g. excluding some segments of society), pricing is still used widely as a management mechanism. It is seen as a means of controlling demand (Robinson *et al.* 1994). Westminster Abbey (UK) uses entrance fees to manage visitation:

> To ward off the ravages of 900 years of visitors, Westminster Abbey has introduced this measure in an attempt to reduce the impact on the fabric of the building of nearly three million visitors a year. The dean . . . defended the measures as essential both to restoring the calm of the abbey as a place of prayer, and as a protection against environmental degradation (Fyall and Garrod 1998: 226).

There is a seasonal element as well. Admission charges can be used as a tool for decreasing overcrowding during the busiest times of the day, week or year. Raising fees during busy periods and lowering them during slow times can achieve a steadier and more balanced flow of visitors (Fyall and Garrod 1998).

Despite the suggestion that the pricing of fees can be used to manage visitor flows, several studies demonstrate that this may not always be the case. Most findings confirm that most of the time, visits to heritage attractions are quite price inelastic, which means that even when prices rise, demand remains reasonably unaffected (Fyall and Garrod 1998; Moscardo 2000; Prentice 1989a). This might be because the total benefits associated with visiting an important site are worth more to visitors than just the amount charged for entrance fees. Powe and Willis (1996) estimated that the total benefits provided by the Warkworth Castle heritage site were estimated to be nearly three times the financial revenue derived from entrance charges. This suggests that there may be a willingness to pay for concept associated with visiting heritage that has not been well researched and utilised by heritage managers. Nonetheless, as the Taj Mahal example provided earlier demonstrates, pricing is still considered a useful management tool.

Providing a way for visitors to leave their mark

One line of thinking suggests that if visitors are provided with a place to 'leave their mark', they will be less inclined to scribble graffiti on, or vandalise, heritage sites (Pearson and Sullivan 1995). Guest books, for example, allow individuals to write comments and feelings, and they provide a medium (instead of a wall or gravestone) where tourists can inform the world of their visit. Similarly, Pearson and Sullivan (1995) suggest that providing merchandise that people can take with them (e.g. high-quality souvenirs and books) will not only enhance the experience, but might also prevent unwanted 'souvenir hunting' behaviours by fulfilling their need to take a piece of the place home.

Providing high-quality experiences

Even if the primary goal of a site is resource conservation, it is important to remember that tourism is also involved, and tourism is a service industry. Research has shown that good visitor service can increase the likelihood that people will enjoy themselves more, which can lead to more respect for the site and less contention. 'Visitors' attitudes to the heritage place are undoubtedly coloured by the level and type of attention they receive. A pleasant, helpful reception is a good insurance against direct damage' (Pearson and Sullivan 1995: 284). Similarly, 'high-quality experiences which satisfy visitors' expectations, motivations, and needs . . . can modify and influence the behaviour of visitors in such a way as to ensure that the values of the heritage resource are maintained' (Hall and McArthur 1993a: 13). Knudson et al. (1995: 104–5) suggest some helpful suggestions for creating a quality visitor experience:

- Provide good service. Service is not a special favour to visitors, it is an essential part of the work of heritage management and employees.

- Be receptive. Being friendly, encouraging and giving visitors individual attention will make their visit a good experience.
- Be helpful. Staff should take the time to help find answers.
- Be accurate. Staff should be able to use maps and brochures effectively.
- Be informed. Knowing the maps and brochures well and knowing answers to common questions and management techniques will help create an enjoyable environment.

Another way of heightening the visitor experience is by keeping the facilities clean and tidy. Clean restrooms, good quality displays, tidy landscapes and orderly communities help create satisfied customers. Parkin *et al.* (1989) suggested that communities surrounding and adjacent to historic sites should be maintained in an attractive manner, since visitors often have to travel through town to arrive at their intended destination. Thus, perceptions of the surrounding community can affect attitudes about the entire experience. They suggest that it is in the best interest of heritage managers, business people and community members that the drive through town be as attractive and pleasant as possible. Improvements like clean pavements, tree-lined streets, hanging baskets, attractive street furniture and good, clear road signs provide a high-quality sense of arrival:

> If the town is itself attractive and welcoming then visitors are likely to stay longer to enjoy the streets, shops, churches, and museums, and not just the castle. By staying longer visitors will spend more, thereby bringing economic benefit to the town and its people, creating jobs, raising incomes and the general standard of living. It is therefore important to consider a heritage attraction in its wider context (Parkin *et al.* 1989: 109).

Creating a quality environment is a challenging job for heritage managers, but ultimately it is up to the tourists to produce their own beneficial experiences (McIntosh 1999).

Heritage staff might want to consider actions that will reduce the effects of boredom and other sources of irritation. Some sites have found success in providing costumed musicians and other entertainers to perform for visitors queuing to enter a building. Likewise, queues might be directed so that people will stand in the shade as much as possible (McCaskey 1975). Offering inexpensive refreshments might also boost visitors' level of tolerance if waiting lines are too long.

Special considerations for certain groups of visitors, such as people with disabilities and families with small children, can also help raise satisfaction levels. Adapted interpretive programmes for people with disabilities and providing easy access, where possible, will go a long way to appeal to a large group of potential visitors. Likewise providing special changing and nursing lounges will help families with babies have a much better experience. These issues will be discussed in greater depth in the next chapter within the context of interpretation.

Knowing what visitors remember most from their visits can be a valuable way of knowing how best to create pleasant experiences for them. From their

Table 5.6 What visitors remember most from heritage site visits

Activities – picnics, trails, walking, riding. People tend to remember well the activities they undertook

Companions – parents, colleagues, friends, spouses. People remember whom they were with and the people they met

Information – they remember concrete facts and new information they learned (e.g. who the inhabitants were, what kinds of beds they had, and dates when things were built)

Built environment – types of buildings, old town, general store, schools, artefacts, the buildings' appearances and condition

Site personnel – the people they came in contact with, such as guides, good interpreters and ill-informed interpreters

Culture – ways of life depicted in the displays, cultural heritage of indigenous peoples, handicrafts, clothes and food

Nature – features of the natural environment, such as trees, shrubberies and the natural landscape

Source: After Masberg and Silverman (1996).

research, Masberg and Silverman (1996) identified seven things heritage tourists remember about their visits: activities, companions, site personnel, information, built environment, nature and culture (Table 5.6). Such knowledge can help direct managers in understanding what changes might need to be implemented.

According to a study by Fyall and Garrod (1998: 227), heritage tourists identified the following items as being critical in making their visit enjoyable and satisfying. The attraction:

- should be inexpensive;
- should be user friendly;
- should be physically and intellectually accessible to as many different visitor groups as possible;
- must be managed in a way that balances the needs of visitors with those of conservation;
- must have its integrity and authenticity maintained;
- must give visitors good value for their money.

Marketing/promotion

The most effective use of marketing and promotional efforts to manage tourists is by encouraging more of them to visit in the off season and less in the high season. Published literature and websites can extol the virtues of visiting when crowds are smaller and more personal attention can be provided.

Selective marketing also has potential to reduce impacts, as certain groups and group sizes are targeted in favour of other groups (McArthur and Hall

1993c). Promotional efforts might also de-emphasise the use of places as venues of mass tourism, such as efforts in Canterbury to play down the city's role as a day-trip destination (Page 1992). Additionally, promotional literature can be used to inform potential visitors of appropriate behaviour in fragile environments and place more stress on less vulnerable sites.

Hardening the resource

As a means of reducing the negative ecological impacts of heritage tourism, managers can harden the resource, which according to McArthur and Hall (1993c) involves activities such as surfacing access routes and walkways, and increasing the number and range of facilities (Plate 5.3). Care must be taken, though, for despite the 'best intentions and "environmentally sound" materials and techniques, hardening may compromise heritage values' (McArthur and Hall 1993c: 21). Hardening must be done in the most environmentally sensitive manner possible, and environmental aesthetics should be kept at the forefront in deciding what type of hardening to employ. Local designs and local materials provide the most ecologically sensitive format. Otherwise, problems arise when, in the name of enhancement, landscape features that are entirely alien to the local character are added, which in the words of Booth (1993: 22), is 'disregard for quality or appropriateness in the crude pursuit of quantity'. Booth (1993) proposes that landscaping and formal design in

Plate 5.3 Hardening the site at Point Pelee National Park, Canada

Plate 5.4 Litter bins on US National Parkland in Arizona, USA

historic areas should include: natural, not imitation, materials; as similar conditions to originals as possible; local detail in paving, street furniture and architecture; and a limitation on the range of building materials. Good examples of this can be found at the Arctic Circle crossing just north of Rovaniemi, Finland, where bus stops and litterbins are made of wood and are built in traditional design. The United States national parks provide a further example, as the National Parks Service has done a good job of fitting parking lot pavement, walkways and waste stations in with local environmental conditions (Plate 5.4).

Interpretation

Interpretation is an education-based activity that reveals meanings behind historic sites, their people and their stories. It takes several forms, including displays and exhibits, printed brochures and maps, signs, audio presentations and guided tours. These will all be discussed in greater detail in Chapter 6, so they are not covered here in depth. Interpretation, like marketing, has the ability to direct people away from sensitive areas and educate them about the need to behave respectfully (Shackley 1998a). Brochures and guidebooks can be designed to emphasise other attractions and de-emphasise the most delicate artefacts. Interpretive signs that warn of penalties have been effective, but they are most effective when mixed with softer interpretive signs. It is important to inform visitors that particular activities, such as touching delicate surfaces or antique furniture, which they might not normally consider unacceptable behaviour, are not permitted, but it is important to let them know why it is not allowed (Pearson and Sullivan 1995: 285).

Creating mindful visitors

Many of these approaches to visitor management come together with other associations to create what Moscardo (1996, 1999, 2000) calls 'mindful visitors'. Based on the psychological work of Langer (1989), Moscardo has explored this concept in considerable depth in the context of tourism and tourist attractions. Moscardo's expansion of this concept forms the foundation of this section.

When people are mindful they pay more attention to the world around them. It is a state of being receptive and learning and seeing the world from various perspectives. Langer's (1989) research shows that it is also linked to better decision-making, better health and higher levels of self-esteem (Moscardo 2000). In the context of heritage, when visitors are mindful, they are more sensitive to context, they process historical information more actively and they have better personal control of various situations, resulting in a greater understanding of, and appreciation for, the past (McIntosh 1999; Moscardo 1996). Mindless visitors are less able to learn new information and change their perspectives (Moscardo 1999, 2000). Table 5.7 demonstrates the key characteristics of mindfulness and mindlessness.

Table 5.7   Key qualities of mindfulness and mindlessness

Mindfulness	Mindlessness
Main features	*Main features*
Receptive to learning	Use of existing routines
Awareness of the setting	Little attention to the setting
Development of new routines	Use of existing routines
Conditions	*Conditions*
New and different settings	Familiar settings
Control and choice	Little control, few choices
Different and changing situations	Recurring situations
Personal significance	No personal relevance
Outcomes	*Outcomes*
Feelings of control	Feelings of helplessness
Feelings of achievement	Feelings of incompetence
Feelings of fulfilment	Feelings of dissatisfaction
Ability to deal with problems	Limited capability to handle problems
Learning and recall	No learning, poor recall

Source: After Moscardo (1999: 25).

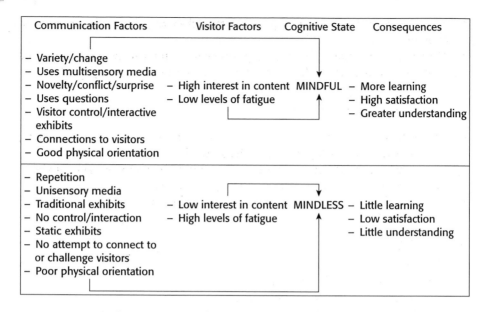

Figure 5.5   Communication and mindfulness model
Source: After Moscardo (1996).

Figure 5.5 describes the factors involved in creating mindful and mindless visitors and the role of heritage site communications in doing so. The model demonstrates that two sets of issues influence visitors: communication and visitor factors. Communication factors refer to the features of the communication or interpretation offered. Visitor factors are things that visitors bring with them to the attraction. These two sets of factors combine to determine whether a visitor will be mindful or mindless (Moscardo 1999: 26).

Moscardo's (1999) book outlines five things that tourist attraction managers and staff can do to encourage mindfulness and communicate effectively with visitors. These are:

1. help visitors find their way around;
2. make connections to visitors and involve them;
3. offer variety;
4. tell a good story that makes sense;
5. know and respect visitors.

Each of these is highlighted in more detail below.

Help visitors find their way around

- Make paths simpler and places easier to recognise.
- Develop a comprehensive orientation system. Use an assortment of devices (i.e. maps and signs) and consider how they balance each other.

- Make sure that maps are aligned so that they match the perspective of tourists.
- Design effective maps, highlighting important sites and using a variety of symbols and colours with not too much information (Moscardo 1999: 55).

Make connections to visitors

- Make personal connections by engaging tourists in conversation, using analogies from everyday life, and telling stories they can relate to.
- Allow visitors some degree of control by giving them choices, asking about their interests and encouraging them to participate.
- Use activities that involve many senses (Moscardo 1999: 71).

Offer variety

- Use a variety of senses.
- Provide diverse social experiences.
- Require different levels of physical activity.
- Provide activities that require different levels of mental activity.
- Involve a diversity of interpretive media.
- Present a variety of physical settings (Moscardo 1999: 82).

Tell a good story

- Use themes and stories to organise and present information.
- Stories need to be clear and well organised.
- Communicators must share some level of common ground with their audiences (Moscardo 1999: 94).

Know the visitors

- Find out what visitors know and understand.
- Learn what their expectations and motives are.
- Learn their characteristics and whom they like to travel with.
- Observe the visitors and how they respond to different communications efforts.
- Interview them, survey them and organise focus groups to learn more about them (Moscardo 1999: 108).

Such efforts, Moscardo (1996, 1999, 2000) argues, are worthwhile because mindful tourists will understand the consequences of their actions and be able to behave in ways that minimise their impacts on the site. 'Mindful visitors will also have a greater appreciation and understanding of a site, and such understanding can provide both support for changing their behaviors on site and for the conservation of the site' (Moscardo 1996: 393).

Mindful visitors have the power to create their own personal experience and take what makes sense to them from what is presented by the interpreters. Mindfulness can itself be encouraged by giving visitors greater power or control over the interpretation they experience. Control encourages mindfulness as it requires choices or decisions and these in turn require active information processing (Moscardo 2000: 14).

Having discussed visitor management frameworks, and special tools that can be used to manage visitors, the discussion now turns to look at the potential to create a broad sustainable framework for heritage tourism, where management is an integral component.

Sustainable heritage tourism framework

The debate around tourism and sustainability has long been discussed within the academic literature and there is no intention to repeat it (Budowski 1976; Butler 1991; Hall and Lew 1998; Mathieson and Wall 1982; McKercher 1993; Wahab and Pigram 1997). What have emerged are broad criteria that appear to be useful in understanding how tourism can be developed in line with sustainability (e.g. Butler 1999; Hall and Lew 1998; Nelson *et al.* 1993). The focus, therefore, of this section is to highlight the key principles and planning and management considerations that are relevant to heritage tourism and when combined offer managers a sustainable heritage tourism development framework. Much of the following discussion has been taken from existing work of one of the authors in which a similar type of framework was developed and applied to national park environments (Boyd 2000c). This framework is adapted to relate specifically to heritage tourism, accommodating heritage within the natural, cultural and built contexts. It should be pointed out that many elements within the framework will receive greater attention elsewhere in the book (complete chapters are devoted to principles such as interpretation and authenticity), and the purpose of naming these here is to illustrate the nature of a sustainable heritage tourism framework for managers to utilise. The framework comprises principles, planning and management considerations.

Key principles include ensuring authenticity, interpretation, access and inter- and intra-generational equity. Authenticity is central to much of heritage tourism as the product(s) on display are often re-creations of a region's past both in terms of the built and cultural landscapes. There is a need to ensure that authenticity is not staged, that it remains real, but one that will vary given the culture involved (MacCannell 1973; Craik 1995; Herbert 1995a). The issue to be raised in Chapter 7 is the extent to which authenticity matters to tourists, and how managers are creating opportunities against which experiences are being realised. This ties closely with the second principle – interpretation (Prentice 1995; Light 1995a). Much of the overall tourist experience here is comprised of learning about the past and this is often best provided through interpretation, in the form of detailed on-site literature, displays, re-enactments and guided tours to name but a few. Access differs according to the form of existing heritage tourism. In a natural heritage setting, the focus must be on controlling access to sites to ensure the safety of the tourist. Where cultural heritage tourism is concerned, access relates to the level of intrusion that is considered acceptable (Butler and Hinch 1996), the extent to which access can and should be granted, and that the privacy of certain aspects of the host culture are respected (Mercer 1994; Grekin and Milne 1996). The final principle of 'equity' implies that heritage attractions are open to all, both now and in the future. While this is both laudable and noble, often the practicalities mean that not all heritage tourism attractions are set up to be able to accommodate all sections of society, particularly the elderly, and the physically and mentally challenged. Furthermore, heritage attractions can often reflect a distorted past with emphasis on a particular history alone, which will influence who will be attracted (Tunbridge and Ashworth 1996).

With respect to planning, the ideals of long-term, integrative and conservation-focused are advanced. A long-term focus is needed if sustainability is to be realised. However, in planning heritage attractions there also needs to be consideration given to whether or not a long-term market actually exists and if certain attractions have a long-term product and experience to offer visitors. Here the nature of ownership of attractions must be taken into account, given that most public sector bodies/agencies are constrained by the short-term mandates of their political masters. Integrative planning acknowledges other uses and users within the region involved. This may include other forms of heritage tourism or tourism in general, as well as non-tourism uses. The overall aim is to promote a position where heritage tourism is viewed as being compatible with other tourism uses of the region, thereby providing diversity of attractions for the visitors. A conservation focus particularly for built attractions, has been promoted through buildings being listed as representative of selective elements of the past (Larkham 1995). With respect to natural heritage, a conservation focus requires that the ecological integrity of the attraction itself be protected against abuse and overuse. In contrast, conserving cultural heritage requires a community-based perspective, where the community that 'owns' the cultural attraction collectively decides the extent to which it is open to visitors (Murphy 1985; Prentice 1993).

Heritage tourism requires management that ensures acceptable limits of use, encourages zoning and is participatory. The issue of use limits varies according to type of heritage tourism. Where built attractions are involved, use levels can be controlled through stating a maximum party size on tours, running a set number of tours as well as stating maximum numbers permitted to ensure visitor safety and compliance with codes and regulations. Visitor levels are less easily managed for cultural and natural heritage tourism attractions and too often the evidence of impacts from overuse demonstrates that acceptable limits/numbers have been overreached. Zoning is a common and well-accepted management tool, increasingly used at many World Heritage Sites, that helps mitigate the extent of impacts occurring by restricting access to the most sensitive sites and directing visitors elsewhere (Wager 1995). In so doing, the integrity of the sites is maintained, but providing visitors access to secondary sites and attractions has altered the overall experience. Management that has a participatory element should be encouraged where the visitor is empowered to respect the sites and attractions and that management should not be solely the preserve of the managers. The fact that heritage tourists are more willing to be educated on site, where learning is a principal element of the overall visit, makes this all the more feasible.

The following case study is presented to show how these aspects may be applied at the level of individual heritage attractions (Boyd 1999).

CASE STUDY   Old Bushmills Distillery

Famous for being the world's oldest licensed distillery (operating since 1608, but with few records prior to 1704), Old Bushmills Distillery is regarded as one of the premier industrial heritage tourist attractions in Northern Ireland and a key stop within the Irish Whisky Trail (McCroskery 1997). Opening as a free tourist attraction in 1975, aided by a grant from the Northern Ireland Tourist Board for carparking, landscaping, bar and coffee shop, and the provision of an audio-visual theatre, visitor numbers have risen from 5,000 to approximately 100,000 over a 20-year period. It has only been since 1993 that visitors have had to pay for admission.

Many of the aspects within the framework are evident within the industrial heritage experience. Authenticity is demonstrated in that the original formula and method of production have not been altered; changes have only taken place in the regions that supply the raw materials. Interpretation is evident in the form of comprehensive tours by qualified guides that take visitors through all stages of production to the point of even sampling the end products. Access is appropriately restricted with visits through the distillery only possible as part of a guided tour. As for the principle of equity, the needs of foreign tourists are accommodated through multilingual guides. However, much of the tour within the distillery buildings is not wheelchair accessible, and therefore restrictive to people with physical disabilities. With regard to planning, a long-term view is in place with increased international marketing, often on the basis of recognition of brand names. Plans are developing to promote Bushmills as one stop on a specialty Malt Whisky tour, and to encourage the development of private and evening functions at the distillery. An integrative aspect to planning is present with the distillery promoted as only one attraction within the larger north coast region. So far there is not a problem of accommodating too many visitors. However, the massive rise in numbers post-1994 did take the managers by surprise. This was accommodated particularly within the summer peak season by extending the hours in which tours were provided and increasing their party size (McCroskery 1997). Restricting the general public from viewing the distillery unsupervised acts as a form of zoning and one that limits interference caused by visitors while at the same time ensures their safety. The participatory management aspect requires more attention, where the focus is not directed at visitors but rather the local community. Management is cognisant that more involvement with the local community where Bushmills is located is needed as few visitors spend money within the town itself, beyond that of accommodation. Overall, however, albeit a different type of tourist attraction, this example reflects an attraction that is being promoted on a sustainable basis.

Managing local residents

It is important to understand that local residents are a part of the tourism product; they should be treated with respect, and their concerns and ideas have to be addressed. This in theory is supposed to reduce the negative social impacts of tourism in destination communities. The notion follows that if residents are empowered to determine their own futures, they will be less inclined to criticise development efforts and have higher tolerance levels for tourists.

Many authors have advocated a community-based approach to tourism development, wherein decision-making power rests primarily in the hands of the public (Dowling 1993; Haywood 1988; Murphy 1985, 1988; Reed 1997; Scheyvens 1999; Simmons 1994; Timothy 1999c; Tosun 1999). Public participation in tourism development by the community can be seen in at least two ways: participation in decision-making and participation in the benefits of tourism (Timothy 1999b; Timothy and Tosun in press). Likewise, in conjunction with the benefits of tourism, local educational, or awareness-building, campaigns can assist in managing local communities and their resources.

Participation in decision-making

Participation in decision-making means that residents have opportunities to voice their own hopes, desires and fears for heritage tourism development and contribute to the planning process from their own expertise and experiences, thereby gaining a meaningful voice in the organisation and administration of tourism (Timothy 2002b, 1999c). In this context 'it is important for heritage managers, by every means in their power, to stay close to the "grass roots", where history is made, and remade' (Pearson and Sullivan 1995: 33). Representing a step in this direction, development specialists now see the value of indigenous knowledge and environmental management practices (Berger 1996; Boyd and Ward 1993; Cloher and Johnston 1999; Strang 1996) and argue that solutions to numerous problems in host environments can be found in the communities themselves, for in most instances, traditional societies do not see themselves as separate from nature. Indigenous systems of pastoralism, hunting and agriculture are frequently the most sustainable forms of resource management (Berger 1996; Timothy 2002b; Timothy and Tosun in press).

In terms of heritage tourism, resident involvement in planning gives communities an opportunity to voice their concern for the way(s) their heritage will be protected and demonstrated to tourists. It should allow them a say in which artefacts, buildings and places they would like to have promoted as tourism resources and which ones they would prefer to keep hidden. This can cultivate community pride and a sense of ownership of heritage and tourism (McArthur and Hall 1993b; Tabata 1989), as it helps them reclaim their own cultural history and allows them to decide how it will be portrayed to the broader society (Walker 1987: 131). This is particularly crucial in indigenous communities, as there are fewer people with each passing generation who know and understand the meanings of traditions, cultures and artefacts. It is also important among ethnic minorities, for there is a danger that dominant ethnic groups and their heritage may overpower and eventually eliminate (intentionally or unintentionally) the heritage of minorities (Boyd and Ward 1993; Caffyn and Lutz 1999).

As a means of promoting the principles of sustainable development (e.g. harmony, equity, holistic development), all stakeholders ought to be encouraged to participate in heritage tourism development. Heritage conservation advocacy groups, public agencies, business associations that might benefit from tourism's growth, and non-governmental organisations are all stakeholders that have an interest in heritage conservation and heritage tourism.

Involving residents and other stakeholders is not a simple task, but it is the most sustainable approach that can be taken. Such efforts require time, money and patience, and are sometimes arduous to co-ordinate. Moderated, open town meetings, surveys, round-table discussions and site visits for residents have all been proposed as appropriate ways of involving local communities (Gill 1996; Fitton 1996; Haywood 1988; Timothy 2002b). These participatory techniques are important in developing heritage tourism, for 'clearly, if communities do not want to be involved in tourism it is difficult and counter-productive to insist' (Fitton 1996: 169).

Participation in the benefits of tourism

The other part of participatory tourism, taking part in the benefits of tourism, means that residents should have opportunities to gain financially and in other ways from the industry's development. Community-based tourism planning should also include creating opportunities for people to own businesses, to work in industry-related employment, to receive training and to be educated about the role and effects of heritage tourism in their regions (Timothy 1999c).

Although this seems like common sense, in many parts of the world, significant sociocultural, political and economic conditions still constrain many would-be entrepreneurs from participating in tourism in this way.

Small-scale, locally owned businesses tend to have the best influences by supporting local people and minimising economic leakages to the outside (Hatton 1999; Smith 1998). Some sustainability advocates in recent years have argued that this kind of small-scale tourism will remain more financially and economically viable in the long term than rapid mass tourism development that is sometimes taken over by outside conglomerates (Mowforth and Munt 1998). As an example, Hatton (1999) describes the Huangshan Mountain region of China, which has experienced remarkable community-based tourism in recent years. While the form of government in place in China has historically precluded popular participation in tourism decision-making, strides are being made to include residents in the benefits of tourism at least. From its inception, the Huangshan tourism development initiative has benefited local residents. For instance, during its development of infrastructure, the Huangshan Mountain Scenic Development Area (HMSDA) committee actively guided and encouraged locals to construct supplementary tourist facilities, services and attractions. This has resulted in increased community incomes and regional prosperity in recent years. As part of these efforts, the HMSDA worked closely with villagers to establish a tourist attraction based on the local wildlife – monkeys. While the area has always been known for spectacular natural beauty, few tourists were attracted there until the monkey reserve was created. Now, thousands of tourists visit each year, generating millions of RMB yuan. This and other developments have had major impacts on the region. The Monkey Park created many local jobs, which brought economic stability and regular wages. Villagers have used tourism receipts to invest in educational facilities and financial aid for children who might not otherwise afford an education, and assistance to elderly and disabled residents has also been funded through the project (Hatton 1999).

The following case example of Uluru National Park, Australia, illustrates how the resident community is involved in participating in decision-making where the park is concerned, as well as participating in the benefits of tourism (Singh and Boyd in press).

CASE STUDY   Uluru National Park, Australia

Uluru (Ayers Rock) is internationally recognised as one of Australia's leading heritage attractions. Tourists are overwhelmingly motivated by the desire to see the spectacular inselberg, but they unfortunately rank learning about Aboriginal culture in the area low (Hall 2000a). Aboriginal communities take a different view and have decided to become involved in tourism, defining their relationship with tourism as having control and exercising choice (Mercer 1994). They have representation on the management board that administers the park, and have control over how tourism is presented, ensuring that the cultural and religious significance that Aboriginal people attach to the park is accorded the highest degree of protection and respect (Wells 1996). As for choice, the Aboriginal communities can decide if they want to be involved with tourism or not. Much of this involvement has recently become symbolised by the interpretive and educational services they offer visitors at the Uluru–Kata Tjuta Cultural Centre located in the park. Their position is summed up in the words of a senior Anangu traditional owner:

> we want tourists to learn about our place, to listen to us Anangu, not just to look at the sunset and climb the puli (Uluru) . . . In the Cultural Centre we will teach the minga (tourists) better. We will teach them about the Tjukurpa (law creation period), teach them inma (dancing), show them how we make punu (woodcarving). We will teach them about joint management. We are always saying, 'Pukulpa pitjama Ananguku ngurakutu – Welcome to Aboriginal land'.

A win–win relationship between tourism and the community has been achieved. Local communities in the park benefit economically, as all businesses in the Cultural Centre are Aboriginal-owned. They also benefit from a sociocultural perspective as the park's interpretive and educational programmes place greater emphasis on Anangu explanation of the surrounding landscape. One could also argue that as a result tourism has benefited. Uluru remains a top tourist attraction, despite the fact that Anangu ask tourists not to photograph them or climb on the rock. Instead they offer tourist walks around its base (the Mala and the Mutitjulu) to highlight better their living traditions.

Public awareness-building efforts

When the people who inhabit tourist communities understand the dynamics of tourism, its impacts and their capacities to benefit from it, they will be in a much better situation to take part in development decision-making and in the benefits of tourism (Din 1993; Lynn 1992; Timothy 1999b, 2000). In the realm of heritage tourism, the more knowledge community members have, the more power they will have. Despite the fact that people in less developed regions have little first-hand knowledge about being tourists, since few have ever had opportunities to travel outside their home regions, they may have fundamental knowledge that is needed for heritage tourism to develop, for they tend to be the ones familiar with local customs, traditions and built heritage. This knowledge, coupled with an understanding of tourism, can empower people to participate better in tourism (Timothy 2000; Tosun and Jenkins 1998).

Some destination communities are making important strides in building awareness of tourism among local populations. In recent years, Yogyakarta, Indonesia, has attempted to educate its residents about the prospective benefits of tourism and their potential role in its development. Efforts were under way in the mid-1990s to heighten public awareness of tourism through official educational campaigns. These involved various media, such as television ads, newspapers and leaflets that were circulated throughout the community. Additionally, short courses in foreign languages and cultures, small business management and accounting were offered by the local tourism development office to community members who were most likely to be involved with tourists (e.g. taxi and pedicab drivers, guesthouse and restaurant owners, and street vendors) (Timothy 2000; Timothy and Tosun in press).

Heritage marketing

Since one of the main purposes of heritage tourism management is to protect and conserve the past, marketing of heritage places does not necessarily entail attempts to increase visitor numbers through advertising. Instead, it means that managers have opportunities to target certain consumers and control their visits while improving conservation standards (Pearson and Sullivan 1995: 286). Nonetheless, much effort has occurred in recent years to promote visitations at heritage sites and to increase public awareness of them, despite the fact that historic sites often have small marketing, advertising and promotional budgets. Information technology (e.g. the Internet) has played a pivotal part in inexpensive advertising and no doubt has contributed to a wider interest in this form of tourism (Bennett 1997). Wigle (1994: 96) argues that the best way to make a small marketing budget go further is to emphasise the aspects that people already find exciting and attractive, and implement this strategy with miserly tactics.

Strategic marketing planning involves three primary elements, or questions: (1) Where are we now? (2) Where do we want to be in the future? (3) How do we get there? (Middleton 1994: 130). With an understanding of these questions, Hall and McArthur (1993b: 40–1) identified five stages, or steps, in the marketing planning process of heritage attractions as follows:

1. internal and external situation analysis;
2. setting marketing objectives and strategies;
3. marketing activities;
4. marketing management;
5. marketing evaluation.

Each of these is examined in more detail in the following sections.

Market situation analysis

No heritage site can be all things to all people. Therefore, it is essential that managers should incorporate an understanding of the behavior of visitors into their marketing and promotional strategies. For example, in many instances inter-pretation has a tendency to aim for the 'average visitor', since different people respond in different ways to different forms of interpretation. However, the result can often be bland, repetitive, or superficial, satisfying few people (Hall and McArthur 1993b: 41).

As the name of this step denotes, heritage managers must understand the present situation. From a marketing perspective, the situation analysis entails an identification of who the visitors are and how the site is currently meeting their needs. One important part of this phase is market segmentation, or the identification of existing tourism demand. The division of the heritage market is useful for knowing what types of people utilise different types of heritage attractions, which will assist managers in knowing what the best approaches to marketing will be. This is very important, for as Light and Prentice (1994a) acknowledge, there are opportunities for individual sites to be developed and packaged in different ways for different types of visitors.

As outlined in Chapter 3, the three most common ways of segmenting the heritage market are by demographic characteristics, geographic origins and psychographic characteristics. Another is product/benefit segmentation, which allows markets to be identified by the product characteristics they fav-our, for example a specific type of heritage experience or attraction (Hall and McArthur 1993b: 43).

Regardless of how the market is segmented, it is important to note that good heritage markets are:

1. sufficiently large to make the attraction feasible;
2. compatible with the qualities and attributes of the site;
3. able to grow or at least maintain their current visitation levels;
4. not 'taken' by existing sites;
5. unsatisfied enough with existing attractions that the site will satisfy their needs (Hall and McArthur 1993b: 43).

The situation analysis sometimes also needs to include a competitor ana-lysis, which is particularly important in the private sector. Competitor analysis is useful for at least two reasons: (1) it reinforces the analysis of the market and (2) it helps managers understand their own strengths and weaknesses in relation to those of their competitors (Heath and Wall 1992). The primary aim of a competitor analysis is to see how the heritage site in question com-pares to others of a similar nature in terms of the attraction itself, access-ibility, market segments, facilities and services, marketing strategies, cost and maintenance.

Ways of measuring the effectiveness of current marketing strategies and plans should also be devised as part of the situation analysis (e.g. importance-performance evaluations). Such tools and their implementation will allow managers see how effective their marketing efforts have been and make decisions regarding what future directions need to be taken.

Establishing marketing objectives and strategies

Once the present situation has been assessed managers can, based on what they learned, formulate goals and objects and establish strategies for reaching these goals. Goals and objectives are where site management would like to be in the future. Strategies are their selected routes for getting there, and plans are the action programmes for moving along these routes (Middleton 1994: 130). Heritage site objectives can range anywhere from creating a positive image for a site to increasing income levels in local communities. Clearly defined goals and objectives can assist site management in the following ways:

- by providing direction towards appropriate organisational behaviour;
- by reducing uncertainty and lack of direction in developing events and programmes;
- by motivating people to work at achieving specific aims;
- by providing a measure which can help gauge the success of site management;
- by providing a focal point for co-ordinating site organisation and management (Hall and McArthur 1993b: 44).

The purpose of developing marketing strategies is to 'translate current conditions . . . into desired situations' (Heath and Wall 1992: 74). To achieve the goal of building general awareness of a newly discovered heritage site, for instance, the organisation in charge might initiate an advertising campaign through various forms of media to let the public know what exists there and how it can be used in a sustainable fashion. Another strategy might be targeting specific market segments as a way of bringing more money into the local economy.

Marketing activities

As part of marketing activities, managers must determine the most correct marketing mix for achieving their stated goals and objectives. The market mix, which is simply a set of variables that can be manipulated to achieve goals and objectives, is important in allowing the heritage attraction to compete for selected target markets (Heath and Wall 1992). Traditionally, the marketing mix has consisted of various elements related to product, price, promotion and place (the four Ps). In heritage terms the product can be seen as the physical characteristics of the attraction, the historic relics, methods of interpretation, the staff, support services, image and branding (Swarbrooke 1995). Price covers a range of issues like admissions, discounts, concessions, value, methods of payment, and cost of getting to the site. Promotion deals specifically with issues such as marketing endeavours, advertising, various promotional media and media design. Finally, place generally refers to the location of the experience and the distribution of the product (Swarbrooke 1995). The physical layout of the attraction and the level of accessibility as are issues like cleanliness, landscaping and spatial patterns.

Recent thinking has expanded the original 4 Ps to include elements such as people, programming and partnerships. Boyd (in press) has examined each of these in considerable detail, and a summary is provided below.

People – from a marketing perspective, the focus is often on the product itself, with less attention to the experiences on offer. The heritage industry has emerged from how a region's past has been commodified and sold to the visitor, where emphasis has been on the tangible products of the industry. The 'people' element suggests that equal attention be focused on the experiences behind the heritage settings themselves, and that while tourism is product driven, ultimately tourists are in search of the intangible within settings where focus is on the actual experiences they seek to take away from visits. This experiential dimension to heritage is often tied to the learning aspect of heritage tourism.

Programming focuses on how the products and experiences can be better packaged for the customer. In tourism this is often in the form of running special events, and in the case of heritage tourism much attention has focused on festivals and how they can be representative of places themselves (Getz 1991). In addition, packaging can involve putting together a mix of product and experience by linking a number of attractions together. Recognised as cluster development, or attraction clusters, this type of programming is often only accomplished through the presence of partnerships between tourist operators.

Partnership is linked to wider ideas of collaboration and network development. Defined by Bramwell and Lane (1999: 179) as 'regular, cross-sectoral interactions between parties, based on at least some agreed rules or norms, intended to address a common issue or to achieve a specific policy goal or goals', it is emerging as almost standard practice within tourism management to involve some sort of partnership agreement, or dialogue between different parties. It is not a new concept, but one that has been around for several decades particularly within management and corporate sectors. It is relatively new within tourism research circles, where the focus has been descriptive and centred around presenting case studies. There has emerged some work that has developed a conceptual dimension to this area of inquiry focussing on heritage tourism. Working in the context of World Heritage Sites, Boyd and Timothy (2001) stressed the importance of three key elements within any partnership: type (informal to formalised), the approach taken (grassroots to agency led) and the extent of co-operation between partners (full to limited).

Another marketing activity used to achieve a site's objectives is target marketing, wherein managers decide which specific groups of visitors they will focus on in their marketing efforts. According to Hall and McArthur (1993b: 45), the identification of target markets involves three stages. First, there must be a decision about how many market segments will be targeted. This will usually be based on its management objectives and the nature of the heritage resources. Second, managers must develop a clear market profile for each segment. Finally, a marketing strategy needs to be developed that is appropriate to the site and the selected market segments.

Heritage managers can market in a number of different ways. One way is to offer the same marketing mix to all potential visitor groups. This approach, usually known as undifferentiated marketing, has the advantage of reaching a wide range of market segments and people who fall within more than one category. It is a 'one size fits all' approach and can involve some wasted financial resources on groups that might not be interested in visiting a particular type of heritage site. Single segmentation, or differentiated marketing, is where a specific target market is selected. This has the advantage of directing all resources to a single segment that managers know will have an interest in visiting. Instead of aiming for a small share of the larger market, an attraction can aim at getting a large share of the specific market that has been identified. Another approach is selective segmenting, which lies somewhere between undifferentiated and single segmenting. Here, a few groups are chosen, which provides some of the advantages of single segmentation while eliminating some of the risks (Heath and Wall 1992: 106). Several approaches have been used in attraction marketing. A common one is to identify attraction clusters (Gunn 1994), and market around the mix of attractions making up individual clusters. Boyd (2000b) in his examination of heritage tourism in Northern Ireland, identified several clusters, comprised of heritage attractions all within relatively close proximity to each other. Another approach that has been used in Canada is marketing through what are known as product clubs, which have a specific clientele, as the following case study demonstrates (Boyd 2002).

CASE STUDY   Product development clubs in Canada

The Canadian Tourism Commission (1998) described product development clubs to involve consortiums of small and medium-sized businesses that agree to work together to develop new tourism products or enhance existing ones. Through pooling knowledge, efforts and resources, key objectives of the product club are to: (1) increase the range and quality of tourism products in Canada; (2) build business networks to increase the exchange of information; and (3) encourage co-operative ventures and partnerships (Boyd 2002). There are currently 12 in operation across Canada (see Table 5.8). With respect to heritage, these range from the independent innkeepers cultural and ecotourism club that develops new packages to complement stays at high-quality heritage inns in Ontario to a festivals network product club that brings together organisers of festivals in association with the tourism industry for the National Capital Region.

One of the most successful is the Conservation Lands Product Club in south-western Ontario. The Conservation Lands of Ontario is an alliance of the Grand River, Halton Region, Hamilton Region, Long Point Region and Niagara Peninsula Conservation authorities in south-western Ontario, designed to market natural heritage tourism (ecotourism along with soft adventure) within their

Table 5.8 Canadian product development clubs

Type and title of product club	Characteristics
Ski and Snowboard Industry	Developing alliances between the ski and snowboard sector and the tourism industry to make product stronger and more competitive
Atlantic Economuseum Network*	Supports tourism product development at economuseums throughout the Atlantic provinces
Tourists with Special Needs*	Develops new specialised packages for people with restricted physical abilities
Independent Innkeepers Cultural/Ecotourism*	Develops new packages to complement stays at high-quality heritage inns in Ontario
Ontario East Adventure*	Develops new packages focusing on the region's abundance of heritage assets in combination with its waterway and adventure products
Conservation Lands*	Develops a model for co-operative product development and sustainable ecotourism/heritage in urban fringe areas
Saskatchewan River Basin*	Packages and markets natural heritage and ecotourism products in the Saskatchewan River Basin
Festivals Network*	Brings together festival organisers and the tourism industry in the National Capital Region to jointly develop a strategy for product development in markets with greatest potential
Quebec Maritime	Brings together tourism tour operators, travel agents, transportation and accommodation sectors to improve the professionalism, the quality of supply and the positioning of small businesses in the eastern regions of Quebec
Aboriginal Waterways*	Develops, packages and markets aboriginal heritage and culture through the creation of destination areas within Saskatchewan and Manitoba
Western Golf Alliance	Develops an approach to increase the saleability of the golf product, to package information and to evaluate delivery mechanisms with a view to increasing product quality and service levels
Greektown*	Brings together 400 businesses to expand cultural tourism potential through a partnership approach

* Denotes those product clubs that have an association with heritage tourism.
Source: Canadian Tourism Commission (1998).

watersheds (Bruno 1998). Over 50 private-sector partners have joined the Conservation Lands, ranging from outfitters (e.g. Grand Experiences), to specific attractions (e.g. Wellington County Museum). Combined, they offer visitors and tour operators the opportunity to enjoy the near urban experience of the outdoors/heritage across 39 conservation areas west of Toronto and Niagara Falls. With respect to specific heritage attractions, the visitor can view within the Conservation Lands of Ontario the following sites: Dundas Valley, a spectacular Carolinian habitat (Hamilton Region); Ball's Falls, a nineteenth-century industrial village (Niagara Peninsula); Crawford Lake, a reconstructed Iroquois village (Halton Region) and Backus Heritage, Backus Woods pioneer village (Bruno 1998). Given that the Conservation Lands of Ontario is a relatively new initiative, it is too early to measure the success of this partnership. What is probably going to emerge over the long term is the attraction of a few key places above the rest, but key attractions that cater to either adventure or heritage visitor experiences. In terms of marketing, this example illustrates the importance of developing networks that focus on niche areas, where a range of attractions, operators and accommodation providers exist in clusters that can easily be accessed by visitors. Furthermore, while the product club involves a mix of partners, it is essential that an overall project manager oversees the partnership. The success of the product development clubs across Canada will be linked to how well project managers can integrate individual partners with the overall visitor experience provided in those regions where the clubs exist.

Marketing management

Once marketing activities have been decided, heritage managers must ensure that selected marketing strategies can be implemented and the key target markets can be reached through the development of appropriate management strategies and mechanisms. As part of this marketing management, managers must be sure that financial and human resources are available for developing and marketing the heritage product. This may result in the need to hire more staff, retrain existing staff, spend money on repairing the site and seeking additional funding. A plan of action should be developed for each action that is required in the marketing strategy. The purpose of these is to delineate tasks, timelines for implementation, cost estimates, tasks, responsibilities and priorities. Action plans, therefore, can make the process more efficient and better assure that the marketing activities are successful (Hall and McArthur 1993b: 46).

Marketing evaluation

It is critical for managers to determine if a marketing strategy was successful against the initial marketing objectives. In some cases, some goals might have been met while others remained unfulfilled (Hall and McArthur 1993b). Within the field of leisure services, Henderson and Bialeschki (1995) suggested several reasons why evaluation is important. These are as follows and have been adapted here to reflect evaluations of marketing efforts:

1. to determine accountability;
2. to assess and establish baseline data;
3. to assess the attainment of goals and objectives;
4. to understand the outcomes and impacts of marketing programmes;
5. to help determine successes and failures in marketing campaigns;
6. to improve quality control;
7. to assist in making decisions on future marketing directions.

Measuring usage and establishing visitor profiles are the most frequent forms of marketing evaluation because visitor numbers are relatively easy to collect, as use is usually based on numbers of people who visited. While visitor numbers can be a useful indicator, they rarely offer information that can be used to make critical decisions (McArthur and Hall 1993a: 256). Evaluation research uses essentially the same data-collecting methods and analytical tools as other forms of research (e.g. questionnaires, interviews, observations, focus groups). However, the primary purpose is to assist managers in understanding issues such as marketing effectiveness, image creation/enhancement, and the number of people who visited the heritage sites based on advertising efforts and media usage (i.e. conversion studies), not necessarily to develop broad-based theories.

Summary and conclusions

This chapter has provided an overview of the management of heritage, offering a broad brushstroke of areas linked to managing heritage tourism: ownership, economics, managing staff, visitors and local residents, visitor management frameworks, elements of a sustainable heritage tourism framework, as well as marketing from a heritage perspective. Co-operation and the creation of partnerships have been advanced in this chapter as important practices in addressing the management of heritage tourism. With respect to economics, what emerges is that while heritage is not cheap, many revenue sources exist that heritage managers can turn to. The user-pays debate was revisited, and while there are reasons some heritage providers are opposed to this philosophy, there are some positive outcomes of charging admission fees at heritage sites, primary among these being the contribution to sustainable management and conservation. An important part of heritage management are the issues associated with human resource management. These have been given only scant attention, but it is important to recognise that issues will vary between paid workers, both from the private and public sector, and those who volunteer. A mix of challenges emerges for managers dealing with employees within the private and public sectors. As for the non-profit sector, managers are faced with creating conditions where workers are given the opportunity to be involved in all aspects of the heritage attraction.

A great deal of attention was paid in this chapter to how visitors are managed, arguing that this is as important as managing the heritage resource itself. A range of visitor management frameworks has been described, which provide managers of natural and cultural sites the option of seeking maximum opportunity or imposing limits to what activities are acceptable and limits to numbers of tourists. More specific management tools and methods were also outlined to demonstrate the options available to managers. A discussion was also provided regarding what elements are useful in constituting a sustainable management framework suitable for heritage tourism development. Where management of local residents is concerned, the focus here has been on ensuring their participation in the planning, protection and management of heritage presented to tourists, as well as their receiving benefits from tourism. Finally the chapter focused on heritage marketing, with an emphasis on the need to target tourists whose actions can be controlled, the promotion of visitor sites, and increasing public awareness about heritage. Such activities require strategic marketing planning, which was also highlighted.

Heritage management is not an easy task, for it is multidimensional and complex. One of the primary dimensions of management is to promote learning about heritage places. As such, interpretation forms an integral part of any visit and can shape the visitor experience. The next chapter focuses on heritage interpretation.

Questions

1. How does ownership of heritage influence how it is managed?
2. What are the pros and cons of asking visitors to pay to see heritage?
3. Along what lines have visitor management frameworks developed?
4. How is heritage marketing linked to managing heritage?

Further reading

Hall, C.M. and McArthur, S. (1998) *Integrated Heritage Management: Principles and practice*, The Stationery Office, London.

Harrison, R. (ed.) (1994) *Manual of Heritage Management*, Butterworth Heinemann, Oxford.

Howard, P. (2002) *Heritage: Management, interpretation, identity*, Continuum, London.

Leask, A. and Yeoman, I. (1999) *Heritage Visitor Attractions: An operations management perspective*, Cassell, London.

McKercher, B. and Du Cros, H. (2002) *Cultural Tourism: The partnership between tourism and cultural heritage management*, Haworth, New York.

Moscardo, G. (1999) *Making Visitors Mindful*, Sagamore, Champaign, Ill.

Nuryanti, W. (ed.) (1997) *Tourism and Heritage Management*, Gadjah Máda University Press, Yogyakarta.

Shackley, M.L. (ed.) (1998) *Visitor Management: Case studies from World Heritage Sites*, Butterworth Heinemann, Oxford.

CHAPTER 6

Heritage interpretation

The concept of interpretation was introduced in the last chapter as a useful way of managing heritage visitors and their potential impacts. This is expanded on in this chapter. Interpretation, viewed here, is essentially a process of communicating or explaining to visitors the significance of the place they are visiting (Alderson and Low 1985; Barrow 1994; Machlis and Field 1984; Moscardo and Woods 1998; Sharpe 1982a; Stansfield 1983). Its purpose is to assist tourists and other visitors in experiencing a resource or event in a way they might not otherwise experience without it (Hammitt 1984: 13). Interpretation involves many aspects of town and country planning (e.g. protection and access), marketing (e.g. user groups and visitor wants and desires) and education-related theories (e.g. what people learn, how they learn and what to teach) (Barrow 1994; Fennell 1999). According to Tilden (1977), interpretation is an educational activity that reveals meaning and relationships through the use of objects, by direct experience, and by instructive media, rather than simply to communicate facts and figures. He also noted that personal interpretation is the most effective form of interaction, but he cautioned that poor quality live interpretation is worse than nothing at all (Risk 1994: 320). Nearly always, interpretation is seen in a positive light as it educates and entertains visitors and causes them to reflect on environmental values.

Nonetheless, criticism of interpretation has arisen over the years. The most common concern is that interpretation interferes with visitors' own experience of a heritage place. According to O'Toole (1992: 14), 'the whole notion of the interpretative centre can be seen as the product of an overactive mind, a mind that must always substitute meaning for experience'. The heart of this argument lies in the belief that places that are seen by managers to need interpretation could in fact stand on their own, and once an individual experiences someone else's interpretation he/she will never be able to have his/her own direct experience (Moscardo 2000: 12). However, the flawed assumptions in this argument are that people have sufficient background and understanding to comprehend the significance of the place on their own and that they come without their own biased interpretations already established. Nonetheless, as Moscardo (2000: 13) points out, it is possible that interpretation might interfere with an experience when an overzealous interpreter provides propaganda instead of presentation.

Bramwell and Lane (1993) identified a number of additional problems. First, when interpretation is propelled by economic motives there is a danger that it is done for the wrong reasons (e.g. profit making). Second, heritage events and places are sometimes simplified to meet the harried needs of visitors. Third, there is some danger in over-interpretation, which can lead to trivialisation of historic events and places and diminish the personal excitement in visiting (Urry 1990). Finally, it is problematic when interpretation turns into a show where significant places are commodified into quaint tourist landscapes, where the show itself becomes more important than the message it is aiming to convey to visitors.

Several aspects of heritage interpretation are presented in this chapter. First, the origins and development of interpretation are addressed. This is followed by an explanation of the roles that can be played by interpretation, namely, education, entertainment, conservation and sustainable development. Discussion moves on to describe the six principles of interpretation as outlined by Freeman Tilden as the basis to introduce interpretative planning and the steps this type of planning involves. Following this, the focus of the chapter shifts towards the challenges that managers face in delivering interpretation programmes, for example the need to offer multilingual services, to acknowledge cross-cultural differences and to adapt programmes to accommodate the special needs sector of society. Finally, the chapter examines the tools that managers can use in heritage interpretation. Both personal and non-personal media are examined along with the opportunities that new technology can play in interpretation, as well as how visitors themselves make use of interpretative media.

Origins and development of interpretation

According to Weaver (1982: 29), interpretation originated very early with ancient storytelling by hunters, fishermen, traders and artisans of the Middle East and Asia. Later Greek and Roman philosophers (e.g. Aristotle, Democritus and Socrates) began to explain 'natural causes for supernatural phenomena' to their students. As commented on in the introductory chapter, one early predecessor of cultural heritage interpretation was present in the Grand Tour, which involved travel within Europe between the sixteenth and nineteenth centuries, where young men of British and European gentry travelled for educational purposes to experience important cultural and historic sites, including art collections, museums, historic sites and universities (Towner 1985). Such movements, which were undoubtedly influenced by religion, philosophy, natural science, literature and the arts, have been reinforced and refined throughout history by exploration, discovery, record keeping and scientific research into what is known today as interpretation (Weaver 1982).

Modern-day interpretation has its roots in nature guiding during the 1800s and early 1900s in the Rocky Mountains of western North America and in places like New Zealand and Australia (Booth and Simmons 2000; Hall 2000a; Molloy 1993; Weaver 1982). As the national parks developed in North America, many of the principles of interpretation that were created spread throughout the Western world, and many have been adopted in the developing world too (Light 1991). Later in the 1900s following this initial phase and largely in response to it, interpretation of the built, or cultural, environment developed. Old buildings, museums and archaeological sites began to be the focus of intense interpretive efforts, taking off from the principles and practices developed in the realm of nature (Light 1991; Weaver 1982). Finally, Light (1991) argues that a third phase has occurred in the development of interpretation; that is, the growth of the heritage industry, which is marked by changing aims and interpretive philosophies and advances in new forms of interpretative media.

The roles of interpretation

According to Herbert (1989a: 191), the role of interpretation is 'to make people more aware of the places they visit, to provide knowledge which increases their understanding and to promote interest which leads to greater enjoyment and perhaps responsibility'. Inherent in this definition are three clear objectives: (1) to educate people about the place they are visiting; (2) to provide an enjoyable, and even entertaining, experience for visitors; and (3) these two elements work together to increase visitors' respect for heritage and take responsibility for caring for it (Bradley 1982; Knudson et al. 1995; Sharpe 1982a). In the words of Tilden (1977: 38), 'he that understands will not willfully deface, for when he truly understands, he knows that it is in some degree a part of himself'. Several authors have described additional, yet similar and overlapping objectives as well (e.g. Knudson et al. 1995; Rennie 1980; Sharpe 1982a). Nonetheless, the three primary objectives described here provide a useful framework for examining the importance and value of interpretation.

Education

Education forms the basis of interpretation and involves a learner and a teacher (the visitor and interpreter, respectively). Interpretation uses heritage properties and objects to demonstrate the past to visitors in hopes of increasing their understanding and appreciation of the resource being presented (Dewar 1989;

Herbert 1989a; Hooper-Greenhill 1992; Moscardo and Woods 1998; Prentice *et al.* 1998). According to Nuryanti (1997), interpretation helps visitors to feel something that the interpreter feels, a sense of wonder at the beauty, variety and complexity of the historic environment.

The educational value of interpretation can be seen from the perspective of formal or informal education. Formal education refers to people attending sites as part of a formal educational programme, such as in schools and universities. Informal education, though, is where tourists receive education and knowledge indirectly, that is not part of a formal educative programme, from interpretive demonstrations (Prentice and Prentice 1989). According to Prentice and Prentice (1989: 148), the market for informal education is greater than that for formal education since it is generally a part of people's vacation/tourism experiences, thereby constituting a larger share of the total visitation.

Within the formal realm, heritage sites are very popular among school groups for experiential learning, and much curriculum includes visits to historic sites, primarily for their educational role in history and geography. The most popular cultural heritage destinations for student field visits are historic buildings, museums, theatres, castles and technology centres (Prentice 1995). Student field trips, according to Prentice (1995: 149), have the potential to increase the experience of place by getting the students to recognise the distinctiveness of a place compared to others, to know a place more intimately, and to use their imaginations. Typically, from the perspective of heritage managers, educational groups are seen as a younger generation, a fresh audience that can be educated about the site and its conservation (Carter 1994).

Heritage site visits can also be key in providing informal educational experiences for visitors, which simply means that they visit not as part of a formal course of study, but attend for some other reason and learn from their visits. In this case, interpretation is nearly always required because the meanings of places and their significance are difficult to grasp without the assistance of interpreters and interpretive media. These enhance the visitors' understanding of the place and their experiences visiting it (Pearson and Sullivan 1995: 288). Some people attend interpretive programmes or facilities because they find acquiring knowledge enjoyable and an enriching experience in its own right. By having more knowledge about the cultural or natural resources of an area, their visits become more meaningful and enjoyable (Knudson *et al.* 1995). As discussed previously, 'mindful' visitors (i.e. inquisitive, alert, participatory) are more inclined to learn than mindless visitors, who tend to be passive and who do not care to ask questions or participate actively in discussions. Interpretation can be an important ingredient in creating mindful visitor behaviour to ensure that correct messages about the site were received (Moscardo 1999; Prentice *et al.* 1998; Stewart *et al.* 1998).

Thus, mindfulness can be a product, in part at least, of the nature of interpretation and its presentation. More mindful heritage visitors can learn many things at historic sites through interpretation. For example, according to a study undertaken by Prentice *et al.* (1998: 15) at Discovery Point, Dundee,

Scotland (home of the ship *Discovery*), when departing visitors were given questions to answer based on information covered in their visit, a majority of respondents selected the correct answer for five of the seven questions, and for many of those who chose correctly, their knowledge was gained from their present visit, although significant numbers claimed to have known the answer prior to their visit (Table 6.1). Similarly, Table 6.2 illustrates the results of a

Table 6.1 What visitors learned from their visit*

	%
Which person was known as 'The Inspiration' for the first Discovery *expedition?*	
Could you have answered this before your visit today?	
No	37.4
What year did Scott sail to Antarctica on the Discovery*?*	
Could you have answered this before your visit today?	
No	70.0
Where was the official launch ceremony of the Discovery*?*	
Could you have answered this before your visit today?	
No	51.3
When locked in the ice during the first expedition to the Antarctic how was the Discovery *eventually released?*	
Could you have answered this before your visit today?	
No	60.6
Which of the following professions was not represented on the Discovery*?*	
Could you have answered this before your visit today?	
No	47.1
Which of the following did Discovery *not do in its lifetime?*	
Could you have answered this before your visit today?	
No	31.4
Which of the following extreme geographical conditions of the continent Antarctica is false?	
Could you have answered this before your visit today?	
No	46.1

* Only the visitors who chose the correct answer are included in this table.
Source: After Prentice *et al.* (1998).

Table 6.2 Responses to: 'You have not learned anything from your visit here today' (%)

	All sites (*n*=1197)	Caerphilly (*n*=324)	Raglan (*n*=355)	Tintern (*n*=969)	Tretower (*n*=149)
Agree	7	12	4	5	7
No opinion	1	1	–	1	2
Disagree	92	87	96	94	91

Source: After Light (1995a: 134).

study by Light (1995a) about learning outcomes from heritage site visits. In his study of four ancient monuments in Wales, Light found that 92 per cent of all visitors to heritage sites felt they learned something from their visit. They also answered many test questions correctly based upon the materials presented to them.

It is a safe conclusion to suggest that most heritage site visitors learn something, either in a formal or informal context, from their visits. Figure 6.1 outlines the elements that influence the effectiveness of informal education at heritage places and their interrelations. In this model Light (1995a) argues that visitor motives, their extent of background knowledge, and their interest in the history of the place, together with the visitor's use of, and attention to, the interpretive media, will result in some level of education and learning. The more interested and knowledgeable a visitor is, and the better the interpretive materials are presented, the more learning will take place. For many people, learning is a major motivation for attending heritage presentations and places

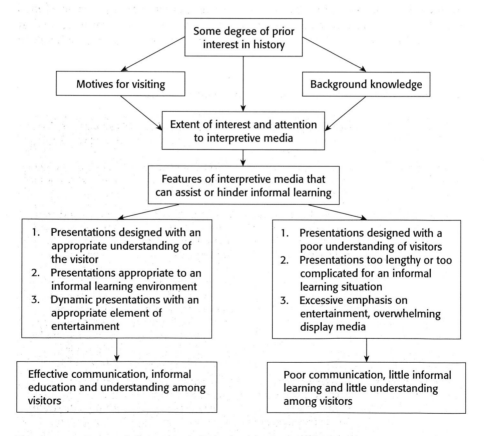

Figure 6.1   Factors influencing informal education at historic sites
Source: After Light (1995a).

(Light 1995a). This is especially so for frequent visitors, while for infrequent and non-visitors, learning is generally less important (Hood 1983; Thomas 1989). For example, from an educational perspective, Miles (1986) categorised museum visitors into three groups: (1) a small group of highly motivated visitors who want to learn; (2) a small group who have little interest in learning; and (3) a larger group with varying degrees of willingness to learn but who might be motivated to learn (Table 6.3) (Light 1995a: 129).

While the focus in this section has been on the educational value, both formal and informal, of interpretation aimed at visitors, a third type of interpretation is starting to emerge within destinations that focuses on the resident community (Boyd 2002a, 2002b) and their understanding (or lack) of heritage surrounding them. The premise behind offering programmes for residents that build local knowledge of heritage is that they in turn will use the knowledge to explain to visitors the type(s) of heritage they can experience in their visit. As such, it is anticipated that this exchange of information and education will enhance the experience visitors take away from visiting the region. In Banff National Park, Canada, for example, a heritage tourism strategy was developed in 1994, which included a programme to educate community members so that they could become conduits of knowledge, which they could share with park

Table 6.3 Visitor segments at museums and heritage sites

Segment	Motives for visiting	Requirements from the visit	Implications for interpretation
Highly motivated to learn	To learn about and understand the history of the sites	Detailed learning and understanding	Extensive attention and likely extensive learning
Can be motivated to learn	Various, but probably with some element of interest and curiosity in the past	Some degree of intellectual stimulation, informal learning and understanding. For some people an element of entertainment and fun may be important	Some attention to interpretation and at least some learning, more so among more motivated visitors. Less motivated folk might be motivated to pay more attention by good quality interpretation
Not at all motivated to learn	Somewhere to take children, somewhere to pass a rainy afternoon, somewhere to kill time	Few specific requirements or expectations	Little if any attention to interpretation, little or no learning

Source: After Light (1995a – based on Miles 1986).

visitors, thereby enhancing visitor experiences and empowering local people with the ability to interact with tourists and actually become part of the product (Boyd 2002b).

Since the orientation programme was introduced in 1997, it has been well received by residents within Banff and while it is a voluntary programme, many businesses have encouraged their employees to participate. This programme stands as an example of how education should not only be aimed at visitors, but that the local community is often in need of understanding the heritage environment in which they live. The local community lives and breathes the heritage every day. Who is better suited than residents to communicate that heritage and experience to visitors? The success of the programme in Banff has opened up the wider utility of using this approach in other Canadian national parks where communities are either present within or adjacent to parks.

Entertainment

Education has been such a core value in interpretation for so long that heritage managers have traditionally viewed pleasure and enjoyment as dichotomous and incompatible with education (Light 1995a). However, today, it is more commonly recognised that fun and learning are not on opposite ends of a continuum. In an early paper, Putney and Wagar (1973: 43) demonstrated tremendous foresight regarding this – 'by helping recreationists enjoy and understand the areas they visit, interpretation of natural and cultural history can add substantially to the quality of visitor experiences and therefore to the stream of benefits produced by such areas'. There has always been a fundamental problem in knowing when the entertainment stops, and the education starts. That is not to say that the two are necessarily mutually exclusive, but rather that there is a clear problem with the medium of representation drowning out the intended educational information (Walsh 1992: 105). More scholars are beginning to realise that even the most explicitly entertaining presentations have, broadly speaking, some educational value, even if it is limited to providing experiences and broadening horizons (Light 1995a: 131).

With the gradual acceptance that entertainment and learning are compatible, and can in fact be quite symbiotic, heritage managers are beginning to realise that the visitor experience can be enhanced by educational entertainment. This balanced approach can assist a site in competing for the public's leisure time by adding appeal to a heritage property (Dewar 1989; Timothy and Wall 1997). Likewise, Knudson et al. (1995) argued that for this very reason, it is important for managers to remember that all interpretation should be recreational, and 'the cornerstone of any policy on visitor care in museum and heritage management is, first of all, pleasure' (Schouten 1995b: 260). Schouten (1995b: 260) suggests that interpretation can make heritage visits UNIQUE experiences, UNIQUE standing for: Uncommon, Novelty, Informative, Quality, Understanding and Emotions.

A significant part of this experience is humour, which some researchers have found to be effective in an educational and interpretive context (e.g. Bruner 1994). While care must be taken in trying to translate humour for foreign visitors, humour plays an important role in many forms of interpretation. It can be a means of retaining visitors' attention and can make the learning environment more interesting, participatory and enjoyable. Bruner (1994: 410) provides an interesting example of this ludic approach to interpretation:

One time on the reconstructed *Mayflower* in Plymouth, which does first-person interpretation, I saw a woman guide in period dress. She told me that it was a long and arduous journey across the ocean, that she had lost her husband on the voyage, and that she felt so lonely in this vast new country. Then she looked me straight in the eye and winked, and I could not tell if it was a 1620s wink or a 1990s wink.

This approach can unlock visitors' imaginations. The goal of interpretive presentations should not be a simple description of historic events and peoples, but to inspire a feeling for a moment of history (Craig 1989: 108). According to one historic site manager (quoted in McAndrew 1995: 19), 'if you can get history across in an entertaining and accurate way, you're going to be more effective'. The following is an example of this:

At a castle in England, visitors are escorted through dark candle-lit corridors by hooded monks to share their meager meal, only to be interrupted by the king's troops who, pounding at the door, force their way into the dining hall. A transformation occurs and a medieval feast is laid on, the only eating utensil a short dagger at each visitor's place (Risk 1994: 325).

Despite the potentially beneficial relationship between education and entertainment in interpretation, there is a danger of entertainment being taken too far and overpowering, and even rendering inaccurate, the information being presented. Stevens (1989), for example, argues that there has been a trend for the medium (especially high-tech and designer media) itself to become the message, rather than the information it is supposed to disseminate. Perhaps because of the need for economic self-reliance, in part at least, many heritage attractions are attempting to win customers, and this is increasingly being done by making the past more palatable and less 'boring' to the public (McAndrew 1995; Stevens 1989). Some attractions thus strive for the 'Disney effect', an experience of far-fetched spectacle, emphasising titillation *instead* of education (Walsh 1992: 97; Wallace 1996). In the words of the director of one historic preservation agency, 'We're competing with Disneyland, lakes in Wisconsin, casino boats and the like, so we have to have a program that's both entertaining and worthwhile. You can't have display boxes [at historic sites] and expect people to go home thrilled' (quoted in McAndrew 1995: 19).

Against this background, interpretation should be seen as part of the attraction base. Good quality interpretation can act as an added appeal to heritage places (Goodey 1979; Light 1995b; Moscardo and Woods 1998; Uzzell 1989a, b), and can be adopted as a form of product development. This appears especially to be the case with the re-enactment of events. Light (1995b) found that many people visited Caerphilly Castle, Wales, specifically to see re-enacted events. Visitors tended to enjoy themselves more on event days than regular days, and they generally stayed longer when a re-enactment was taking place. One of the most effective ways of interpreting historic events is to involve the visitors themselves in the re-enactment process. A number of historic sites in North America have begun involving visitors more in their interpretive programmes. For example, in a small Maine (USA) community, visitors themselves may sign up to be participants in the community's interpretation efforts and special events. Tourists take the parts of people who actually occupied the village during the 1700s. They live in eighteenth-century houses and for an entire weekend they 'work, eat and live in the past, experiencing history in a way few will equal' (Risk 1994: 325).

Conservation and sustainable development

From a conservation perspective, the underlying value of the educative and entertaining roles of interpretation is to enhance awareness, create a sense of ownership, and instil a desire to interact with relics of the past in a sustainable manner. Many interpretation experts have argued that quality interpretive programmes will raise the value of a site in the eyes of tourists, and greater value will lead to a greater realisation of the need to preserve and protect (Herbert 1989a; Pearson and Sullivan 1995; Prentice and Prentice 1989; Tilden 1977). This is done through inspiration – inspiring visitors to richer living, higher levels of sensitivity and actions that favour their natural and cultural heritage now and in the future (Knudson *et al.* 1995: 60).

Bramwell and Lane (1993) identified five areas in which interpretation can assist in developing more sustainable forms of tourism: visitor management, economic benefits, environmental benefits, community involvement and attitudes and values.

Visitor management

In the area of visitor management, interpretation can be used to help direct visitors to less crowded and sensitive areas by offering alternative attractions or making subtle suggestions to visitors about additional routes and areas that can be visited (Millar 1989; Moscardo and Woods 1998; Sharpe 1982a). Interpretation can also be used as a means of developing previously under-utilised attractions and regions.

Economic benefits

By functioning as a part of the existing attraction base and also by attracting attention to previously ignored areas, interpretation can attract additional visitors and cause them to stay longer in the destination community. This of course means increased employment opportunities and increased external spending. Skilled interpretive managers can also help spread the positive economic benefits of tourism throughout the community by highlighting the historical significance of various businesses in town and encouraging visitors to use local services, such as restaurants, shops, accommodation, laundries and banks. It can also get visitors thinking about some of the local handicrafts of local significance and which might be tied to part of the history of the area (Bramwell and Lane 1993).

Environmental benefits

Interpretation obviously has the ability to further the cause of local environmental conservation. Interpretation makes visitors aware of their place in the environment and offers them a better understanding of the complexities of coexisting with that environment (Sharpe 1982a: 8). It can further visitors' knowledge and appreciation of the place being visited, and as a result, may help them modify their behaviour and show more respect for local history and traditions (Bramwell and Lane 1993).

Community involvement

In common with all aspects of tourism (Murphy 1985; Timothy 1999c; Tosun 1999), interpretation has greater potential to promote sustainability when local residents are allowed and encouraged to promote and support the aspects of their heritage that are important to them (Ambler 1995; Walker 1987). Interpretation informs the public, and an informed public can make wiser decisions on matters related to heritage resource management than an uninformed public (Nuryanti 1997; Sharpe 1982a). Residents need to be given an opportunity to decide what should be interpreted and how it should be interpreted. This type of empowerment can result in increased community pride and modification of behaviour towards local physical and sociocultural environments (Bramwell and Lane 1993).

Attitudes and values

If interpretation does increase interest and respect for local communities among tourists, then it may result in different attitudes and values than those negative ones traditionally attributed to mass tourists (Mathieson and Wall 1982). In this way, tourists may become less exploitative of local residents and desire to seek more rewarding interactions with them. This can go further to create civic pride and public support in destination residents, resulting in stronger desires to preserve local traditions and customs (Bramwell and Lane 1993; Sharpe 1982a).

Sharpe (1982a) and Rennie (1980) suggest that an additional purpose of interpretation is to build public awareness of an agency's goals and operations. This is important, for such activities can quell public concerns about many things, including tourism, conservation and other site functions. Rudd and Davis (1998) provide a detailed case of the Bingham Canyon Copper Mine, an old and distinctive industrial heritage establishment in Utah (USA), which has used interpretation and guest relations as a way of improving its image and building community approval of its activities without attempting to increase profits directly from tourism. Kennecott Utah Copper Company, the mine owner and operator, has developed its interpretive programme along two primary themes: its commitment to the environment and its commitment to the community. The mine is presented as a natural landscape rather than a ravaged landscape, and to assuage public concern about pollution, Kennecott uses its interpretive centre to assure visitors of its own concerns for the environment. It also attempts to assure the public of its positive contribution to the local economy and the company's long-term financial stability. The company portrays itself as a good neighbour, one that is stable and a compassionate member of the community, and to prove it, all tourism receipts are donated to charities (Rudd and Davis 1998: 89).

Tilden's guiding principles of interpretation

One of the pioneering experts in interpretation was Freeman Tilden, who proposed six fundamental principles of interpretation that have guided much interpretive planning and the development of many interpretive programmes throughout the world since the mid-twentieth century. His ideas have become standard practice in both natural and cultural realms of interpretation, and many scholars have attempted to build on them (e.g. Field and Wagar 1982; Nuryanti 1997; Uzzell 1994). Tilden's (1977: 9) six principles are as follows:

1. Interpretation should relate what is being displayed or described to something within the personality and life experiences of the visitor. If what the interpreter presents to the audience does not activate a cognitive model from within the experiential realm of the visitor, it will be of little interest to the visitor (Hammitt 1984). People construct their understandings of experiences and the world around them by seeking patterns and adapting the situation to what they already know (Moscardo 2000: 13). According to the president of Henry Ford Museum and Greenfield Village, 'history can't just be about dead people from three generations ago. The point is to inspire people. You need to tell a story and make it meaningful to someone's life' (quoted in Lassen 1999: 44).

2. Information itself is not interpretation. Interpretation is revelation based on information. It is therefore critical to provide visitors with new information and transmit it in a way that inspires. This is different for each individual, and different stimuli might be necessary for different cognitive models in different individuals (Hammitt 1984). This is why, according to Nuryanti (1997: 117), 'it is fundamental to interpretation to realize that meaning lies within the observer or participant . . . rather than as some objective quality inherent in the object itself'.

3. Interpretation is an art that brings together many other arts, whether the materials being presented are historical, architectural or scientific. This highlights the importance of good people and communications skills. The 'art' that Tilden referred to is the 'creativity and imaginativeness of interpreters to present the emotional and enjoyable side of interpretation' (Hammitt 1984: 16).

4. The primary objective of interpretation is not instruction but rather pro-vocation. One of the primary responsibilities of heritage managers is to provoke positive action on the part of tourists. This can be done by bring-ing the past alive for people and, as mentioned in principle (1), drawing out personal meaning for visitors (Beck and Cable 1998). The job of inter-preters, therefore, is to assist visitors in developing relationships of their own between themselves and the heritage place being visited. Tilden's provocation also means to get visitors involved physically and mentally in the interpretive process (Hammitt 1984).

5. Interpretation should be more holistic rather than be made up of simple parts. Hammitt (1984) explains this to mean that interpretation needs to target the whole person, by relating to many different sensory and cognitive facets of information processing. Tilden is also referring to holism in the sense that entire natural and cultural areas are essentially one ecosystem that needs to be considered singly and in its entirety.

6. Interpretation addressed to different visitor groups should follow a fundamentally different approach. Here, Tilden refers to varying degrees of capability in understanding history, cultural systems and natural pro-cesses. Children, for example, process information differently from adults, and these differences need to be considered in interpretive planning.

Interpretive planning

At its simplest, planning is a way of organising the future in order to achieve some desired goal(s). The goals (and roles) of interpretation can best be met by careful and systematic planning. Several reasons for interpretive planning can be identified:

1. It helps establish intentions and goals from the very beginning.
2. The place of interpretation within the context of financial and time constraints will be defined.
3. Resources and markets are assessed at an early stage.
4. Consultation with various agencies and professions are assured and valuable networks are created.
5. Funding opportunities are usually understood.
6. The planning document itself can provide a basis for seeking financial assistance.
7. The timeline to achieve the plan may provide a neutral management tool.
8. The plan provides a clear statement of the professional role of interpreters.
9. Similarly, other staff can identify their responsibilities and opportunities within the broader management framework.
10. A plan usually improves the chances of making target dates for seasonal openings (Goodey 1994: 310).

Specifically, the purposes of interpretive planning include developing a successful programme, assuring protection for areas of special interest, and setting forth guidelines for effective operations, management and maintenance programmes (Bradley 1982: 83). According to Bradley (1982: 78–80), several guiding elements should direct the process of interpretive planning. First is livability. Planning for interpretive programmes must provide realistic convenience for all people. Safety is an important consideration in this, as is the provision of wise interaction with interpretive media, while at the same time discouraging the inappropriate use of heritage. The second guideline is efficiency, which means that facilities need to be designed in the most efficient way for the provision of utilities, maintenance and services. Third is the amenity factor. It is vital that the interpretive setting provides unity, practicality, variety and character, while remaining sensitive to the heritage objects being interpreted. The fourth element is flexibility and choice, which allow changes to occur in the planning process if necessary and in the interpretive programme later on, for example when new techniques and themes might need to be introduced. Likewise, interpretive media need to be used in such a way that will allow visitors to observe, understand and progress at their own pace. Fifth, minimum harm to the natural and cultural environments must be considered in interpretive planning. Construction and visitor use must be planned so that they have only minimal disruption on the environment and the functioning of the site. Ways of mitigating impacts should be determined ahead of time. Optimum use of resources is the sixth guideline, which includes decision-making about new developments and establishing priorities in the long and short term for interpretation. Finally, involvement of the local population in decision-making by giving them a voice about their concerns and desires, is a requisite part of planning.

In common with other forms of planning, interpretive planning involves a series of logical and sequential steps. Planning should be viewed as an ongoing

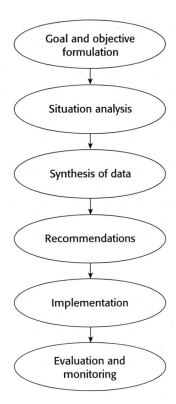

Figure 6.2 Interpretive planning process

process that will guide interpreters and site managers to meet their goals and deal with problems that might arise. The main steps in the planning process are shown in Figure 6.2 and are outlined in detail below, although it is important to realise that this is a formal pattern and that not all projects necessarily follow these steps directly, for each situation is different and must be adapted to meet present needs.

Goal and objective formulation

Goals and objectives for the interpretive programme should be developed in a way that will guide the entire planning process. They should be developed with consistency and commitment. Sometimes these are formed in tentative terms since they might need to be altered once the situation analysis has been completed. Goals are generally stated in very broad or abstract terms. For example, an agency might set a goal for an interpretive programme to 'build awareness among visitors of the need to protect natural and cultural assets in the community'. Objectives, on the other hand, are more specific, and they usually describe ways in which the goal(s) can be achieved. It is important that objectives be kept specific and feasible. In the context of the goal just described, two objectives might be to 'assist each visitor in understanding the ecological processes at play', and to 'provide opportunities for visitors to participate in historical re-enactments'.

Situation analysis/data collection

The old adage, 'you can't know where you're going unless you know where you're coming from' is foundational in planning. It is difficult to enact changes and make recommendations without understanding the current situation. Thus, it is important to carry out a situation analysis, which in many cases entails a thorough inventory of existing infrastructure, interpretive media and natural and cultural resources, as well as the identification of potential natural and cultural resources and interpretative tools that have yet to be utilised. Also as part of this process, a market, or demand, analysis should be conducted where possible to understand the needs and expectations of heritage visitors. This helps define the audience and provides foundational information to form the basis upon which further directions in management and development can be taken.

A strong group of experts is usually necessary in this phase of the planning process. Such a group of experts will reduce the likelihood that important elements of the resource base, market and interpretive programme are missed. For example, an interpretative specialist may not have a thorough understanding of the particular site being inspected. A cultural historian, anthropologist or architect, who specialises in built heritage, or a biologist specialising in natural heritage, could contribute much insight into this stage of the planning process.

Analysis and synthesis of data

The role of this phase is to assemble and analyse the information that was collected, which can result in the identification of themes that are critical in a well-balanced interpretive programme. Rarely do the raw data collected from the inventory result in usable information on their own. Some kind of systematic analysis and cross-examination with other information is usually required, creating a more holistic view of the situation. The data collected are analysed in such a way that a big picture begins to form from which stories can be told. Analysis also allows managers to acknowledge trends in visitor use and impacts, which can help in making decisions for future efforts.

Potential resources should be categorised and analysed in light of the potentials and problems associated with existing resources. Once the information has been analysed, new interpretive themes might become evident, such as new types of vegetation, distinctive types of wildlife or even a new feature of the cultural landscape.

Also during this phase, it is important, based on what managers now know from the data collection and analysis, to develop alternative plans or alternative programmes. This allows significant flexibility and can make interpretive management less complicated later on when issues and problems occur that might not have been foreseen.

Recommendations/the plan

Following the analysis and synthesis, managers should be able to make recommendations and plans of action. If a new building was discovered in a historic city or a new archaeological site near an existing attraction, a useful recommendation might be to excavate it and begin restorative or preservation work so that an interpretive programme can be developed that will include it in the entire interpretive package. The situation analysis might also reveal that an existing interpretive medium is ineffective. Therefore, a recommendation might be to update it or make more drastic changes. Timelines and steps for implementing recommendations are usually developed as part of the interpretive plan.

Implementation

This step is not an easy one, for it is often constrained by fiscal and temporal limitations. Managers must decide what recommendations they will implement and when, which is often determined by budgets and human resources. Included in this step should be a careful scheduling of details to ensure a proper sequence of action (Sharpe 1982a). Incremental implementation is highly recommended in the planning literature as a way of ensuring that unforeseen changes can be made if necessary. Flexibility, adaptability and efficiency (elements of sustainable development) can be better ensured if programmes' are implemented in an incremental manner. For example, if a programme is implemented non-incrementally, and it is later discovered that some of the interpretive programme and media selected are ineffective, it can be costly, time consuming and irritating to have to undo/redo what could have been prevented in the beginning. Of great importance is to combine incremental implementation with a continuous course of evaluation and monitoring, which is the subject of the next section.

Evaluation and monitoring

The final planning phase, and perhaps the longest, is evaluation and monitoring. This requires a long-term commitment on the part of managers, as monitoring and evaluation must be a continuous process. Evaluation and monitoring are necessary to ensure that a plan will continue to meet its objectives, and like incremental implementation, they can help ensure flexibility,

Table 6.4 Purposes for evaluating interpretation

- To provide feedback regarding the successes and failures of the current programme
- To provide information to enlighten future research
- To understand how different audiences react to different interpretive media
- To know about staff effectiveness and training
- To guide the agency in relation to its objectives
- To assess the recreational and educational impacts of interpretation
- To convince other individuals and agencies of the value of interpretation
- To assist in making planning and policy decisions
- To measure safety and security issues in relation to media and facilities
- To provide the public with a way of voicing their concerns
- To enforce accountability, particularly in the area of cost-effectiveness

Source: Compiled from Knudson *et al.* (1995), and Light (1992).

adaptability and efficiency. Evaluative research on visitor behaviour, interpreter effectiveness and facility use should be a part of the continuous monitoring phase of planning since it allows managers to make changes and improve the programme based on their findings. These and other issues are outlined in Table 6.4, which shows the primary reasons for evaluating interpretation. In addition, three dimensions of interpretive programme evaluation have been identified: (1) self-evaluation (i.e. appraising individual professional standards of quality); (2) peer evaluation (i.e. appraisals by other interpreters); and (3) visitor evaluation (objective assessment of visitors' reaction) (McArthur and Hall 1993a: 258). Several types of information are important to know about interpretive programmes and facilities, which can be learned by finding answers to questions such as those below:

- What do visitors say and think about the programme?
- What do visitors learn from the presentations?
- What do visitors think about the exhibits?
- Do visitors read labels?
- How long do visitors study the exhibits?
- What do they learn from the exhibits/signs?
- Who are the visitors?
- How does the audience change through the year and over the years?
- What do staff members say about the visitors? (Knudson *et al.* 1995: 442–3).

Cross-cultural and special needs issues

As was demonstrated in Chapters 3 and 5, heritage visitors are not a homogeneous group of people with undifferentiated interests and needs, and heritage places are becoming ever more prominent places of cross-cultural interface.

While the largest share of the world's heritage sites do not attract a great deal of international attention, this situation is changing as more people from every corner of the globe are beginning to travel. As a result, more and more heritage sites are beginning to be added to international travellers' itineraries, and more destinations are desirous to include their heritage offerings on tour circuits. Likewise, more people with special needs are travelling now more than ever, as laws and practice have required tourist facilities to accommodate their special needs. In light of these changes, as part of good management, interpretive programmes must adapt to address the issues of multilingual interpretation, cross-cultural understanding and special needs visitors.

Bilingual and multilingual interpretation

Very little research has been done on bilingual and multilingual heritage interpretation despite the fact that more places are increasingly including foreign languages in their interpretive media. Light (1992) is perhaps the most obvious exception to this trend, and his work provides the foundation for much of this discussion.

In Wales, heritage attractions have for some time been providing bilingual interpretation in both English and Welsh. In one sense this is indicative of broader sociopolitical efforts to redirect the fate of the Welsh language (Light 1992). In countries such as Canada, Finland and Switzerland, which have more than one official language, interpretation at publicly operated parks and historic sites is generally presented in both or all official languages. This at least allows domestic visitors from key linguistic regions to read or hear the interpretive programme in the primary language.

In countries where only one language dominates, it is becoming more common for museums and heritage places to provide interpretive programmes in the languages of their largest international visitor groups (Plate 6.1). One study of a historic site in England found that only 31 per cent of visitors were British. For approximately half of the people interviewed, English was not their first language. Of these, 6 per cent said they were unable to understand English commentaries or graphic materials. At this site, this ratio amounted to about 20,000 visitors, indicating that there is a clear need for foreign language support (Harrison 1994: 319). Thus, it is critical for managers to know their visitors, where they are from and what their primary languages are.

In addition to adding verbal or written dialogue in other languages, accommodations can be made by doing physical demonstrations of activities that do not require a great deal of explanation. Likewise, direct participation in simple activities and skills where knowledge of the host language is unnecessary can be more productive than long lectures or storyboards (Knudson *et al.* 1995: 117). Even though many foreign groups arrive at historic sites with their own translators, it is essential to adapt the presentations out of common courtesy and to provide them with valuable learning experiences. It must also be kept in

Plate 6.1   Bilingual interpretive sign in China – makes no sense in English

mind that certain language-specific things like idioms, jargon and humour, do not translate well into foreign languages.

Light (1992: 181–3) provided a useful overview of a study he conducted at several heritage sites in Wales, where the Welsh language has diminished significantly in recent decades in favour of English, sparking fervent efforts within much of the population to preserve the language and restore it to everyday usage. As expected, he found that the majority of Welsh-speaking residents (75 per cent) agreed that a Welsh-language guidebook would be very useful, but among non-Welsh residents there was less support (62 per cent). The findings indicate that Welsh speakers are strongly in favour of bilingual (Welsh and English) interpretation at historic sites, and they are less satisfied with the extent of Welsh language they encounter.

Three visitor groups were identified by Light (1992) at heritage sites in Wales, and bilingual interpretation, he argues, has different roles for each group. The first group is fluent Welsh speakers. Since relatively few people speak and understand Welsh fluently today, Welsh language interpretation is unlikely to be cost-effective, particularly at sites in south and east Wales where fewer native speakers live. At one site, Caerphilly Castle, it was found that only 1.8 per cent of the visitors were Welsh speaking, while over 8 per cent were from mainland Europe. Thus, in simple demand terms, 'there is a strong case for providing French and German interpretation before Welsh at such sites' (Light 1992: 182). However, the issue in Wales is not one of simple demand or economics. Instead the benefits are seen as intangible and futuristic as an investment in the future of the language.

Light's second group of visitors is those people who are visitors to Wales. English-speaking travellers do not (and cannot) ignore the Welsh language. In fact, his study showed that the majority of non-Welsh visitors were aware of the use of Welsh at the study sites, and the Welsh language is a definite part of the heritage experience in Wales. Thus, the Welsh-language media signs became part of the attraction, as many visitors claimed to have enjoyed seeing Welsh around them and that it created a part of the experience of being in Wales. Several respondents reported being fascinated by the problems of pronouncing the language or trying to find any connections to English. In a very real sense then, 'interpretation is intended to explain place, but simply the presence of another language, although incomprehensible to many people, acts to give meaning to place' (Light 1992: 183).

The third group of visitors was those residents of Wales who do not speak Welsh. These individuals appear to identify with the Welsh language as a significant element of 'Welshness'. Consequently they demonstrate greater support for bilingual interpretation and are more aware of the amount of Welsh they encounter.

Bilingual or multilingual interpretation, while a worthwhile effort, may be difficult, costly and ineffective in some places where many languages are spoken (e.g. Ghana and other West African countries). Instead, the main lingua franca might be used – in the case of Ghana this would be English even though several languages are spoken there. Sometimes the lingua franca is chosen for efficiency reasons, but it may also be used to avoid conflict that might occur if one indigenous language is selected over another. Having multiple language signs might make them too large to be considered environmentally sensitive, and it can be confusing and aesthetically polluting to have too many languages printed on interpretive signs and other media.

Cultural differences

Cross-cultural sites are places where encounters between cultures occur (Upitis 1989). Such encounters can enhance the heritage experience or, conversely, they might create problems, especially when different cultures have divergent historic understandings of a common place. Interpretation can have a crucial role to play in mitigating some of the problems that might be created through cultural differences.

When interpreting cross-cultural sites interpreters must be sensitive to differing cultural perspectives. By way of example, for the Maori people of New Zealand, to interpret indigenous historic sites and the activities of Maori ancestors in the conventional European manner could be taken as sacrilege. Even oral interpretation might be deemed an unworthy action. 'As one Maori interpreter has stated: "when Maori visit a sacred place, they go to feel rather than to see. Interpretation panels are an encumbrance, there for the use of the ignorant, those who cannot see with their minds nor feel with their hearts"' (Molloy 1993: 67).

Programmes with a cross-cultural element should be founded on three basic perspectives, which can help eliminate much of the contestation among visitors that so often accompanies heritage interpretation (see Chapter 8):

1.   There must be recognition of human dignity and the right of others to have beliefs and values different from one's own.
2.   Positive attitudes towards people from other groups must prevail, such as fair-mindedness, respect for feelings, empathy and friendliness.
3.   It is critical to accept differences with interest and pleasure, as an enrichment of one's own life and understanding rather than as an assumption of inferiority on the part of the different culture (Upitis 1989: 154).

Interpretation and people with disabilities

Interpreters and heritage site managers have the responsibility to accommodate people with special needs, particularly those with learning and physical disabilities, and the elderly. Harrison (1994) mentions four groups of people with special needs that need to be taken into account in providing access to interpretive facilities and interpretive programmes. These are the wheelchair borne, the blind and partially sighted, those with hearing difficulties and the elderly and less mobile. Their specific needs include sufficient floor space for wheelchairs, displays that are visible and readable from a wheelchair, supplementary audio or reading material for the deaf, good light and sufficient print sizes for the partially sighted, Braille and other touchable media for the blind, and seating and resting places for the elderly and less mobile (Harrison 1994: 318). It is important to be certain that obstacles and hazards are removed immediately and that changes of level and changes in floor texture are kept to a minimum. For people with hearing impairments, devices exist that can assist them in hearing interpretive presentations (Cox 1994; Hartley 1995).

Heritage sites have gained enough knowledge through the years that interpretation can be a fun and learning experience for people with learning disabilities as well. The aim here is to increase intellectual accessibility for people who might otherwise feel intimidated or left out of places that should be accessible to all members of society (Cox 1994: 354). Much of these efforts are assisted by the use of new devices that also assist with the learning of disabled people.

In addition to mechanisms that help people to hear, feel and access interpretation, it is important that interpreters are trained in a sensitive manner. Careful use of terminologies and words demonstrates that staff care about the feelings, needs and experiences of all visitors. Phrases such as 'now look at . . .' can be replaced by 'here, we find . . .'. Likewise, visually impaired people like to hear descriptions of objects and colours because some might be able to see a little, they might be able to remember images and they might have good imaginations. The best advice about developing scripts for tapes used by visually impaired people is for the script to be written by a person who has visual disabilities (Cox 1994: 353).

In 1992, President Bush signed the Americans with Disabilities Act (ADA), the aim of which was to eliminate discrimination (intentional and inadvertent) against people with disabilities. As discussed in Chapter 3, this civil rights law has significant implications for interpretation at heritage sites. Since the ADA requires that everyone, regardless of disability, should have full enjoyment and equal opportunity of services and facilities, interpretive programmes fall within its purview. Knudson *et al.* (1995: 118) described several ways in which the ADA affects interpretation and general heritage management in the United States by illustrating a number of situations that would constitute discrimination under the law:

- Outdoor and nature sites cannot assume that an individual with disabilities would not want to climb rocks or climbing towers or that it would not be safe and therefore prohibit participation. In this case, management must do whatever they can to accommodate safe participation by carrying out an individualised assessment.

- If a programme is open, it must accommodate people with disabilities. For example, allowing someone with a disability to register for a heritage trail hike but failing to identify accessible access points is discriminatory.

- Interpretive programmes for individuals with disabilities must be equal to those for people without disabilities. For instance, if a heritage property offers 25 programmes, but only 5 are for people with disabilities, this is considered discriminatory.

- Interpretation must take place in the most integrated setting possible. If interpreters do not learn techniques to reduce negative interaction among people with and without disabilities, they might be found in violation of the law.

- Putting on special showings at separate times for people with disabilities is discriminatory, for example requiring disabled people to attend a programme at 10 a.m. when other visitors can go any time during the day.

- Charging higher fees to visitors with disabilities in an effort to recoup the cost of compliance is a violation.

- Museums and heritage sites must provide supporting aids such as raised letters, special signage, sign-language interpreters, and cassette tapes to facilitate communication.

- Structural changes to facilities (e.g. wheelchair ramps) and other ways of making interpretation accessible to everyone are required.

Again, as mentioned in Chapter 3, some historic structures are exempt from this if their heritage value is deemed to be jeopardised by such additions, although it is incumbent on managers in this situation to try finding some alternative to accommodate visitors with disabilities.

Interpretive media

Most interpretive media fit within one of two (or both) categories: personal and non-personal (Ham 1992; Regnier *et al.* 1994; Sharpe 1982b). Personal media are those that utilise a living person as the actual medium for disseminating information. Non-personal media are mechanisms and set-ups that require no intervention on the part of staff for visitors to obtain the information they need.

Personal media

Several forms of personal media have found considerable success at heritage sites throughout the world. One of the most common forms is conducted activities, which include guided tours (Plate 6.2), trail hikes, walks and train and stagecoach trips. These are used to show large and small groups around historic sites and museums, and they are one of the most rewarding approaches

Plate 6.2   Guided interpretation at ancient Greek ruins in Sicily

to person-based interpretation. Similarly, group talks or lectures are presentations that take place before groups at set times in venues such as amphitheatres, campfires and conference rooms. With smaller groups, two-way communication may be possible, but this generally involves more of a lecture format (Sharpe 1982b). These are very useful media for explaining the historical and natural background and context to large groups of visitors.

Information attendants are an important part of interpretation. Here the staff member is stationed in one location (e.g. an information booth), and visitors seek her/him out to ask questions, get directions and inquire about additional information. Museums sometimes have guides stationed at entrances to orient visitors before they begin a guided or self-guided tour (Butcher-Younghans 1993). Likewise, stationary guides can be placed strategically throughout museums and outdoor sites to answer questions that relate specifically to the place where they are stationed.

Perhaps the most rapidly growing form of personal interpretation, and certainly among the most common at heritage theme parks and outdoor village museums, is living characters and cultural demonstrations (Light 1991; Walsh 1992). Often interpreters portray non-specific characters dressed in period costumes, speaking with period dialects, and taking on a first-person approach to information giving. They are commonly involved in the production of activities and goods that would have been common during the period under examination and specific to the place. Examples include candle pouring, baking, horse shoeing, cheese making, washing clothes with a washboard and place-specific activities such as making wooden shoes in the Netherlands (Plate 6.3).

Plate 6.3 Dutch artisan demonstrating the art of wooden shoe making

Role-playing is another important form of living character interpretation. In role-playing, the staff member presents a real person from the past who might have been associated with the site. It is important that the person being portrayed has been well researched and thoroughly rehearsed (Butcher-Younghans 1993). A third form of living characters is living history performances. These are re-enactments or skits performed by actors, such as bank robberies, cowboy shootouts, civil war battles, cultural ceremonies and rituals. Research into these is also important, particularly in the details of clothing, storytelling and activity (Butcher-Younghans 1993). McAndrew (1995) argues that one of the strengths of the living interpretation is that it tends to be less formal, thereby allowing visitors to feel more comfortable asking questions, and it provides them with an 'enjoyable visit, rich in novelty' (Light 1991: 8).

Related to this approach are special events, which can also be seen as a method of interpretation. English Heritage's programme of special events, for example, began in 1985 and has since developed into a major annual activity. By 1993, the programme had developed into more than 200 events on 50 different themes at some 70 properties, examples being 'The Fury of the Norseman'; 'Everyday Life in the Time of Richard III'; 'The Bard's Best Falconry'; 'Fourth National Longbow Championship'; and even a 'Grand Catastrophe' (Griffin and Giles 1994: 332). Although the boom began in the UK, heritage events are becoming more commonplace in North America (Janiskee 1996) (Plate 6.4) and Asia (Peleggi 1996). Of special events as interpretive media, Janiskee (1996: 412) stated that their production 'can greatly increase public awareness of historic house values and enhance the economic, educational and sociocultural benefits' associated with their preservation.

Non-personal

Non-personal media are common at most heritage locations and include both visual and audio devices. Written material is a very common interpretive medium throughout the world. Brochures, guidebooks, labels and maps are good examples of written media that can be printed in various languages. Sometimes these are offered to visitors as part of the entrance fee, although at some locations a nominal fee is charged, which most visitors are willing to pay.

Signs, another visual medium, are probably the most common form of interpretation (Plate 6.5). Interpretive signs allow a great deal of material to be included at each stop along the trail or alongside the display path. Visual images on signs can catch and keep people's attention and assist in articulating important messages. It is important that signs are made of durable materials that will withstand harsh weather and visitors leaning on and touching them (Sharpe 1982b). In historic urban areas it is important to provide signs so that visitors can find their way around. Very old cities tend to be crowded, with

Plate 6.4   Re-enactment of history at Fort George, Canada

Plate 6.5   A tourist utilising interpretive signs at the Grand Canyon

narrow streets and a mix of residential housing, businesses and industrial buildings. Traversing such an urban landscape can be confusing for visitors who are not familiar with the place, and signs posted along main tourist routes can be valuable in assisting visitors in navigating their way around.

Related to signs are exhibitions, which are used most commonly at outdoor sites (e.g. indigenous ruins) and are essentially panels containing text on a neutral background together with maps, photographs and graphics. They sometimes also include artefacts recovered from the site. Their primary objective is to provide a general introduction, orientation and overview of the attraction (Light 1995b: 135). Exhibitions are usually distinct from museums, according to Light (1995b), for in museums the objects themselves are the principal means of communication, while the purpose of an exhibition is to interpret a historic monument.

Self-guided audio tours are a useful non-visual medium. This involves audio devices being used by visitors to describe the objects in view and often includes sound effects as well. Typically, the objects or displays are numbered, and a number in the audio guide corresponds to what tourists are viewing (Sharpe 1982b). This method is very important in allowing foreign visitors an opportunity to experience the site in their own language, and otherwise, it adds animation and flavour to the scenes being described and the stories being told. These tours are effective because they allow visitors to set their own pace, spend time in areas that interest them and spend less time in places that do not (Butcher-Younghans 1993; Light 1995b).

Media selection

Managers should review several questions in determining what media to focus on in any given situation. Questions related to economics and efficiency must be considered, including how much it costs and whether or not it requires continuous maintenance, electricity or a person to operate it. Likewise, issues of visitor use must be considered, such as how readily visitors can tamper with it, what the primary audience is, and how effective it is (Sharpe 1982b). Additionally, Sharpe (1982b) proposed three factors that ought to be considered in guiding the media selection process: the resource, the visitors and the interpreters. This, together with the questions listed first, can help determine the suitability of a specific medium.

Visitor issues

Traditionally interpretation has treated heritage visitors as one homogenous audience in terms of education level, ethnic background, mental and physical capability, language, age, place of origin and reason for travel. However, as Uzzell (1994: 299) notes, 'there is no such body as the general public. The so-called general public is made up of different audiences with different needs and different expectations.' These differences need to be recognised and planned for to ensure effective interpretation and to avoid conflict (Field and Wagar 1982). Different groups, such as the elderly and children, will be looking for different experiences.

   Likewise, managers should realise that not all visitors can understand the site in the same way they do. If they do not, interpretation might be conducted at the level of the interpreter[a] rather than the level of visitors. Visitors need orientation, direction and instructions; they need to be led to understand from their own life experiences what is being presented. This is particularly important among foreign visitors who come from divergent backgrounds with different sets of expectations. In essence, visitors need to be told what is unique about the place they are visiting (Uzzell 1994: 298). Generally, heritage visitors are limited in the amount of information they can understand, so interpretation should be provided at different levels to reflect the interest and abilities among different groups. It is usually better that fewer features are interpreted and understood well by visitors than many features interpreted and not understood (Uzzell 1994).

   Managers need to consider what visitors need to know about the place to make their visit stimulating and memorable. Thus, in choosing the media, interpreters must also take into account what visitors perceive as being the most important forms of interpretation and characteristics of museum interpretive exhibits. In one study (Herbert 1989a), visitors were asked to rate the various

Table 6.5 Effectiveness of various media forms according to visitors (%)

Media type	Very important	Quite important	Not important
Notices that give facts and details	77	22	1
Diagrams showing things as they were	74	25	1
Guide cards for a self-conducted tour	55	36	9
Maps showing the site in its region	53	41	7
Exhibitions	39	54	7
Historical tableaux	30	46	24
Guided tours	27	40	33
Audio-visual presentations	18	44	39
Sound commentaries	16	38	47

Source: Adapted from Herbert (1989a).

Table 6.6 Top 10 attributes of an interpretive exhibit

1. It arouses interest in the subject
2. The information is presented clearly
3. It teaches something new
4. It catches people's attention
5. It relays the message quickly
6. It involves the visitor
7. Visitors can use it at their own pace
8. It is a memorable experience
9. It respects the intelligence of the visitor
10. It uses familiar items or experiences to make the point

Source: After Alt and Shaw (1984 – cited in Moscardo 1999: 37).

forms of interpretation in terms of their effectiveness (Table 6.5). Likewise, based on an early study by Alt and Shaw (1984), Table 6.6 presents the top 10 most important characteristics of museum exhibits according to museum visitors in the 1980s. Clarity, poignancy, attractiveness and dynamics are key qualities described in this survey. It is clear, then, that interpretive tools should attract and keep visitors' attention. According to Moscardo (1999: 64), this can be done by using large, living, touchable, moving and colourful means and involve notions of discovery, interaction and action.

Interactivity is a central element in heritage visitation. A site that offers opportunities to participate in historic activities, to handle and use artefacts, or to view the re-enactment of a historically significant event is much more interesting to most visitors than simply looking at a motionless display of gadgets and photographs. Weiler (1984) has discussed the importance of utilising the world's industrial past, such as factories and areas of natural resource extraction, as attractions, which would offer up-close, hands-on experience with past industrial activities. Interactivity also means that visitor groups should be encouraged to interact with, and learn from, each other (Uzzell 1994).

Resource issues

The nature of the resource can be a major determining factor in deciding what types of media to choose. For example, self-guided audio tours might be important to consider in noise-sensitive places. Films and live guides might be useful before entering a sensitive cave, so that people will know how to behave based on what they learned in the presentation (Sharpe 1982b). Underwater attractions, such as sunken ships, are probably best interpreted using waterproof signs rather than any form of electronic media, although tourist submarines and guided dive tours provide good opportunities for underwater interpretation as well (Tabata 1989). The medium itself may also have a role to play in resource protection by convincing people not to touch, or by actually protecting the artefact itself, such as ropes and interpretive signs.

Light (1995b: 134) argues,

> Ancient monuments are very different from both museums and visitor centres. The simple fact that most monuments are in a ruinous state, and the need to protect the physical fabric of the building, acts as a fundamental constraint on the type of interpretive media which can be employed.

As a result, interpretive media at monuments are generally simpler than those used at other sites. The fact of being a ruin is an important limitation on what can be said about the site and therefore different interpretative strategies will need to be employed. At ancient monuments, the main types of media used are exhibitions, outdoor panels and stereo-audio tours (Light 1995b: 134).

Interpreter issues

Because interpreters are an important part of the heritage experience, they must possess people-related skills and content knowledge. Interpreters need to have excellent communications skills because theirs is the job of communicating meanings and experiences to visitors. They must also possess a friendly disposition and a dynamic personality, avoiding what Risk (1994: 320) considers to be an unacceptable situation where

> stilted, dry and memorized, and presented with little or no enthusiasm and sparkle, the presentation drones endlessly and painfully on to a well deserved termination while visitors, reduced almost to a trance by boredom, drift aimlessly away before the conclusion of the programme or presentation.

This somewhat humorous and unfortunate scenario is common at many heritage places. A charismatic speaker can accomplish much when his or her job is to provoke people to think, absorb and discover (Lewis 1989). The more competent the interpreter is at communicating, the more visitors will get out of their visit (Ryan and Dewar 1995). Good interpreters need to be cordial, good-natured, confident, well organised and humorous (Knudson *et al.* 1995).

Likewise, interpreters need to have a solid understanding of their field of specialisation. At most sites, since interpretation is essentially 'about place and the concept of place, about putting people and things into their environmental context' (Aldridge 1989: 64), geography is an essential area of knowledge. Interpreters should have a firm grasp on the history and facts associated with the specific location where they work. Visitors will always remember the interpreter who provided them with incorrect information! Interpreters also need to understand learning theories and behavioural aspects of interpretation (Fennell 1999), which will help them achieve the desired results of an interpretive programme. Interpreters should be taught many things as part of their training related to visitor behaviour and learning theory. These learning principles are summarised in Table 6.7. Understanding interpreter skills and training can assist management in deciding which person-based media could be used.

New technologies

Many new technological developments have occurred in recent years in the area of heritage interpretation (Velarde and Allen 1994). In the words of Uzzell (1994: 295), traditionally 'interpretation meant leaflets and exhibition panels and maybe an audio-visual programme. The range of interpretive media now used is not only considerably more varied but increasingly technical: computer

Table 6.7 Learning principles for interpreter training

- People learn better when they are actively involved in the learning process
- People learn better when they are using as many senses as appropriate
- People prefer to learn what is of most value to them at the present
- What people discover for themselves generates a special and vital excitement and satisfaction
- Learning requires activity on the part of the learner
- Friendly competition stimulates learning
- Knowing the usefulness of the knowledge being acquired makes learning more effective
- People learn best from hands-on experience
- People learn best when the experience is close to them in time and space
- Questions can be effectively used to help people derive meanings
- Giving people expectations at the beginning of an activity will focus attention and thus improve learning
- The ways in which people are responded to affect their learning

Source: Adapted from Lewis (1989).

simulations, personal stereo guided tours, rides augmented with sounds and smells.' While modernising interpretive programmes is important, managers need to be cautious not to allow the medium to dominate the resource. Too many high-tech mechanisms and gimmicks can detract from the real experience, causing some people to want to stay away. It is easy for new 'designer' interpretive tools to yield 'visitor "oohs" and "aahs" for reasons more related to technology and aesthetics than to heritage interpretation' (Pearson and Sullivan 1995: 298).

Electronic media are quickly replacing many of the human guides at museums throughout the world. For example, electronic guides were introduced at the Roman Baths Museum in Bath, England, in 1995 (Walter 1996).

> On entering the museum, each visitor is handed an electronic guide, which resembles a long telephone handset with press-button dialing. Use of this is included in the admission price and almost everyone takes one. Various sites around the museum are identified by a number and, on pressing the number on the handset, the visitor can listen to information about the site (currently available in six languages) (Walter 1996: 241) (Plate 6.6).

These handsets are becoming commonplace throughout the UK, Western Europe and increasingly so in North America.

Computers are perhaps one of the most significant technological advances to affect interpretation in recent years. Interactive computer displays have

Plate 6.6   Advanced personal interpretive media at the Roman Baths, Bath, England

found significant success, largely because they offer several sensory experiences and allow visitors to control the information they receive (Moscardo and Woods 1998). Computer-related virtual reality may also become significant within the heritage context in the future. Cyber boundaries are already being crossed, and perhaps someday people will be able to experience the Roman Colosseum, the Great Wall of China and the Museum of Natural History all in one afternoon, without ever having to leave home (Timothy 2001c: 175). Additionally, 'virtual reality may also become a useful planning tool for building projects and exhibition development, by allowing the project team to visualize the finished product before it has been built' (Fahy 1995: 94). Computers already benefit site management generally by providing curators with enormous volumes of information storage space and opportunities to cross-examine information from their collections in more innovative ways, making connections that could not have been made easily with a manual system (Fahy 1995: 85).

Multimedia shows are another manifestation of technological change that is becoming more popular at historic sites. Lighting illusions and high-tech sound equipment can contribute significantly to the portrayal of historic events through pageants and other theatrical performances located at historic properties. Such performances usually require large amounts of equipment, which should be hidden during the day if possible so that it does not create a distraction for daytime visitors (Clair 1997). High-tech light and sound shows, such as those at Borobodur and Prambanan temple complexes in Indonesia, can assist in highlighting traditional practices and art forms during performances.

New developments are not without their negative implications, however. Walter (1996) has outlined several criticisms of the use of technological developments at historic sites. Prior to the introduction of the electronic guides at the Bath museum, visitors talked among themselves; they pointed out places of interest and discussed what they were gazing at. Now,

> almost everybody is silent as they listen to their electronic guide. At any one time, no more than one person in 30 is likely to be talking. As a colleague who had visited the baths many times said to me: 'It's like a morgue in there now' (Walter 1996: 242).

What is negative about this is that visitors no longer look for objects, but rather numbers, and few look around independently now. Before, parents geared their conversation to their children as they discovered things together. Once the parents began using the handsets, according to Walter, the children were left without a way of relating to either adults or objects. In conclusion, Walter (1996: 244) laments 'it seems that the technology provides more information to more people but at the cost of isolating visitors from each other and from the site. It is perhaps analogous to the replacement of the cinema by the home television set.'

Visitor use of interpretive media

From their study of visitors to Mount Cook National Park, Stewart *et al.* (1998) identified four types of visitors in relation to their use of interpretive media: seekers, stumblers, shadowers and shunners (see Table 6.8). Stewart *et al.* (1998) characterised seekers by their need to obtain information and interpretive information. This group was divided into learners, gatherers and fillers. *Learners* are visitors who seemed to require information about the place at all stages throughout their visit. This group is the most likely to be stimulated by interpretation and the most aware of the place prior to visiting. Among these visitors, interpretation may not advance their understanding of the place, but it will likely supplement it. *Gatherers* are visitors who collect information about the site to help them undertake selected activities. In common with learners, gatherers make use of interpretation throughout their visit; however, their motives are different. Instead of gathering information to enhance their understanding of place, they tend to collect information (e.g. times and locations of activities) that will enable them to do certain activities. The last type of seeker is the *filler*. Fillers are people who are forced to take an interest in interpretation, when it would not otherwise have been a major part of their experience. For example, fillers would generally seek out interpretation centres, such as visitor centres or covered exhibitions, as shelter from inclement weather. In this case, visitors are obliged to take more than a passing interest in interpretation,

Table 6.8   Interpretive users at Mount Cook National Park

Seekers – visitors who actively seek sources of information and interpretation:

- *Learners* – people who seek interpretation specifically to learn about the place
- *Gatherers* – people who seek information (as opposed to interpretation) about a place
- *Fillers* – those who seek information and interpretation to fill time while at a place

Stumblers – visitors who stumble across information and interpretation sources:

- *Satisfied* – people who are satisfied to stumble over interpretation while at the place
- *Frustrated* – people who are frustrated to stumble over interpretation at the place

Shadowers – visitors who were chaperoned by other people through interpretation:

- *Formal* – people who are chaperoned by guides around interpretation sites
- *Informal* – people who are chaperoned informally around interpretation sites

Shunners – visitors who shun sources of information and interpretation:

- *Avoiders* – people who purposefully avoid interpretation
- *Passive* – those who are uninterested in interpretation

Source: Adapted from Stewart *et al.* (1998).

and if the need did not exist to fill time, they probably would not otherwise have spent much time interacting with interpretation.

The second primary category described by Stewart *et al.* (1998) is stumblers, for whom interpretation is simply a chance encounter. The experience of stumbling into interpretation appears to add to the experience of *satisfied stumblers*, who take more than a passing interest in it when they find it. *Frustrated stumblers* appear to be dissatisfied with their happenstance encounter with interpretation. When they eventually find interpretation, they tend to be critical of it. Owing to this experience, they will be unlikely in the future to be interested in interpretation.

Shadowers, according to Stewart *et al.* (1998), are formal and informal. *Formal shadowers* are usually escorted formally through the site and through the interpretive facilities by a paid guide. It appears that this is the only visitor group likely to use the whole range of interpretation prior to and during their visit to a site. *Informal shadowers* are led through interpretation as tag-alongs by friends and relatives who might be active seekers themselves, and while they did not necessarily seek out interpretation on their own initiative, they take an interest in it because of the people/seekers they are with.

Shunners comprise the final group of interpretation users. *Passive shunners* make little effort to experience interpretation, often as a result of time constraints, tiredness, lack of language abilities or lack of interest. They might, however, be influenced by some forms of interpretation that are difficult to avoid (e.g. announcements on a bus). *Avoiders* actively and decisively avoid site interpretation. For one reason or another they resist becoming involved in interpretation, so its effect on their understanding of place is minimal.

The seeker type of visitor, Miles (1986: 78) argues, will learn from the exhibits almost regardless of what the museum does, though the museum can have a major influence on the quality of the learning that takes place. Miles refers to the other types of visitors as 'window shoppers', some of whom visit simply as a way of passing time (e.g. sightseeing, escaping from the rain and somewhere to take bored kids). Few of these are actually interested in having an educational experience.

According to Light's (1995b) study in Wales, in terms of media specifically, heritage visitors used outdoor panels most often, and nearly all visitors saw them, while stereo-audio tours were found to be the least utilised. Reasons for this included:

1. People do not like guided tours or Walkman stereos.
2. People were unaware that such a self-guided tour existed.
3. Some people did not feel they had enough time at the site.
4. Accompanying children kept some people from using the audio tour.
5. Some thought the tour was too costly.

Setting up and learning how to use an audio tour sometimes also acts as a deterrent to visitors (Herbert 1989a; Light 1995b). Despite all this, audio tours and other audio media are valuable tools because they can cause visitors to use their imagination to re-enact certain events or sites in their own minds (Herbert 1989a), and visitors are more likely to listen to the whole audio tape than they are to look at all the visual displays or outdoor panels. What this suggests is that audio interpretation does a better job of retaining heritage tourists' attention than written interpretation (Light 1995b: 138). According to Light (1995b), audio media retain attention more than visual. This is to some degree a result of their novelty value and people's propensity to listen to more information than they are prepared to read.

Live presentations by interpreter tour guides and lectures are also rated quite highly as effective media. These are popular because they allow visitors to interact with the information better and personalise the experience. Interaction with interpreters is generally rated highly by visitors because this allows them to ask questions about information that is most interesting and personally relevant (Moscardo and Woods 1998: 320). Live demonstrations are a good way of communicating to an audience, especially when audience participation is involved (McArthur and Hall 1993c: 29).

The most common types of things visitors get from participating in interpretive programmes are knowledge, personal experience, social benefits and aesthetic encounters (Masberg and Silverman 1996). For most people, knowledge is gained about specific topics such as everyday life during different periods of history, animal life and different cultures. Personal experiences typically include developing a personal relationship with the sights seen and even heard. Social benefits were also important outcomes, such as sharing their experiences with companions (e.g. family members, friends and fellow students), and aesthetic appreciation for features such as nature, food, natural landscape, music and animals can be a memorable experience (Masberg and Silverman 1996: 23–4).

The following case study of interpretation at Hadrian's Wall in northern England demonstrates several of the issues and principles described in this chapter.

CASE STUDY Interpretation at Hadrian's Wall

Hadrian's Wall was built by the Romans between AD 120 and 130 as part of their territorial defensive line on the empire's northern border. The wall, over 3 m thick, stretched from sea to sea in northern England just south of the border of Scotland and included fortresses, towers and milecastles all along its length. Hadrian's Wall today is the best-preserved and most impressive Roman ruin in the UK (also a designated World Heritage Site) and has become a significant tourist attraction in recent years (Cole 1994; Turley 1998; Usherwood 1996) (see Table 6.9). Visitors can travel along much of the wall, which passes through countryside, agricultural land and urban areas, or they can arrive at specific points along it for tours and views of the wall in various degrees of preservation and deterioration.

Table 6.9 Annual visitation at selected Hadrian's Wall sites

Site	1995	1996	1997	1998
Arbeia	74,309	77,559	70,638	87,279
Museum of Antiquities	19,503	18,680	16,748	16,328
Corbridge	22,861	23,188	25,769	23,925
Chesters	68,570	77,809	76,642	77,365
Housesteads	127,389	122,189	123,559	114,033
Vindolanda	68,041	71,770	71,586	68,052
Roman Army Museum	53,701	54,358	48,950	44,749
Birdoswald	34,899	40,607	37,536	36,614
Tullie House	57,034	59,587	61,891	59,573
Senhouse	2,677	2,914	3,396	5,754
Once Brewed	79,735	79,680	78,468	66,474
Total	608,719	628,341	615,183	600,146

Source: Compiled from Hadrian's Wall Tourism Partnership (1999).

Interpretive panels are the most common medium used by English Heritage, the caretaker of the wall, along its route, and interpretive centres (free and paid-entry) exist in some locations. Generally interpretation includes illustrations of what the structure was believed to have looked like in Roman times and are accompanied by descriptions of the wall and its functions. Signs/panels are translated into German, Italian, French and Japanese for the sake of foreign tourists, even though these groups together account for only approximately 10–20 per cent of the visitors to the region. At some points along the wall, different media are utilised. Audiotapes (English only) are provided at Vindolanda and Corbridge, combining music and sounds with general information about the Roman way of life and the wall (Turley 1998: 116).

Despite these positive aspects, Turley (1998: 117) described several negative issues that have plagued interpretation of the wall in the past. First, problems arose because the audiotapes focused on the interpretive panels, creating crowded conditions at times. Second, the main sites along the wall had museums, which displayed many artefacts associated with the Roman period, but the quality of these museums was variable, and some of them and their displays appeared not to have been updated for decades. Third, at some of the museums (e.g. in Chesters), there was no interpretation of the stone works and other artefacts, except for a few single-line, or single-word, comments. Reviews of the Chesters museum were mixed, suggesting that the value of visiting was the ambience, while others suggested that the displays failed to do justice to the artefacts. Fourth, the wall museums have traditionally been unable to retain visitors for more than a few minutes. Finally, relatively few of the sites offered interpretive services to non-English speakers. Efforts to turn this situation around have been made in recent years by English Heritage (1996) by way of improving displays, establishing more orientation centres, gateway sites and places where visitors can find information. Various other media are also being tried, and improvements have been made in catering more to the needs of international visitors. Likewise, it is now recognised that interpretation at various points along the wall will help build awareness among tourists of the need to preserve this relic and to direct larger crowds of people away from the sections that are beginning to fall apart.

Summary and conclusions

Heritage tourism is often differentiated from other types of tourism by visitors' interest and willingness to learn at sites and accept that education is an important aspect of the heritage experience (Boyd 2002a). Interpretation by managers of sites therefore plays an essential role in assisting the visitor's process of learning. This chapter has offered a detailed discussion of heritage interpretation. It has gone beyond the traditional examination of different types of formal education, to viewing interpretation as part of entertainment and an integral part of sustainable development.

An important aspect of the chapter has been the development of the debate around interpretative planning. Having its genesis in Tilden's (1977) fundamental principles of interpretation, this type of planning, if it is to be successful, needs to be based upon several guiding elements: livability, efficiency, amenity, flexibility, minimum harm, optimum resource use and where the local population is involved with the decision-making process. It is also important, however, to accept that these guiding elements exist within a series of logical and sequential steps, common within planning in general, but which may be adapted to meet the requirements of interpretative planning. These have been highlighted to include the following sequential order: goals and objective formulation (where goals are broad-based and abstract as opposed to objectives that are more specific and provide direction as to how goals may be achieved), situation analysis and data collection, analysis and synthesis of data, recommendations and plan of action, implementation, evaluation and monitoring.

With heritage places becoming even more prominent as places of cross-cultural interface, managers are increasingly faced with the challenges of meeting the needs of a growing international clientele where their ability to comprehend will range from those who are able-bodied to those with special needs. Not to cater across this spectrum of abilities would be to ignore central elements of sustainability, which stresses principles such as equity and ethics. Therefore, managers need to know their audience, and be able to adapt interpretation programmes to serve multilingual participation at heritage venues, either through verbal and written means or via dialogue as part of the demonstration of activities. Interpretation needs to be seen as having a crucial role to play in situations where cultural differences exist. As noted in this chapter, managers would do well to follow the guidelines set out by Upitis (1989) and develop programmes from the perspective of respect for human dignity, and having a positive and enriching attitude towards other cultures regardless of the impact this may have on one's own culture and system of beliefs. Where the 'ability' of individuals is concerned, heritage managers are faced with offering equal access and interpretation to all sectors of society. Clearly this represents challenges and greater costs where the special needs population is concerned, but to ignore this heritage market would be wrong and would send a message that heritage is not open to all and that heritage places are the preserve of the elite and non-disabled visitor when clearly this is not the case.

As interest in heritage attractions continues to grow, managers are faced with providing new and exciting ways to convey their messages to visitors. This chapter has revealed the range of interpretative media available, including personal media (tours, guides, cultural demonstrations, living characters and the hosting of special events) and those categorised as non-personal (brochures, signage, exhibitions, exhibitions and self-guided audio tours). The decision as to what medium is best in aiding interpretation requires that managers first acknowledge that all audiences are different; some may need to be told what makes a place unique, while others can rate what is important but require interpretive methods that engender a stimulating and memorable visit.

With the advent of new technology at heritage attractions, interactivity is emerging as having a central role in engaging younger elements of society, as they aspire to learn through experiences that involve their participation and interaction with exhibits and displays. While the ability to interact with inanimate objects can be very educational and worthwhile, managers should be cautious as to how far down the technology road they should travel as high-tech presentations can potentially replace quality with gimmicks that detract from the experience intended. The authors are not advocating that computers should not be part of the interpretation process, instead they suggest caution regarding the extent to which they should be used, for as shown in this chapter using new developments can also have negative implications.

Research has shown that visitors make different use of interpretive media. While it is often amiss to label tourists as falling into certain categories, there is much merit in doing so from the perspective of managers whose challenge is to offer interpretation to all visitors. Recent research such as that by Stewart *et al.* (1998) suggests that there is benefit in developing interpretive media that can cater to the needs of specific types of visitors, be they seekers, stumblers or shadowers, but as Light (1995b) reveals in his research in Wales, while a certain medium (audio interpretation) is preferred by managers to help visitors retain information, preference by visitors may remain with traditional approaches (reading written panels). Despite the range of media used by managers, and the extent to which visitors engage themselves with it, what is essential is that the heritage experience, interpretation and products themselves remain as authentic as possible. This issue of authenticity is the focus of the next chapter.

Questions

1. Is education more important than entertainment regarding heritage interpretation?
2. What are key factors influencing formal and informal education at heritage sites?
3. In what ways are heritage attactions accommodating the special needs visitor?
4. Evaluate the pros and cons of personal and non-personal interpretative media?

Further reading

Butcher-Younghans, S. (1993) *Historic House Museums: A practical handbook for their care, preservation, and management*, Oxford University Press, New York.

Harrison, R. (ed.) (1994) *Manual of Heritage Management*, Butterworth Heinemann, Oxford.

Knudson, D.M., Cable, T.T. and Beck, L. (1995) *Interpretation of Cultural and Natural Resources*, Venture, State College, Pa.

Machlis, G.E. and Field, D.R. (eds) (1984) *On Interpretation: Sociology for interpreters of natural and cultural history*, Oregon State University Press, Corvallis.

Tilden, F. (1977) *Interpreting Our Heritage*, University of North Carolina Press, Chapel Hill.

CHAPTER 7

The authenticity debate

One of the most pressing debates in recent years in the realm of heritage has been the notion of authenticity (Fawcett and Cormack 2001; Fees 1996; Rogers 1996; Selwyn 1996). Authenticity is central to much of heritage tourism as the product(s) on display are often re-creations of a region's past in terms of both the built and cultural landscapes. The association heritage has with history and the built landscape, raises concern over how authentic a representation of the past can be. As Ashworth and Tunbridge (2000) point out, there are many types of authenticity associated with a particular object, building or site (e.g. creator, material, function, concept, history, ensemble, context). With the absence of a conservation and heritage planning culture until the mid-1960s onward, how authentic are aspects of the built environment given that they have been subject to decay, lack of attention, and then when prevented from further decay are subject to restoration, protection, repair and even rebuilding? Perhaps then, if authenticity is accepted as central to heritage, where places are concerned, this can only be found within what Ashworth and Tunbridge term 'heritage gem cities', which they define as 'usually small, cities in which the historic resource is so dramatic, extensive, and complete' (2000: 155), that the past has survived intact with little or no change.

Authenticity is associated with portraying the past in an accurate manner. According to Butcher-Younghans (1993: 189), an accurate account of history is necessary for sound interpretation, 'whether it be a resident's political life, a historical event that took place at the site, or the history of the house itself being unraveled', ensuring that any story told is grounded in and related to solid fact. This, however, does not solve the problem of ensuring accuracy in the written record of history itself. Heritage, while it can mean many different things as described in the introductory chapter, is often the re-creation of the selective past, those elements that society values as part of its heritage, wants to remember and feels proud about. Heritage should also be about those elements that society is not so keen to reveal, and so accuracy and authenticity should reflect both. The challenge will be for heritage managers to 'tread carefully to avoid producing constructed histories on the backs of cliché-ridden concepts of popular memory and heritage' (Kavanagh 1983: 140).

In contrast to heritage settings, the authenticity debate equally applies to the experiences that tourists take home with them. The tourism literature is full of examples of how heritage events are often challenged on the extent to which products are staged as opposed to being real and authentic (cf. MacCannell 1973; Craik 1995; Herbert 1995a), although this may vary given the culture involved, and authenticity can be reaffirmed in the actual consumption of the experience itself (McIntosh and Prentice 1999).

Within the realm of heritage, Bruner (1994: 399–400) has established a four-part typology of authenticity. First, there is what may be termed 'authentic reproduction'. This form of authenticity refers to giving the appearance of being original, with most interpreters and managers aiming to make the site and its functions credible and convincing. This, Bruner argues, is the primary task of museum professionals – to make a site believable to the visiting public. The second meaning of authenticity is when the site not only resembles the original conditions, but is a complete and flawless replication that is historically accurate, as far as accuracy can be guaranteed by scholarly research. The third sense of authenticity means original instead of copied. In this sense of the word, though, any form of reproduction or alterations would render sites inauthentic. At many historic sites this level of authenticity is difficult to achieve, for although some buildings or artefacts are original, in most cases others are brought in to complete the exhibit. In most cases, therefore, this form of authenticity is not achieved. The fourth meaning of authenticity implies a sense of authority or legal recognition, although questions often arise as to who has the authority and power to authenticate. In this sense, a site can be authentic because it is the duly authorised and representative location of something of historical importance. The outdoor living museum in New Salem, Illinois (home to President Abraham Lincoln in his young adult years), for example, is legitimised by the state of Illinois as the state's true New Salem. In this case, there is only one state-approved New Salem (Bruner 1994). Thus, in this regard it is the authentic location.

The authenticity debate offered in this chapter is centred on two main strands of thought. First, the tourists' search for authenticity, and second the all-too-often reality that what they are shown are distortions of the past. With respect to the former, the debate revolves around the desire of tourists to search out authentic experiences and places and the heritage industry's acknowledgment of this, and whether in the end the tourists will recognise or care that what they are experiencing is staged and that the heritage on offer has been commodified. In terms of the latter, five different types of distorted pasts are addressed in the chapter, namely, invented places, relative authenticity, ethnic intruders, sanitised and idealised pasts, and the unknown past. The debate starts by looking at the tourists and their search for authenticity.

Tourists and the search for authenticity

It has long been the view that people travel in search of authentic experiences and places (MacCannell 1973, 1976; Moulin 1991), although the academic view of authenticity is very often quite different from the form of authenticity that tourists seek (Cohen 1988). Research by Moscardo and Pearce (1986) shows that for tourists, authenticity is an important aspect of historic sites and comprises much of the appeal for visiting them. Visitor satisfaction, in fact, is somewhat determined by their perceptions that an experience was real or authentic. This is expected to increase in the future, for in today's harried world of 'Disney-ised or Vegas-ised' places, people will have a deeper need and desire to visit authentic natural and cultural environments (O'Meara 2000: 44). For many tourists, this is manifested in the desire to visit indigenous peoples for it is they who, in the minds of tourists, represent real natives living in real places and living real history (Moulin 1991; Ryan and Crotts 1997).

Tour operators and other travel service providers appear to agree that people seek authentic experiences, as they have started using terms like 'real', 'authentic' and 'genuine' excessively in their promotional literature. According to Herbert (1995a: 45), 'some visitors, though probably a small minority, are extremely interested in the authenticity of the sites and are likely to be disappointed if things are not "real"'. The following example demonstrates this in the situation of an initiation ritual in Papua New Guinea that was performed for tourists:

> This assertion of collective male power had lasted about twenty minutes when one of the hazers said in pidgin: 'The law is finished now; we will stand up and the tourists will take pictures.' Then all four of the hazers moved behind the initiates and stood in a row, facing the tourists, who were then instructed: 'Clap your hands. The rule of Kwolimopan . . . is over; it's finished now; we have completed it. OK, you can take pictures of us now. Clap your hands.' The tour guide informed the tourists in English that they should applaud and had been invited to take pictures. The tourists did applaud, and most took a picture or two – although with some reluctance. They seemed annoyed and confused at this point. The hazers had suddenly defined the performance as staged, at least in part, for tourists rather than for the Chambri themselves and this called into question its authenticity (Errington and Gwertz 1989: 49, quoted in Balme 1998: 68–9).

Arguments suggesting that tourists, whether they know it or not, do not actually seek authentic experiences have intensified in recent years. To Boorstin (1964), pseudo-events, artificial products and contrived experiences are endemic to tourism because this is what tourists desire as they embrace a false sense of reality. MacCannell (1976) and Burnett (2001), however, argue that this might not be intentional because they might simply be unknowing victims of tourism's inclination to present fairy tales as facts and replicas as reality.

They appear to be happy with inauthentic places because they are incapable of recognising them as such (Moscardo 2000).

In contrast, Urry (1990, 1995) argues that tourists are capable of perceiving the simulated nature of tourism, but that postmodern tourists sometimes actively seek contrived experiences as part of their desire for fun and the 'value they place on eclecticism' (Moscardo 2000: 8). Some tourists want extra authenticity, that which is better than reality. People want a fantastic, hyperreal experience of what they believe the past should have been (Boniface and Fowler 1993; Bruner 1994). Thus, although many people desire an authentic experience, animation may be more important than authenticity (Wall 1989), for the commercial reproduction of heritage may be just as good as an authentic product in satisfying the needs of tourists (Robb 1998; Tuan 1977). Visitors in most cases are not looking for scientific historical evidence. They may even be only partly interested in historical reality. Instead, they are looking for an experience (Schouten 1995a: 21). Brown (1996) calls historic sites that provide these experiences 'genuine fakes' – fundamentally phoney but still able to stir up genuine feelings of nostalgia.

This latter argument is important for heritage attractions, for as one author argues

> . . . most tourist destinations, and certainly those aimed at the mass market, are not intended, and never were intended to be examples of the real world. A holiday destination to most visitors is not the real world, it is generally an imaginary world, a wishful world, or a Shangri-La . . . In the case of present day tourists, it would appear that most wish the gaze to fall on pleasant, even if artificial or staged vistas. What they wish to take back home with them, most importantly, are themselves, intact, refreshed, happy, and with good feelings and memories (Butler 1996: 93).

Staged authenticity and commodified heritage

The desire of tourists to experience authentic heritage, coupled with their common lack of discernment between reality and fabrication, has led to the presentation of what MacCannell (1973, 1976) termed 'staged authenticity', referring to a series of phases in which local conditions and regions go through a process of being staged for tourist consumption. He suggests that front regions, or the locations where tourists come in contact with local environments and peoples, become decorated and superficially presented to resemble places, peoples and practices of back regions to which visitors have limited access. Backstage in this context means the authentic and true, while front stage is the staged, or inauthentic, front, which tourists see and experience.

Buck's (1978) research on the Old Order Amish in Pennsylvania showed how that community used staged authentic experiences (front stage) purposefully to pacify tourists and thereby minimise direct contact (in the backstage) with the outside world. Similar actions taken by Kuzaki villagers in Japan consciously create artificial traditions and events for tourists so that they can keep their real traditions hidden from them (Creighton 1997). In this way, travel service providers have gone about setting up pseudo back regions for outsiders, and tourists are virtually unable to escape this staged set up (Desmond 1999; MacCannell 1976; Moscardo and Pearce 1986).

In many cases, as described above, tourists appear to be unable to differentiate between staged authenticity and real heritage experiences. However, Cohen (1979) argues that many do recognise the difference. In fact, he proposed a typology of situations in relation to authentic tourist experiences (Figure 7.1) that takes MacCannell's ideas a step further. The first type is truly authentic experiences wherein the situation is 'objectively real' and accepted by the tourists as being real. These encounters are more likely to be found off the beaten tourist path in MacCannell's backstage areas. Second is staged authenticity. In this condition, the situation is staged or made up for the tourists, but the tourists are unable to distinguish this from reality. Here the destination or service provider passes off a spurious account as reality. Cohen refers to this as 'covert tourist space'. The third part of the matrix is denial of authenticity where although the scene is presented as genuine, tourists question its authenticity. Contrived authenticity is the fourth type of experience. In this situation the event or place is overtly inauthentic and presented as such by the tourist establishment and perceived as such by the tourist. This situation is termed 'overt tourist space'. Cohen (1979) also pointed out that this could be a dynamic model where situation one becomes situation two and two becomes situation four in time.

Pearce and Moscardo (1986) argued that the earlier theorists of authenticity neglected the possibility of tourists achieving/perceiving authentic experiences through interaction with people in tourist settings. Heritage visitors who feel they have learned and gained insight from their visits have obviously found some degree of authenticity (Moscardo and Pearce 1986), although Cohen and MacCannell would imply that they have not. From this perspective, Pearce and Moscardo (1986) suggested that tourist scenes can be classified into four types:

	Tourists view the experience as real	Tourists view the experience as staged
Real scenes are provided	1. Authentic experience	3. Denial of authenticity (staging suspicion)
Staged scenes are provided	2. Staged authenticity (covert tourist space)	4. Contrived authenticity (overt tourist space)

Figure 7.1 Types of authenticity in tourist situations
Source: After Cohen (1979: 76).

1. authentic people in authentic environments, akin to MacCannell's (1979) backstage people in a backstage region;
2. authentic people in inauthentic environments (backstage people in a front stage situation);
3. inauthentic people in inauthentic situations (front stage people in front stage contexts);
4. inauthentic people in authentic environments (front stage people in a backstage region).

This concept of staged authenticity is closely linked to a similar notion called commoditisation, which suggests that tourists' inability to distinguish between authentic and inauthentic places and experiences and service providers' willingness to provide inauthentic (front stage) experiences, objects and events that once had cultural and spiritual meaning become commodified for tourist consumption and in the process they change their form and function, resulting in the loss of much of their heritage value. 'Where there is a gulf between historical realities and tourists' expectations, the fantasies will be packaged and sold' (Keesing 1989: 32). Likewise, tourist commodification 'undermines minority cultures through simplifying and packaging cultures into "30-minute" entertainments and cheap souvenirs' (Ryan and Crotts 1997: 900). In this way, cultural heritage is modified and sometimes destroyed by its treatment as a tourist attraction because it becomes 'meaningless to the people who once believed in it' (Greenwood 1989: 173).

Traditional dances and other performances are one of the most often cited cultural forms that are affected in this way as the dances themselves when pre- sented to tourists 'become a set of signs rather than a set of symbols' (Simpson 1993: 167). Various authors have examined this in a variety of locations (Balme 1998; Boissevain 1996; Hughes-Freeland 1993; Picard 1990; Tahana and Oppermann 1998), and one of the most widely scrutinised cases is the 18-ha Polynesian Cultural Center (PCC) in Hawaii. Criticisms of the PCC's imper- sonation of various Polynesian dances, craft making and cultural performances focus on the staged and overly performance-oriented programmes that have little connection to reality in terms of costumes, dance forms and performers (Douglas and Douglas 1991; Webb 1994) (Plate 7.1). For instance, Balme (1998: 62) decries the cultural mimicry in PCC performances and routines that involve the audience, such as when one performer said to the spectators 'When I come out, I want you to give me a round of applause' or when he involved them in clapping and rhythm practising, and perhaps even worse, when audience mem- bers are invited on to the stage to don grass skirts and dance, which inspired Douglas and Douglas (1991: 64) to conclude that 'all this had a stronger ele- ment of vaudeville than cultural tradition about it'. Similarly, the PCC has been judged harshly because of its lack of breadth and depth in not providing glimpses of all Polynesian islands (Douglas and Douglas 1991).

In defence of the PCC, one author suggested that staff and managers realise the product they are offering is superficial, but in the relatively short span of time visitors can spend at the PCC, some portrayal and glimpses into

Plate 7.1 Performers at the Polynesian Cultural Center, Hawaii

Polynesian cultures are 'better than none at all' (Stanton 1989: 249). The centre does not claim to provide truly authentic views of Polynesian cultures. 'As a model and not the reality, the process of selecting the cultural elements to be shown admittedly creates a "fake culture", one which would not be found today anywhere in the various Polynesian Islands' (Stanton 1989: 252). The PCC aims instead to share bits and pieces of culture that might have been in the past in an entertaining fashion, and what cannot be helped is 'naïve or uninformed tourists' expectations' (Stanton 1989: 253).

One of the most commonly cited examples of commoditised culture is the Alarde – a centuries-old celebration in Fuenterrabia, Spain, that at one time was an important commemoration of local history. With its eye to meeting tourist demand, the municipal government ordered the Alarde celebrations to be performed twice in one day to attract more visitor attention. In only two years, the celebration had lost its appeal for the local population and had ceased being a celebration for the villagers and had become a tourist spectacle, and community leaders found it difficult to incite enthusiasm among residents to participate. What 'was a vital and exciting ritual became an obligation to be avoided' (Greenwood 1989: 178). No longer do residents participate for themselves. Community leaders have had to pay them to participate, because through commoditisation

the ritual has become a performance for money. The meaning is gone . . . this decision directly violated the meaning of the ritual, definitively destroying its authenticity and its power for the people . . . Making their culture a public performance took the municipal government a few minutes; with that act, a 350-year-old ritual died (Greenwood 1989: 178–80).

Commoditisation entails more than just the simple packaging of culture and heritage for tourist consumption. It is also blamed for creating extra-spectacular events, and objects, for tourists have become dissatisfied with the ordinary (or real) world. There is a need to offer tourists ever more exotic and titillating experiences that are decorated to appear authentic (Cohen 1988). Specific to heritage tourism, 'nostalgia has lengthened and deepened to such an extent that the cult of the everyday now competes with the bias towards the more spectacular and monumental relics of the past' (Lowenthal 1985: 3). Nostalgia for the past causes people to reach deeply for the meanings of yesterday, despite the fact that what they want might not have been. People want commodified places, artefacts, and experiences that are beyond belief with extraordinary meaning, a McDisneyisation of the past (O'Meara 2000). 'In the sacral festival of tourism we turn inanimate matter into "monuments" . . . objects are given meanings that would have astounded their originators' (Horne 1984: 29), something Boon (1982) described as an 'exaggeration of cultures'.

The concepts of cultural exaggeration and gigantism have therefore emerged to denote this attitude of better than the best, more spectacular than the magnificent and more authentic than reality. Demand is now for products that are 'most authentic', or most exotic (Burnett 2001; Cohen 1988). So, tourism has emerged as a tool for accomplishing this to meet the fantasies of spectators (Swarbrooke 1994), particularly within the realm of culture and heritage, which has 'led not only to a distortion of the past, but to a stifling of the culture of the present' (Hewison 1987: 10). Hewison believes that the promotion of heritage creates fantasies of a world that never was, that it allows the replacement of true history, which is often uncomfortable, with a more comfortable, nostalgic form.

Distorted pasts

The tourist demand for 'authentic' experiences and the resultant staging of cultures, places and events result in several different types of distorted pasts. Figure 7.2 outlines five types of distorted past that are created by various intentional actions, economic and business processes, political pressures and tourist expectations – all forces that play a part in distorting the past.

Invented places

Commodification of heritage results in the creation of replicas of historic sites and objects, non-original renditions of the past, and the development of imaginary, invented or contrived places, people and events. One side of this perspective

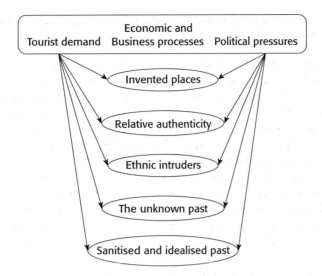

Figure 7.2 Types of distorted pasts

is invented, or imaginary places, for tourists will travel in search of the original, even where it never existed. One example from the United States is Liberal, Kansas, the 'real' location of Dorothy's farm in the tale of the Wizard of Oz (Plate 7.2). In truth there is no 'real' farm or Land of Oz in Kansas, but the invented past, created by the medium of film, has constructed such a place in the minds of visitors. This is common within the phenomenon of literary heritage, as outlined in Chapter 2. Places that become real in the minds of children and remembered throughout life (e.g. Beatrix Potter's farm), are in fact a part of those people's heritage, and when people visit houses where writers lived and worked and the landscapes that provided the settings for their novels, 'the lines blur as imagined worlds vie with real-life experiences' (Herbert 1995a: 33).

Another form of this, though not based on literary or media images, is invented ethnicity. One popular example is Leavenworth, Washington, a small town that grew during the nineteenth century as a mining and railroad town. During the Depression, the community's economic base began to falter, resulting in derelict buildings, high levels of unemployment and a steady stream of outmigration. Tourism was subsequently selected in the 1960s as a means of reviving the local economy and society, but not just any form of tourism; Leavenworth was successfully reinvented as an authentic-looking Bavarian village where residents of Seattle and other communities in the state and across the country could experience 'authentic' German foods, music, architecture and shopping. At issue here, however, is that neither Leavenworth nor its residents were in any way Bavarian, despite how they were promoted (Frenkel 1997; Price 1996).

Similarly, Raivo (2000: 146) describes the replica landscapes of war that are prominent throughout much of Finland. In this case, heritage landscapes

Plate 7.2   Oz and the Yellow Brick Road, Liberal, Kansas, USA

depicting features of the Winter War against Russia and other battles (e.g. dugouts, trenches, front-line barricades) are reproduced throughout the country in diverse places as a way of creating a sense of place and period, and building a Finnish national identity 'far away from the historical front line' and at sites that 'never existed as such in the past'.

In Singapore, the commodification of heritage has led to the construction of the Cultural Theatre where visitors can get a taste of 'Instant Asia'. Here, staged performances of invented traditions comprising Chinese, Malay and Indian cultural elements are blended with foods and other forms of entertainment. Visitors are presented with 'a package of cultures, wrapped up in 45 minutes of staged spectacle', inauthentic because they contrast with reality – dances and operas performed that are not part of the local culture, depictions of peasants planting rice when rice was never grown in Singapore, and the selling of 'native' arts and crafts that are imported from abroad (Leong 1989: 366).

In a process termed here 'the modernisation of antiquity', societies of the developed world imitate historic buildings and landscapes in everyday modern life, such as a bank with a Greek colonnade façade and castles in amusement parks (Lowenthal 1985). This may be seen as a means of authenticating modern-day structures by making them look old. This process is common in urban and rural areas as new buildings are thatched and façades created.

A final argument is that moving buildings and other artefacts to non-original places diminishes their heritage value, for historical resources acquire a higher value for the public when developed in their original sites and in their original settings. This relates to what Boniface and Fowler (1993: 121) call the 'moving object' phenomenon, which refers to artefacts that are moved from their original location to a different cultural and geographic context. The object may still be authentic, but its location is not. This raises questions of whether or not this is authentic heritage (Swarbrooke 1994). There are countless examples of artefacts that have been removed from their original locations and placed in museums or private collections. In addition, examples exist where, for a variety of reasons, entire structures have been relocated, including the temples of Abu Simbel in Egypt, which were moved to a more elevated location so they would not be destroyed with the creation of Lake Nasser.

This has been said of Greenfield Village, Michigan (USA), an eclectic collection of historic memorabilia (e.g. the cycle shop where the Wright Brothers built their first aeroplane and the small courthouse where young Abraham Lincoln practised law), spanning some 300 years of history. Although the buildings themselves are original, and therefore in one regard, authentic, their displacement from Ohio and Illinois to a theme park in Michigan is said by some to render them inauthentic. While today it is argued that moving such buildings destroys history, there was no precedent at the time Henry Ford moved them to Greenfield Village (1920s and 1930s). Instead it was a time when not many people cared about history, and much of the past was being demolished. 'Edison's New Jersey laboratory – the site of some of the nation's most noteworthy inventions – was, in fact, in ruins, with pieces of Edison's buildings being used for scrap wood' when Ford went back through the community and re-collected the wood from barns and chicken coops to rebuild the lab (Lassen 1999: 46).

Relative authenticity

Amidst the debate it is important to realise that authenticity is a relative term. Authenticity is, according to many theorists, a subjective phenomenon created by personal experience, cultural influences and national history. In terms of the latter, history is usually told from the perspective of the winners of wars, not from the perspective of the defeated.

Dominant culture affects the public's understanding of 'reality'. For example,

> We depict the *Pithecanthropus erectus* in an Indonesian museum with Malay facial features, not because there is any evidence of them, but because that is the way Indonesians perceive humans. In the Museum of Natural History in Washington, DC, the Neanderthal man is shown giving a dominating gesture over his wife. We actually have no clue whether this was the case and the presentation tells us a lot more about our way of perceiving the world around us than it does about our ancestors (Schouten 1995a: 26).

The meanings of heritage objects should not be seen as being directly derived from the object itself. Instead, it is the way the object is presented and the sociocultural background of the person viewing it that produces meaning (Laenen 1989; McLean 1998; Pearce *et al.* 1996). Thus, the meaning of heritage and authenticity is culturally constructed and changes from one context to the next (McLean 1998: 247). Even UNESCO has recognised this fact in its Nara Document on Authenticity, which states that the meaning of authenticity does vary between cultures and depends on various contextual sources of information (Burnett 2001).

Just as authenticity may be influenced and ultimately defined by cultural and social representations, it is also context and place specific. Ghost towns provide a good example of this, as they are different from other types of heritage places in this regard. Ghost towns' authenticity is measured by the degree of decay and tarnish. At most of these types of places, maintenance workers endeavour to carry out a policy of 'arrested decay', or 'keep[ing] it standing but mak[ing] it look like it's still falling down' (DeLyser 1999: 614). DeLyser provides an interesting look at Bodie State Park, California, a ghost town based on gold mining. What remains today has not been altered. None of the buildings have been reproduced; no fallen buildings have ever been reassembled; no new buildings have been added to the site; and no building has been restored, painted or repaired to look new again. In this sense, it is an authentic ghost town (DeLyser 1999: 623). Other types of sites derive their sense of authenticity based on the notion that they have been restored and reconstructed to an accurate state of a time in the past.

Similarly, according to Swarbrooke (1994), part of the authenticity dilemma is whether ancient ruins should be left as ruins or should be reconstructed to look as near as possible how they would have appeared in their days of operation. Some people feel that ruins should be left alone; reconstruction can detract from the authenticity of the site. This reflects the fact that people want old things to seem old, enforced by decay (Larkham 1995; Lowenthal 1985). The older something is, the more value it seems to possess. 'Much of our aesthetic pleasure in the ancient lies in the belief that such objects really do come from the remote past' (Lowenthal 1975: 18). However, according to Lowenthal (1975: 26), 'because we feel that old things should look old, we may forget that they originally looked new'. Likewise, people have a tendency to want to conserve the ancient past, not being concerned for the recent past (Winks 1976).

Plate 7.3 Wupatki Indian ruins, Arizona, USA

This is clearly visible in Arizona (USA), where a drive through the Navajo Nation Reservation reveals many derelict hogans (traditional mud houses) dotting the landscape. Most have only been abandoned since the 1970s and 1980s and do not attract tourist attention. However, abandoned Native American homes and communities from 500 years ago are major attractions and are being conserved by the US National Park Service (Plate 7.3). Thus, the 'age factor' adds value to ruined Indian structures from both tourist and archaeological perspectives.

Authenticity is also subjective on a personal level. According to one line of thinking, tourists can achieve an authentic experience through relationships with people at tourist settings, because authenticity emerges from individual experiences (Cohen 1988; Moscardo 2000; Pearce and Moscardo 1986). Thus, one tourist may have an authentic experience, while another at the same location may not (Cohen 1988). Herbert (1995a: 45) alludes to this when he declares,

> If visitors seek an experience from their visit which is meaningful to them . . . should we be concerned whether that experience draws upon fact or reality, or whether or not the two can be distinguished? The answer to that question is 'probably not'. If the experience is authentic to the visitor, that is sufficient.

McIntosh and Prentice (1999) discovered three distinct psychological processes that explain people's abilities to create their own authentic experiences. Reinforced assimilation involves a reflection on the differences between the past and the present. How things were in the past is grasped and causes people to appreciate their lives in modern times. One quote by a participant in McIntosh and Prentice's (1999: 602) study highlights this process:

> I would say I've gained an insight into the past. It makes you reflect upon life then and today, and it made me think about what it would've been like for my child if he had been living then; he would have started work at ten years of age; to think of the working machinery; that it must have been a terrifying place with all those machines going at once; and health-related issues. We take things like medical help and education so much for granted these days . . . I'm glad I'm living now. I feel more appreciative of my life today.

The cognitive perception process is where people attain new insights or information, something they did not know before. In this category the new insights gained are not assimilated with personal experience, the cultural experience usually being unfamiliar. The following statements by one of their participants is characteristic of this:

> I gained a view of what the world was like then, in very vivid terms; a real feeling of what it was like; it was very authentic. The surprise is the biggest thing. It taught me about a way of life I knew nothing about. I knew about the Industrial Revolution, but not about the life conditions. I feel I've learnt a lot and identified with their hardships (McIntosh and Prentice 1999: 603).

The third process, retroactive association, involves people being able to relate their experience to a past they can personally remember. It entails the reliving of memories, as the new experience triggers them. In this experience, objects and their interpretation become highly personalised and bring back memories of childhood or earlier years. For example,

> I grew up living with my grandmother in a cottage not far from here, so I remember what it was like. I can remember being bathed in a tin tub; I remember the mangle and the grate, and my granny cooking fresh bread and home made jam . . . I sat in the school classroom and it felt so realistic; the school had the same desks as we used to have in our school (McIntosh and Prentice 1999: 604).

Ethnic intruders

Against the premises of the last section, Douglas and Douglas (1991) undertook a critique of the authenticity of the PCC in Hawaii, arguing that ethnic flexibility, together with other entertainment factors in place in cultural presentations, renders events and entire attractions inauthentic. They argue that authenticity is significantly diminished in cultural events and ethnic demonstrations when non-local people play the part of interpreters in a setting that is said to be authentic. For example, at the PCC, ethnicity . . . seems to be flexible, as . . . some dancers of indeterminate authenticity: a male dancer with the Fijians appeared shortly after as a Tahitian boatman and later as a Maori. The Tongan contingent also included – with a quick change of costume – a Fijian girl who was the only identifiable Fijian on Fiji's canoe moments before, and the blue raffia skirts on the husky Tongan men seemed slightly over the top (Douglas and Douglas 1991: 62).

Still other observers subscribe to the idea of diminishing authenticity when outsiders are utilised to conserve and interpret. In the Cayman Islands, for example, most of the professionals employed in conservation in museums, the National Trust and the National Archives and Cultural Foundation are expatriate foreigners working on short-term contracts. A visiting American, in fact, founded the National Trust, and most board members are foreigners, which has in the words of Amit-Talai (1997: 61), created 'an identity crisis'. Such evidence, Amit-Talai (1997: 62) argues, in effect 'contract[s] out the enterprise of nation building'.

Sanitised and idealised pasts

There is a common belief that tourists, while in search of authentic experiences in some form, if faced with truly authentic experiences, would cease visiting heritage sites, for they would appear in conditions that most people would find tasteless, dirty and otherwise unimaginable and unacceptable. This is because people can only see the past through the eyes of the present. Historical accuracy, therefore, is not always compatible with visual and sensory harmony (Barthel 1990). In this case heritage and authenticity are said to be sanitised or made palatable to cater to the tastes and desires of tourists (Burnett 2001; Hewison 1987; Hubbard and Lilley 2000; Leong 1989), but also for practical/logistical reasons.

At outdoor heritage museums, which Barthel (1990) calls staged symbolic communities, several examples of sanitised pasts are notable (Plate 7.4). Idealised social environments are usually portrayed as happy, industrious communities where representations of conflict, antisocial behaviour, death, disease, divorce, orphanages and starvation are notably absent (Barthel 1990; Walsh 1992). This led Colonial Williamsburg critic, Huxtable (1992: 24–5, quoted in Gable and Handler 1996), to conclude that outdoor living museums encourage the 'replacement of reality with selective fantasy' and perversion of the way Americans think, because it has taught them to

> prefer – and believe in – a sanitized and selective version of the past, to deny the diversity and eloquence of chance and continuity, to ignore the actual deposits of history and humanity that make our cities vehicles of a special kind of art and experience, the gritty accumulations of the best and worst we have produced.

Similar sentiments have been expressed by other living heritage museum observers (e.g. Barthel 1990; Gable and Handler 1993; Uzzell 1994; Van West and Hoffschwelle 1984; Walsh 1992; Wells 1993). According to some critics

Plate 7.4   Mystic Seaport Living Village, USA

(e.g. Hardy 1988: 336), scholars and interpreters should refrain from demonstrating only the 'noble past' in favour of portraying 'real history', by seeking 'warts and all' in a more honest context.

In physical environmental terms, authenticity speculators also point out that much of the infrastructure provided to make a site functional for interpretation and other visitor use causes the place to be less than truly authentic, because these would not have been a part of the original site. Examples include gutters on log cabins to redirect rainwater, animals fenced in so their waste is not dispersed throughout town, paved roads, restrooms with flushing toilets, air conditioning and heating units, rubbish bins around town and electric spinning machines (Bruner 1994). Ancient castles, for example, originally did not have flushing toilets or central heating systems, but these are provided in the modern-day context to make places usable for tourists. If historic towns and buildings were left strictly in their original condition, modern-day tourists would most certainly be offended by the smells, plumbing problems, darkness and cold (Timothy and Wall 1997). In the words of Barthel (1990: 87), out-door museums 'are clean beyond reason. They also don't smell bad. The stench that would have permeated a whaling town like Mystic is totally absent.' They also look newer than they should, but this might reflect people's desires for artefacts not to look old, even if they are historic (Lowenthal 1977: 254).

Something even as seemingly innocuous as lawn-mowing methods may be seen as detracting from historical accuracy. Many institutions cut the grass with electric or gas lawn mowers, yet many of the landscapes being interpreted were from periods before the advent of motorised mowers (Reid 1989).

In idealising the past there is also an element of selective memory. Nostalgia is a odd thing, for in the process of remembering, people tend to remember the good times, or the pleasant things from history, disregarding or expunging from their memories the negative times and situations (Lowenthal 1996). In this sense, heritage becomes distorted on both societal and personal levels. A negative experience on a vacation trip can change in meaning with the passing of time. Eventually, as details fade, the memories of the trip are placated, becoming recollections of enjoyment and beliefs that 'it wasn't all that bad'. On a societal level, the same can be true. Selective memory dictates that

> plantation houses . . . once horrific scenes of the disease, lack of hygiene, squalor and torture associated with slavery, are portrayed instead as symbols of genteel living associated with the colonial plantocracy, and then projected as part of the Third World nation's patrimony to be enjoyed by tourists (Dann 1998: 40).

The unknown past

This line of thinking suggests that true authenticity is impossible because people in the modern day cannot possibly understand precisely the lives of people from history or know enough about the details of their everyday lives to make interpretation accurate. In the words of Lowenthal (1985: 214),

> no historical account can recover the totality of any past events, because their content is virtually infinite. The most detailed historical narrative incorporates only a minute fraction of even the relevant past; the sheer pastness of the past precludes its total reconstruction.

Researchers, managers and interpreters lack sufficient knowledge to provide precise depictions of the past. The past is not a known entity, for 'no account can recover the past as it was, because the past was not an account, it was a set of events and situations' (Lowenthal 1985: 215). Thus, because people necessarily view the past from current perspectives, and authenticity is socially constructed (Barthel 1996; Craig 1989; Burnett 2001; Simpson 1993), the past is enigmatic, and all that can be done is to imagine what it was like (Hewison 1991). Even if details are known, some are too difficult or unimaginable to portray. 'I went to work in the sawmills because I was desperate, the wage form was exploitation, every day was purgatory, but there was no other local alternative. How do you make a museum of an experience like that?' (West 1988: 58).

Sometimes places are preserved at a time about which more is known and from which more artefacts are available. Barthel (1990: 81) writes that because Old Sturbridge Village, Massachusetts, was recreated at an approximate historical moment, 'it will always be 1830 in Sturbridge'. At Beamish, England, everything (regardless of its age) is frozen at the same point in time (Bennett 1988: 68). At both of these locations, issues and decisions that arise will be settled not by 1830 residents, but by 2002 curators and interpreters.

Often, interpreters and historic site managers concentrate almost all of their attention on the portrayal of buildings and other human-created structures. However, Reid (1989) argues that not only do historic buildings at open-air museums need to be as accurate and authentic as possible, but that the surrounding landscape and grounds need to be as well. Also, these should be included in the interpretive programme, for the natural landscape surrounding the communities, or artefacts being considered, are also a part of the historic environment. This, she argues, can be done through continuous research into the types of vegetation and land use that would have existed at the time of the place being interpreted. She gave one example of a historic site, Clayville Rural Life Center in central Illinois, doing research into the physical characteristics that would have been present during the communities' pioneer days at the confluence of the prairie and woodlands nature zones. In this example, such research was very important, for the native growth and available water supply significantly influenced the settlement patterns in the Clayville region.

Summary and conclusions

This chapter has provided a detailed review of authenticity within heritage tourism. Heritage tourism is often differentiated from other types of tourism by the importance placed on the quality of experiences people take home with them. In Chapter 6, it was argued that interpretation is an important principle for heritage tourism. The same position needs to be taken where authenticity is concerned, as this influences both how managers interpret and present heritage, which in turn shapes the tourist experience. This may be true from the perspective of the scholar and researcher, but it is unclear whether or not tourists see authenticity in the same vein. Are academics too often caught up with notions of authenticity that bear little resemblance to what tourists really value in the end? There are some heritage tourists who do seek real and authentic experiences, but most tourists as Butler (1996: 93) stated, simply want to take away from a visit 'good feelings and memories'. Staged authenticity has resulted to ensure that there are good feelings and memories to take home, and while this chapter has illustrated many examples where this is practised, watching demonstrations and interacting with people are often enough in the eyes of most tourists, even heritage tourists, to qualify as being authentic. An unfortunate consequence of 'staging' to create certain experiences has generated a commodified product. Heritage providers feel the need to entertain tourists more, and in so doing run the risk of diluting the experience and alienating the local population. In a sense they are caught up with what were referred to in the chapter as cultural exaggeration and gigantism, where heritage providers in their zeal to entertain create extra-spectacular events and develop products that are 'most authentic and exotic' but really only serve to provide tourists with fantasies and distorted pasts.

If tourists accept that they are being shown distorted worlds, should scholars be concerned about imaginary places (e.g. the Land of Oz), invented ethnicity (e.g. the Cultural Theatre in Singapore), inauthentic locations (e.g. built features within open-air museums), if they are still taking away memorable experiences? Perhaps it is more important to allow people to 'create' their own authentic experiences as pointed out by McIntosh and Prentice (1999), be that through reinforced assimilation, cognitive perception or retroactive association, and accept that authenticity is both relative and subjective when reduced to the personal level. As for the debate over ethnic intruders and whether or not this detracts from visitors' experiences, surely it is more important to ensure that local people feel a part of the experience rather than being kept from it.

There is no escaping the fact that most heritage sites have been sanitised, and in a sense 'made ready for the visitors' and therefore have created idealised pasts. Heritage providers may run the risk of offending some visitors if they try to make conditions as close to reality as possible in modern times. But in doing this they create the opportunity for tourists to take away memorable and lasting experiences. However, there is also the real danger that by beautifying the past, they may dilute the impact they can have on tourists. To be fair to heritage providers, the past is often unknown and what is presented is simply segments of history that we are fortunate enough to understand. From this perspective, the extent to which the past can be presented in an authentic manner is brought into proper context.

While authenticity has assumed central importance within tourism studies, its limited application outside of ethnic, heritage or cultural tourism, has led some to rethink its meaning in order to justify and enhance its explanatory power (Wang 1999). In this sense there may be more of an opportunity to emphasise quality rather than authenticity. Quality has recently been associated with service and heritage management from the perspective of stakeholders and is a process that requires implementation (Hall and McArthur 1998). Similarly, quality can refer to the experiences being offered, where the argument can be made that expectations and experiences sought are met through the provision of quality products. As the demographic profile of heritage tourists tends increasingly to reflect the middle to latter stages of the life cycle (Prentice 1993), the issue of quality may hold greater importance over authenticity in how places and experiences in the future are presented to tourists.

Questions

1. What are the four types of authenticity described by Cohen? To what extent is it possible to shift from one type to another?
2. To what extent is authenticity within heritage shaped by culture, context and place?
3. Are heritage places guilty of sanitising and idealising the past?

Further reading

Barthel, D. (1996) *Historic Preservation: Collective memory and historical identity*, Rutgers University Press, New Brunswick, NJ.

Cohen, E. (1988) 'Authenticity and commoditization in tourism', *Annals of Tourism Research*, 15: 371–86.

McCannell, D. (1976) *The Tourist*, Schocken Books, New York.

Moscardo, G. and Pearce, P. (1986) 'Historic theme parks: an Australian experience in authenticity', *Annals of Tourism Research*, 13: 467–79.

Selwyn, T. (ed.) (1996) *The Tourist Image: Myths and myth making in tourism*, Wiley, Chichester.

CHAPTER 8

The politics of heritage

The underlying premise of this chapter is that heritage and its designation are inherently political concepts. Societies, cultural groups and governments collectively interpret the past in a subjective manner to meet their own ideological goals (Barthel 1990; Graham 1998b; Hobsbawm and Ranger 1983; Lowenthal 1985). In the words of Johnson (1999: 187), 'heritage tourism is not just a set of commercial transactions, but the ideological framing of history and identity'.

Politics is in its very essence about power, and heritage by its very nature is a political phenomenon, since history is always told from the perspective of winners of wars and people in positions of power (Hall 1994, 1997, 2000b). Thus, place identities are always in a state of transition in the midst of multifarious 'political, cultural and economic struggles over the meaning of the past' (Hubbard and Lilley 2000: 223). The recording of historic buildings is, according to Bold (1994), a political act that is defined by perceptions of historical significance.

Particular ideologies are conserved and represented for tourists through museums, historic houses, monuments and markers, tours, heritage districts, tourism landscapes and other public spaces (Hall in press). The tourist gaze is not politically neutral, for the representation of heritage in tourism can act to legitimise existing social and political values and structures (Hall in press). Thus, by definition, heritage is a representation of values and is commonly used (intentionally or otherwise) to manipulate, exclude and reinvent the past (Norkunas 1993; Shaw *et al.* 1997).

According to Ashworth (1995), all heritage involves choices from a vast array of pasts, many of which will not be selected. Ultimately, what heritage will be conserved depends on the ideological issues of those in power. Some artefacts will become heritage, while others will be discarded (Graham 1994a: 135). For example, until quite recently, most heritage tourism and heritage in general excluded the past of the powerless and minorities in society, favouring instead artefacts, places and events of the upper-class elites, such as castles, cathedrals and palaces. Vestiges of the lives of commoners were generally overlooked. Norkunas (1993: 97) argues that 'the ruling class carefully controls the form and content of historical re-creations and tourist landscapes, legitimizing itself by projecting its own contemporary sociocultural values upon the past'. This has been especially apparent in developing countries where it is customary for places associated with royalty or other upper-class elites to be shown to tourists, at the expense of artefacts that depict the life of peasants (Boniface and Fowler 1993). However, as the travelling public has become increasingly more aware of the role that common people have played throughout history, everyday vestiges of the past (e.g. villages, small cottages, industrial plants, farmhouses and workshops) have increased in popularity as tourist attractions, and the role of marginal peoples has been enhanced (Hollinshead 1992).

Against this background, this chapter examines issues related to power in heritage tourism, of which societal amnesia (heritage exclusion), erasure of the dominant past, dissonance and contested pasts, and the use of heritage propaganda to create nationalism and place image, are the primary results. The chapter also considers political conflict and its impact on heritage and heritage conservation, particularly focusing on heritage as deliberate target and heritage as innocent bystander. Community participation in, and control of, heritage tourism is also discussed as an important political issue. It is political because the process of heritage designation, protection and interpretation must involve empowerment and participation where people understand and are able to control facets of their own heritage (Marks 1996).

Collective amnesia and the excluded past

The heritage portrayed to tourists in many locations reflects what some observers call collective amnesia. This has a connotation of the deliberate forgetting of some aspects of the past, referring to the fact that entire societies elect to disregard, exclude or suppress certain aspects of history because they are uncomfortable, embarrassing, or by so doing, the society or its leaders can achieve some political/ideological objective(s), often with a racist slant. Ashworth (1995) terms this 'disinheritance' whereby some social and ethnic groups are written out of the script of history. This societal memory loss has resulted in many diverse heritages throughout the world being excluded from conservation and interpretation, and being hidden from the tourist gaze (Boniface and Fowler 1993; Graham 1996; Leong 1989; Powell 1997; Robinson 1999a).

> The history which is part of the fund of knowledge or the ideology of nation, state, community, or movement is not necessarily what has actually been preserved by popular memory, but what has been selected, written, pictured, popularized, and institutionalized by those with the power to do so . . . Heritage therefore represents the power of the winners (Hall 1997: 95).

One of the primary methods used to exclude certain pasts is through education and official curricula. MacKenzie and Stone (1990: 3–4; Stone and MacKenzie 1989) described four primary reasons why an 'excluded past' exists in education:

- School curricula are already overcrowded, and educational leaders argue that time cannot be used up on 'new' subjects when the survival of many long-established (e.g. mathematics and social studies) disciplines is in question.

- Teachers' own ignorance has allowed some important aspects of the past to be excluded. Many textbooks, for example, ignore contemporary understandings of the past.

- Studying some pasts is commonly seen as an extravagant luxury that has little direct relevance to today's society.

- Aspects of the past are sometimes excluded intentionally for political or ideological reasons.

While all of these reasons have some political undertones, it is the last element that is of most concern in this chapter. Through education, dominant institutions can, based on their ideological goals, reveal only what is congenial and disregard what is inconvenient or what opposes what they want the public to know (Gawe and Meli 1990: 101).

One of the best examples of intentional amnesia, or excluded pasts, is found in the United States in the relationship between indigenous peoples and the European/white immigrants. According to traditional teaching in US schools, American history began at the moment the 'white man', in this case Christopher Columbus, 'discovered' the Americas in 1492. This overtly Eurocentric view all but completely ignores thousands of years of human habitation in North America prior to the European arrival (Boniface and Fowler 1993). This is particularly notable in history textbooks, which commonly devote only 10–15 pages of coverage to life in America before European settlement and hundreds of pages to the period following the arrival of Columbus, which according to Kehoe (1990: 201) is very telling about the dominant American social view of the past: 'America hardly existed before European colonization.' This has been the non-native view of the past since the 1400s, and the notion that native peoples could possibly have contributed anything to the development of American society is seen as ignorant or revolutionary (Blancke and Slow Turtle 1990). The relegation of American Indians into stereotypical roles as unprogressive, savage warriors by 'official' history and Hollywood media has long been the focus of children's play and perpetuated childhood fears of these 'untamed savages' (Blancke and Slow Turtle 1990: 109). This treatment of indigenous patrimony and its resultant stereotypes have their roots in the national myth of Manifest Destiny, wherein European Christians were committed to subdue the earth and have dominion over all living things thereon (Kehoe

1990: 202). This so-called 'discovery' view of American settlement reflects the self-centred superiority complex endemic to Western civilisation. This kind of treatment of indigenous heritage has existed in all parts of the world and with nearly every colonised ethnic group (Holland 1990; Jones 1997).

Similar conditions have long existed in the treatment of the heritage of Americans and Britons of African lineage. For centuries, black heritage has been hidden from public view in both the United States and Great Britain. Since the abolition of slavery, the issue has been an embarrassment for both nations, and the more politically powerful majority (white) has elected to keep the African past at a fair distance. The disgraceful and inhumane treatment of Africans at the hands of white Americans and Europeans did not end with the abolition of slavery, but continued well into the twentieth century in many places. The suppression of black heritage in both nations until quite recently is indicative of this. However, African and white Americans alike have finally begun to realise the need to resurrect this forgotten element of history, resulting in increasing attention to preserving and interpreting elements of the heritage of slavery and subsequent African-American/British legacies (Hayes 1997). The rapid development of black heritage attractions in the United States in recent years is indicative of changing power structures within that country (Morgan and Pritchard 1998; Pritchard and Morgan 2001) brought about largely by African-American 'pressure for history to be rewritten from a perspective unbiased against, if not positively pro, the [African]-American' (Boniface and Fowler 1993: 19). Although, as of 1990, there still was not any kind of national institution responsible for preserving or documenting the black presence in Great Britain, but efforts were under way to establish a black cultural archives museum to accommodate artefacts, documents and other objects related to the African presence in the UK (Garrison 1990: 231).

Throughout North America, African/slave-related heritage is now coming to the fore as major tourist attractions in places like Birchtown, Nova Scotia, Canada, where some of the first black Canadian settlers arrived more than 200 years ago and which is being developed into an important tourist destination. An African heritage tourism centre, a church and school on the Birchtown site are being planned (*Globe and Mail* 2000). The story of the underground railway is being told through the creation of a black heritage trail in Brant County, Ontario, which played an important part in the smuggling of slaves into Canada. The black heritage trail traces the lives of leading individuals within the African community that formed in Brant County, and tells stories of the operation of the underground railroad (Boyd 2002a). Similar efforts are under way in the south-eastern United States. For example, slave cabins have been renovated and reconstructed on plantations in Virginia and other southern states. Until now, tourism to the plantations focused primarily on the mansions and lives of the wealthy white landlords and slave owners.

Today, however, considerable strides are being made to tell the 'whole story', including the harsh conditions and treatment of the slaves. According to one interpretive supervisor at Mount Vernon, Virginia, 'it wasn't comfortable in the 1970s to talk about slaves. Today, it's just part of what we do. It's part of history, and you have to present it' (quoted in Smith 2000: 16). The state of Virginia, one of the first North American destinations for slaves from Africa, is taking the largest strides in promoting African-American heritage and revealing what life was like for the slaves, inasmuch as this can be done in the modern context. African-American sites in Virginia include historic places of the Revolutionary and Civil wars, homes of prominent black Americans, renovated slave dwellings, outdoor slave exhibits staffed by costumed personnel, slave routes, the Legacy Museum of African-American History, the Robert R. Morton Museum: A Center for the Study of Civil Rights in Education and several other museums (Bartlett 2001).

Similar racial or ethnic exclusion has long existed in the United States towards the Hispanic population, one example being the Alamo complex in San Antonio, Texas, which has been culturally refashioned by Anglo interests to harmonise with predominant notions of an Anglo 'us' and Latino 'them' (de Oliver 1996: 19). However, in common with African-American heritage, the American Latino pasts and cultures have begun to be recognised in official circles as an important part of the collective national heritage.

CASE STUDY South Africa

The United States and the UK are not the only two countries having to deal with racially excluded pasts. South African heritage, for instance, excludes a black African past. Apartheid history failed to recognise an African presence in much of the country, and the 1960s Coloured Labour Preference policy attempted to keep African workers entirely from the western Cape region of the country. 'In the process, the African presence was conveniently forgotten' (Worden 1996: 65). In South Africa, history was manipulated to justify inequitable land distribution and to establish the whites' oppressive power over the indigenous Africans, for according to official (pre-1994) history, 'it was only the arrival of the Whites that brought peace to a land of people mutually hostile and incapable of living together in harmony' (Gawe and Meli 1990: 103). The white view supported two notions: (1) the country was an 'empty land' into which European pioneers could put down their roots, and (2) there could be no common heritage in a place divided between two races (Worden 1997).

With the democratisation of South Africa and the end of apartheid in 1994, indigenous heritage, which had previously been disregarded, became a primary concern, and efforts to revive, preserve and promote it began. Museum curators, researchers and community organisations have now begun to correct racial and cultural biases that have long existed. Initiatives, such as the National Monuments Council's declaring the house of Sol T. Plaatje (an indigenous author and secretary of the South African Native National Congress) a national monument, were pioneering in this regard, for it was the first museum in the country to commemorate the life of a black person. Another initiative was the founding of the KwaMuhle Museum in Durban, where scenes from the daily life in black townships are depicted together with settings about political trade unions and cultural organisations under apartheid (Goudie *et al.* 1996: 71).

The apartheid form of exclusion meant that the National Monuments Council traditionally had emphasised heritage buildings and places that represented colonial heritage more than indigenous heritage. In 1990, for instance, 97 per cent of all declared monuments were representative of the values of the immigrant white community (Worden 1997: 46). This fact has produced problems in post-apartheid South Africa in promoting heritage tourism, owing to the difficulties of establishing new tourist markets and heritage sites of interest (Goudie *et al.* 1996, 1999).

Many similar accounts exist throughout the world. In Nazi Germany, for example, thousands of museums were built to reinforce the myth of the super-race. Hitler's followers even planned the 'museum of a vanished race', to exhibit looted Judaica and demonstrate the success of the 'ultimate solution' (Cameron 1995: 52). In the 1980s the Malaysian government declared that Yap Ah Loy, the Chinese immigrant who founded the village that later became Kuala Lumpur, was no longer founder of the capital. Instead, official sources now identify the local Malay *raja* as the city's true founder. With this act, the minority Chinese role has been concealed (Cartier 1996: 50). Likewise, by playing down the evidence from archaeological sources in Africa, Western archaeologists have been able to deny African people a claim to their own historic monuments. Colonialists saw fit to disprove claims of the Great Zimbabwe site's African origin by developing theories that suggested its builders were Persians, Phoenicians, Portuguese, Arabs or Chinese (Garrison 1990: 235). Finally, the Israel National Parks Authority has long practised unequal treatment of different Jewish ethnic and social groups and has, according to Bauman (1995: 21), 'required that the Palestinian presence be ignored and forgotten'.

In addition to race, the pasts of other sectors of society have also long been held from the purview of interpreted or even accepted heritage. In a critique of Beamish, in England, Bennett (1988: 67) argued that the museum completely ignored the important labour and trade union movements in the region, as well as the activities of women in suffrage and feminist campaigns. The heritage industry has traditionally promoted the dominant power base, focusing on the great men of history while overlooking the women, children, disabled groups and ethnic minorities, who are typically depicted (if at all) as lending support to the male, central figure (Hubbard and Lilley 2000; McLean 1998). Other newer social groups, such as refugees and 'historical strangers' (e.g. Somalians in northern Europe), are also casualties of selective heritage. Their past is no past at all in the new land, where they are generally excluded from mainstream history and heritage interpretation (Tunbridge 1994; Worden 1996). This selective version of heritage demonstrates a history of hegemonic notions about class, ethnicity and gender (Waitt and McGuirk 1997: 350). In fact, there is more than a suggestion of a lack of democracy in the process of ascribing meaning and value, where the process itself is hidden from the public gaze or informed by dominant codes of significance. These . . . invariably favour the privileged classes . . . with their blindness to class struggle, gender inequalities, and racist legacy (West 1988: 51–2).

Erasing the dominant past

During the past half-century, many oppressive colonial superpowers and autocratic administrations, which during their reigns performed unspeakable cruelties and enacted strict measures of repression upon their subordinates, have granted independence to their former colonies and given way to democratic, capitalist societies. Such was the legacy of many executive powers that upon achieving freedom from their hegemonic grasp, some new nations have desired to erase the records and signs that such a hurtful, oppressive and sometimes embarrassing, legacy ever existed.

In the case of Eastern Europe, during the early and mid-twentieth century, monuments were erected and conserved around three primary themes: pre-socialist, socialist and religious edifices. These emphases by the communist states allowed the leaders to propagandise their people against fascism, partisanship and class distinctions, as well as highlight the importance of birthplaces of leading socialist thinkers and 'liberation' by the Soviet army (Carter 1982). Later, following the collapse of communism in the early 1990s, the new governing ideologies are attempting to veil the communist past and its remnant landscapes comprised of monuments, place and street names and public iconography. The removal or demolition of such elements and the renaming of places are indicative of these changes being wrought. Such endeavours, it is believed, will aid in the recovery from communist-era trauma and social division. However, there are strong movements to preserve at least some of the communist past so that a pluralist heritage can be created. Much of the current struggle among new administrations is how much of this heritage should be removed and what should replace it (Ashworth and Tunbridge 1999: 107–8). This dilemma is difficult in the emerging market economies of Central and Eastern Europe (CEE), for in one sense they are forced to choose between identity and economy (Hall, D.R. 1991; Hall, C.M. 1994; Tunbridge 1994) – identity because they want to recreate, or at least move beyond, their past to reflect new national ideals, and economy because the communist past is a marketable heritage resource that attracts tourists and produces revenue (Light 2000b). For the countries of CEE, the main priority in this regard is to 'place the communist period – now widely regarded as a historical aberration – firmly behind them' (Light 2000b: 159). Budapest came up with a fairly unique solution to this predicament. In 1990, Budapest's city council voted to remove some 40 political effigies from Hungary's communist era to a park near the edge of town, which has since become one of the city's most significant tourist attractions (Light 2000a). Light (2000a: 154) summarises the situation of erasure as follows in the context of Romania:

> Although Romania's communist past is an object of interest for curious Western tourists, Romanians see this period of their country's history through very different eyes. Given their especially harsh experience of totalitarianism, economic austerity, and systematic repression, most Romanians are understandably eager to draw a line completely under the communist period. Political discourse since 1990 has been dominated by reform and the construction of a 'new' Romania . . . Accordingly, there has been little concern with retaining the material legacy of the communist period. For Romanians this was an unwelcome reminder of the former regime. Instead, in the early post-communist period there was a concerted effort to erase the physical traces, as far as was possible, of Ceauşescu's regime. Some of the most obvious examples include the removal of banners on factories praising Ceauşescu, the toppling of statues of communist leaders, and the widespread renaming of both individual streets and entire settlements whose names were a reminder of the previous regime.

Half a century following the Second World War, Germany is still attempting to move past its disgraceful period of Nazi rule, and debates continue there over how best to preserve some of the controversial heritage from that era (Ashworth 1991). Likewise, in some urban centres of Malaysia, officials are attempting to rewrite local heritage with a Malay focus and an overt neglect (or destruction) of colonial features (Shaw *et al.* 1997). This is to be expected, for according to Graham (2000: 77), the process of nation building is often 'as much about forgetting the past as commemorating it'.

Dissonant and contested heritage

Tunbridge and Ashworth (1996: 20) have provided a comprehensive examination of dissonance in the context of heritage, which they define as 'a discordance or a lack of agreement and consistency' in understanding and portraying what is or is not heritage. When communities are complex and multidimensional in ethnic and social terms, there is bound to be some degree of dissonance and contestation regarding the treatment of heritage. In this case, questions nearly always arise as to which community of many is being considered, who represents it and do its interests conflict with those of other communities (Ashworth in press; Graham 1996). As conservation and interpretation involve the presentation of messages, sometimes dissonance or contestation is created between groups who share the same heritage (Charlesworth 1994; Graham 1996; McBryde 1995; Olsen 2000; Tunbridge and Ashworth 1996).

Olsen (2000) identified three types of contested heritage. The first involves two or more groups claiming the same or overlapping heritage. Here, same places have different meanings for different groups, and each group believes that its view is correct, while that of the other group(s) is not. Lowenthal (1996) gives an example in discussing how differing versions of Indian history aggravate Hindu–Muslim relations. 'To Pakistanis, Nehru is a shallow playboy, Gandhi a religious hypocrite; Indians depict a Pakistan spawned by feudal lords and greedy merchants, its founder, Jinnah, a Westernized opportunist and British stooge' (Lowenthal 1996: 235). While both groups share some similar colonial and indigenous heritages, their views and interpretations of those heritages have led to contestation between the two groups (Olsen and Timothy 2002).

The second form of contested heritage is division within one group. In some cases there are divisions within a group over what aspects of their heritage to emphasise and share with the public. Tunbridge and Ashworth (1996: 29) term this division 'undesirable transmission', when there are 'messages that society, or sections of it, would rather not hear themselves or permit others to hear'. Lowenthal (1996: 156) notes that 'what heritage does not highlight it often hides'. In this way, 'heritage shapes an embraceable past' through the 'celebrating of [some aspects of a heritage] and forgetting others' (Lowenthal 1996: 162). Lowenthal (1979a) gave an example of this where a women's league in a small California town wished to commemorate the prostitutes who worked there during the gold rush with the dedication of a memorial plaque. The city council opposed the action because members were ashamed to share that portion of their past with outsiders.

The third form of contested heritage is indigenous versus colonial, which really refers to two different groups with parallel heritages, often leading to questions about which, or whose, heritage should be preserved. This area of contestation has been a focus of post-colonial studies concerned with the interpretation and use of colonial heritage in areas where the indigenous population has begun to rediscover and assert its own collective identities. This has subsequently led to the development of an atmosphere where cultural and racial diversity and multicultural sensitivities are high (Tunbridge 1998b). In many instances, 'indigenous peoples have histories of sustained exploitation and abuse of human rights which continue into present times' (Sofield and Birtles 1996: 412).

Multiple groups sharing the same heritage

It is common for several different accounts of individual events to exist as different groups interpret them. Battles between Native Americans and white settlers, for example, commonly take on different perspectives when told by each side. Buchholtz (1998) tells of this situation where the US National Park Service and Crow Indians both re-enact Custer's Last Stand at the Battle of Little Bighorn. The events are scheduled on the same weekend at approximately the same time, but each has a separate version of the original event. The two events depict many of the same historic occurrences and both desire to present an authentic reproduction, although each side tells a slightly different story. Likewise, differences are present in the Indian attire, cavalry uniforms, riding equipment, and even the places where the events occurred, and the number of people and deaths occurring had some notable differences.

This category of dissonance occurs when competing paradigms of social understanding apportion different meanings to the same artefacts, places and events (Graham 1996: 12). Stonehenge is perhaps one of the best-known examples of this. The heritage value of Stonehenge has various meanings for several groups, each wanting something different from it. English Heritage owns Stonehenge, the National Trust owns 1,500 acres surrounding it and the Ministry of Defence owns large areas in its vicinity on Salisbury Plain (Addyman 1989; Bender and Edmonds 1992; Crouch and Colin 1992; Fowler 1992). However, this is not the only source of contestation. There are also differing views about the conservation and use of the site, especially for scientific, religious and tourism purposes. The Druids, who claim the site as their own spiritual heritage, want access to it on the summer solstice, scientists want continuous access so they can study its origins and curious tourists desire access for heritage enjoyment.

Concurrent claims to Jerusalem and its holy sites between Jews, Muslims and even Christians is certainly one of the most hotly contested heritage locations in the world. Here particularly, the words of Tunbridge (1984: 171) are relevant: 'one person's landmark may be an object of . . . hostility to another'. Similar politically motivated contestation exists in Northern Ireland between Catholics and Protestants, and in the Republic of Ireland there is overt conflict between Anglo and Gaelic heritage (Boyd 2000b; Graham 1994a, 1998a). One way to lessen this contestation is to focus on how events are remembered by different groups within society. In the case of Northern Ireland, the Somme Heritage Centre does not commemorate the cost the Unionist/ Protestants paid to Britain during this battle alone in the First World War, but includes nationalists that fought and lost their lives. By broadening the heritage to the battle itself and thereby eliminating the element that creates the feeling of dissonance, both sectors of Northern Ireland will be allowed to share in this history and this heritage attraction.

Even in 'peaceful' tourist destinations, opposing views of spaces exist. For instance, differing political views of Niagara Falls, which is divided by the US–Canadian border, have created contrasting landscapes, land uses and meanings of place at Niagara (Timothy 2001c). The US side is notorious for its derelict and dirty industrial landscape owing to the long-term practice of factory construction adjacent to the Falls, while the Canadian side of the border is known for its parklands and well-groomed scenery owing to its designation as a provincial park in the 1800s. Several observers explain the ideological differences that have created two divergent heritage landscapes in essentially one location. McGreevy (1991) argued that the difference emanates from the meaning each country places on the Falls. For Canada, Niagara is like a welcoming front entrance:

It has been embellished and manicured. To find the part of the lot that corresponds to America's Niagara, we must travel around the house to the back alley. There, behind the garage, is a row of garbage cans. This is a utilitarian place to which we are not meant to direct our attention. Niagara is like a dark, back alley of the United States, an appropriate place for dioxin and nuclear waste, but apparently not for gardens (McGreevy 1991: 4).

Heritage divisions within one group

Very often within one broad group of people, contestation occurs between various factions who interpret their common history in different ways. Because many groups are heterogeneous, divergent views are to be expected (Graham 1994b; Kavanagh 1983). 'Since there is no single culture common to all members of a society who reside within the territory of the state, nationalism is always an artificial construct, a myth or ideology created by state intellectuals' (Leong 1989: 358). In urban areas especially, the heritage values tend to be those of whichever social group is in power. The dominant group does not necessarily have to be the majority, but it typically moulds the city according to its unconscious (or conscious) bias (Tunbridge 1984: 171). This results in dissonances between various ethnic groups regarding their heritage representations (Tunbridge 1998b: 102). This is the case in Canadian cities like Montreal and Ottawa between Anglo- and Franco-Canadians, and throughout much of Canada. The French-Canadian approach to history is somewhat different from that of Anglo-Canadians (Tunbridge 1998b).

Parallel heritages

The most common aspect of this type is the conflict that occurs between indigenous and colonial heritage. Tunbridge (1984) suggested that the politically dominant groups in society usually marginalise the heritage of disadvantaged people. This is very much the case with colonial–colony relationships where in most cases colonialism suppresses a nation's right to a national heritage (Hinz 1990). The situations of Native Americans and South Africans mentioned earlier, where history was deleted to achieve political and nationalist goals, are a good example of this. This is the nature of the colonial–colony relationship. History was in essence falsified or distorted to support the intentions of the rulers (Gawe and Meli 1990).

Tourism often relegates indigenous people to the margins of society and enhances the colonial relationship between dominant and subordinate peoples (Ryan and Crotts 1997). This influences the nature of heritage presented to tourists. To most white tourists and European residents of Zimbabwe, for example, Matobo National Park represents an area rich in natural beauty and political heritage, because it is where Cecil Rhodes, the British founder of Rhodesia (today Zimbabwe), is buried. To indigenous Africans, however, the park is symbolic of ethnic nationalism, for Mzilikazi, a celebrated Ndebele leader, is also buried there (Ranger 1989). Differences are also notable in New Zealand between the native Maoris and the European (white) population. Among European New Zealanders, heritage usually identifies with elements of the built environment or cultural landscape – in a sense, that humans are separate from nature. The indigenous view, however, sees humankind as an integral part of nature, so that heritage is part of an indivisible whole, an every-day lived experience (Hall and McArthur 1993a: 3).

In some places many phases of colonisation occurred, resulting in several different and overlapping colonial histories. In Ghana for instance, there is a call for the 500-year history of Elmina Castle, a major site on the slave route, to be represented and interpreted as accurately as possible (Plate 8.1). However, this raises a difficult question: which period should be presented for different sections of the castle? The functions of many rooms changed over time, especially with successive takeovers by foreign powers – first the Portuguese, then the Dutch, followed by the British (Bruner 1996: 293). Bruner (1996: 293–4) explains the confusing situation as follows:

> Which story should be told? Vested interests and strong feelings are involved. Dutch tourists are interested in the two centuries of Dutch rule in Elmina Castle, the Dutch cemetery in the town, and the old Dutch colonial buildings. British tourists want to hear about colonial rule in the Gold Coast. Many Ashanti people have a special interest in the rooms where . . . their king was imprisoned in Elmina Castle in 1896, after the defeat of the Ashanti forces by the British army.

Plate 8.1   Elmina Slave Fort, Ghana

The king was later exiled to the Seychelles Islands and only returned to Ghana in 1924. He is important to all Ghanaians as a representation of resistance to British colonialism.

To solve just this type of dilemma, Longstreth (1992: 224) argues that what is needed 'is an integrative, holistic view of the past, one that looks with equal seriousness at all periods, phases, episodes, and phenomena that have ceased their currency'.

Propaganda and place: creating images through heritage

It is not uncommon for presiding governments to utilise heritage in one form or another to shape public opinion, to build nationalism and to create images that reflect their political ideals. This is typically done by destroying or forgetting heritage (e.g. the Eastern European examples described earlier), creating pasts that never existed (e.g. the examples of invented authenticity described in Chapter 7), and manipulating history and heritage – the focus of this section.

Heritage and its material objects can be used as a means of affirming and reinforcing national identities both for tourists and for citizens (Hobsbawm and Ranger 1983; Light 2000a; McLean 1998; Rogers 1996). Of this and the ideas of heritage suppression, Graham et al. (2000: 12) state that the 'nation-state required national heritage for a variety of reasons. It supported the consolidation of this national identification, while absorbing or neutralizing potentially competing heritages of social-cultural groups or regions.' Such an approach has long been used by newly independent countries, where leaders have attempted to unify and manage their new national populace by manufacturing nationhood, national identity and patriotism through special events, re-creations of culture and developing xenophobia and public disdain towards other ethnicities, especially previous ruling groups (Graham 1996; Hall 1998; Howell 1994; Leong 1989). Aspects of heritage like superstitions, crafts, folk songs and folk life are part of the underlying elements of national identity that are often tapped. Some states establish folk museums in an effort to preserve national culture and identity precisely for this purpose, as in the case of the Welsh Folk Museum, which aimed to 'remake' rural Wales for the Welsh population (Gruffudd 1995).

According to Ashworth (1990b), war arouses powerful nationalist emotions. This is why so many countries emphasise war heritage, including battlefields, national cemeteries, tombs of unknown soldiers and so on, to engender a sense of collective patriotism. In Finland, war landscapes of monuments and memorials have been highlighted, and even created to support a 'nationalistic narrative' (Raivo 2000). According to Raivo (2000: 139), 'these marked sites of the national past do not tell us so much about what really happened as how we should remember these happenings and commemorate them'. Such heritages have been endowed with national soul and memory for a unique purpose. In this way, battlefields and other nationalist memorials become ideologically encoded landscapes (Raivo 2000: 145).

Correspondingly, as part of its national patriotism-building efforts, the United States has created an admirable past. 'Americans have extended it, reinterpreted it, and reinvented it' (Lowenthal 1977: 255). Like many nations, Americans have magnified their ancestors' heroic traits and minimised their disgraceful ones. 'The past [in the United States] is more a chronicle of national greatness than an account of actual events and persons', an assertion supported by Hobsbawm and Ranger (1983), for Americans reject Benedict Arnold and 'historic sites associated with Jay Gould and Wild West prostitutes' (Lowenthal 1977: 261). Thus, the past is reconstructed and truth reconfigured to persuade insiders that this is real history (Norkunas 1993). According to the Director of the American Holocaust Museum, even the Holocaust is recast in order to teach fundamental American values: pluralism, democracy, restraint on government and individual rights (cited in Lennon and Foley 1999: 49). In the communist countries of CEE, heritage was promoted by the governments not for tourism purposes per se, but instead to indoctrinate a sense of achievement and identity within the citizenry of each country (Hall 1998: 350).

Heritage can also be used to build supranationalist identity/unity, as in the case of the European Union, where the European Commission and other bodies (e.g. Council of Europe) are attempting to solidify and promote a common European heritage to build unity among member nations (Ashworth 1995; Graham 1998b). However, such a heritage, according to Graham (1998b: 45), cannot comprise everything common to all of Europe. Instead, it must embrace heterogeneity of cultures and highlight notions of multiculturalism and overlap if it is to validate and legitimate European integration. Many difficulties, not least of which are individual national identities grounded in linguistic and religious traditions, stand in the way of the Commission's efforts to build unity through common heritage (Tunbridge 1998a).

Heritage is commonly used also to create a nationalist fervour and image that can transcend the world. McCrone et al. (1995) discuss this at great length in the context of Scotland. This allows images to be created abroad, desirable images that will lend credence to newly independent nations or nations who desire a heightened global image. States thus use tourism, heritage and heritage tourism to manipulate or alter people's perceptions of them (Leong 1989; San Roman 1992). China is an interesting example, where Porter (1997) speculated on the country's potential use of Macao after its return in 1999 to create an image of power and Portuguese colonial defeat or cross-national harmony.

CASE STUDY   Heritage politics in Singapore

The varied cultural and colonial history of Singapore has resulted in multidimensional views of heritage. Different communities were influenced in different ways, which has now resulted in complications in current heritage meanings and perceptions. For example, each of the dominant ethnic communities – Malays, Chinese and Indians – had its own experience with the Second World War and the Japanese occupation, and the younger generations of all these communities believe it to have little relevance to their own lives (Henderson 1997: 40). This has resulted in various interpretations of the war and the development of several different war-related tourist attractions that favour different ethnicities.

This collage of cultures within such a small country has created various levels and types of heritage contestation. Race is a major source of tension in this, particularly between the Indians and Chinese. National policy states that regardless of race, any person who can afford it is welcome in Little India, which has resulted in many Chinese shopkeepers setting up shop. Indian merchants do not generally like this idea, for they feel Little India is 'their space', which Chinese shops would spoil. This attitude is fed by the knowledge that Singapore's majority population is Chinese and Little India is somewhat of a sanctuary for the minority Indians (Chang 1999). Between the two groups, tensions have emerged throughout the years owing to conflicting ideas about who constitutes the 'true insider' (Chang 1999: 96).

The public-sector manipulation of heritage to create an image and instil nationalism has also been a part of heritage politics in Singapore (Chang *et al.* 1996). In fact, much of the country's heritage was destroyed and then reconstructed to fit an idealised notion of what it should be.

By the end of 1993, all rural villages in Singapore had been demolished and the inhabitants relocated into high-rise apartments. When the last village was bulldozed in May 1993, it meant the 'end of the country's rural heritage and a way of life which had predated the arrival of Sir Stamford Raffles in 1819 . . . As agriculture was judged not to make the most effective use of limited land, state emphasis was placed on manufacturing industries' (Powell 1997: 86). This economic restructuring was rapid and did not therefore allow much time for nostalgia to play into the situation. Many beautiful, historic buildings were destroyed, including the Adelphi Hotel (built in the 1880s), the Arcade (built 1909), the Panglima Prang mansion (built 1860), and the Kandang Kerbau Market. Additionally, the Raffles Institution, a school founded by Sir Stamford Raffles himself in 1823, was torn down to facilitate the building of Raffles City, a large shopping mall (Powell 1997). The government rationalised such mass destruction of mixed local and colonial heritage by its heavy emphasis on modernisation and technological change in economic development. In the process, leaders convinced Singaporeans that rapid modernisation is more favourable than nostalgia for the past (James 1995; Powell 1997).

Such endeavours to rid the island of its built heritage were later recompensed by the building of new and often invented heritage. For example, in 1989, an uninhabited Malay village was built by the Housing and Development Board to represent an idealised re-creation of an indigenous *kampong* (Powell 1997).

This is one example of real traditions and places being replaced by contrived traditions and places (Leong 1989).

Another example is the New Asia–Singapore cultural and heritage park that was recently constructed. Its identity is basically a state-led initiative to reposition tourism, improve the urban landscape and create a new identity for Singaporeans. Its story tells of a country proud of both its traditions and its modernity. The Museum Precinct relates the country's voyage to nationhood. The Singapore River tells about the country's colonial past and the entrepreneurship of its people. The representations of Little India and Chinatown depict a multicultural society living and working harmoniously (Chang and Huang in press; Chang and Yeoh 1999).

Other efforts since the mid-1980s to revitalise tourism have included the redevelopment of key ethnic neighbourhoods and historic districts to enhance the 'oriental mystique and charm' of the island state. Efforts then and presently focus on trying to bring back much of the local colour that once typified Little India, Chinatown and other historic zones before the widespread redevelopment of the 1960s and 1970s (Chang and Huang in press).

War and conflict

Wars and other political conflicts necessarily restrict the growth of heritage tourism. Research has shown that nearly any degree of political discord will result in major downturns in global travel, even in regions not directly involved in the conflict (Pizam and Mansfeld 1996; Sönmez 1998). Tourism is a volatile industry, and the lingering effects of the Yugoslavian wars, for example, have so far had long-lasting repercussions in terms of tourism development. What is left of the former federation and the new independent states that emerged from its dissolution (e.g. Croatia, Slovenia, Bosnia-Hercegovina, Macedonia) are all faced with image problems that can be traced directly to the wars. They are still very much considered by potential travellers as dangerous places to visit (Panic-Kombol 1996) (Plate 8.2). In addition to tourism development and growth, political unrest can prevent effective conservation of historic sites and heritage places, as well as physically destroy the sites and artefacts upon which tourism is based, especially when they are targeted for destruction by opposing forces.

Heritage as target

Because built heritage is typically seen as an emblem of society, ethnic pride, spiritual unity or nationhood, adversaries commonly target historic artefacts and places for destruction as a way of crushing national patriotism and solidarity.

Plate 8.2   Signs of war/conflict at Medurgorje pilmigrage site, Bosnia-Hercegovina

The term 'heritage genocide' was used by Talley (1995) to describe the destruction of heritage through violent means. The deliberate aims of destroying heritage for political purposes is assisted, according to Talley (1995: 59), by humankind's inherent and irresistible urge to destroy – a 'primordial impulse to wreak havoc'.

One of the most recent examples of heritage genocide to have received worldwide attention was the destruction of the Buddhist statues at Bamyam, Afghanistan, early in 2001 by that country's then ruling Taliban government. While this was not a result of war or even any kind of international battle per se, it was an attempt by an extremist government to purify Afghanistan's cultural landscape into one that reflected only an Islamic heritage. By doing this, the heritage of Buddhists around the world, and indeed an important part of the entire world's heritage, was destroyed for ever, despite global efforts to convince the Taliban not to carry out this atrocity (Ashworth forthcoming).

Another prominent example of heritage genocide is the Yugoslav shelling of Dubrovnik, a world heritage town on the south Croatian coast, in 1992 during the Yugoslavian wars (Bumbaru 1992). Many rooftops of ancient buildings, including churches, shops and private homes, were destroyed as the entire walled community was targeted and damaged. Today, most of the damage, with the exception of bullet holes in walls, fountains and cobblestone streets, has been repaired, and once again Dubrovnik is a vibrant heritage city (Plate 8.3). The medieval Mostar Bridge over the Neretva River in Mostar, Bosnia-Hercegovina, also a UNESCO site, succumbed to a similar fate, although it was destroyed completely during the dissolution of the Yugoslavian Federation.

Plate 8.3   The refurbished Old Town of Dubrovnik, 2001

Plate 8.4   The destroyed Mostar Bridge and its reconstruction

Current efforts, however, are under way to rebuild the bridge (Plate 8.4) using original stones retrieved from the river and financed by the European Union and other international organisations. Not only was the physical heritage of Mostar destroyed, so was the people's common heritage identity, which will still be healing once the bridge's reconstruction is complete.

Terrorism, too, is a major political force that has existed for a very long time, but which received renewed worldwide attention following the 2001 September 11 attacks on New York City and Washington, DC. Icons of the United States' political and economic heritage were the target selected by terrorists fighting against a heritage of capitalism and Westernisation.

Heritage as innocent casualty

Even when heritage structures are not the deliberate targets of political violence, they are commonly damaged and even destroyed as innocent bystanders in the way of violence. A good example of this is the Angkor Wat temples of Cambodia, which suffered considerable damage during that country's civil wars of the 1970s and 1980s, primarily through acts of deliberate destruction, not inadvertent shelling or bombing. Actually, relatively little bombing occurred in the area, but bullet holes can still be seen throughout the complex, especially in the carved reliefs and statues caused by vandalising soldiers for the sheer enjoyment of being destructive (Dauge 1997: 166). Many of the Buddhas and other statues were crushed or blown apart by dynamite. This destruction began in 1970, when Angkor was invaded and overrun by the Khmer Rouge and it quickly became one of the rebel strongholds. Despite these tragic actions, which did enormous damage to the site itself, one of the most critical impacts of the war was that it depleted precious financial resources that could have been used for conservation (Timothy 1999a) and did not allow regular maintenance for nearly 20 years because it was occupied by warring factions and its surrounding environment was laced with land mines. As a result, much of it had been overgrown by vegetation, flooded by water and deterioration related simply to abandonment (Dauge 1997; Hornik 1992; Wager 1995). In addition to the relicts themselves, visitor facilities and highways to Angkor were destroyed, and the road to recovery has been long, tedious and costly (Wager 1995).

Another type of battle that commonly ensues between nations, but which does not always take the form of active combat, is border disputes. Several border disputes directly involve important heritage places. For more than a century, Thailand and Cambodia have been involved in a territorial dispute involving the Preah Vihear ancient temple complex located near the border of the two countries. It is one of the best examples of Khmer architecture and one of the most impressive temples in South-East Asia. The main problem is that the temple is located in the territory that was strongly contested between the two countries, and each one has at some point controlled ownership of it. Several clashes have ensued over the years, forcing the complex to change hands on a number of occasions between the Thais and Cambodians. In 1962, however, the location of the international boundary was fixed by a decision of the International Court of Justice, which confirmed that the temple was located just a few hundred metres inside Cambodia, where it remains today (St John 1994; Timothy 2001c).

War as attraction

As was discussed at length in Chapter 2, the aftermath of war is a major attraction in many parts of the world, for people are interested in human-created disasters, loss of life, and destruction of natural and built environments. Sarajevo, Bosnia-Hercegovina, is a good example where this phenomenon is presently taking place. While tourism in Sarajevo has not yet recovered to anywhere near its previous level prior to the wars of the early 1990s, war tourism is something that helps keep local hotels and other services afloat in desperate economic times. Thus, there has been a growth of 'morbid' tourism since 1995, wherein tourists follow trails through sites of destruction to 'gaze on the physical remnants of human suffering' (Hall 1998: 351).

An interesting type of war tourism has developed in recent years wherein veterans travel back to places where they fought during war times. This is particularly popular among American veterans who fought in Vietnam, Korea and Western Europe (Smith 1996). An additional unique and relatively new feature of this is tours for veterans who suffer from post-traumatic stress disorder. Apparently, according to some research, veterans can heal some of their psychological disorders by visiting war heritage sites where they might have fought and learn to deal with the fears that these places created within them (Watson *et al.* 1995).

Community involvement in planning and development

The issue of community-based planning, discussed in Chapter 5, is a highly political issue that ought to be addressed again briefly in the context of the politics of heritage tourism. The degree to which tourism communities are permitted and encouraged to participate in tourism development and planning and receive benefits from its growth is an issue of power. Many governments and political systems throughout the world discourage this form of community-based tourism, while other systems require it. In South Africa, for example, not only was the heritage of indigenous Africans not included in the development of heritage tourism (Goudie *et al.* 1996), indigenous people were not included in any forms of decision-making, and few were ever encouraged to be involvedin tourism from an entrepreneurial viewpoint. The exclusion of local people from policy decision-making and planning has been the traditional paradigm throughout the world, and still is in many more traditional societies (Saugee 1992; Timothy 1999c; Tosun and Jenkins 1998; Tosun and Timothy 2001), although the situation is beginning to change.

Recently, researchers have concentrated intensively on this issue of community empowerment, and in the realm of heritage tourism the focus has related primarily to the plight of indigenous peoples. It is now realised that the involvement of indigenous people in heritage planning and heritage tourism development is critical. Since they were the ones who traditionally were excluded from heritage conservation and interpretation, it is vital for them in today's development climate to determine and control the fate of their own heritage (Hall 1997). According to Keelan (1993: 101), interpretation strategies relating to indigenous heritage, art and culture must be developed from a basis that recognises the indigenous ownership of the product and indigenous participation through all stages of the planning and information delivery process, especially since displaying culture and history can create antagonisms. Local people are important, for they can help heritage tourism developers appreciate local histories and the pasts of ordinary people, and in some way help reduce the commodification of places or help temper the destruction of cultures (Teo and Yeoh 1997: 210).

Very often indigenous people are the ones with the most knowledge about places, artefacts and traditions. Likewise, their traditions in relation to nature are very often more sustainable than those proposed by outside experts. For example, 'Maori sustainability has its basis in a spiritual metaphysical approach . . . Sustainability is the maori that keeps things in existence – it is a life force, a vitality or vital essence' (Cloher and Johnston 1999: 48). Cloher and Johnston (1999: 48) provide an example wherein Maori handicrafts are sensitive to ecological processes:

> The flax has to be cut with sensitivity taking the outer leaves and leaving the inner core intact. The remains are to be returned to the mother plant to enable re-growth. The kit therefore has more than a utilitarian value – as it represents its vital origin . . . The spiritual enters into every activity.

Maori traditions also promote cultural, social and economic sustainability in various ways. Cultural sustainability is confirmed by cultural expressions through ethics and values, shrines and sacred places, rituals, myths and legends, dances, songs, art and ceremonies. Social sustainability is assured through traditional practices of communalism and kinship bonding (*whanaungatanga*) where the greater good of the community is more important than the individual and where common lineages create a sense of belonging. Economic sustainability exists by 'economies of affection' based primarily on providing for one's own kin. They share food and property; they are compassionate and share what they have with people less fortunate than themselves (Cloher and Johnston 1999).

For many years, the Maori image was used to market tourism to New Zealand. Maoris were stereotyped in menial roles without consultation or commercial benefit (Barnett 1997: 471). Today the tides have turned, however, and the Maori have much more control of their images and the heritage tourism that exists based largely on their culture. The Maori are well-established stakeholders in tourism in New Zealand. In 1996 it was estimated that 153 tourism operations in New Zealand were owned or operated by Maori or providing a Maori product. This included entertainment, arts and crafts, history/display of artefacts and guided tours (Barnett 1997). At its broadest, Maori tourism includes any tourist experience of Maori culture. A Maori tourism product is generally viewed as 'an opportunity provided within the composite tourism product for the tourist to have contact with Maori culture', which in 1995 and 1996 was experienced by some 36 per cent of international visitors to New Zealand (Zeppel 1997: 475). Today, heritage tourism is seen as a way of legitimising the Maori struggle for political and economic recognition (Ryan and Crotts 1997).

Summary and conclusions

The issue of politics is important when addressing heritage, and this relationship has been the focus of this chapter. In places, the tone and language used have been strong and critical, and this has been deliberate, for throughout the world heritage too often reflects only those who hold positions of power within society. It goes back to what was stressed in the introductory chapter that heritage is selective on the basis of power and who is able to exercise it to suit their own ends. As seen in this chapter, this has allowed the distortion, exclusion and deliberate forgetting of certain elements of national pasts, whether this has been achieved via the education process (which in itself is a sad reflection on society) or done for higher political and ideological reasons. However, what is beginning to emerge is a revisioning of the past, where stories of the Native American and African/slave past, for example, are starting to be told as part of the national heritage. It would be naive not to suppose that part of this rethinking is linked to opportunities for heritage tourism. What is important, however, is that heritage is beginning to reflect a holistic story of the past, as much as can be known of it. The case study of South Africa would suggest this country still has a long way to go in representing an equitable and balanced heritage.

Because of the type of power structure that has existed in many places, national foci have turned to erasing anything that reminds of undesirable pasts. This is true for the countries of CEE, as well as for a Germany keen to erase its Nazi past. While some memories are difficult for citizens in these regions, there is a danger that rapid erasure could result in some heritages being lost for ever. It may be better that reminders of this time in history are preserved as a way of avoiding its reoccurrence in the future.

Dissonant heritage was an important discussion in this chapter, raising questions about heritage in conflict between different social and cultural groups.

Heritage cannot be divorced from identity (Graham *et al.* 2000). In fact it is often used in the shaping of a country's identity as has been illustrated by examples within this chapter. Likewise, heritage has a role to play in building nationalism, reinforcing national identity, patriotism and creating fervour, out of which favourable images have emerged and which is now being sold to tourists. The issue lies in the extent to which these images of nationalism are distortions of the truth, and in one sense the extent to which heritage and heritage tourism have been used to manipulate perceptions of place as the Singapore case study demonstrated.

Unfortunately, much cultural and natural heritage will be lost in regions where wars and violence are an all too common occurrence. This is particularly unfortunate when heritage is deliberately targeted as a means of removing elements of a group's past, or even when it is damaged as an innocent casualty of a war. In both situations, preservation efforts need to be encouraged as soon after the conflict as possible, to ensure that some elements can be saved. As revealed here, where heritage genocide has taken place, a greater desire exists to rebuild those icons of heritage, for they are often a reflection of a people's common heritage. For some people war zones are a tourist attraction. They contain a different kind of heritage, often a personal one for those who played a role in battling or a morbid appeal for those who wish to see sites of death and destruction.

Finally, heritage is a community resource, and thus all sectors of a community should be involved in its planning and development. While some societies deny full involvement by community groups, it has been encouraging to see recently that where heritage is concerned, indigenous peoples are being allowed a stronger voice in how their heritage is both presented and marketed to tourists, and in so doing are able to control to some degree at least their own heritage. Since heritage is so often connected to power and the abuse of power, this is a positive note to end this chapter.

Questions

1. Why is heritage a political concept?
2. How have power arrangements influenced and shaped heritage tourism?
3. Can the 'contestation' element ever be removed from heritage tourism?
4. How has war and conflict impacted upon and affected heritage and heritage tourism?
5. What are the benefits of heritage tourism planning being devolved to the community level?

Further reading

Hall, C.M. (1994) *Tourism and Politics: Policy, power and place*, Wiley, Chichester.
Hobsbawn, E. and Ranger, T. (eds) (1983) *The Invention of Tradition*, Cambridge University Press, Cambridge.

Leong, W.T. (1989) 'Culture and the state: manufacturing traditions for toursim', *Critical Studies in Mass Communication*, 6(4): 355–375.

Norkunas, M.K. (1993) *The Politics of Public Memory: Tourism, history, and ethnicity in Monterey, California*, State University of New York Press, Albany.

Shaw, B.J. and Jones, R. (eds) (1997) *Contested Urban Heritage: Voices from the periphery*, Ashgate, Aldershot.

Tunbridge, J. and Ashworth, G.J. (1996) *Dissonant Heritage: The management of the past as a resource in conflict*, Wiley, Chichester.

CHAPTER 9

Reflections and futures

Heritage tourism has emerged as an important leisure activity and area of scholarly research. This book is about heritage tourism; it has been written from the perspective that other texts cover heritage in general (e.g. Graham *et al.* 2000), the societal implications of heritage and tourism (e.g. Herbert 1995b), and specifically heritage management (e.g. Hall and McArthur 1998). The approach taken here has been broad-based in an attempt to cover the main issues from a theoretical/research perspective, as well as from a practical viewpoint. This book has covered a wide range of concepts and issues, and this concluding chapter aims to highlight some of the issues raised in previous chapters, and discusses potential future developments in the study of heritage tourism.

Defining heritage tourism

Defining concepts is never an easy task, and in the course of writing this book, the authors were tempted to provide yet another new definition of heritage tourism. Instead, it was decided to provide a discussion of its meaning based on existing definitions and models, which show the linkages between heritage and tourism. A critical point to make here is that the heritage 'environment' transcends any particular type of tourism, and the extent to which heritage tourism overlaps with other forms needs to be acknowledged. There are problems associated with compartmentalising experiences to conform to specific types of tourism, and perhaps there is justification in moving the debate away from narrow interpretations into a more holistic framework of thinking. Heritage is important in peoples' lives as the magnitude of the industry appears to suggest, and the significance and value that lie within heritage are not in how it is defined, but in how it is used to create meaningful experiences for tourists, while promoting conservation values.

Supply and demand

An acceptance that heritage is present across many environments has allowed many types of heritage attractions to emerge or, more accurately, be created. However, it is difficult to say if this has been a positive development. On the one hand, it is important that heritage attractions are developed for all possible environments, provided they reflect heritage attributes of their locations. However, there seems to be a significant concern among some observers that there is now an oversupply of heritage, and a creation of attractions that are far divorced from their settings. This is especially concerning where there is no guarantee that demand will continue to grow in the future, although it probably will. It is important for heritage attractions to be connected to the attributes of place, otherwise this form of tourism will continue to be 'McDisneyised' to an extent that only selective facets of the past are presented. The current level of interest in heritage is creating a situation where destinations seeking to capitalise on this market are continuously expanding their attraction bases, often placing the ever more popular heritage label on existing features to create new demand, for example, 'heritage rivers', 'heritage coasts', 'heritage railways'. Owing to the societal trends underscored in this book this heritage naming is a popular trend in modern society where tourism services elect to adopt such a name (e.g. the Heritage Inn or the Heritage Café) as a promotional tactic in the same way many non-tourism establishments (e.g. Heritage School, Heritage Farms Produce, Heritage Supermarket and Heritage Place Credit Union) do.

Attractions should be developed in association with the support services they require. Failure to do so may result in supply being underused, or for more popular attractions, an inability to cater to the needs of visitors. As for demand, the challenge does not rest with current demand, for much is known about the demographics, origins and motivations of heritage visitors. Instead, the focus should be on understanding unmet demand and how to turn this into actual use, overcoming the obstacles (e.g. inaccessibility, lack of educational preparation, disabilities, psychological constraints) that prevent people from visiting heritage sites.

Conserving the past

While heritage is one of the oldest forms of travel, the importance placed on conserving the past is a relatively recent phenomenon, despite the fact that awareness regarding preservation can be traced back several centuries (Graham *et al.* 2000; Ashworth and Tunbridge 2000). In some parts of the world, there is a real danger of losing heritage. Heritage places within the developed *scot.* world have benefited from long-standing legislation and the establishment of conservation bodies, while in the developing world other priorities have tended to take precedence over heritage matters. As heritage is under the control of individual nations, it is difficult, and perhaps wrong in some ways, for the Western world to insist that developing countries give higher priority to conserving their past, particularly if the past is associated with a colonial legacy many citizens wish to forget. Where conservation is possible, the adoption of the process outlined in the book is encouraged, which connects conservation to the development of the tourism infrastructure, including long-term management and interpretation. Also, decisions have to be taken concerning the extent of conservation efforts. Should a more passive approach (e.g. preservation) or an active approach (e.g. renovation) be undertaken? This is a difficult question to answer, and the response will vary in every situation depending on goals, management traditions, budget limitations and the nature of the site and its surrounding environment. Whatever approach is used, there is a need to ensure that the heritage value of place remains.

Management

Management of heritage is never easy; it is multifaceted, and issues vary according to ownership, type of attraction and the nature of the environment where sites are located. Through experience, many tools have developed to assist managers in dealing with staff and visitors, and in managing the heritage resource base. The outcome of good management is sustainable environments both for visitors and the local community. Where tourists are concerned, a balance has to be struck by managers over how much of the market opportunity should, and can, be capitalised upon, and at what stage should limits apply and restrictions be imposed. As for the relationship with the local population, the approach should not be one of managing, but rather one of facilitating involvement and public participation. It is important to remember that the heritage displayed to tourists is also the heritage of the local people, and it is essential that they feel some degree of attachment to it, have an effective voice in how it is managed and receive some kind of benefit from sharing it with outsiders. In attempting to achieve sustainability, managers are also faced with the reality of how they can generate sufficient funds to ensure their attractions remain economically viable. While a range of options exists, and these were debated at length, decisions will have to be reached regarding whether or not to impose user fees, which is an unpopular prospect for some public and non-profit sector managers. Marketing is an important part of heritage management. It can assist in promoting awareness of a site and result in increased revenues. When done properly, it can also be a useful tool for managing visitors and their impacts.

Interpretation and authenticity

Interpretation plays an essential role in assisting the visitors' learning process. Not only does it educate and entertain, it also offers a means to convey conservation and sustainable development principles. However, managers need to be cautious in not letting interpretation diminish visitor experiences. An assumption is often made that heritage tourists are a more education-oriented people, who are keen on learning new things through heritage experiences. While that may be true for some, it cannot be assumed to apply to the majority of visitors. Therefore, the challenge is to provide interpretation across a range of capabilities and willingness, requiring that the right message be conveyed through the most appropriate medium. In theory, interpretation should form an important part of any heritage attraction, but in reality a flexible approach may need to be adopted regarding its importance in relation to site goals and objectives. As regards authenticity, a strong argument was made to challenge thinking that its existence or absence affects the experiences of tourists. It is probably safe to assume that most tourists are aware that performances and events are staged to some extent, have been altered and do not entirely reflect what conditions were like in pre-tourist eras. One of the most pressing challenges facing site managers today is the creation of authentic environments. However, as complete reality is unrealistic and simply impossible, perhaps it is becoming more important for managers to focus on being as authentic as possible within bounds of logic and providing visitors with satisfying experiences.

Relationship with politics

The last topic examined in the book was the connection between heritage and politics/power. Heritage and its designation are inherently political concepts, and as such, certain heritages have been manipulated to suit the ideological goals of people and systems in power. This has meant that heritage reflects the stories told by winners of wars and aristocratic elites who have seen heritage as a tool to legitimise political control. Because heritage entails a choice, the choice should be made to maintain a balance between the aristocratic past of nobility, dominant racial groups and autocratic rulers and that of common folks, ethnic minorities and others whose past might have been conveniently forgotten. Should uncomfortable pasts be eliminated? This is a difficult question, especially for nations that are trying to right the wrongs of history, but the answer is 'probably not'. Despite this potential discomfort and embarrassment some heritages may bring to certain groups, the present and future generations have a right to know, and perhaps assist in the healing process. Because heritage reflects power, it also reflects conflict. There is little doubt that it will remain an issue of dissonance, but heritage providers and leaders should aim to lessen intra-group (and inter-group) tensions by creating situations that involve people instead of excluding them.

Heritage of the future

It has been well accepted that tourism is not a static phenomenon; it is subject to sizeable change (Butler and Pearce 1995; Pigram and Wahab 1998), affected by both exogenous and endogenous factors. It is likely that the heritage supply will continue to grow in the future. A number of factors may account for this. First, the number of sites being ascribed with World Heritage status continues to increase every year, and many of these become key tourism attractions for individual nations, although it is worth pointing out that achieving World Heritage status does not always assure higher levels of visitation. Second, at lower scales, supply will be fuelled by the desire to create more opportunities nationally, regionally and locally and as more and more places seek to cash in on tourism as a means of economic development. Third, it is anticipated that the supply will become more segmented as new forms are added and as existing types are further refined and redefined. Finally, as Western societies become more culturally diverse, and as minority groups continue to gain political strength and their voices begin to be heard more clearly, there will surely be a surge of new heritage attractions that reflect the dismissed pasts of indigenous and politically inferior peoples.

In terms of heritage demand, the trend will probably be one of growth. This is based on several observations. First, larger populations in major source regions are ageing, and members of the retiring generation today are better educated, more affluent, more mobile and more adventurous than their predecessors. This, coupled with a tendency for people to become more nostalgic and interested in heritage as they age, will more than likely result in increased demand. Second, because today's tourist is better travelled and more knowledgeable about travel than previous generations, there exists greater marketability for heritage. If one accepts the argument that tourists are in the business of collecting places, then heritage, particularly that attached to culture and ethnic groups, will have a continual appeal. Heritage continues to witness rejuvenation in terms of the magnitude of the industry and the numbers of people who cite heritage as an integral part of their travels. It is unlikely that this will show a marked decline, as heritage environments offer tourists a different experience than places associated with purely relaxation-oriented destinations. As people continue to travel, it is this difference that, over time, will continue to generate the greater appeal. Thus, good management will remain critical, and if numbers continue to rise, then good management is needed at heritage places to ensure sustainability of resources, communities and tourism.

In terms of interpretation, one area of future growth will be exhibits becoming more interactive. While interactivity reflects current advances in technology, it should not be seen as a replacement for conventional interpretation, which also has the capacity to involve and educate visitors. As for the experiences created at heritage sites, the danger is that sites and artefacts could become secondary in their appeal, losing visitors' attention to technology and other fancy media. The role of virtual reality in potentially providing surrogate heritage experiences cannot be ignored. Perhaps someday it will be possible to visit the Roman ruins, the Pyramids of Egypt or the rainforest of Brazil without ever having to get on an aeroplane.

Likewise, in the future, heritage may be changed to become more appealing to the masses and designed to conform to contemporary fashions and in a way reduce heritage to the status of spectacles in a theme park. Tourism destinations change over time, and heritage places are not immune from this process. While it is not easy to prevent change, there is danger in allowing too much change to occur at heritage and cultural sites, which might cause the attraction to lose its appeal and ultimately cease to exist. Butler (1996) cautioned about trying to promote heritage to mass markets, suggesting that attractions and sites could move through a cycle of original use, tourist use, interpretation, restoration, elaboration and end up as increasingly fabricated and commoditised objects whose original heritage appeal is ruined. Thus, changing the original features and uniqueness of place should be avoided where heritage tourism is concerned.

This book is about heritage and tourism. A holistic approach has been used to explore various aspects that combine to make up heritage tourism. The focus has ranged between description, explanation and critique in the hope of generating further discussion and debate. There is much more to understand about the management, magnitude, meaning and depth of heritage tourism than can possibly be provided in one single volume. However, it is hoped that this book has provided a step in that direction and that a useful framework has been created to guide students and researchers in understanding many of the issues and implications surrounding heritage tourism.

Questions

1. Can a consensus be reached over what is meant by heritage tourism?
2. Which of the two is more important – heritage tourism supply or the demand for heritage tourism?
3. What role(s) can technology play in heritage interpretation?
4. Does heritage tourism have a long-term future?

Further reading

Ashworth, G.J. and Tunbridge, J.E. (2000) *The Tourist-Historic City: Retrospect and prospect of managing the heritage city*, Pergamon, New York.

Graham, B. Ashworth, G.J. and Tunbridge, J.E. (2000) *A Geography of Heritage: Power, culture and economy*. Arnold, London.

Hall, C.M. and McArthur, S. (eds) (1996) *Heritage Management in New Zealand and Australia: The human dimension*, Oxford University Press, Melbourne.

Hall, C.M. and McArthur, S. (1998) *Integrated Heritage Management: Principles and practice*, The Stationery Office, London.

References

Adams, J.S. and McShane, T.O. (1992) *The Myth of Wild Africa: Conservation without Illusion*, W.W. Norton, New York.

Addyman, P.V. (1989) 'The Stonehenge we deserve', in H. Cleere (ed.), *Archaeological Heritage Management in the Modern World*, Unwin Hyman, London, 265–71.

Airey, D. and Shackley, M. (1998) 'Bukhara (Uzbekistan): a former oasis town on the Silk Road', in M. Shackley (ed.), *Visitor Management: Case studies from World Heritage Sites*, Butterworth Heinemann, Oxford, 10–25.

Alderman, D.H. (2002) 'Writing on the Graceland wall: on the importance of authorship in pilgrimage landscapes', *Tourism Recreation Research*, 27(2): 27–33.

Alderson, W.T. and Low, S.P. (1985) *Interpretation of Historic Sites*, 2nd edn, American Association for State and Local History, Nashville.

Aldridge, D. (1989) 'How the ship of interpretation was blown off course in the tempest: some philosophical thoughts', in D.L. Uzzell (ed.), *Heritage Interpretation*, vol. 1: *The natural and built environment*, Belhaven, London, 64–87.

Alfrey, J. and Putnam, T. (1992) *The Industrial Heritage: Managing resources and uses*, Routledge, London.

Alt, M.B. and Shaw, K.M. (1984) 'Characteristics of ideal museum exhibits', *British Journal of Psychology*, 75: 25–36.

Ambler, C. (1995) 'Small historic sites in Kansas: merging artifactual landscapes and community values', *Great Plains Quarterly*, 15: 33–48.

Amit-Talai, V. (1997) 'In pursuit of authenticity: globalization and nation building in the Cayman Islands', *Anthropologica*, 39(1/2): 53–63.

Ansprenger, F. (1989) *The Dissolution of the Colonial Empire*, Routledge, London.

Ashworth, G.J. (1988) 'Marketing the historic city for tourism', in B. Goodall and G. Ashworth (eds), *Marketing in the Tourism Industry: The promotion of destination regions*, Croom Helm, London, 162–75.

Ashworth, G.J. (1990a) 'Accommodation and the historic city', *Built Environment*, 15(2): 92–100.

Ashworth, G.J. (1990b) 'Swords into ploughshares: defense heritage tourism as the peaceful uses of the artefacts of war', *Visions in Leisure and Business*, 9(1): 61–72.

Ashworth, G.J. (1990c) 'The historic cities of Groningen: which is sold to whom?', in G. Ashworth and B. Goodall (eds), *Marketing Tourism Places*, Routledge, London, 138–55.

Ashworth, G.J. (1991) *War and the City*, Routledge, London.

Ashworth, G.J. (1995) 'Heritage, tourism and Europe: a European future for a European past?', in D.T. Herbert (ed.), *Heritage, Tourism and Society*, Mansell, London, 68–84.

Ashworth, G.J. (1997) 'Elements of planning and managing heritage sites', in W. Nuryanti (ed.), *Tourism and Heritage Management*, Gadjah Mada University Press, Yogyakarta, 165–91.

Ashworth, G.J. (1999) 'Heritage dissonance and Holocaust tourism: some cases from European planning', paper presented at the Annual Meeting of the Association of American Geographers, Honolulu, Hawaii, March.

Ashworth, G.J. (forthcoming) 'Bamyam: whose heritage was it and what should we do about it?', *Current Issues in Tourism*.

Ashworth, G.J. (in press) 'Heritage, identity and places: for tourists and host communities', in S. Singh, D.J. Timothy and R.K. Dowling (eds), *Tourism in Destination Communities*, CAB International, Wallingford.

Ashworth, G.J. and Tunbridge, J.E. (1990) *The Tourist-Historic City*, Belhaven, London.

Ashworth, G.J. and Tunbridge, J.E. (1999) 'Old cities, new pasts: heritage planning in selected cities of Central Europe', *GeoJournal*, 49: 105–16.

Ashworth, G.J. and Tunbridge, J.E. (2000) *The Tourist-Historic City: Retrospect and prospect of managing the heritage city*, Pergamon, New York.

Ashworth, G.J. and Voogd, H. (1990) *Selling the City: Marketing approaches in public sector urban planning*, Belhaven, London.

Aziz, H. (1995) 'Understanding attacks on tourists in Egypt', *Tourism Management*, 16: 91–5.

Bainbridge, S. (1979) *Restrictions at Stonehenge: The reactions of visitors to limitations in access*, HMSO, London.

Baker, S.M. and Kennedy, P.F. (1994) 'Death by nostalgia: a diagnosis of context-specific cases', *Advances in Consumer Research*, 21: 169–74.

Balcar, M.J.O. and Pearce, D.G. (1996) 'Heritage tourism on the West Coast of New Zealand', *Tourism Management*, 17: 203–12.

Balme, C.B. (1998) 'Staging the Pacific: framing authenticity in performances for tourists at the Polynesian Cultural Center', *Theatre Journal*, 50(1): 53–70.

Balsas, C.J.L. (2000) 'City center revitalization in Portugal: lessons from two medium size cities', *Cities*, 17(1): 19–31.

Barke, M. and Harrop, K. (1994) 'Selling the industrial town: identity, image and illusion', in J.R. Gold and S.V. Ward (eds), *Place Promotion: The use of publicity and marketing to sell towns and regions*, Wiley, Chichester, 93–114.

Barnett, S. (1997) 'Maori tourism', *Tourism Management*, 18: 471–3.

Barrow, G. (1994) 'Interpretive planning: more to it than meets the eye', *Environmental Interpretation*, 9(2): 5–7.

Barthel, D. (1990) 'Nostalgia for America's village past: staged symbolic communities', *International Journal of Politics, Culture, and Society*, 4(1): 79–93.

Barthel, D. (1996) *Historic Preservation: Collective memory and historical identity*, Rutgers University Press, New Brunswick, NJ.

Bartlett, T. (2001) 'Virginia develops African-American tourism sites', *Travel Weekly*, 4 June: 16.

Baum, T. (1995) 'Ireland – the peace dividend', *Insights*, July: 9–14.

Bauman, J. (1995) 'Designer heritage: Israeli national parks and the politics of historical representation', *Middle East Report*, 25(5): 20–3.

Bazin, C.M. (1995) 'Industrial heritage in the tourism process in France', in M.F. Lanfant, J.B. Allcock and E.M. Bruner (eds), *International Tourism: Identity and change*, Sage, London, 113–26.

Beck, L. and Cable, T. (1998) *Interpretation for the 21st Century: Fifteen guiding principles for interpreting nature and culture*, Sagamore, Champaign, Ill.

Beckett, J.C. (1988) *Belfast: The making of the city*, Appletree, Belfast.

Belk, R.W. (1990) 'The role of possessions in constructing and maintaining a sense of past', in M.E. Goldberg, G. Gorn and R.W. Pollay (eds), *Advances in Consumer Research*, vol. 17, Association for Consumer Research, Provo, Utah, 669–76.

Bender, B. and Edmonds, M. (1992) 'Stonehenge: Whose past? What past?', *Tourism Management*, **13**: 355–7.

Bennett, M.M. (1997) 'Heritage marketing: the role of information technology', *Journal of Vacation Marketing*, **3**(3): 272–80.

Bennett, T. (1988) 'Museums and "the people"', in R. Lumley (ed.), *The Museum Time Machine*, Routledge, London, 63–85.

Bennett, T. (1995) *The Birth of the Museum: History, theory, politics*, Routledge, London.

Berger, D.J. (1996) 'The challenge of integrating Maasai tradition with tourism', in M.F. Price (ed.), *People and Tourism in Fragile Environments*, Wiley, Chichester, 175–97.

Berry, S. and Shephard, G. (2001) 'Cultural heritage sites and their visitors: too many for too few?', in G. Richards (ed.), *Cultural Attractions and European Tourism*, CAB International, Wallingford, 159–71.

Bessière, J. (1998) 'Local development and heritage: traditional food and cuisine as tourist attractions in rural areas', *Sociologia Ruralis*, **38**(1): 21–34.

Blancke, S. and Slow Turtle, C.J.P. (1990) 'The teaching of the past of the Native peoples of North America in US schools', in P. Stone and R. MacKenzie (eds), *The Excluded Past: Archaeology in education*, Unwin Hyman, London, 109–33.

Boasberg, T. (1992) 'A new paradigm for preservation', in A.J. Lee (ed.), *Past Meets Future: Saving America's historic environments*, Preservation Press, Washington, DC, 145–51.

Boissevain, J. (1996) 'Ritual, tourism and cultural commoditization in Malta: culture by the pound?', in T. Selwyn (ed.), *The Tourist Image: Myths and myth making in tourism*, Wiley, Chichester, 105–20.

Bold, J. (1994) 'Defining and recording the resource: the built environment', in R. Harrison (ed.), *Manual of Heritage Management*, Butterworth Heinemann, Oxford, 79–84.

Boniface, P. (1995) *Managing Quality Cultural Tourism*, Routledge, London.

Boniface, P. (2001) 'Touring world heritage in AD 2000', *Tourism Recreation Research*, **26**(1): 73–9.

Boniface, P. and Fowler, P.J. (1993) *Heritage and Tourism in 'The Global Village'*, Routledge, London.

Boon, J.A. (1982) *Other Tribes, Other Scribes: Symbolic anthropology in the comparative study of cultures, histories, religions and texts*, Cambridge University Press, Cambridge.

Boorstin, D. (1964) *The Image: A guide to pseudo events in American society*, Harper, New York.

Booth, E.A. (1993) 'Enhancement in conservation areas', *The Planner*, **79**: 22–3.

Booth, K.L. and Simmons, D.G. (2000) 'Tourism and the establishment of national parks in New Zealand', in R.W. Butler and S.W. Boyd (eds), *Tourism and National Parks: Issues and implications*, Wiley, Chichester, 39–49.

Borley, L. (1996) 'Heritage and environment management: the international perspective', in W. Nuryanti (ed.), *Tourism and Culture: Global civilization in change*, Gadjah Mada University Press, Yogyakarta, 180–8.

Bowes, R.G. (1989) 'Tourism and heritage: a new approach to the product', *Recreation Research Review*, 14(4): 35–40.

Boyd, S.W. (1995) 'Sustainability and Canada's National Parks: suitability for policy, planning and management', unpublished Ph.D. thesis, Department of Geography, University of Western Ontario, Canada.

Boyd, S.W. (1999) 'North–south divide: the role of the border in tourism to Northern Ireland', *Visions in Leisure and Business*, 17(4): 50–71.

Boyd, S.W. (2000a) 'Heritage tourism in the old town, Mombasa', paper presented at the Atlas Africa conference, Mombasa, 14–16.

Boyd, S.W. (2000b) 'Heritage tourism in Northern Ireland: opportunities under peace', *Current Issues in Tourism*, 3(2): 153–74.

Boyd, S.W. (2000c) 'Tourism, national parks and sustainability', in R.W. Butler and S.W. Boyd (eds), *Tourism and National Parks: Issues and Implications*, Wiley, Chichester, 161–86.

Boyd, S.W. (2002a) 'Cultural and heritage tourism in Canada: opportunities, principles and challenges', *International Journal of Tourism and Hospitality Research*, 3(3): 211–33.

Boyd, S.W. (2002b) 'Partnership in the mountains: heritage tourism in Banff National Park', paper presented at the Royal Geographical Society/Institute of British Geographers Annual Conference, Belfast, 2–6 January.

Boyd, S.W. (in press) 'Marketing challenges and opportunities for heritage tourism', in A. Fyall, A. Leask and B. Garrod (eds), *Managing Visitor Attractions: New directions*, Butterworth Heinemann, Oxford.

Boyd, S.W. and Butler, R.W. (1996) 'Managing ecotourism: an opportunity spectrum approach', *Tourism Management*, 17: 557–66.

Boyd, S.W. and Butler, R.W. (2000) 'Tourism and national parks: the origin of the concept', in R.W. Butler and S.W. Boyd (eds), *Tourism and National Parks: Issues and implications*, Wiley, Chichester, 13–27.

Boyd, S.W. and Spawforth, H. (2001) 'Rural community involvement through tourism partnership: case study of the LUMO Community wildlife sanctuary, Kenya', in *Proceedings of the International Conference on New Directions in Managing Rural Tourism and Leisure: Local impacts, global trends*. Scottish Agricultural College, Ayr.

Boyd, S.W. and Timothy, D.J. (1999) 'Heritage trails: opportunities and implications for management', paper presented at the Sustaining Rural Environments: Issues in Globalization, Migration and Tourism International Conference, Flagstaff, Ariz., 20–23 October.

Boyd, S.W. and Timothy, D.J. (2001) 'Developing partnerships: tools for interpretation and management of World Heritage Sites', *Tourism Recreation Research*, 26(1): 47–53.

Boyd, W.E. and Ward, G.K. (1993) 'Aboriginal heritage and visitor management', in C.M. Hall and S. McArthur (eds), *Heritage Management in New Zealand and*

Australia: Visitor management, interpretation and marketing, Oxford University Press, Auckland, 103–18.

Bradley, G.A. (1982) 'The interpretive plan', in G.W. Sharpe (ed.), *Interpreting the Environment*, Wiley, New York, 74–99.

Bramwell, B. and Lane, B. (1993) 'Interpretation and sustainable tourism: the potential and the pitfalls', *Journal of Sustainable Tourism*, 1(2): 71–80.

Bramwell, B. and Lane, B. (1999) 'Collaboration and partnerships for sustainable tourism', *Journal of Sustainable Tourism*, 7(3/4): 179–81.

Bramwell, B. and Lane, B. (eds) (2000) *Tourism Collaboration and Partnerships: Politics, practice and sustainability*, Channel View Publications, Clevedon.

Bramwell, B. and Rawding, L. (1996) 'Tourism marketing images of industrial cities', *Annals of Tourism Research*, 23: 201–21.

Bredemeier, J. (1999) 'Jordan to open historic baptism park', *Leisure Travel News*, 20 December: 6.

Brett, D. (1996) *The Construction of Heritage*, Cork University Press, Cork, Ireland.

Britton, S. (1982) 'The political economy of tourism in the Third World', *Annals of Tourism Research*, 9: 331–58.

Broadhurst, R. (1989) 'The search for new funds', in D.L. Uzzell (ed.), *Heritage Interpretation*, vol. 2: *The visitor experience*, Belhaven, London, 29–43.

Brown, D. (1996) 'Genuine fakes', in T. Selwyn (ed.), *The Tourist Image: Myths and myth making in tourism*, Wiley, Chichester, 33–48.

Brown, I.J. (1989) 'Mining and tourism in Southern Australia', *Industrial Archaeology Review*, 12(1): 55–66.

Browne, L. (1994) 'Tourism in Northern Ireland: a sustainable approach', paper presented at the International Institute for Peace Through Tourism, Second Global Conference, Montreal.

Browne, S. and Stevens, T. (1996) 'The role of heritage attractions in sustainable tourism strategies: the experience in Ireland', *Visions in Leisure and Business*, 15(1): 43–64.

Brownill, S. (1994) 'Selling the inner city: regeneration and place marketing in London's Docklands', in J.R. Gold and S.V. Ward (eds), *Place Promotion: The use of publicity and marketing to sell towns and regions*, Wiley, Chichester, 133–52.

Brubacher, M., Kelley, E. and Strickert, F. (2000) 'Holy land pilgrimage reports', *Washington Report on Middle East Affairs*, 19(4): 14.

Bruner, E.M. (1994) 'Abraham Lincoln as authentic reproduction: a critique of post-modernism', *American Anthropologist*, 96(2): 397–415.

Bruner, E.M. (1996) 'Tourism in Ghana: the representation of slavery and the return of the Black Diaspora', *American Anthropologist*, 98(2): 290–304.

Bruno, S. (1998) Interview with the Product Manager for the Conservation Land of Ontario, Grand River Conservation Authority, Cambridge, Ontario, 22 June.

Buchholtz, D. (1998) 'The Battle of the Little Bighorn: history, identity, and tourism in the 1990s', in A.A. Lew and G.A. Van Otten (eds), *Tourism and Gaming on American Indian Lands*, Cognizant, New York, 113–27.

Buck, R.C. (1978) 'Boundary maintenance revised: tourist experience in an Old Order Amish Community', *Rural Sociology*, 43: 221–34.

Buckley, P.J. and Klemm, M. (1993) 'The decline of tourism in Northern Ireland', *Tourism Management*, 14: 184–94.

Budowski, G. (1976) 'Tourism and environmental conservation: conflict, coexistence, or symbiosis?', *Environmental Conservation*, 3: 27–31.

Bumbaru, D. (1992) 'Dubrovnik: heritage and culture as targets', *Impact*, **4**(5): 1–2.

Burnett, K.A. (2001) 'Heritage, authenticity and history', in S. Drummond and I. Yeoman (eds), *Quality Issues in Heritage Visitor Attractions*, Butterworth Heinemann, Oxford, 39–53.

Burton, S. (1993) 'History with a bottom line', *Time*, 12 July: 36–7.

Butcher-Younghans, S. (1993) *Historic House Museums: A practical handbook for their care, preservation, and management*, Oxford University Press, New York.

Butler, R.W. (1980) 'The concept of a tourist area cycle of evolution and implications for management of resources', *Canadian Geographer*, **24**(1): 5–12.

Butler, R.W. (1991) 'Tourism, environment, and sustainable development', *Environmental Conservation*, **18**(1): 201–9.

Butler, R.W. (1996) 'The role of tourism in cultural transformation in developing countries', in W. Nuryanti (ed.), *Tourism and Culture: Global civilization in change*, Gadjah Mada University Press, Yogyakarta, 91–101.

Butler, R.W. (1997) 'The destination life cycle: implications for heritage site management and attractivity', in W. Nuryanti (ed.), *Tourism and Heritage Management*, Gadjah Mada University Press, Yogyakarta, 44–53.

Butler, R.W. (1999) 'Sustainable tourism: a state-of-the-art review', *Tourism Geographies*, **1**(1): 7–25.

Butler, R.W. and Boyd, S.W. (2000) 'Tourism and parks – a long but uneasy relationship', in R.W. Butler and S.W. Boyd (eds), *Tourism and National Parks: Issues and implications*, Wiley, Chichester, 4–11.

Butler, R.W. and Hinch, T. (eds) (1996) *Tourism and Indigenous Peoples*, International Thomson Business Press, London.

Butler, R.W. and Pearce, D. (eds) (1995) *Change in Tourism: People, places, processes*, Routledge, London.

Butler, R.W. and Smale, B.J.A. (1991) 'Geographic perspectives on festivals in Ontario', *Journal of Applied Recreation Research*, **16**(1): 3–23.

Butler, R.W. and Waldbrooke, L.A. (1991) 'A new planning tool: the tourism opportunity spectrum', *Journal of Tourism Studies*, **2**(1): 1–14.

Butts, D.J. (1993) 'Institutional arrangements for cultural heritage management in New Zealand: legislation, management, and protection', in C.M. Hall and S. McArthur (eds), *Heritage Management in New Zealand and Australia: Visitor management, interpretation and marketing*, Oxford University Press, Auckland, 169–87.

Caffyn, A. (1998) 'Rural regeneration through tourism: evidence from the single regeneration budget', in D. Hall and R. O'Hanlon (eds), *Proceedings of the Rural Tourism Management: Sustainable Options Conference*, Scottish Agricultural College, Ayr, 109–28.

Caffyn, A. and Lutz, J. (1999) 'Developing the heritage tourism product in multi-ethnic cities', *Tourism Management*, **20**: 213–21.

Cameron, C.M. (1989) 'Cultural tourism and urban revitalization', *Tourism Recreation Research*, **14**(1): 23–32.

Cameron, D.F. (1995) 'The pilgrim and the shrine: the icon and the oracle. A perspective on museology for tomorrow', *Museum Management and Curatorship*, **14**(1): 47–55.

Canadian Tourism Commission (1998) *Product Development Clubs*, CTC, Ottawa.

Carter, B. and Grimwade, G. (1997) 'Balancing use and preservation in cultural heritage management', *International Journal of Heritage Studies*, **3**(1): 45–53.

Carter, F.W. (1982) 'Historic cities in Eastern Europe: problems of industrialization, pollution and conservation', *Mazingira*, 6(3): 62–76.

Carter, G. (1994) 'Heritage interpretation and environmental education', in R. Harrison (ed.), *Manual of Heritage Management*, Butterworth Heinemann, Oxford, 359–64.

Cartier, C. (1996) 'Conserving the built environment and generating heritage tourism in peninsular Malaysia', *Tourism Recreation Research*, 21(1): 45–53.

Cassia, P.S. (1999) 'Tradition, tourism and memory in Malta', *Journal of the Royal Anthropological Institute*, 5(2): 247–63.

Chance, S. (1994) 'The politics of restoration', *The Architectural Review*, 196(10): 80–3.

Chang, T.C. (1999) 'Local uniqueness in the global village: heritage tourism in Singapore', *Professional Geographer*, 51(1): 91–103.

Chang, T.C. and Huang, S. (in press) ' "New Asia – Singapore": a seductive concoction of tourism, place and image', in C. Cartier and A.A. Lew (eds), *The Seduction of Place*, Routledge, London.

Chang, T.C., Milne, S., Fallon, D. and Pohlmann, C. (1996) 'Urban heritage tourism: the global–local nexus', *Annals of Tourism Research*, 23: 284–305.

Chang, T.C. and Yeoh, B.S.A. (1999) ' "New Asia – Singapore": communicating local cultures through global tourism', *Geoforum*, 30(2): 101–15.

Charlesworth, A. (1994) 'Contesting places of memory: the case of Auschwitz', *Environment and Planning D: Society and Space*, 12: 579–93.

Chen, J.S. (1998) 'Travel motivation of heritage tourists', *Tourism Analysis*, 2(3/4): 213–15.

Cheung, S.C.H. (1999) 'The meanings of a heritage trail in Hong Kong', *Annals of Tourism Research*, 26: 570–88.

Clair, L. (1997) 'The role of technology in heritage site interpretation', in W. Nuryanti (ed.), *Tourism and Heritage Management*, Gadjah Mada University Press, Yogyakarta, 105–13.

Clark, R.N. and Stankey, G.H. (1979) *The Recreation Opportunity Spectrum: A framework for planning, management, and research*, USDA, Washington, DC.

Cloher, D.U. and Johnston, C. (1999) 'Maori sustainability concepts applied to tourism: a North Hokianga study', *New Zealand Geographer*, 55(1): 46–52.

Clout, H.D. (1998) 'The European countryside: contested space', in B. Graham (ed.), *Modern Europe: Place, culture and identity*, Arnold, London, 287–309.

Cohen, E. (1978) 'The impact of tourism on the physical environment', *Annals of Tourism Research*, 5: 215–37.

Cohen, E. (1979) 'Rethinking the sociology of tourism', *Annals of Tourism Research*, 6: 18–35.

Cohen, E. (1988) 'Authenticity and commoditization in tourism', *Annals of Tourism Research*, 15: 371–86.

Cohen, E. (1992) 'Pilgrimage centers: concentric and excentric', *Annals of Tourism Research*, 19: 33–50.

Cole, A. (1994) 'The development of Hadrian's Wall National Trail', in R. Harrison (ed.), *Manual of Heritage Management*, Butterworth Heinemann, Oxford, 70–1.

Confer, J.C. and Kerstetter, D.L. (2000) 'Past perfect: explorations of heritage tourism', *Parks and Recreation*, 35(2): 28–38.

Cossons, N. (1989a) 'Heritage tourism: trends and tribulations', *Tourism Management*, 10: 192–4.

Cossons, N. (1989b) 'Plural funding and the heritage', in D.L. Uzzell (ed.), *Heritage Interpretation*, vol. 2: *The visitor experience*, Belhaven, London, 16–22.

Cox, J. (1994) 'Interpretation for persons with a disability', in R. Harrison (ed.), *manual of heritage management*, Butterworth Heinemann, Oxford, 353–5.

Craig, B. (1989) 'Interpreting the historic scene: the power of imagination in creating a sense of historic place', in D.L. Uzzell (ed.), *Heritage Interpretation*, vol. 1: *The natural and built environment*, Belhaven, London, 107–12.

Craig-Smith, S.J. (1995) 'The role of tourism in inner-harbor redevelopment', in S.J. Craig-Smith and M. Fagence (eds), *Recreation and Tourism as a Catalyst for Urban Waterfront Redevelopment: An international survey*, Praeger, Westport, Conn., 15–35.

Craik, J. (1995) 'Are there cultural limits to tourism?', *Journal of Sustainable Tourism*, 3(2): 87–98.

Crain, M.M. (1996) 'Contested territories: the politics of touristic development at the Shrine of El Rocío in southwestern Andalusia', in J. Boissevain (ed.), *Coping with Tourists: European reactions to mass tourism*, Berghahn Books, Providence, 1–26.

Crawford, D.W. and Godbey, G. (1987) 'Reconceptualizing barriers to family leisure', *Leisure Sciences*, 9: 119–27.

Creighton, M. (1997) 'Consuming rural Japan: the marketing of tradition and nostalgia in the Japanese travel industry', *Ethnology*, 36(3): 239–54.

Crookston, M. (1998) 'Conservation and regeneration: two case studies in the Arab world', in E. Laws, B. Faulkner and G. Moscardo (eds), *Embracing and Managing Change in Tourism: International case studies*, Routledge, London, 264–78.

Crouch, D. and Colin, A. (1992) 'Rocks, rights and rituals', *Geographical Magazine*, 64(6): 14–19.

Culture Plus (1992) 'Cultural tourism', *Culture Plus*, 9: 16.

Dann, G.M.S. (1998) ' "There's no business like old business": tourism, the nostalgia industry of the future', in W.F. Theobald (ed.), *Global Tourism*, 2nd edn, Butterworth Heinemann, Oxford, 29–43.

Dauge, V. (1997) 'Post-war recovery in Cambodia', *Museum Management and Curatorship*, 16(2): 164–72.

Davies, S. (1993) 'Planning in a crisis', *Museums Journal*, 93(7): 31–3.

Davies, A. and Prentice, R. (1995) 'Conceptualizing the latent visitor to heritage attractions', *Tourism Management*, 16: 491–500.

Davis, F. (1979) *Yearning for Yesterday: A sociology of nostalgia*, The Free Press, New York.

Dawson, D. (1991) 'Panem et circenses? A critical analysis of ethnic and multicultural festivals', *Journal of Applied Recreation Research*, 16(1): 35–52.

de Oliver, M. (1996) 'Historical preservation and identity: the Alamo and the production of a consumer landscape', *Antipode*, 28(1): 1–23.

Dearden, P. and Rollins, R. (eds) *Parks and Protected Areas in Canada: Planning and management*, Oxford University Press, Oxford.

Delafons, J. (1997) 'Conservation of the historic heritage', *Town & Country Planning*, 66(5): 136–7.

DeLyser, D. (1999) 'Authenticity on the ground: engaging the past in a California ghost town', *Annals of the Association of American Geographers*, 89: 602–32.

Desmond, J.C. (1999) *Staging Tourism: Bodies on display from Waikiki to Sea World*, University of Chicago Press, Chicago.

Dewar, K. (1989) 'Interpretation as attraction', *Recreation Research Review*, **14**(4): 45–9.

Din, K. (1993) 'Dialogue with the hosts: an educational strategy towards sustainable tourism', in M. Hitchcock, V.T. King and M.J.G. Parnwell (eds), *Tourism in South-East Asia*, Routledge, London, 327–36.

Douglas, N. and Douglas, N. (1991) 'Where the tiki are wired for sound and poi glow in the dark: a day at the Polynesian Cultural Center', *Islands Business Pacific*, **17**(12): 60–4.

Dove, J. (1993) 'Human impact on Egypt's past', *Geography Review*, **7**(1): 25–8.

Dowling, R.K. (1993) 'An environmentally-based planning model for regional tourism development', *Journal of Sustainable Tourism*, **1**(1): 17–37.

Dowling, R.K. and Getz, D. (2000) 'Wine tourism futures', in B. Faulkner, G. Moscardo and E. Laws (eds), *Tourism in the Twenty-First Century: Reflections on experience*, Continuum, London, 49–66.

Drohan, M. (1995) 'Bloody tourists: invasion of the foreign hordes', *The Globe and Mail* (Toronto), 7 October: 2.

Drost, A. (1996) 'Developing sustainable tourism for World Heritage Sites', *Annals of Tourism Research*, **23**: 479–84.

Duerksen, C.J. (1992) 'Managing growth with preservation', in A.J. Lee (ed.), *Past Meets Future: Saving America's historic environments*, Preservation Press, Washington, DC, 109–13.

Duff-Brown, B. (2001) 'Taj Mahal tickets costly: foreign tourists refusing to pay, hurting business', *The Arizona Republic*, 3 September: A27.

Eagle, D. and Carnell, H. (1977) *The Oxford Literary Guide to the British Isles*, Clarendon Press, Oxford.

Eastaugh, A. and Weiss, N. (1989) 'Broadening the market', in D.L. Uzzell (ed.), *Heritage Interpretation*, vol. 2: *The visitor experience*, Belhaven, London, 58–67.

Ebony (1990) 'Georgia's black history trail', *Ebony*, **45**(4): 167–72.

Eckstein, J. (1993) 'Heritage under threat', *Leisure Management*, **13**(5): 30–2.

Edginton, C.R., Hudson, S.D. and Lankford, S.V. (2001) *Managing Recreation, Parks, and Leisure Services: An introduction*, Sagamore, Champaign, Ill.

Edwards, J.A. (1989) 'Historic sites and their local environments', in D.T. Herbert, R.C. Prentice and C.J. Thomas (eds), *Heritage Sites: Strategies for marketing and development*, Avebury, Aldershot, 272–93.

Edwards, J.A. and Llurdés, J.C. (1996) 'Mines and quarries: industrial heritage tourism', *Annals of Tourism Research*, **23**: 341–63.

English Heritage (1996) *Hadrian's Wall World Heritage Site Management Plan*, English Heritage, London.

English Heritage (2002 – copyright) 'Visit English Heritage Properties and Sites' <www.english-heritage.org.uk>

English Tourist Board (1979) *English Cathedrals and Tourism*, English Tourist Board, London.

Errington, F. and Gwertz, D. (1989) 'Tourism and anthropology in a post-modern world', *Oceania*, **60**: 37–54.

Evans, G. (2001) 'World heritage and the World Bank: culture and sustainable development?', *Tourism Recreation Research*, **26**(1): 81–4.

Evans, K. (1998) 'Competition for heritage space: Cairo's resident/tourist conflict', in D. Tyler, Y. Guerrier and M. Robertson (eds), *Managing Tourism in Cities: Policy, process and practice*, Wiley, Chichester, 179–92.

Fagence, M. (in press) 'Interactions in socio-cultural space', in S. Singh, D.J. Timothy and R.K. Dowling (eds), *Tourism in Destination Communities*, CAB International, Wallingford.

Fahy, A. (1995) 'New technologies for museum communication', in E. Hooper-Greenhill (ed.), *Museum, Media, Message*, Routledge, London, 82–96.

Falk, J.H. and Dierking, L.D. (1992) *The Museum Experience*, Whalesback Books, Washington, DC.

Fawcett, C. and Cormack, P. (2001) 'Guarding authenticity at literary tourism sites', *Annals of Tourism Research*, **28**: 686–704.

Fees, C. (1996) 'Tourism and the politics of authenticity in a North Cotswold town', in T. Selwyn (ed.), *The Tourist Image: Myths and myth making in tourism*, Wiley, Chichester, 121–46.

Fennell, D.A. (1999) *Ecotourism: An introduction*, Routledge, London.

Field, D.R. and Wagar, J.A. (1982) 'People and interpretation', in G.W. Sharpe (ed.), *Interpreting the Environment*, Wiley, New York, 52–73.

Fitton, M. (1996) 'Does our community want tourism? Examples from south Wales', in M.F. Price (ed.), *People and Tourism in Fragile Environments*, Wiley, Chichester, 159–74.

Fladmark, J.M. (ed.) (1998) *In Search of Heritage: As pilgrim or tourist?*, Donhead Publishing, Shaftesbury, UK.

Fletcher, J. (1997) 'Heritage tourism: enhancing the net benefits of tourism', in W. Nuryanti (ed.), *Tourism and Heritage Management*, Gadjah Mada University Press, Yogyakarta, 134–46.

Florin, L. (1993) *Ghost Towns of the West*, Promontory Press, New York.

Foley, M. and Lennon, J.J. (1996) 'JFK and dark tourism: a fascination with assassination', *International Journal of Heritage Studies*, **2**: 198–212.

Fowler, P. (1989) 'Heritage: a post-modernist perspective', in D.L. Uzzell (ed.), *Heritage Interpretation*, vol. 1: *The natural and built environment*, Belhaven, London, 57–63.

Fowler, P. (1992) *The Past in Contemporary Society: Then, now*, Routledge, London.

Frenkel, S. (1997) 'Alluring landscapes: the symbolic economy of "Bavarian" Leavenworth', paper presented at the Association of American Geographers annual conference, Fort Worth, Texas, April.

Fyall, A. and Garrod, B. (1998) 'Heritage tourism: at what price?', *Managing Leisure*, **3**: 213–28.

Fyson, N. (1991) 'Shoring up the past', *Geographical Magazine*, **63**(9): 18–21.

Gable, E. and Handler, R. (1993) 'Deep dirt: messing up the past at colonial Williamsburg', *Social Analysis*, **34**(3): 3–16.

Gable, E. and Handler, R. (1996) 'After authenticity at an American heritage site', *American Anthropologist*, **98**(3): 568–78.

Ganguly, M. (2001) 'At the Taj Mahal, grime amid grandeur', *Time*, 10 September: 6.

Garrison, L. (1990) 'The Black historical past in British education', in P. Stone and R. MacKenzie (eds), *The Excluded Past: Archaeology in education*, Unwin Hyman, London, 231–44.

Garrod, B. and Fyall, A. (2000) 'Managing heritage tourism', *Annals of Tourism Research*, **27**: 682–708.

Garrod, B. and Fyall, A. (2001) 'Heritage tourism: a question of definition', *Annals of Tourism Research*, **28**: 1049–52.

Gauch, S. (1991) 'Slum spreads at feet of sphinx', *Christian Science Monitor*, 14 January: 12–13.

Gawe, S. and Meli, F. (1990) 'The missing past in South African history', in P. Stone and R. MacKenzie (eds), *The Excluded Past: Archaeology in education*, Unwin Hyman, London, 98–108.

George, W.E. (1976) 'Historic buildings: procedures for restoration', in S. Timmons (ed.), *Preservation and Conservation: Principles and practices*, National Trust for Historic Preservation, Washington, DC, 397–402.

Getz, D. (1991) *Festivals, Special Events and Tourism*, Van Nostrand Reinhold, New York.

Getz, D. (1993) 'Tourist shopping villages: development and planning strategies', *Tourism Management*, 14: 15–26.

Getz, D. and Frisby, W. (1988) 'Evaluating management effectiveness in community-run festivals', *Journal of Travel Research*, 27(1): 22–7.

Gilbert, D. and Clark, M. (1997) 'An exploratory examination of urban tourism impact, with reference to residents' attitudes in the cities of Canterbury and Guildford', *Cities*, 14(6): 343–52.

Gill, A.M. (1996) 'Rooms with a view: informal settings for public dialogue', *Society and Natural Resources* 9, 633–43.

Glasson, J., Godfrey, K. and Goodey, B. (1995) *Towards Visitor Impact Management: Visitor impacts, carrying capacity and management responses in Europe's historic towns and cities*, Avebury, Aldershot.

Globe and Mail (2000) 'Birchtown, Nova Scotia', *Globe and Mail*, 7 February: A6.

Goodey, B. (1979) 'The interpretation boom', *Area*, 11: 285–8.

Goodey, B. (1994) 'Interpretive planning', in R. Harrison (ed.), *Manual of Heritage Management*, Butterworth Heinemann, Oxford, 303–11.

Goodwin, H. (2000) 'Tourism, national parks and partnerships', in R.W. Butler and S.W. Boyd (eds), *Tourism and National Parks: Issues and implications*, Wiley, Chichester, 245–62.

Goudie, S.C., Khan, F. and Kilian, D. (1996) 'Tourism beyond apartheid: black empowerment and identity in the "New" South Africa', in P.A. Wells (ed.), *Keys to the Marketplace: Problems and issues in cultural and heritage tourism*, Hisarlik Press, Enfield Lock, UK, 65–86.

Goudie, S.C., Khan, F. and Kilian, D. (1999) 'Transforming tourism: black empowerment, heritage and identity beyond apartheid', *South African Geographical Journal*, 81(1): 22–31.

Graefe, A.R. (1990) 'Visitor impact management', in R. Graham and R. Lawrence (eds), *Towards Serving Our Visitors and Managing Our Resources*, Tourism Research and Education Centre, University of Waterloo, Waterloo, Ontario.

Graham, B. (1994a) 'Heritage conservation and revisionist nationalism in Ireland', in G.J. Ashworth and P.J. Larkham (eds), *Building a New Heritage: Tourism, culture and identity in the new Europe*, Routledge, London, 135–58.

Graham, B. (1994b) 'No place of the mind: contested Protestant representations of Ulster', *Ecumene*, 1: 257–81.

Graham, B. (1996) 'The contested interpretation of heritage landscapes in Northern Ireland', *International Journal of Heritage Studies*, 2(1/2): 10–22.

Graham, B. (1998a) 'Contested images of place among Protestants in Northern Ireland', *Political Geography*, 17(2): 129–44.

Graham, B. (1998b) 'The past in Europe's present: diversity, identity and the construction of place', in B. Graham (ed.), *Modern Europe: Place, culture and identity*, Arnold, London, 19–49.

Graham, B. (2000) 'The past in place: historical geographies of identity', in B. Graham and C. Nash (eds), *Modern Historical Geographies*, Pearson, Harlow, 70–99.

Graham, B., Ashworth, G.J. and Tunbridge, J.E. (2000) *A Geography of Heritage: Power, culture and economy*, Arnold, London.

Graham, B. and Murray, M. (1997) 'The spiritual and the profane: the pilgrimage to Santiago de Compostela', *Ecumene*, 4: 389–409.

Graham, R., Nilsen, P. and Payne, R.J. (1988) 'Visitor management in Canadian national parks', *Tourism Management*, 9: 44–62.

Greenwood, D.J. (1989) 'Culture by the pound: an anthropological perspective on tourism as cultural commoditization', in V.L. Smith (ed.), *Hosts and Guests: The anthropology of tourism*, 2nd edn, University of Pennsylvania Press, Philadelphia, 171–85.

Grekin, J. and Milne, S. (1996) 'Toward sustainable tourism development: the case of Pond Inlet, NWT', in R.W. Butler and T. Hinch (eds), *Tourism and Indigenous Peoples*, International Thomson Business Press, 76–106.

Grenville, J. (ed.) (1999) *Managing the Historic Rural Landscape*, Routledge, London.

Griffin, J. and Giles, H. (1994) 'Bringing history alive: special events at English Heritage', in R. Harrison (ed.), *Manual of Heritage Management*, Butterworth Heinemann, Oxford, 331–2.

Gruffudd, P. (1995) 'Heritage as national identity: histories and prospects of the national pasts', in D.T. Herbert (ed.), *Heritage, Tourism and Society*, Mansell, London, 49–67.

Gunn, C. (1994) *Tourism Planning: Basics, concepts, cases*, 3rd edn, Taylor and Francis, Washington, DC.

Gupta, V. (1999) 'Sustainable tourism: learning from Indian religious traditions', *International Journal of Contemporary Hospitality Management*, 11(2/3): 91–5.

Hadrian's Wall Tourism Partnership (1999 – copyright) 'Hadrian's Wall World Heritage Sites, Tourism Facts & Figures', <http://www.hadrians-wall.org/tourstats.htm>

Hall, C.M. (1994) *Tourism and Politics: Policy, power and place*, Wiley, Chichester.

Hall, C.M. (1996) 'Tourism and the Maori of Aotearoa, New Zealand', in R. Butler and T. Hinch (eds), *Tourism and Indigenous Peoples*, International Thomson Business Press, London, 155–75.

Hall, C.M. (1997) 'The politics of heritage tourism: place, power and the representation of values in the urban context', in P.E. Murphy (ed.), *Quality Management in Urban Tourism*, Wiley, Chichester, 91–101.

Hall, C.M. (2000a) 'Tourism and the establishment of national parks in Australia', in R.W. Butler and S.W. Boyd (eds), *Tourism and National Parks: Issues and implications*, Wiley, Chichester, 29–38.

Hall, C.M. (2000b) *Tourism Planning: Policies, processes and relationships*, Prentice Hall, Harlow.

Hall, C.M. (in press) 'Politics and place: an analysis of power in tourism communities', in S. Singh, D.J. Timothy and R.K. Dowling (eds), *Tourism in Destination Communities*, CAB International, Wallingford.

Hall, C.M. and Lew, A.A. (eds) (1998) *Sustainable Tourism: A geographical perspective*, Longman, Harlow.

Hall, C.M. and McArthur, S. (1993a) 'Heritage management: an introductory framework', in C.M. Hall and S. McArthur (eds), *Heritage Management in New Zealand and Australia: Visitor management, interpretation, and marketing*, Oxford University Press, Auckland, 1–17.

Hall, C.M. and McArthur, S. (1993b) 'The marketing of heritage', in C.M. Hall and S. McArthur (eds), *Heritage Management in New Zealand and Australia: Visitor management, interpretation, and marketing*, Oxford University Press, Auckland, 40–7.

Hall, C.M. and McArthur, S. (1993c) 'Towards sustainable heritage management?', in C.M. Hall and S. McArthur (eds), *Heritage Management in New Zealand and Australia: Visitor management, interpretation, and marketing*, Oxford University Press, Auckland, 274–8.

Hall, C.M. and McArthur, S. (eds) (1996) *Heritage Management in New Zealand and Australia: The human dimension*, Oxford University Press, Melbourne.

Hall, C.M. and McArthur, S. (1998) *Integrated Heritage Management: Principles and practice*, The Stationery Office, London.

Hall, C.M. and Macionis, N. (1998) 'Wine tourism in Australia and New Zealand', in R.W. Butler, C.M. Hall and J. Jenkins (eds), *Tourism and Recreation in Rural Areas*, Wiley, Chichester, 197–224.

Hall, C.M., Mitchell, I. and Keelan, N. (1992) 'Maori culture and heritage tourism in New Zealand', *Journal of Cultural Geography*, **12**(2): 115–28.

Hall, C.M. and Piggin, R. (2001) 'Tourism and world heritage in OECD countries', *Tourism Recreation Research*, **26**(1): 103–5.

Hall, C.M. and Zeppel, H. (1990a) 'Cultural and heritage tourism: the new grand tour?', *Historic Environment*, 7(3/4): 86–98.

Hall, C.M. and Zeppel, H. (1990b) 'History, architecture, environment: cultural heritage and tourism', *Journal of Travel Research*, **29**(2): 54–5.

Hall, D.R. (1991) 'Contemporary challenges', in D.R. Hall (ed.), *Tourism and Economic Development in Eastern Europe and the Soviet Union*, Belhaven, London, 282–9.

Hall, D.R. (1998) 'Central and Eastern Europe: tourism, development and transformation', in A.M. Williams and G. Shaw (eds), *Tourism and Economic Development: European experiences*, 3rd edn, Wiley, Chichester, 345–73.

Ham, S.H. (1992) *Environmental Interpretation: A practical guide for people with big ideas and small budgets*, North American Press, Golden, Colo.

Hammitt, W.E. (1984) 'A theoretical foundation for Tilden's interpretive principles', *Journal of Environmental Education*, **12**: 13–16.

Hanna, M. (1993) 'Monitoring heritage', *Leisure Management*, **13**(10): 20–2.

Hardy, D. (1988) 'Historical geography and heritage studies', *Area*, **20**: 333–8.

Harris, F. (1989) 'From the industrial revolution to the heritage industry', *Geographical Magazine*, **61**(5): 38–42.

Harrison, R. (1994) 'London's Tower Bridge', in R. Harrison (ed.), *Manual of Heritage Management*, Butterworth Heinemann, Oxford, 315–19.

Hartley, E. (1995) 'Disabled people and museums: the case for partnership and collaboration', in E. Hooper-Greenhill (ed.), *Museum, Media, Message*, Routledge, London, 151–5.

Hatton, M.J. (1999) *Community-Based Tourism in the Asia-Pacific*, Canadian International Development Agency, Ottawa.

Hayes, B.J. (1997) 'Claiming our heritage is a booming industry', *American Visions*, **12**(5): 43–8.

Haywood, K.M. (1988) 'Responsible and responsive tourism planning in the community', *Tourism Management*, **9**: 105–18.

Heath, E. and Wall, G. (1992) *Marketing Tourism Destinations: A strategic planning approach*, Wiley, Chichester.

Henderson, J.C. (1997) 'Singapore's wartime heritage attractions', *Journal of Tourism Studies*, 8(2): 39–49.

Henderson, K.A. and Bialeschki, M.D. (1995) *Evaluating Leisure Services: Making enlightened decisions*, Venture, State College, Pa.

Henson, F.G. (1989) 'Historical development and attendant problems of cultural resource management in the Philippines', in H. Cleere (ed.), *Archaeological Heritage Management in the Modern World*, Unwin Hyman, London, 109–17.

Herbert, D.T. (1989a) 'Does interpretation help?', in D.T. Herbert, R.C. Prentice and C.J. Thomas (eds), *Heritage Sites: Strategies for marketing and development*, Avebury, Aldershot, 191–230.

Herbert, D.T. (1989b) 'Leisure trends and the heritage market', in D.T. Herbert, R.C. Prentice and C.J. Thomas (eds), *Heritage Sites: Strategies for marketing and development*, Avebury, Aldershot, 1–14.

Herbert, D.T. (1995a) 'Heritage as literary place', in D.T. Herbert (ed.), *Heritage, Tourism and Society*, Mansell, London, 32–48.

Herbert, D.T. (ed.) (1995b) *Heritage, Tourism and Society*, Mansell, London.

Herbert, D.T. (2001) 'Literary places, tourism and the heritage experience', *Annals of Tourism Research*, **28**: 312–33.

Hewison, R. (1987) *The Heritage Industry: Britain in a climate of decline*, Methuen, London.

Hewison, R. (1991) 'The heritage industry revisited', *Museums Journal*, **91**: 23–6.

Hills, A. (1997) 'Two-way tourism in Eastern Europe', *History Today*, 47(3): 29–30.

Hinz, M.O. (1990) 'The right to a past: Namibian history and the struggle for national liberation', in P. Stone and R. MacKenzie (eds), *The Excluded Past: Archaeology in education*, Unwin Hyman, London, 61–7.

Hitchcock, M. and Nuryanti, W. (eds) (2000) *Building on Batik: The globalization of a craft community*, Ashgate, Aldershot.

Hobsbawm, E. and Ranger, T. (eds) (1983) *The Invention of Tradition*, Cambridge University Press, Cambridge.

Holcomb, B. (1994) 'City make-overs: marketing the post-industrial city', in J.R. Gold and S.V. Ward (eds), *Place Promotion: The use of publicity and marketing to sell towns and regions*, Wiley, Chichester, 115–32.

Holdsworth, D. (1985) *Reviving Main Street*, University of Toronto Press, Toronto.

Holland, L. (1990) 'Whispers from the forest: the excluded past of the Aché Indians of Paraguay', in P. Stone and R. MacKenzie (eds), *The Excluded Past: Archaeology in education*, Unwin Hyman, London, 134–51.

Hollinshead, K. (1992) ' "White" gaze, "red" people – shadow visions: the disidentification of "Indians" in cultural tourism', *Leisure Studies*, **11**: 43–64.

Hood, M.G. (1983) 'Staying away: why people choose not to visit museums', *Museum News*, **61**: 50–7.

Hooper-Greenhill, E. (1988) 'Counting visitors or visitors who count?', in R. Lumley (ed.), *The Museum Time-Machine: Putting cultures on display*, Routledge, London, 213–32.

Hooper-Greenhill, E. (1992) *Museums and the Shaping of Knowledge*, Routledge, London.

Horne, D. (1984) *The Great Museum: The re-presentation of history*, Pluto Press, London.

Hornik, R. (1992) 'The battle for Angkor', *Time*, 6 April: 54–6.

Hovinen, G.R. (1995) 'Heritage issues in urban tourism: an assessment of new trends in Lancaster County', *Tourism Management*, **16**: 381–8.

Hovinen, G.R. (1997) 'Lancaster County, Pennsylvania's heritage tourism initiative: a preliminary assessment', *Small Town*, 27(6): 4–11.

Howell, B.J. (1994) 'Weighing the risks and rewards of involvement in cultural conservation and heritage tourism', *Human Organization*, 53(2): 150–9.

Hubbard, P. and Lilley, K. (2000) 'Selling the past: heritage-tourism and place identity in Stratford-upon-Avon', *Geography*, 85(3): 221–32.

Hudman, L.E. and Jackson, R.H. (1992) 'Mormon pilgrimage and tourism', *Annals of Tourism Research*, 19: 107–21.

Hughes-Freeland, F. (1993) 'Packaging dreams: Javanese perceptions of tourism and performance', in M. Hitchcock, V.T. King and M.J.G. Parnwell (eds), *Tourism in Southeast Asia*, Routledge, London, 138–54.

Huxtable, A.L. (1992) 'Inventing American reality', *New York Review of Books*, 39(20): 24–9.

Ioannides, D. and Ioannides, M.C. (2002) 'Pilgrimages of nostalgia: patterns of Jewish travel in the United States', *Tourism Recreation Research*, 27(2): 17–25.

Isar, Y.R. (1986) 'Collision course: heritage preservation versus the demands of modernization', in Y.R. Isar (ed.), *The Challenge to Our Cultural Heritage: Why preserve the past?*, Smithsonian Institute, Washington, DC, 21–30.

Jackowski, A. and Smith, V.L. (1992) 'Polish pilgrim-tourists', *Annals of Tourism Research*, 19: 92–106.

Jackson, E.L. and Scott, D. (1999) 'Constraints to leisure', in E.L. Jackson and T.L. Burton (eds), *Leisure Studies: Prospects for the twenty-first century*, Venture, State College, Pa, 299–320.

Jago, L.K. and Deery, M.A. (2001) 'Managing volunteers', in S. Drummond and I. Yeoman (eds), *Quality Issues in Heritage Visitor Attractions*, Butterworth Heinemann, Oxford, 194–216.

James, S.E. (1995) 'The future of Asia's past', *Silver Kris*, 22(6): 54–8.

Janiskee, R.L. (1996) 'Historic houses and special events', *Annals of Tourism Research*, 23: 398–414.

Jansen-Verbeke, M. (1999) 'Industrial heritage: a nexus for sustainable tourism development', *Tourism Geographies*, 1(1): 70–85.

Jansen-Verbeke, M. and Lievois, E. (1999) 'Analysing heritage resources for urban tourism in European cities', in D.G. Pearce and R.W. Butler (eds), *Contemporary Issues in Tourism Development*, Routledge, London, 81–107.

Jansen-Verbeke, M. and van Rekom, J. (1996) 'Scanning museum visitors: urban tourism marketing', *Annals of Tourism Research*, 23: 364–75.

Johnson, D.G. and Sullivan, J. (1993) 'Economic impacts of Civil War battlefield preservation: an ex-ante evaluation', *Journal of Travel Research*, 32(1): 21–9.

Johnson, N. and Sharpe, A. (1994) 'The assessment of Cornish mine engine houses', in R. Harrison (ed.), *Manual of Heritage Management*, Butterworth Heinemann, Oxford, 88–92.

Johnson, N.C. (1999) 'Framing the past: time, space and the politics of heritage tourism in Ireland', *Political Geography*, 18: 187–207.

Johnson, P. and Thomas, B. (1995) 'Heritage as business', in D.T. Herbert (ed.), *Heritage, Tourism and Society*, Mansell, London, 170–90.

Jones, G.A. and Bromley, R.D.F. (1996) 'The relationship between urban conservation programmes and property renovation: evidence from Quito, Ecuador', *Cities*, 13(6): 373–5.

Jones, R. (1997) 'Sacred sites or profane buildings? Reflections on the Old Swan Brewery conflict in Perth, Western Australia', in B.J. Shaw and R. Jones (eds), *Contested Urban Heritage: Voices from the periphery*, Ashgate, Aldershot, 132–55.

Jutla, R.S. (2002) 'Understanding Sikh pilgrimage', *Tourism Recreation Research*, 27(2): 65–72.

Kavanagh, G. (1983) 'History and the museum: the nostalgia business?', *Museums Journal*, 83: 139–41.

Keelan, N. (1993) 'Māori heritage: visitor management and interpretation', in C.M. Hall and S. McArthur (eds), *Heritage Management in New Zealand and Australia: Visitor management, interpretation and marketing*, Oxford University Press, Auckland, 95–102.

Keesing, R.M. (1989) 'Creating the past: custom and identity in the contemporary Pacific', *The Contemporary Pacific*, 1(1/2): 19–42.

Kehoe, A.B. (1990) ' "In fourteen hundred and ninety-two, Columbus sailed . . .": the primacy of the national myth in US schools', in P. Stone and R. MacKenzie (eds), *The Excluded Past: Archaeology in education*, Unwin Hyman, London, 201–16.

Kerstetter, D., Confer, J. and Bricker, K. (1998) 'Industrial heritage attractions: types and tourists', *Journal of Travel and Tourism Marketing*, 7(2): 91–104.

Kia, B. and Williams, V. (1989) 'Saving Sana'a', *Geographical Magazine*, 61(5): 32–6.

Kieron, S. (ed.) (1992) *Regeneration: Toronto's waterfront and the sustainable city*, Royal Commission on the Future of the Toronto Waterfront, Toronto.

Kirk, W. (1963) 'Problems of geography', *Geography*, 48: 357–71.

Kirshenblatt-Gimblett, B. (1998) *Destination Culture: Tourism, museums, and heritage*, University of California Press, Berkeley.

Knudson, D.M., Cable, T.T. and Beck, L. (1995) *Interpretation of Cultural and Natural Resources*, Venture, State College, Pa.

Konrad, V.A. (1982) 'Historical artifacts as recreational resources', in G. Wall and J.S. Marsh (eds), *Recreational Land Use: Perspectives on its evolution in Canada*, Carleton University Press, Ottawa, 393–417.

Koščak, M. (1999) 'Heritage trails through Dolenjska and Bela Krajina in southeast Slovenia – bordering region between Slovenia and Croatia', *Zemědělská Ekonomika*, 45(2): 71–7.

Kostyal, K.M. (1996) 'Coal diggers' ways', *National Geographic Traveler*, 13(5): 116.

Krakover, S. and Cohen, R. (2001) 'Visitors and non-visitors to archaeological heritage attractions: the cases of Massada and Avedat, Israel', *Tourism Recreation Research*, 26(1): 27–33.

Laenen, M. (1989) 'Looking for the future through the past', in D.L. Uzzell (ed.), *Heritage Interpretation*, vol. 1: *The natural and built environment*, Belhaven, London, 88–95.

Laganside Corporation (1999) *Cathedral Quarter*, Laganside Corporation, Belfast.

Landy, W. (1999) 'The importance of being Ernest: Key West celebrates 100 years of Hemingway', *Air Currents*, Summer: 27–33.

Langer, E. (1989) *Mindfulness*, Addison Wesley, Reading, Mass.

Larkham, P.J. (1992) 'Conservation and the changing urban landscape', *Progress in Planning*, 37: 83–181.

Larkham, P.J. (1995) 'Heritage as planned and conserved', in D.T. Herbert (ed.), *Heritage, Tourism and Society*, Mansell, London, 85–116.

Lassen, T. (1999) 'Back to the future', *World Traveler*, 31(7): 42–8.

Law, C.M. (1993) *Urban Tourism: Attracting visitors to large cities*, Mansell, London.

Leask, A. and Fyall, A. (2001) 'World heritage site designation: future implications from a UK perspective', *Tourism Recreation Research*, 26(1): 55–63.

Lennon, J.J. and Foley, M. (1999) 'Interpretation of the unimaginable: the U.S. Holocaust Memorial Museum, Washington, D.C., and "dark tourism"', *Journal of Travel Research*, 38(1): 46–50.

Lennon, J.J. and Foley, M. (2000) *Dark Tourism: In the footsteps of death and disaster*, Cassell, London.

Leong, W.T. (1989) 'Culture and the state: manufacturing traditions for tourism', *Critical Studies in Mass Communication*, 6(4): 355–75.

Leslie, D. (1999) 'Terrorism and tourism: the Northern Ireland situation – a look behind the veil of certainty', *Journal of Travel Research*, 38(1): 37–40.

Leung, Y.F. (2001) 'Environmental impacts of tourism at China's world heritage sites: Huangshan and Chengde', *Tourism Recreation Research*, 26(1): 117–22.

Lew, A.A. and Van Otten, G.A. (1998) 'Prospects for Native American reservation tourism in the 21st century', in A.A. Lew and G.A. Van Otten (eds), *Tourism and Gaming on American Indian Lands*, Cognizant, New York, 215–25.

Lewis, W.J. (1989) 'Training interpreters', in D.L. Uzzell (ed.), *Heritage Interpretation*, vol. 1: *The natural and built environment*, Belhaven, London, 209–13.

Light, D. (1991) 'The development of heritage interpretation in Britain', *Swansea Geographer*, 28: 1–13.

Light, D. (1992) 'Bilingual heritage interpretation in Wales', *Scottish Geographical Magazine*, 108(3): 179–83.

Light, D. (1995a) 'Heritage as informal education', in D.T. Herbert (ed.), *Heritage, Tourism and Society*, Mansell, London, 117–45.

Light, D. (1995b) 'Visitors' use of interpretive media at heritage sites', *Leisure Studies*, 14: 133–49.

Light, D. (1996) 'Characteristics of the audience for "events" at a heritage site', *Tourism Management*, 17: 183–90.

Light, D. (2000a) 'An unwanted past: contemporary tourism and the heritage of communism in Romania', *International Journal of Heritage Studies*, 6(2): 145–60.

Light, D. (2000b) 'Gazing on communism: heritage tourism and post-communist identities in Germany, Hungary and Romania', *Tourism Geographies*, 2(2): 157–76.

Light, D. and Prentice, R.C. (1994a) 'Market-based product development in heritage tourism', *Tourism Management*, 15: 27–36.

Light, D. and Prentice, R.C. (1994b) 'Who consumes the heritage product? Implications for European heritage tourism', in G.J. Ashworth and P. Larkham (eds), *Building and New Heritage: Tourism, culture and identity in the new Europe*, Routledge, London, 90–116.

Lilieholm, R.J. and Romney, L.R. (2000) 'Tourism, national parks and wildlife', in R.W. Butler and S.W. Boyd (eds), *Tourism and National Parks: Issues and implications*, Wiley, Chichester, 137–51.

Lindberg, K., McCool, S. and Stankey, G. (1997) 'Rethinking carrying capacity', *Annals of Tourism Research*, 24: 461–5.

Lloyd, D.W. (1998) *Battlefield Tourism: Pilgrimage and the commemoration of the Great War in Britain, Australia and Canada, 1919–1939*, Berg, Oxford.

Llurdés, J.C. (2001) 'Heritage tourism and textile "model villages": the case of River Park, Barcelona, Spain', *Tourism Recreation Research*, 26(1): 65–71.

Longstreth, R. (1992) 'When the present becomes the past', in A.J. Lee (ed.), *Past Meets Future: Saving America's historic environments*, Preservation Press, Washington, DC, 213–25.

Louder, D.R. (1989) 'Le Québec et la Franco-Américanie: a mother country in the making', in S. Hornsby, V. Konrad and J. Herlan (eds), *Four Hundred Years of Borderland Interaction in the Northeast*, Acadiensis Press, Fredericton, 126–39.

Lowenthal, D. (1975) 'Past time, present place: landscape and memory', *Geographical Review*, 65(1): 1–36.

Lowenthal, D. (1977) 'The bicentennial landscape: a mirror held up to the past', *Geographical Review*, 67(3): 253–67.

Lowenthal, D. (1979a) 'Age and artifact: dilemmas of appreciation', in D.W. Meinig (ed.), *The Interpretation of Ordinary Landscapes: Geographical essays*, Oxford University Press, New York, 103–28.

Lowenthal, D. (1979b) 'Environmental perception: preserving the past', *Progress in Human Geography*, 3(4): 549–59.

Lowenthal, D. (1985) *The Past is a Foreign Country*, Cambridge University Press, Cambridge.

Lowenthal, D. (1992) 'A global perspective on American heritage', in A.J. Lee (ed.), *Past Meets Future: Saving America's historic environments*, Preservation Press, Washington, DC, 157–63.

Lowenthal, D. (1996) *Possessed by the Past: The heritage crusade and the spoils of history*, The Free Press, New York.

Lujan, C.C. (1998) 'A sociological view of tourism in an American Indian community: maintaining cultural integrity at Taos Pueblo', in A.A. Lew and G.A. Van Otten (eds), *Tourism and Gaming on American Indian Lands*, Cognizant, New York, 145–62.

Luthy, D. (1994) 'The origin and growth of Amish tourism', in D. Kraybill and M. Olshan (eds), *The Amish Struggle with Modernity*, University Press of New England, Hanover, 113–29.

Lynch, K. (1972) *What Time is This Place?*, MIT Press, Cambridge, Mass.

Lynn, W. (1992) 'Tourism in the people's interest', *Community Development Journal*, 27(4): 371–7.

McAndrew, T.M. (1995) 'Making history: when historic site interpreters try to entertain visitors, do they make history come alive or do they reshape the past?', *Illinois Issues*, 21(7): 18–20.

McArthur, S. and Hall, C.M. (1993a) 'Evaluation of visitor management services', in C.M. Hall and S. McArthur (eds), *Heritage Management in New Zealand and Australia: Visitor management, interpretation and marketing*, Oxford University Press, Auckland, 251–73.

McArthur, S. and Hall, C.M. (1993b) 'Strategic planning for visitor heritage management: integrating people and places through participation', in C.M. Hall and S. McArthur (eds), *Heritage Management in New Zealand and Australia: Visitor management, interpretation and marketing*, Oxford University Press, Auckland, 241–50.

McArthur, S. and Hall, C.M. (1993c) 'Visitor management and interpretation at heritage sites', in C.M. Hall and S. McArthur (eds), *Heritage Management in New Zealand and Australia: Visitor management, interpretation and marketing*, Oxford University Press, Auckland, 18–39.

McBoyle, G. (1996) 'Green tourism and Scottish distilleries', *Tourism Management*, 17: 255–63.

McBryde, I. (1995) 'Dream the impossible dream? Shared heritage, shared values, or shared understanding of disparate values?', *Historic Environment*, **11**(2/3): 8–14.

MacCannell, D. (1973) 'Staged authenticity: arrangements of social space in tourist settings', *American Journal of Sociology*, **79**(3): 589–603.

MacCannell, D. (1976) *The Tourist*, Schocken Books, New York.

McCaskey, T.G. (1975) 'Conservation of historic areas: management techniques for tourism in the USA', in A.J. Burkart and S. Medlik (eds), *The Management of Tourism*, Heinemann, London, 151–9.

McCrone, D., Morris, A. and Kiely, R. (1995) *Scotland – the Brand: The making of Scottish heritage*, Edinburgh University Press, Edinburgh.

McCroskery, S. (1997) Interview with manager of Old Bushmills Distillery, August.

McGreevy, P. (1991) *The Wall of Mirrors: Nationalism and perceptions of the border at Niagara Falls*, University of Maine, Orono.

Machlis, G.E. and Field, D.R. (eds) (1984) *On Interpretation: Sociology for interpreters of natural and cultural history*, Oregon State University Press, Corvallis.

McIntosh, A.J. (1999) 'Into the tourist's mind: understanding the value of the heritage experience', *Journal of Travel and Tourism Marketing*, **8**(1): 41–64.

McIntosh, A.J. and Prentice, R.C. (1999) 'Affirming authenticity: consuming cultural heritage', *Annals of Tourism Research*, **26**: 589–612.

McIntyre, G. (1993) *Sustainable Tourism Development: Guide for local planners*, World Tourism Organization, Madrid.

MacKenzie, R. and Stone, P. (1990) 'Introduction: the concept of the excluded past', in P. Stone and R. MacKenzie (eds), *The Excluded Past: Archaeology in education*, Unwin Hyman, London, 1–14.

McKercher, B. (1993) 'The unrecognized threat to tourism: can tourism survive sustainability?', *Tourism Management*, **14**: 131–6.

McLean, F. (1998) 'Museums and the construction of national identity: a review', *International Journal of Heritage Studies*, **3**(4): 244–52.

Mahony, C. (1999) 'Heritage tourism: strategies for implementation and the model of "the Civil War Discovery Trail"', *History News*, **54**(1): 21–4.

Makens, J.C. (1987) 'The importance of U.S. historic sites as visitor attractions', *Journal of Travel Research*, **25**(3): 8–12.

Mallam, M. (1989) 'Can heritage charities be profitable?', in D.L. Uzzell (ed.), *Heritage Interpretation*, vol. 2: *The visitor experience*, Belhaven, London, 44–50.

Mansfeld, Y. (1992) '"Industrial landscapes" as positive settings for tourism development in declining industrial cities: the case of Haifa, Israel', *GeoJournal*, **28**(4): 457–63.

Marks, R. (1996) 'Conservation and community: the contradictions and ambiguities of tourism in the stone town of Zanzibar', *Habitat International*, **20**(2): 265–78.

Marris, T. (1985) 'The importance of our architectural heritage for England's tourism', *The Tourist Review*, **40**(1): 23–6.

Marsh, J. (1989) 'Recreation and tourism at historic sites', *Recreation Research Review*, **14**(4): 7–9.

Marsh, R. (1991) 'Selling heritage', *Leisure Management*, **11**(10): 38–40.

Masberg, B.A. and Silverman, L.H. (1996) 'Visitor experiences at heritage sites: a phenomenological approach', *Journal of Travel Research*, **34**(4): 20–5.

Mathieson, A. and Wall, G. (1982) *Tourism: Economic, physical and social impacts*, Longman, London.

Mercer, D. (1994) 'Native peoples and tourism: conflict and compromise', in W.F. Theobold (ed.), *Global Tourism: The next decade*, Butterworth Heinemann, Oxford, 124–45.

Merriman, N. (1989) 'The social basis of museum and heritage visiting', in S.M. Pearce (ed.), *Museum Studies in Material Culture*, Leicester University Press, Leicester, 153–71.

Merriman, N. (1991) *Beyond the Glass Case: The past, the heritage and the public in Britain*, Leicester University Press, Leicester.

Middleton, V.T.C. (1994) *Marketing in Travel and Tourism*, Butterworth Heinemann, Oxford.

Middleton, V.T.C. (1997) 'Marketing issues in heritage tourism: an international perspective', in W. Nuryanti (ed.), *Tourism and Heritage Management*, Gadjah Mada University Press, Yogyakarta, 213–19.

Miles, R.S. (1986) 'Museum audiences', *International Journal of Museum Management and Curatorship*, 3: 73–80.

Millar, S. (1989) 'Heritage management for heritage tourism', *Tourism Management*, 10: 9–14.

Min, Z. (1989) 'The administration of China's archaeological heritage', in H. Cleere (ed.), *Archaeological Heritage Management in the Modern World*, Unwin Hyman, London, 102–8.

Mohit, R.S. and Kammeier, H.D. (1996) 'The fort: opportunities for an effective urban conservation strategy in Bombay', *Cities*, 13(6): 387–98.

Molloy, L. (1993) 'The interpretation of New Zealand's natural heritage', in C.M. Hall and S. McArthur (eds), *Heritage Management in New Zealand and Australia: Visitor management, interpretation and marketing*, Oxford University Press, Auckland, 59–69.

Morgan, N.J. and Pritchard, A. (1998) *Tourism Promotion and Power: Creating images, creating identities*, Wiley, Chichester.

Morinis, A. (1992) 'Introduction: the territory of the anthropology of pilgrimage', in A. Morinis (ed.), *Sacred Journeys: The anthropology of pilgrimage*, Greenwood Press, Westport, Conn., 1–30.

Morton, W.B. (1986) 'Saving Indonesia's Borobudur: a high-tech triumph in international cooperation', in Y.R. Isar (ed.), *The Challenge of our Cultural Heritage: Why preserve the past?*, Smithsonian Institution Press, Washington, DC, 113–22.

Moscardo, G. (1996) 'Mindful visitors: heritage and tourism', *Annals of Tourism Research*, 23: 376–97.

Moscardo, G. (1999) *Making Visitors Mindful*, Sagamore, Champaign, Ill.

Moscardo, G. (2000) 'Cultural and heritage tourism: the great debates', in B. Faulkner, G. Moscardo and E. Laws (eds), *Tourism in the 21st Century: Lessons from experience*, Continuum, London, 3–17.

Moscardo, G. and Pearce, P.L. (1986) 'Historic theme parks: an Australian experience in authenticity', *Annals of Tourism Research*, 13: 467–79.

Moscardo, G. and Woods, B. (1998) 'Managing tourism in the Wet Tropics World Heritage area: interpretation and the experience of visitors on Skyrail', in E. Laws, B. Faulkner and G. Moscardo (eds), *Embracing and Managing Change in Tourism: International case studies*, Routledge, London, 307–23.

Moulin, C.M. (1991) 'Cultural heritage and tourism development in Canada', *Tourism Recreation Research*, 16(1): 50–5.

Mowforth, M. and Munt, I. (1998) *Tourism and Sustainability: New tourism in the Third World*, Routledge, London.

Muinzer, L. (1993) 'Norway's heritage trail', *Scandinavian Review*, **81**(1): 90–4.

Murphy, P.E. (1985) *Tourism: A community approach*, Methuen, New York.

Murphy, P.E. (1988) 'Community driven tourism planning', *Tourism Management*, **9**: 96–104.

Murray, M. and Graham, B. (1997) 'Exploring the dialectics of route-based tourism: the Camino de Santiago', *Tourism Management*, **18**: 513–24.

Myles, K. (1989) 'Cultural resource management in sub-Saharan Africa: Nigeria, Togo and Ghana', in H. Cleere (ed.), *Archaeological Heritage Management in the Modern World*, Unwin Hyman, London, 118–27.

Nelson, J.G., Butler, R.W. and Wall, G. (eds) (1993) *Tourism and Sustainable Development: Monitoring, planning, managing*, University of Waterloo, Department of Geography, Waterloo, Ontario.

Newcomb, R.M. (1979) *Planning the Past: Historical landscape resources and recreation*, Dawson, Folkestone.

Newman, D.R. and Hodgetts, R.M. (1998) *Human Resource Management: A customer-oriented approach*, Prentice Hall, Upper Saddle River, NJ.

Newsome, D., Moore, S.A. and Dowling, R.K. (2001) *Natural Area Tourism: Ecology, impacts and management*, Channel View Publications, Clevedon.

New York Times (2001) 'Trees enshrine Angkor temples: roots threaten ancient structures', *New York Times*, 19 August: A22.

Norkunas, M.K. (1993) *The Politics of Public Memory: Tourism, history, and ethnicity in Monterey, California*, State University of New York Press, Albany.

Northern Ireland Tourist Board (1993) *Tourism in Northern Ireland: A sustainable approach*, NITB, Belfast.

Northern Ireland Tourist Board (1999a) *Report of the Industrial Heritage Product Working Group: New directions for industrial heritage tourism in Northern Ireland*, NITB, Belfast.

Northern Ireland Tourist Board (1999b) *Tourism Facts, 1998*, NITB, Belfast.

Northern Ireland Tourist Board (2000) *Building the Proposition: Foundations of future tourism in Northern Ireland*, NITB, Belfast.

Northern Ireland Tourist Board (2001a) *Tourism Facts, 2000*, NITB, Belfast.

Northern Ireland Tourist Board (2001b) *Visitor Attractions Survey 2000: Annual report*, NITB, Belfast.

Norton, P. (1989) 'Archaeological rescue and conservation in the North Andean area', in H. Cleere (ed.), *Archaeological Heritage Management in the Modern World*, Unwin Hyman, London, 142–5.

Nuryanti, W. (1996) 'Heritage and postmodern tourism', *Annals of Tourism Research*, **23**: 249–60.

Nuryanti, W. (1997) 'Interpreting heritage for tourism: complexities and contradictions', in W. Nuryanti (ed.), *Tourism and Heritage Management*, Gadjah Mada University Press, Yogyakarta, 114–22.

Olinda, P. (1991) 'The old man of nature tourism: Kenya', in T. Whelan (ed.), *Nature Tourism: Managing for the environment*, Island Press, Washington, DC, 23–38.

Olsen, D.H. (2000) 'Contested heritage, religion and tourism', unpublished master's thesis, Bowling Green State University, Bowling Green, Ohio.

Olsen, D.H. and Timothy, D.J. (1999) 'Tourism 2000: selling the millennium', *Tourism Management*, **20**: 389–92.

Olsen, D.H. and Timothy, D.J. (2002) 'Contested religious heritage: differing views of Mormon heritage', *Tourism Recreation Research*, **27**(2): 7–15.

O'Meara, K. (2000) 'Adventure tourism's future: keeping it real', *Travel Weekly*, 59(77): 44.

Orbaşli, A. (2000) *Tourists in Historic Towns: Urban conservation and heritage management*, E & FN Spon, London.

O'Toole, F. (1992) 'The emperor's map makes us tourists in our own land', *Interpretation Journal*, 51: 13–14.

Page, S.J. (1992) 'Managing tourism in a small historic city', *Town & Country Planning*, 61(7/8): 208–11.

Page, S.J. (1993) 'Perspectives on urban heritage tourism in New Zealand: Wellington in the 1990s', in C.M. Hall and S. McArthur (eds), *Heritage Management in New Zealand and Australia: Visitor management, interpretation and marketing*, Oxford University Press, Auckland, 218–30.

Page, S.J. (1995a) *Urban Tourism*, Routledge, London.

Page, S.J. (1995b) 'Waterfront revitalization in London: market-led planning and tourism in London Docklands', in S.J. Craig-Smith and M. Fagence (eds), *Recreation and Tourism as a Catalyst for Urban Waterfront Redevelopment*, Praeger, Westport, Conn., 53–70.

Page, S.J. and Dowling, R.K. (2001) *Ecotourism*, Prentice Hall, Harlow.

Page, S.J. and Getz, D. (1997) *The Business of Rural Tourism: International perspectives*, International Thomson Business Press, London.

Panic-Kombol, T. (1996) 'The cultural heritage of Croatian cities as a tourism potential', *World Leisure and Recreation*, 38(1): 21–5.

Parkin, I., Middleton, P. and Beswick, V. (1989) 'Managing the town and city for visitors and local people', in D.L. Uzzell (ed.), *Heritage Interpretation*, vol. 2: *The visitor experience*, Belhaven, London, 108–14.

Patullo, P. (1997) 'Reclaiming the heritage trail: culture and identity', in L. France (ed.), *The Earthscan Reader in Sustainable Tourism*, Earthscan Publications, London, 135–48.

Payne, R.J. and Graham, R. (1993) 'Visitor planning and management in parks and protected areas', in P. Dearden and R. Rollins (eds), *Parks and Protected Areas in Canada: Planning and management*, Oxford University Press, Oxford, 185–210.

Pearce, D.G. (1987) 'Motel location and choice in Christchurch', *New Zealand Geographer*, 43: 10–17.

Pearce, D.G. (1997) 'The roles of the public sector in conservation and tourism planning', in W. Nuryanti (ed.), *Tourism and Heritage Management*, Gadjah Mada University Press, Yogyakarta, 88–100.

Pearce, D.G. (1998) 'Tourist districts in Paris: structure and functions', *Tourism Management*, 19: 49–65.

Pearce, J. (1993) *Volunteers: The organizational behaviour of unpaid workers*. Routledge, London.

Pearce, P.L. and Moscardo, G.M. (1986) 'The concept of authenticity in tourist experiences', *Australian and New Zealand Journal of Sociology*, 22(1): 121–32.

Pearce, P.L., Moscardo, G.M. and Ross, G. (1996) *Tourism Community Relationships*, Pergamon, Oxford.

Pearson, M. and Sullivan, S. (1995) *Looking after Heritage Places: The basics of heritage planning for managers, landowners and administrators*, Melbourne University Press, Carlton.

Peleggi, M. (1996) 'National heritage and global tourism in Thailand', *Annals of Tourism Research*, 23: 432–48.

Picard, M. (1990) ' "Cultural tourism" in Bali: cultural performances as tourist attraction', *Indonesia*, 49: 37–74.

Picard, M. (1995) 'Cultural heritage and tourist capital: cultural tourism in Bali', in M.F. Lanfant, J.B. Allcock and E.M. Bruner (eds), *International Tourism: Identity and change*, Sage, London, 44–66.

Picard, M. (1997) 'Cultural tourism in Bali: the construction of a cultural heritage', in W. Nuryanti (ed.), *Tourism and Heritage Management*, Gadjah Mada University Press, Yogyakarta, 147–64.

Pigram, J.J. and Wahab, S. (1998) 'Sustainable tourism in a changing world', in J.J. Pigram and S. Wahab (eds), *Tourism, Development and Growth: The challenge of sustainability*, Routledge, London, 17–31.

Pizam, A. and Mansfeld, Y. (eds) (1996) *Tourism, Crime and International Security Issues*, Wiley, Chichester.

Plog, S. (1973) 'Why destination areas rise and fall in popularity', *Cornell Hotel and Restaurant Administration Quarterly*, 14(3): 13–16.

Plog, S. (1991) *Leisure Travel: Making it a growth market . . . again!* Wiley, New York.

Pocock, D.C.D. (1992) 'Catherine Cookson country: tourist expectation and experience', *Geography*, 77: 236–43.

Poria, Y., Butler, R.W. and Airey, D. (2001) 'Clarifying heritage tourism', *Annals of Tourism Research*, 28: 1047–9.

Porter, J. (1997) 'Macau 1999', *Current History*, 96: 282–6.

Powe, N.A. and Willis, K.G. (1996) 'Benefits received by visitors to heritage sites: a case study of Warkworth Castle', *Leisure Studies*, 15: 259–75.

Powell, R. (1997) 'Erasing memory, inventing tradition, rewriting history: planning as a tool of ideology', in B.J. Shaw and R. Jones (eds), *Contested Urban Heritage: Voices from the periphery*, Ashgate, Aldershot, 85–100.

Prentice, M.M. and Prentice, R.C. (1989) 'The heritage market of historical sites as educational resources', in D.T. Herbert, R.C. Prentice and C.J. Thomas (eds), *Heritage Sites: Strategies for marketing and development*, Avebury, Aldershot, 143–90.

Prentice, R.C. (1989a) 'Pricing policy at heritage sites: how much should visitors pay?', in D.T. Herbert, R.C. Prentice and C.J. Thomas (eds), *Heritage Sites: Strategies for marketing and development*, Avebury, Aldershot, 231–71.

Prentice, R.C. (1989b) 'Visitors to heritage sites: a market segmentation by visitor characteristics', in D.T. Herbert, R.C. Prentice and C.J. Thomas (eds), *Heritage Sites: Strategies for marketing and development*, Avebury, Aldershot, 1–61.

Prentice, R.C. (1993) *Tourism and Heritage Attractions*, Routledge, London.

Prentice, R.C. (1994) 'Heritage: a key sector of the "new" tourism', *Progress in Tourism, Recreation and Hospitality Management*, 5: 309–24.

Prentice, R.C. (1995) 'Heritage as formal education', in D.T. Herbert (ed.), *Heritage, Tourism and Society*, Mansell, London, 146–69.

Prentice, R.C., Guerin, S. and McGugan, S. (1998) 'Visitor learning at a heritage attraction: a case study of Discovery as a media product', *Tourism Management*, 19: 5–23.

Price, T. (1996) *Miracle Town: Creating America's Bavarian village in Leavenworth, Washington*, Price and Rogers, Vancouver, Wash.

Prideaux, B. (in press) 'Creating visitor attractions in peripheral areas', in A. Fyall, A. Leask and B. Garrod (eds), *Managing Visitor Attraction: New directions*, Butterworth Heinemann, Oxford.

Prideaux, B. and Kininmont, L. (1999) 'Tourism and heritage are not strangers: a study of opportunities for rural heritage museums to maximize tourist visitation', *Journal of Travel Research*, 37(1): 299–303.

Pritchard, A. and Morgan, N.J. (2001) 'Culture, identity and tourism representation: marketing Cymru or Wales?', *Tourism Management*, 22: 167–79.

Putney, A.D. and Wagar, J.A. (1973) 'Objectives and evaluation in interpretive planning', *Journal of Environmental Education*, 5(1): 43–4.

Raivo, P.J. (2000) 'Landscaping the patriotic past: Finnish war landscapes as a national heritage', *Fennia*, 178(1): 139–50.

Ranger, R. (1989) 'Whose heritage? The case of Matobo National Park', *Journal of Southern African Studies*, 15: 217–49.

Rasamuel, D. (1989) 'Problems in the conservation and restoration of ruined buildings in Madagascar', in H. Cleere (ed.), *Archaeological Heritage Management in the Modern World*, Unwin Hyman, London, 128–41.

Reed, M.G. (1997) 'Power relations and community-based tourism planning', *Annals of Tourism Research*, 24: 566–91.

Regnier, K., Gross, M. and Zimmerman, R. (1994) *The Interpreter's Guidebook: Techniques for programs and presentations*, 3rd edn, University of Wisconsin, Stevens Point.

Reid, D.A. (1989) 'Open-air museums and historic sites', *Association for Preservation Technology Bulletin*, 21(2): 21–7.

Rennie, F. (1980) 'Interpretive evaluation: an applied methodology for self-guided trails', unpublished master's thesis, University of Guelph, Canada.

Rghei, A.S. and Nelson, J.G. (1994) 'The conservation and use of the walled city of Tripoli', *Geographical Journal*, 160: 143–58.

Richards, G. (1996) 'Production and consumption of European cultural tourism', *Annals of Tourism Research*, 23: 261–83.

Richards, G. (2001a) 'The development of cultural tourism in Europe', in G. Richards (ed.), *Cultural Attractions and European Tourism*, CAB International, Wallingford, 3–29.

Richards, G. (2001b) 'The market for cultural attractions', in G. Richards (ed.), *Cultural Attractions and European Tourism*, CAB International, Wallingford, 31–53.

Risk, P. (1994) 'People-based interpretation', in R. Harrison (ed.), *Manual of Heritage Management*, Butterworth Heinemann, Oxford, 320–30.

Robb, J.G. (1998) 'Tourism and legends: archaeology of heritage', *Annals of Tourism Research*, 25: 579–96.

Robinson, M. (1999a) 'Cultural conflicts in tourism: inevitability and inequality', in M. Robinson and P. Boniface (eds), *Tourism and Cultural Conflicts*, CAB International, Wallingford, 1–32.

Robinson, M. (1999b) 'Tourism development in deindustrializing centres of the UK: change, culture and conflict', in M. Robinson and P. Boniface (eds), *Tourism and Cultural Conflicts*, CAB International, Wallingford, 129–59.

Robinson, R., Wertheim, M. and Senior, G. (1994) 'Selling the heritage product', in R. Harrison (ed.), *Manual of Heritage Management*, Butterworth Heinemann, Oxford, 381–99.

Rodgers, W.P. (1982) 'The conservation of buildings within developing countries: the state of the art', in R. Zetter (ed.), *Conservation of Buildings in Developing Countries*, Oxford Polytechnic, Department of Town Planning, Oxford, 14–19.

Rogers, M. (1996) 'Beyond authenticity: conservation, tourism, and the politics of representation in the Ecuadorian Amazon', *Identities*, 3(1/2): 73–125.

Rossides, N. (1995) 'The conservation of the cultural heritage in Cyprus: a planner's perspective', *Regional Development Dialogue*, 16(1): 110–25.

Rudd, M.A. and Davis, J.A. (1998) 'Industrial heritage tourism at the Bingham Canyon Copper Mine', *Journal of Travel Research*, **36**(3): 85–9.

Russell, P. (1999) 'Religious travel in the new millennium', *Travel and Tourism Analyst*, **5**: 39–68.

Ryan, C. (1999) 'Some dimensions of Maori involvement in tourism', in M. Robinson and P. Boniface (eds), *Tourism and Cultural Conflicts*, CAB International, Wallingford, 229–45.

Ryan, C. and Crotts, J. (1997) 'Carving and tourism: a Maori perspective', *Annals of Tourism Research*, **24**: 898–918.

Ryan, C. and Dewar, K. (1995) 'Evaluating the communication process between interpreter and visitor', *Tourism Management*, **16**: 295–303.

Sadek, H. (1990) 'Treasures of ancient Egypt: preserving civilization's legacy in world cultural parks', *National Parks*, **64**(5): 16–17.

Sadek, H. (1994) 'A future for the past', *National Parks*, **68**(1/2): 38–42.

St John, R.B. (1994) 'Preah Vihear and the Cambodia–Thailand borderland', *Boundary and Security Bulletin*, **1**(4): 64–8.

Sakya, K. (1996) 'Nature and cultural heritage management in Nepal', in W. Nuryanti (ed.), *Tourism and Culture: Global civilization in change*, Gadjah Mada University Press, Yogyakarta, 201–11.

San Roman, L. (1992) 'Politics and the role of museums in the rescue of identity', in P.J. Boylan (ed.), *Museums 2000: Politics, people, professionals and profit*, Museums Association and Routledge, London, 25–41.

Santos, X.M. (2002) 'Pilgrimage and tourism at Santiago de Compostela', *Tourism Recreation Research*, **27**(2): 41–50.

Saugee, D.B. (1992) 'Keepers of the native treasures', in A.J. Lee (ed.), *Past Meets Future: Saving America's historic environments*, Preservation Press, Washington, DC, 189–95.

Scheyvens, R. (1999) 'Ecotourism and the empowerment of local communities', *Tourism Management*, **20**: 245–9.

Schofield, P. (1996) 'Cinematographic images of a city: alternative heritage tourism in Manchester', *Tourism Management*, **17**: 333–40.

Schouten, F.F.J. (1995a) 'Heritage as historical reality', in D.T. Herbert (ed.), *Heritage, Tourism and Society*, Mansell, London, 21–31.

Schouten, F.F.J. (1995b) 'Improving visitor care in heritage attractions', *Tourism Management*, **16**(4): 259–61.

Seale, R.G. (1989) 'National historic parks and sites, recreation, and tourism', *Recreation Research Review*, **14**(4): 15–19.

Seale, R.G. (1996) 'A perspective from Canada on heritage and tourism', *Annals of Tourism Research*, **23**: 484–8.

Seaton, A.V. (1996) 'Guided by the dark: from thanatopsis to thanatourism', *International Journal of Heritage Studies*, **2**: 232–44.

Seaton, A.V. (2000) ' "Another weekend away looking for dead bodies": Battlefield tourism on the Somme and in Flanders', *Tourism and Recreation Research*, **25**(3): 63–78.

Seaton, A.V. (2002) 'Thanatourism's final frontiers? Cemeteries, churchyards and funerary sites as sacred and secular pilgrimage', *Tourism Recreation Research*, **27**(2): 73–82.

Selwyn, T. (1996) 'Introduction', in T. Selwyn (ed.), *The Tourist Image: Myths and myth making in tourism*, Wiley, Chichester, 1–32.

Setiawan, B. and Timothy, D.J. (2000) 'Existing urban management frameworks and heritage conservation in Indonesia', *Asia Pacific Journal of Tourism Research*, **5**(2): 76–9.

Shackley, M. (1996) 'Too much room at the inn?', *Annals of Tourism Research*, **23**: 449–62.

Shackley, M. (1998a) 'Conclusions: visitor management at cultural World Heritage Sites', in M. Shackley (ed.), *Visitor Management: Case studies from World Heritage Sites*, Butterworth Heinemann, Oxford, 194–205.

Shackley, M. (1998b) 'Introduction: world heritage sites', in M. Shackley (ed.), *Visitor Management: Case studies from World Heritage Sites*, Butterworth Heinemann, Oxford, 1–9.

Shackley, M. (2001) 'Sacred world heritage sites: balancing meaning with management', *Tourism Recreation Research*, **26**(1): 5–10.

Sharpe, G.W. (1982a) 'An overview of interpretation', in G.W. Sharpe (ed.), *Interpreting the Environment*, Wiley, New York, 3–26.

Sharpe, G.W. (1982b) 'Selecting the interpretive media', in G.W. Sharpe (ed.), *Interpreting the Environment*, Wiley, New York, 100–23.

Shaw, B.J., Jones, R. and Ling, O.G. (1997) 'Urban heritage, development and tourism in Southeast Asian cities: a contestation continuum', in B.J. Shaw and R. Jones (eds), *Contested Urban Heritage: Voices from the periphery*, Ashgate, Aldershot, 169–96.

Shoji, N. (1991) 'The privatization of Borobudur', *Inside Indonesia*, **28**: 13–14.

Silberberg, T. (1995) 'Cultural tourism and business opportunities for museums and heritage sites', *Tourism Management*, **16**: 361–5.

Simmons, D.G. (1994) 'Community participation in tourism planning', *Tourism Management*, **15**: 98–108.

Simons, M.S. (2000) 'Aboriginal heritage art and moral rights', *Annals of Tourism Research*, **27**: 412–31.

Simpson, B. (1993) 'Tourism and tradition: from healing to heritage', *Annals of Tourism Research*, **20**: 164–81.

Simpson, F. (1999) 'Tourist impact in the historic centre of Prague: resident and visitor perceptions of the historic built environment', *Geographical Journal*, **165**(2): 173–83.

Singh, S. and Boyd, S.W. (in press) 'Destination communities: structure, definitions, and types', in S. Singh, D.J. Timothy and R.K. Dowling (eds), *Tourism in Destination Communities*, CAB International, Wallingford.

Singh, T.V. and Singh, S. (2001) 'The emergence of voluntary tourism in the Himalayas: a case of Kanda Community', paper presented at the IAST Conference, Macau, 10–14 July.

Sizer, S.R. (1999) 'The ethical challenges of managing pilgrimages to the Holy Land', *International Journal of Contemporary Hospitality Management*, **11**(2/3): 85–90.

Slater, T.R. (1984) 'Preservation, conservation and planning in historic towns', *The Geographical Journal*, **150**(3): 322–34.

Smith, L. (2000) 'Slave cabin opens at Virginia plantation', *Washington Post*, 8 October: 16.

Smith, S. (1989) 'Funding our heritage', in D.L. Uzzell (ed.), *Heritage Interpretation*, vol. 2: *The visitor experience*, Belhaven, London, 23–8.

Smith, S.L.J. (1985) 'Location patterns of urban restaurants', *Annals of Tourism Research*, **12**: 581–602.

Smith, S.L.J. (1988) 'Defining tourism: a supply-side view', *Annals of Tourism Research*, **18**: 312–18.

Smith, V.L. (1992) 'The quest in guest', *Annals of Tourism Research*, **19**: 1–17.

Smith, V.L. (1996) 'War and its tourist attractions', in A. Pizam and Y. Mansfeld (eds), *Tourism, Crime and International Security Issues*, Wiley, New York, 247–64.

Smith, V.L. (1998) 'Privatization in the third world: small-scale tourism enterprises', in W.F. Theobald (ed.), *Global Tourism*, 2nd edn, Butterworth Heinemann, Oxford, 205–15.

Soemarwoto, O. (1992) *Cultural Tourism Development, Central Java-Yogyakarta. Activity Report No. 8, Environmental Aspects of Tourism*, Directorate General of Tourism/UNESCO/UNDP, Yogyakarta.

Sofield, T.H.B. and Birtles, R.A. (1996) 'Indigenous peoples' cultural opportunity spectrum for tourism (IPCOST)', in R. Butler and T. Hinch (eds), *Tourism and Indigenous Peoples*, International Thomson Business Press, Boston, 396–433.

Sönmez, S. (1998) 'Tourism, terrorism, and political instability', *Annals of Tourism Research*, **25**: 416–56.

Sönmez, S. and Graefe, A.R. (1998) 'Influence of terrorism risk on foreign tourism decisions', *Annals of Tourism Research*, **25**: 112–44.

Squire, S.J. (1993) 'Valuing countryside: reflections on Beatrix Potter tourism', *Area*, **23**: 5–10.

Squire, S.J. (1994) 'The cultural values of literary tourism', *Annals of Tourism Research*, **21**: 103–20.

Stabler, M. (1998) 'The economic evaluation of the role of conservation and tourism in the regeneration of historic urban destinations', in E. Laws, B. Faulkner and G. Moscardo (eds), *Embracing and Managing Change in Tourism: International case studies*, Routledge, London, 235–63.

Stankey, G.H., Cole, D.N., Lucas, R.C., Peterson, M.E. and Frissell, S.S. (1985) *The Limits of Acceptable Change (LAC) System for Wilderness Planning*, USDA Forest Service, Odgen, Utah.

Stansfield, G. (1983) 'Heritage and interpretation', *Museums Journal*, **83**: 47–51.

Stanton, M.E. (1989) 'The Polynesian Cultural Center: a multi-ethnic model of seven Pacific cultures', in V. Smith (ed.), *Hosts and Guests: The anthropology of tourism*, 2nd edn, University of Pennsylvania Press, Philadelphia, 248–62.

Stebbins, R.A. (1996) 'Cultural tourism as serious leisure', *Annals of Tourism Research*, **23**: 948–50.

Stevens, T. (1989) 'The visitor: who cares? Interpretation and consumer relations', in D.L. Uzzell (ed.), *Heritage Interpretation*, vol. 2: *The visitor experience*, Belhaven, London, 103–7.

Stevens, T. (1995) 'Heritage as design: a practioner's perspective', in D.T. Herbert (ed.) *Heritage, Tourism & Society*, Mansell, London, 191–211.

Stewart, E.J., Hayward, B.M., Devlin, P.J. and Kirby, V.G. (1998) 'The "place" of interpretation: a new approach to the evaluation of interpretation', *Tourism Management*, **19**(3): 257–66.

Stoddard, V.G. (1999) 'The keys to Ernest Hemingway', *USA Today*, 16 July: D1–2.

Stoke-on-Trent (1997) *Visitor Survey, 1997*, Hanley, Stoke-on-Trent.

Stokes, S.N. (1992) 'America's rural heritage', in A.J. Lee (ed.), *Past Meets Future: Saving America's historic environments*, Preservation Press, Washington, DC, 197–203.

Stone, P. and Mackenzie, R. (1989) 'Is there an "excluded past" in education?', in D.L. Uzzell (ed.), *Heritage Interpretation*, vol. 1: *The natural and built environment*, Belhaven, London, 113–20.

Strang, V. (1996) 'Sustaining tourism in far north Queensland', in M.F. Price (ed.), *People and Tourism in Fragile Environments*, Wiley, Chichester, 109–22.

Strange, I. (1997) 'Planning for change, conserving the past: towards sustainable development policy in historic cities?', *Cities*, 14(4): 227–33.

Stratton, M. (1994) 'Working with other interests: the built environment and museums', in R. Harrison (ed.), *Manual of Heritage Management*, Butterworth Heinemann, Oxford, 225–32.

Surgohudujo, S. (1971) 'Borobudur temple', *Indonesian Perspectives*, July: 40–5.

Sutton, M.D. (1982) 'Interpretation around the world', in G.W. Sharpe (ed.), *Interpreting the Environment*, Wiley, New York, 644–63.

Swarbrooke, J. (1994) 'The future of the past: heritage tourism into the 21st century', in A.V. Seaton (ed.), *Tourism: The state of the art*, Wiley, Chichester, 222–9.

Swarbrooke, J. (1995) *The Development and Management of Visitor Attractions*, Butterworth Heinemann, Oxford.

Tabata, R. (1989) 'Implications of special interest tourism for interpretation and resource conservation', in D.L. Uzzell (ed.), *Heritage Interpretation*, vol. 2: *The visitor experience*, Belhaven, London, 68–77.

Tahana, N. and Oppermann, M. (1998) 'Maori cultural performances and tourism', *Tourism Recreation Research*, 23(1): 23–30.

Talley, M.K. (1995) 'The old road and the mind's internal heaven: preservation of the cultural heritage in times of armed conflict', *Museum Management and Curatorship*, 14(1): 57–64.

Telfer, D.J. (2001) 'Strategic alliances along the Niagara Wine Route', *Tourism Management*, 22: 21–30.

Teo, P. and Yeoh, B.S.A. (1997) 'Remaking local heritage for tourism', *Annals of Tourism Research*, 24: 192–213.

Thomas, C.J. (1989) 'The roles of historic sites and reasons for visiting', in D.T. Herbert, R.C. Prentice and C.J. Thomas (eds), *Heritage Sites: Strategies for marketing and development*, Avebury, Aldershot, 62–93.

Thorsell, J. and Sigaty, T. (2001) 'Human use in world heritage natural sites: a global inventory', *Tourism Recreation Research*, 26(1): 85–101.

Tiesdell, S., Oc, T. and Heath, T. (1996) *Revitalizing Historic Urban Quarters*, Architectural Press, Oxford.

Tilden, F. (1977) *Interpreting Our Heritage*, University of North Carolina Press, Chapel Hill.

Timothy, D.J. (1994) 'Environmental impacts of heritage tourism: physical and socio-cultural perspectives', *Manusia dan Lingkungan*, 2(4): 37–49.

Timothy, D.J. (1997) 'Tourism and the personal heritage experience', *Annals of Tourism Research*, 34: 751–4.

Timothy, D.J. (1999a) 'Built heritage, tourism and conservation in developing countries: challenges and opportunities', *Journal of Tourism*, 4: 5–17.

Timothy, D.J. (1999b) 'Cross-border partnership in tourism resource management: international parks along the US–Canada border', *Journal of Sustainable Tourism*, 7(3/4): 182–205.

Timothy, D.J. (1999c) 'Participatory planning: a view of tourism in Indonesia', *Annals of Tourism Research*, 26: 371–91.

Timothy, D.J. (2000) 'Building community awareness of tourism in a developing country destination', *Tourism Recreation Research*, 25(2): 111–16.

Timothy, D.J. (2001a) 'Benefits and costs of smallness and peripheral location in tourism: Saint-Pierre et Miquelon (France)', *Tourism Recreation Research*, 26(3): 61–70.

Timothy, D.J. (2001b) 'Genealogy, religion and tourism', paper presented at the Association of American Geographers Annual Conference, New York City, 1–3 March.

Timothy, D.J. (2001c) *Tourism and Political Boundaries*, Routledge, London.

Timothy, D.J. (2002a) 'Sacred journeys: religious heritage and tourism', *Tourism Recreation Research*, 27(2).

Timothy, D.J. (2002b) 'Tourism and community development issues', in R. Sharpley and D.J. Telfer (eds), *Tourism and Development: Concepts and issues*, Channel View Publications, Clevedon, UK, 149–64.

Timothy, D.J. and Tosun, C. (in press) 'Tourism planning in destination communities: participation, incremental growth, and collaboration', in S. Singh, D.J. Timothy and R.K. Dowling (eds), *Tourism in Destination Communities*, CAB International, Wallingford.

Timothy, D.J. and Wall, G. (1995) 'Tourist accommodation in an Asian historic city', *Journal of Tourism Studies*, 6(2), 63–73.

Timothy, D.J. and Wall, G. (1997) 'Turismo y patrimonio arquitectonico: temas polemicos (Tourism and built heritage: critical issues)', *Estudios y Perspectivas en Turismo*, 6(3): 193–208.

Tosun, C. (1999) 'Towards a typology of community participation in the tourism development process', *International Journal of Tourism and Hospitality*, 10(2): 113–34.

Tosun, C. and Jenkins, C.L. (1998) 'The evolution of tourism planning in third-world countries: a critique', *Progress in Tourism and Hospitality Research*, 4: 101–14.

Tosun, C. and Timothy, D.J. (2001) 'Shortcomings in planning approaches to tourism development in developing countries: the case of Turkey', *International Journal of Contemporary Hospitality Management*, 13(7): 352–9.

Towner, J. (1985) 'The grand tour: a key phase in the history of tourism', *Annals of Tourism Research*, 12: 298–333.

Towner, J. (1996) *An Historical Geography of Recreation and Tourism in the Western World: 1540–1940*, Wiley, Chichester.

Travel and Tourism Executive Report (1997) '65 million travel to historical, cultural sites and events a year', *Travel and Tourism Executive Report*, 18(5): 1–5.

Travel Industry Association (1997) *1997 Outlook for Travel and Tourism*, Travel Industry Association, Washington, DC.

Travel Weekly (1999) 'Study: "heritage tourists" account for 20% of travel spending', *Travel Weekly*, 20 September: 111.

Travel Weekly (2000a) 'Asia and the Pacific: threatened sites', *Travel Weekly*, 6 January: 13.

Travel Weekly (2000b) 'Eastern Europe: threatened sites', *Travel Weekly*, 13 January: 30.

Trotzig, G. (1989) 'The "cultural dimension of development" – an archaeological approach', in H. Cleere (ed.), *Archaeological Heritage Management in the Modern World*, Unwin Hyman, London, 59–63.

Tuan, Y.F. (1977) *Space and Place: The perspective of experience*, University of Minnesota Press, Minneapolis.

Tunbridge, J. (1981) 'Heritage Canada: the emergence of a geographic agent', *Canadian Geographer*, 25: 271–7.

Tunbridge, J. (1984) 'Whose heritage to conserve? Cross-cultural reflections upon political dominance and urban heritage conservation', *Canadian Geographer*, **28**: 171–80.

Tunbridge, J. (1994) 'Whose heritage? Global problems, European nightmare', in G.J. Ashworth and P.J. Larkham (eds), *Building a New Heritage: Tourism, culture and identity*, Routledge, London, 123–34.

Tunbridge, J. (1998a) 'The question of heritage in European cultural conflict', in B. Graham (ed.), *Modern Europe: Place, culture and identity*, Arnold, London, 236–60.

Tunbridge, J. (1998b) 'Tourism management in Ottawa, Canada: nurturing in a fragile environment', in D. Tyler, Y. Guerrier and M. Robertson (eds), *Managing Tourism in Cities: Policy, process and practice*, Wiley, Chichester, 91–108.

Tunbridge, J. and Ashworth, G.J. (1996) *Dissonant Heritage: The management of the past as a resource in conflict*, Wiley, Chichester.

Turley, S. (1998) 'Hadrian's Wall (UK): managing the visitor experience at the Roman frontier', in M. Shackley (ed.), *Visitor Management: Case studies from World Heritage Sites*, Butterworth Heinemann, Oxford, 100–20.

Turner, V. (1973) 'The center out there: pilgrim's goal', *History of Religion*, **12**(3): 191–230.

UNESCO (1999) *Operational Guidelines for the Implementation of the World Heritage Convention*, UNESCO, Paris.

UNESCO (2001 – updated) 'The World Heritage List', updated 16 December 2001. <www.unesco.org/whc/heritage.htm>

Upitis, A. (1989) 'Interpreting cross-cultural sites', in D.L. Uzzell (ed.), *Heritage Interpretation*, vol. 1: *The natural and built environment*, Belhaven, London, 153–60.

Urry, J. (1990) *The Tourist Gaze: Leisure and travel in contemporary societies*. Sage, London.

Urry, J. (1995) *Consuming Places*, Routledge, London.

U.S. Catholic (2000) 'Unsettled in the Holy Land: a travel advisory to Jubilee Year pilgrims', *U.S. Catholic*, **65**(1): 31.

US National Park Service (2001 – updated) NPS Visitation Database, <http://www2.nature.nps.gov/npstats/>

Usherwood, P. (1996) 'Romans and Barbarians: Hadrian's Wall in modern times', in M. Robinson, N. Evans and P. Callaghan (eds), *Tourism and Culture: Image, identity and marketing*, University of Northumbria, Newcastle, 279–88.

Uzzell, D.L. (1985) 'Management issues in the provision of countryside interpretation', *Leisure Studies*, **4**: 159–74.

Uzzell, D.L. (1989a) 'Introduction: the natural and built environment', in D.L. Uzzell (ed.), *Heritage Interpretation*, vol. 1: *The natural and built environment*, Belhaven, London, 1–14.

Uzzell, D.L. (1989b) 'Introduction: the visitor experience', in D.L. Uzzell (ed.), *Heritage Interpretation*, vol. 2: *The visitor experience*, Belhaven, London, 1–15.

Uzzell, D.L. (1989c) 'The hot interpretation of war and conflict', in D.L. Uzzell (ed.), *Heritage Interpretation*, vol. 1: *The natural and built environment*, Belhaven, London, 33–47.

Uzzell, D.L. (1994) 'Heritage interpretation in Britain four decades after Tilden', in R. Harrison (ed.), *Manual of Heritage Management*, Butterworth Heinemann, Oxford, 293–302.

Uzzell, D.L. (1996) 'Creating place identity through heritage interpretation', *International Journal of Heritage Studies*, **1**(4): 219–28.

Uzzell, D.L. and Ballantyne, R. (eds) (1998) *Contemporary Issues in Heritage and Environmental Interpretation*, The Stationery Office, London.

Van der Borg, J., Costa, P. and Gotti, G. (1996) 'Tourism in European heritage cities', *Annals of Tourism Research*, **23**: 306–21.

Van West, C. and Hoffschwelle, M. (1993) ' "Slumbering on its old foundations": interpretation at colonial Williamsburg', *South Atlantic Quarterly*, **83**(2): 157–75.

Vaske, J., Donnelly, M. and Whittaker, D. (2000) 'Tourism, national parks and impact management', in R.W. Butler and S.W. Boyd (eds), *Tourism and National Parks: Issues and implications*, Wiley, Chichester, 203–22.

Velarde, G. and Allen, R. (1994) 'Design-based interpretation', in R. Harrison (ed.), *Manual of Heritage Management*, Butterworth Heinemann, Oxford, 338–47.

Vukonić, B. (1992) 'Medjugorje's religion and tourism connection', *Annals of Tourism Research*, **19**: 79–91.

Vukonić, B. (1996) *Tourism and Religion*, Pergamon, Oxford.

Vukonić, B. (2002) 'Religion, tourism and economics: a convenient symbiosis', *Tourism Recreation Research*, **27**(2): 59–64.

Wager, J. (1995) 'Developing a strategy for the Angkor World Heritage Site', *Tourism Management*, **16**: 515–23.

Wahab, S. and Pigram, J.J. (eds) (1997) *Tourism, Development and Growth: The challenge of sustainability*, Routledge, London.

Wahyono, H. (1995) 'Developing an historic preservation area as a tourist attraction: the Old City of Semarang, Indonesia', unpublished master's thesis, School of Urban and Regional Planning, University of Waterloo, Ontario.

Waitt, G. and McGuirk, P.M. (1997) 'Selling waterfront heritage: a critique of Millers Point, Sydney', *Tijdschrift voor Economische en Sociale Geografie*, **88**(4): 342–52.

Walker, E.G. (1987) 'Indian involvement in heritage resource development: a Saskatchewan example', *Native Studies Review*, **3**(2): 123–37.

Wall, G. (1982) 'Cycles and capacity: incipient theory or conceptual contradiction?', *Tourism Management*, **3**: 188–92.

Wall, G. (1989) 'An international perspective on historic sites, recreation, and tourism', *Recreation Research Review*, **14**(4): 10–14.

Wall, G. (1996) 'Terrorism and tourism: an overview and an Irish example', in A. Pizam and Y. Mansfeld (eds), *Tourism, Crime and International Security Issues*, Wiley, Chichester, 143–58.

Wall, G. (1997) 'Tourism attractions: points, lines and areas', *Annals of Tourism Research*, **24**: 240–3.

Wall, G., Dudycha, D. and Hutchinson, J. (1985) 'Point pattern analyses of accommodation in Toronto', *Annals of Tourism Research*, **12**: 603–18.

Wallace, M. (1996) *Mickey Mouse History and Other Essays on American Memory*, Temple University Press, Philadelphia.

Walsh, K. (1992) *The Representation of the Past: Museums and heritage in the post modern world*, Routledge, London.

Walter, T. (1996) 'From museum to morgue? Electronic guides in Roman Bath', *Tourism Management*, **17**: 241–5.

Wang, N. (1999) 'Rethinking authenticity in tourism experience', *Annals of Tourism Research*, **26**: 349–70.

Ward, K.G. (1997) 'Coalitions in urban regeneration: a regime approach', *Environment and Planning A*, **29**: 1493–506.

Ward, S.V. and Gold, J.R. (1994) 'Introduction', in J.R. Gold and S.V. Ward (eds), *Place Promotion: The use of publicity and marketing to sell towns and regions*, Wiley, Chichester, 1–17.

Watson, C.G., Tuorila, J., Detra, E., Gearhart, L.P. and Wielkiewicz, R.M. (1995) 'Effects of a Vietnam War memorial pilgrimage on veterans with posttraumatic stress disorder', *Journal of Nervous and Mental Disease*, **183**(5): 315–19.

Wearing, S. (2001) *Volunteer Tourism: Seeking experiences that make a difference*, CAB International, Wallingford.

Weaver, H.E. (1982) 'Origins of interpretation', in G.W. Sharpe (ed.), *Interpreting the Environment*, Wiley, New York, 28–51.

Webb, T.D. (1994) 'Missionaries, Polynesians, and tourists: Mormonism and tourism in La'ie, Hawai'i', *Social Process in Hawaii*, **35**: 195–212.

Weiler, J. (1984) 'Reusing our working past for recreation and tourism', *Recreation Canada*, **42**(2): 36–41.

Wells, C. (1993) 'Interior designs: room furnishings and historical interpretations at colonial Williamsburg', *Southern Quarterly*, **31**: 89–111.

Wells, J. (1996) 'Marketing indigenous heritage: a case study of Uluru National Park', in C.M. Hall and S. McArthur (eds), *Heritage Management in Australia and New Zealand: The human dimension*, Oxford University Press, Melbourne, 222–30.

West, B. (1988) 'The making of the English working past: a critical view of the Ironbridge Gorge Museum', in R. Lumley (ed.), *The Museum Time-Machine: Putting cultures on display*, Routledge, London, 36–62.

West, J. (ed.) (1991) *The Americans with Disabilities Act: From policy to practice*, Milbank Memorial Fund, New York.

Wigle, R. (1994) 'Making history seem tempting: marketing an historic site as a visitor attraction', *Journal of Travel and Tourism Marketing*, **3**(2): 95–101.

Winks, R. (1976) 'Conservation in America: national character as revealed by preservation', in J. Fawcett (ed.), *The Future of the Past: Attitudes to conservation, 1174–1974*, Thames and Hudson, London, 140–7.

Worden, N. (1996) 'Contested heritage at the Cape Town Waterfront', *International Journal of Heritage Studies*, **1**(1/2): 59–75.

Worden, N. (1997) 'Contesting heritage in a South African city: Cape Town', in B.J. Shaw and R. Jones (eds), *Contested Urban Heritage: Voices from the periphery*, Ashgate, Aldershot, 31–61.

Zeppel, H. (1997) 'Maori tourism in New Zealand', *Tourism Management*, **18**: 475–8.

Zeppel, H. and Hall, C.M. (1991) 'Selling art and history: cultural heritage and tourism', *Journal of Tourism Studies*, **2**(1): 29–45.

Zeppel, H. and Hall, C.M. (1992) 'Arts and heritage tourism', in B. Weiler and C.M. Hall (eds), *Special Interest Tourism*, Belhaven, London, 47–68.

Ziegler, A.P. and Kidney, W.C. (1980) *Historic Preservation in Small Towns: A manual of practice*, American Association for State and Local History, Nashville.

Index

Note: Page numbers in **bold** refer to plates.